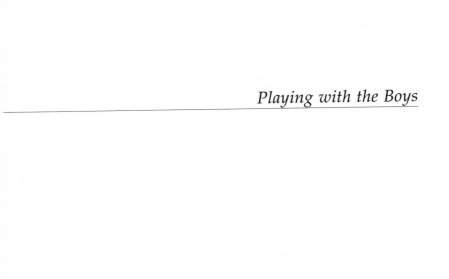

Playing with the Boys

EILEEN MCDONAGH

LAURA PAPPANO

PLAYING WITH THE BOYS

*Why Separate Is
Not Equal in Sports*

OXFORD
UNIVERSITY PRESS
2008

OXFORD
UNIVERSITY PRESS

Oxford University Press, Inc., publishes works that further
Oxford University's objective of excellence
in research, scholarship, and education.

Oxford   New York
Auckland   Cape Town   Dar es Salaam   Hong Kong   Karachi
Kuala Lumpur   Madrid   Melbourne   Mexico City   Nairobi
New Delhi   Shanghai   Taipei   Toronto

With offices in
Argentina   Austria   Brazil   Chile   Czech Republic   France   Greece
Guatemala   Hungary   Italy   Japan   Poland   Portugal   Singapore
South Korea   Switzerland   Thailand   Turkey   Ukraine   Vietnam

Copyright © 2008 by Oxford University Press, Inc.

Published by Oxford University Press, Inc.
198 Madison Avenue, New York, NY 10016

www.oup.com

Oxford is a registered trademark of Oxford University Press

Library of Congress Cataloging-in-Publication Data
McDonagh, Eileen L.
Playing with the boys : why separate is not equal in sports /
Eileen McDonagh and Laura Pappano.
   p. cm.
ISBN 978-0-19-516756-6
1. Sports—Social aspects—United States.   2. Sex discrimination in sports—
United States.   3. Sex discrimination against women–United States.
I. Pappano, Laura, 1962–   II. Title.
GV706.5.M3673 2008
306.4830973—dc22   2007018278

9 8 7 6 5 4 3 2 1

Printed in the United States of America
on acid-free paper

For Edward and Robert, and for Robert Edward,
and in memory of Carol Newsom—E.M.
For Tom, Olivia, Molly, and Donovan—L.P.

Contents

Preface

When radio shock jock Don Imus derided the Rutgers women's basketball team as "nappy-headed ho's" the day after they had played in the NCAA Division I championship game in April 2007, capping an improbable season and play-off run with a powerful showing of heart and skill, it wasn't so shocking.

The comments sparked a firestorm. Sponsors deserted Imus. CBS and MSNBC yanked his show. Pundits intoned. Sports radio hosts went wild, some criticizing him but others defending him, claiming the women had probably heard worse from the stands. What was the big deal, anyhow?

Imus's trash talk triggered expressions of public outrage about the racist nature of his name-calling. Somewhere in the background, with a little less fervor, we heard about gender.

It is easier to talk about race in sports. The deplorable treatment faced by black male athletes like football talent Kenny Washington and baseball star Jackie Robinson provides a clear wrong. We accept that we should judge athletes based on their skill, character, and performance—not the color of their skin.

On the other hand, female athletes, particularly successful women playing the "male" game of basketball, draw a muddier defense. They may shoot from the perimeter, box out, pass and play with a drive that makes watching a thrill, but there remains a background buzz that challenges their identity: They can't be *real* women. At the heart of Imus's remark—and the too faint defense of women college players—was the notion that the serious, powerful female athlete remains a social contradiction.

When we began work on this book more than six years ago, probing the notion that sport is an essential tool for obtaining gender equality in society, some met us with quizzical expressions. Were we really *serious?* The very term "sex-segregated sports" struck some as odd. What did we mean?

As we probed further, however, unearthing parallels between arguments against women's access to workplace, higher education, and voting rights and prevailing beliefs about female athletes and their "place" in society, it became clear that the battle for gender equality had reached a new frontier. Sports mattered to women's power *off the field.*

Sports, in other words, are not just for fun, are not just for guys, are not just so much background yammering (though talk radio can make it sound that way), but a social force that does not merely reflect gender differences, but in some cases, creates, amplifies, and even imposes them. What's more, we found that it isn't just habit or preference that keeps males and females in their separate athletic places; many recreational, educational, and professional sports programs make it a *legal* requirement.

The "real" problem, we came to see, is the very notion of dividing the athletic universe into "male sports" and "female sports," which has long seemed the most obvious and natural thing in the world. And yet, when we began looking at the roots of this and the effects, we found something surprising: Dividing sports by sex—segregating organized athletics based on gender—doesn't reliably reflect actual physical differences between males and females at all. Rather, it reflects antiquated social patterns and false beliefs. And what's more, it enforces, sometimes baldly, sometimes subtly, the notion that men's activities and men's power are the real thing and women's are not. Women's sports, like women's power, are second-class.

The assumption that women are physically different from men translates into the assumption that women are physically inferior to men, which translates into the assumption that women couldn't— and hence shouldn't—compete with men because that would spell immediate injury to women, physically if not also psychologically.

The whole idea that one group is inherently better than another also conflicts with the very American values that we each hold dear, that is, the belief that each of us should be judged as an *individual* and not defined by group membership. While we were well aware of the benefits of Title IX, it became obvious that Title IX is not enough. Yes, this law altered access to educational resources, including sports, but it didn't change the underlying *structure* of the way society treated and viewed male and female athletes. By condoning sex segregation in contact sports, Title IX ended up reinforcing the assumption that girls couldn't—or shouldn't—play with the boys.

In fact, we found that it helps hold in place the stereotypical notions of males and females. Eileen represents the pre–Title IX generation and Laura a post–Title IX generation. No sports were available to girls in Eileen's high school, and so she shaped her passion as a fan of horse racing and dogsled racing and embraced outdoor activities, including hiking, which spurred her on treks through the High Sierras and a climb of Mt. Kilimanjaro. Laura, on the other hand, thanks to Title IX, was allowed to take middle school wood shop, join the *Danbury News-Times* carrier baseball league, and, with her sister, play midfield for the New Milford (CT) town travel soccer team. And yet being "allowed" was different from being welcomed and valued as an equal.

Title IX has gotten girls and women onto the playing field. But the game itself remains off-kilter and poorly refereed. We need a fresh way of thinking about organized sports that contributes to, rather than distracts from, building real gender equality.

Days after Imus's remarks, the Rutgers players found themselves giving a press conference in which their coach, C. Vivian Stringer, painted them as accomplished students and aspiring musicians, doctors, veterinarians. The quest to reveal their nonathletic interests was an apology of sorts, a means for "proving" they were anything but "ho's." Many male college athletes at top Division I basketball schools are not there for an education but for a boost into the NBA. Ironically, no one refers to them as "ho's."

Acknowledgments

This book began as a conversation in the corridors of the Murray Research Center at the Radcliffe Institute for Advanced Study at Harvard, and through these six years conversations have pushed this book forward. Some of these talks have been formal: Thank you to Wheelock College president Jackie Jenkins-Scott and athletic director Diana Cutaia, as well as University of Lowell professor Jeffrey Gerson. Bob Davoli generously provided us with a practice field in the business community where we could test our thesis in the company of unusually tough-minded (if not macho) audiences. Many professional political science associations over the years included us on panels where we benefited enormously from discussants' constructive criticism; political scientist Kristin Goss at Duke University incorporated our work into her courses even before its publication, giving us a prescient preview of student's-eye views. Harvard University's Government Department, American Politics Workshop, was an invaluable forum for trial runs before going into print.

The *Boston Globe Magazine*, including former editors John Koch and Nick King, as well as current editor in chief Doug Most, gave our argument early airings. *New York Times* Education Life editor Jane Karr made room for a sports story in her section. We gained from small meetings and structured conversations with Bill Littlefield, Peter Roby, Cathy Inglese, and Barbara Lee.

This book has also served as the fuel and beneficiary of more dinner party debates than either of us can list here. Special thanks to those who prodded and encouraged us, who never failed to ask, "How's the book going?" Many have offered valuable feedback or opened doors for us, especially Mandy Bass, Andrew Martin, Peter Karoff, Paul Friedberg, Andrea Kelley, Eric Schwarz, Maureen Coffey, Chuck Agosta, Lucy McQuilken, Jerry Grady, Evelyn Kramer, Davi Ellen Chabner, Larry Shulman, Howard Weinstein, Mary Wolf, David Davoli, and Steven George. Athletes Karen Smyers, Emily Watts, Bobbi Gibb, Margaret Murdock, Nikki Darrow, Kim Salma, Shelley Looney, and Ryan Jones generously shared their experiences, as did physicians Dr. Bert Zarins, Dr. Carol Otis, and Dr. Arthur Boland.

In addition, we extend our deepest thanks and gratitude to those who plowed through earlier versions of our manuscript, sometimes in the context of professional academic meetings, and always offering invaluable criticism and advice. To Wade Woodson we are especially indebted, as well as to Lee Ann Banaszak, Nico Cornell, Bob Davoli, Sheila Fiekowsky, Kristin Goss, Mary Katzenstein, Edward Price, Robert Price, Stephano Quatrano, Cindy Rosenthal, Kay Schlozman, Shauna Shames, and Sidney Verba.

We received research help from many quarters, including the Smith College Library archives, The White House Project, Northeastern University, papers from the National Organization for Women, Julie Masters at Scholastic, Inc., and USA Wrestling. Special thanks to the Schlesinger Library at the Radcliffe Institute for Advanced Study at Harvard, particularly to Diana Carey, and to Nicole Zarrett and Leanne Doherty, who were there encouraging us at the start of this enterprise. We also thank Anne Colby for her support while we were at the Murray Research Center, and later Annemette Sørensen and Marty Mauzy. In addition, Eileen McDonagh wishes to offer special thanks to Drew Gilpin Faust for providing an affiliate appointment at the Radcliffe Institute for Advanced Study, which greatly facilitated this project. Eileen also thanks Gary King for appointing her as a Visiting Scholar at the Institute for Quantitative Social Science (IQSS) at Harvard University, an invaluable community of scholars. We also thank research assistants who were crucial for the completion of this project, including Lauren Ernst, Michele Frazier, Anne Guèvremont, Michele

Hearty, Deanne Kallgren, Elizabeth Pipkin, Efrat Procaccia, Rain Robertson, Shauna Shames, and Greg Skidmore. In addition, we thank Robert Price and Shauna Shames for editorial assistance.

This book also owes a large debt to those journalists and academics who have wrangled with issues of gender and sports. We are especially grateful for the work of Deborah Brake, Susan Cahn, Shirley Castelnuovo, Mary Jo Festle, Lynda Ransdell, Sharon Guthrie, Allen Guttmann, John R. Thelin, Elliot J. Gorn, Warren Goldstein, Christine Brennan, Susan Jennings, Jere Longman, Selena Roberts, William C. Rhoden, Welch Suggs, Karen Tokarz, Joseph B. Treaster, and Diane Heckman.

Writing a book is one thing, publishing it is another, and we are the beneficiaries of the continuous contributions of talented, thoughtful, and dedicated individuals at Oxford University Press. Our editor, David McBride, embraced the project and brought his sharp mind and sport-world fluency to the manuscript. This book would not exist without the foresight and enthusiasm of Dedi Felman, whose initial guidance, tough questions, and support were invaluable. Oxford vice president and publisher Niko Pfund was engaged from the start; Laura Lewis's careful and thoughtful work raised critical questions. We are indebted to many others at Oxford, including Brendan O'Neill.

Finally, each of us extends our deepest thanks to our families. Laura Pappano directs special credit to Tom Lynch, whose prodigious sports knowledge has been invaluable, and who has approached this project with as much passion, support, and information (thank you for every rumpled news clipping and anecdote) as any writer or partner dare hope for. Olivia, Molly, and Donovan have lived the mantra of gender equality and even helped with research. There is no family member who has not made a contribution: Thanks to JoAnne, Robert, Nancy, Tom, Barbara, Dante, Ellen, Margaret, Adnan, Andrea, Spence, Christopher, Agnes, Susan, Derek, and Nancy. Eileen McDonagh also counted on her family and on Lesko, a very special *brava hund* always there for her, to see her through this project. She directs her love and thanks to Edward Price, Ellen Price, and Zachary Price, to Robert Price and Alice Bierhorst, and to Bob Davoli whose loyalty and enthusiasm for it all carry the day.

Playing with the Boys

1

WHAT'S THE PROBLEM?

Egalitarianism is the philosophical foundation of our political process.

—*Hoover v. Meiklejohn*[1]

Sports Matter

When two former U.S. presidents, Bill Clinton and George H. W. Bush, sat down the evening of February 6, 2005, at the Fox Network sports desk, they delivered more than the planned message. Ostensibly the two appeared on the Super Bowl pregame show to win support for tsunami relief efforts. However, in choosing this event as their venue, they embraced an unabashed cultural and political fact: Sports matter.[2]

Athletic events, they confirmed, are more than entertainment, exercise, or pastime. Sports—football and the Super Bowl in particular—provide one of the largest and most important stages in American society. Some 86 million U.S. households tuned in to watch Super Bowl XXXIX. By contrast, four days earlier just 38.4 million tuned in to President George W. Bush's State of the Union Address.[3] The NFL may be among the most superbly packaged and marketed athletic products in the world, but the ease with which politics, power, and money intermingle with organized sports is more than a good pitch. The connections run deep.[4] Some sociologists argue that "sports have replaced formal religion as a dominant force in the lives of many Americans."[5] And in educational contexts, as law scholar Julia Lamber notes, the purpose of sports "is for students to learn the kinds of discipline, cooperation, and ability to meet challenges that often produce success in later public and private life."[6]

As political activist Barbara Lee notes, "When a popular male athlete retires, he's often encouraged to run for office. When John Elway retired from the Broncos, people wanted him to run for Congress. When Forty-Niners' Steve Young retired, people encouraged him to run for the Senate."[7] Hence it is no accident that former Major League Baseball players, ex-football players, and retired NBA gamers serve in Congress. When President George W. Bush (former Little Leaguer and baseball team owner) delivered his 2004 State of the Union Address, media outlets made much ado about New England Patriots quarterback Tom Brady appearing in Mrs. Laura Bush's box. A few noted the attendance of WNBA player Tamika Catchings.

Sports and Masculinity

Athletics are a comfortable companion to power. The easy chemistry between sports, politics, and business, as political scientist Varda Burstyn argues, has led to natural alliances.[8] As Michael Messner notes, they all provide a forum for public displays of masculinity.[9] Success in athletics, as in politics and business, defines what it is to be "male" in our society. Organized sports enforce a male power structure that reaches far beyond the field.[10] Organized sports support a form of sex segregation that permeates nearly every aspect and intersection of athletic and popular culture. Courts pronounce athletes individuals, but practice and institutional rules first sort players as male or female. Some individuals courageously challenge sex discrimination in sports, but most accept the status quo.[11]

Such acceptance is not without consequence. Yes, Tamika Catchings attended the State of the Union Address, but her presence, in contrast to Brady's, lacked a broader context. There was no confusion about the meaning of Brady's attendance, either the cachet of being invited or the value to President Bush in hosting a two-time Super Bowl MVP known for handling clutch situations with clear-headed cool.

Sports and Sex Equality

This book addresses the issue of sex equality in the context of sports. We live in a society in which key elements are gendered as male.[12] Winning is male. Power is male. Money is male. Physical dominance is male. And big-time Las Vegas–lined, network-covered, sold-out-venue, sponsor-rich sports are male. We must recalibrate this system. Athletics should be gender-neutral, a human activity and not a pumped-up, artificial rendition of men's strength and women's weakness as a definition of sex identity.[13]

Many see sports as a static system reflecting social and gender realities rather than constructing them. After all, it has been drilled into our heads that female athletes are not as good as male athletes, that female sports are less interesting, that female sporting events are less worthy of promotion or public interest. Open any sports page or tune in to any television news sports segment in the country and see such beliefs confirmed.

This state of affairs has sprung from the same history of bias that pronounced women out of place in jobs other than secretary, nurse, or teacher. It has sprung from times when physicians insisted women are not physically strong enough to handle the stress of higher education, that letting women use their brains too much shrinks their uteruses, rendering them infertile.[14] This bias was born from the gut anger some express at the notion of women serving in the military, particularly in combat. No wonder children once giggled at the very idea of a woman firefighter or police officer. In other words, biases that once seemed untouchable—biases based on beliefs about female physical limitations—now appear absurd.

Athletics Is Not a Special Case

The culture and the structure governing organized sports should not exist apart from the fairness and equality mandated in other sectors of American life. Hold organized sports accountable in this way, and a system out of balance is revealed, one in which male superiority is not merely presumed but artificially constructed and enforced, not only by social norms but also by legal ones.[15] What is more, these patterns are dominant not only in the way sports are organized for the very young but also, as Maree Boyle and Jim McKay note, for the elderly.[16] Thus it is time to examine sports in the context of the American heritage of egalitarian values and constitutional principles.[17] For this reason, we have written a different kind of book about sports and gender. It is about what is recognized but rarely examined: how athletics shape and perpetuate stereotypical gender roles that limit women's social, economic, and political opportunities, thereby maintaining women's inequality in American society compared to men.

Intersectionality

Taken together, human beings constitute an intersection of many ascriptive characteristics acquired at birth, such as their race, class, religious background, language orientation, nationality, historical time period of birth, and, of course, their sex. The complexities of the way ascriptive characteristics interact socially, economically, and politically make it dangerous to single out just one, such as sex, as the definition of a problem. This is because whatever a person experiences due to one ascriptive characteristic, such as sex, is modified greatly by all the other characteristics, such as race, class, nationality, and so on. As legal scholar Rhonda Reaves notes, African American women, for example, often experience discrimination because of their gender *and* their race. Consequently they are particularly vulnerable to the harm of sexual harassment in sports contexts where they are coached by white males.[18]

Consider the sexist and racial slurs directed at the Rutgers University women's basketball team by Don Imus, one of the most influential and financially lucrative "pitchmen in the history of radio, if not broadcasting."[19] Although famous for ridiculing the elite and the powerful in the celebrity world of politics and entertainment, he struck a low blow when he mocked and degraded the mostly African American women basketball players as "nappy-headed ho's."[20] Clearly racism was intersecting with sexism in his attack on these 18-, 19-, and 20-year-old women. The outrage generated by the debacle was more than warranted. As Essence

Carson, captain of the Rutgers basketball team, explained, "It is more than a game of basketball . . . as a society, we're trying to grow . . . and get to the point where we don't classify women as hos and we don't classify African-American women as nappy-headed hos."[21] Exactly.

Thus we wish to establish at the outset that we are cognizant of the need for an appreciation of the intersectionality that is the reality for all human beings.[22] However, we also see another reality, namely, the way assumptions about women's inferiority to men in athletic endeavors cuts across all other ascriptive characteristics. All women are assumed to be athletically inferior to all men, whether the comparison is between or within ascriptive groups. Thus, for example, African American women are viewed as athletically inferior to African American male athletes as well as white male athletes; women from Kenya are assumed to be inferior athletes compared to men from Kenya as well as American men; French-speaking women athletes in Quebec are assumed to be athletically inferior to male French-speaking athletes in Quebec as well as all other male athletes from everywhere.

Something about "Sex"

Thus we argue there is something about sex difference in relation to assumptions about athletic prowess that requires particular attention in spite of the intersectionality principle. No matter how valuable and crucial it is to understand the way sex, race, class, and so on, work together to set parameters for life opportunities and experiences, we also point to the way "sex difference" is assumed by most to be the most determinant ascriptive attribute that accounts for athletic talent and performance. For example, is it likely that Don Imus would have made his racialized remarks about Rutgers' women's basketball team if they had been *men*? Would he have called a *male* basketball team a bunch of "nappy-headed _____ [fill in the blank]"? No, we can assume that it was the women's *sex* that first caught his attention and then their *race*. This is not to say that the racial component of his sexism is unimportant or irrelevant to an analysis of sex discrimination in sports. Rather, it is merely to assume that the starting point for an analysis of sex-segregated sports policies and the harm they impose on all women is assumptions about *sex difference first*, as a foundation for an examination of how other ascriptive characteristics, such as race, nationality, and disability, necessarily intersect with sex difference discrimination. A full analysis of the intersectionality dimension of sex discrimination in sports would go beyond the scope of this book. Our aim is to begin the conversation about intersectionality in sports by addressing the foundation of that intersectionality: sexism in sports in general and coercive sex segregation as an underrecognized form of sexism in particular.[23]

Thus the goal of this book is to address and challenge the way sex difference is tied to the myth of female inferiority and its corollary, a history that prevented women from playing hard or even competing at all—whatever their race, class, and so on. In the case of the United States, this book applauds Title IX's vital and pioneering push but draws attention to its failure to challenge adequately the assumption of women's athletic inferiority, which still pervades the recreational, educational, and professional sports arenas.

Time to Challenge the Way We Think about Sports

This book, therefore, is about how sports matter in American society and how sports do—or do not—promote women's equality. These are relevant questions regardless of one's predilection toward sports. Whether you are passionate about sports and believe athletics matter—or matter too much—this book aims to address everyone by addressing the *meaning* of sports in American society. We aim for this book to serve as a field guide for understanding a fundamental principle: if women cannot compete fairly on the field, they cannot compete fairly off it, either. As long as the phrase "you play like a girl" remains an insult, female abilities are undervalued—for all women, whatever their race, class, or other birth characteristics.

This book challenges how we think about organized sports, as participants, parents, and fans. Athletics are a visible part of American culture and it's tempting to accept what is presented. That is why it's critical to put sports into a legal, historical, and social context and to challenge the gut assumption that Title IX provided a fix and a level playing field for females in athletics. Yes, we can credit Title IX with getting more women involved in sports programs. However, as sports scholars Barrie Houlihan and Anita White argue, sports as a developmental tool for individuals and for society at large involves a lot more than just "getting more people to play more sport."[24] As we will discuss, a serious problem in organized sports today, in spite of and even because of Title IX, is the way policies codify historic myths about female physical inferiority and foster a system which, while offering women more opportunities than ever before, still keeps them from being perceived as equal athletes to men. Sports are too vital not to hold them to principles of fairness, justice, and equality demanded in other sectors of society. This book presents, therefore, a multidimensional argument which coalesces around a single belief: organized athletics are a critical arena for gender equality. The next frontier in the long history of achieving equal rights for women in the United States is *sports*.[25]

The Problem: Coercive Sex Segregation

The Three I's

We begin with the observation that the organization of sports in American society is based on a principle of coercive sex segregation. What is more, we contend that coercive sex segregation does *not* reflect actual sex differences in athletic ability, but instead constructs and enforces a flawed premise that females are inherently athletically inferior to males. Specifically, we argue that coercive sex segregation in sports is based on three false assumptions, what we term the three I's: (1) female *inferiority* compared to males, (2) the need to protect females from *injury* in competition with males, and (3) the *immorality* of females competing directly with males. By virtue of these three false assumptions, we argue that coercive sex-segregated sports policies are instrumentally and normatively unfair and injurious to women. They are also a barrier to the broader goal of achieving gender equality in American society, just as were earlier forms of coercive sex segregation that limited females' access and advancement in education and employment.

Of course, arguments can—and should—be made for voluntary sex segregation for any historically subordinated group, such as women and African Americans. Some American women, for example, living in a male-centered society, appreciate female-only educational

institutions. We have no quarrel with members of historically subordinated groups who voluntarily self-segregate themselves as a
remedial mechanism to compensate for past and present discrimination. However, the key word is *voluntarily*.

At present, sex segregation in sports in the United States is coerced by law, not merely custom or tradition, making it so pervasive
as to be all but invisible. This book aims to bring the flawed premises
and negative consequences of coercive sex-segregated sports policies
to the attention of the American public. In this book, therefore, we
make a clear distinction in sports between coercive sex segregation
and voluntary sex segregation. It is coercive sex segregation as it
appears in virtually every recreational, educational, and professional
sports structure that we identify as "the problem."

Sex-Segregated Sports in America

The key problem with coercive sex segregation in sports policies is
that these policies are not based on the athletic ability of any particular girl or woman who seeks to "play with the boys," but are
based solely on the sex categorization of girls and women as "female." Thus coercive sex-segregated sports policies prescribe such
segregation, regardless of the athletic talent or demonstrated qualifications of any particular girl or woman. Since most such policies
are coercive on the basis of law, not just social more, custom, or
tradition, when a qualified female wishes to "play with the boys,"
she most likely will have to seek a court remedy to do so. When such
challenges have been made, many courts have supported arguments
that being barred from play *solely* on the basis of being female
violates the Equal Protection Clause of the Fourteenth Amendment.
The central question we raise is why a woman who is qualified to play
on a sports team or in a sporting event must go to court to do so.

Sex Segregation: Invisible and Pervasive

Sex segregation is such an ingrained part of athletics at every skill
level that it rarely draws attention, much less protest. To date, for
example, there have been over 500 court cases involving sex discrimination in sports programs, including coaching (hiring, promo-

tion, salaries, resources), scheduling of events, scholarships, wages, academic standards for athletic participation, drug testing, sexual harassment, types of teams sponsored, pregnancy and abortion, rape and sexual violence—and, yes, sex segregation. The latter, however, constitutes a mere 10 percent of all cases on record. Does this mean sex segregation doesn't matter or doesn't even exist? No, it means that sex segregation in sports is so taken for granted that it is only challenged in rare circumstances.

Thus everyone recognizes sex discrimination when coaches with the same educational and training experience, coaching the same sports, are paid different salaries because one coaches girls and the other coaches boys. Everyone sees sex discrimination when girls' teams are scheduled to play in the off-season, practice at off-hours, or on poorly graded fields while well-maintained and cultivated fields are reserved for boys' teams. So too we recognize sex discrimination when female athletes are tested more or less for drugs than male athletic peers. Some may even recognize the unfairness of young women being shunted into "girls' sports" like volleyball or cheerleading, rather than football or baseball—or noting, as one Johnson City, New York, mother did in 2007, the unfair message sent when cheerleaders encourage the boys' high school basketball team but not the girls' team.[26]

Yet why not identify coercive sex segregation as a form of sex discrimination in sports?

For too long, conventional wisdom has held that women simply cannot compete with men, and the point is typically illustrated by making gender comparisons pitting the impressive mass of bulk and muscle of, say, a 350-pound NFL lineman against the delicate stereotype of a petite woman. No one asks how many males can match the height, weight, and strength to challenge a lineman physically. What's more, a lineman—offensive or defensive—has a narrow repertoire of athletic talent, geared primarily to blocking and tackling. Football may be the favorite sport evoked to argue for male "natural" physical superiority, but there are many other physiques and skills that are valuable on a football team, from lanky, fast receivers to power-legged and steel-nerved kickers.

Some middle and high schools have done the unthinkable and allowed females to "play with the boys" on football teams. Obviously middle or high school football players are a world away from NFL-level pros, but that is precisely the point: *We should not sort athletes by what sex they are, but rather by their skill, interest, and ability in relation to the particular sports they wish to play.* Some girls have been terrific additions to boys' teams. In 1993, Yorktown High School soccer star Heather Sue Mercer became the placekicker on the school football team and ended up as the top-scoring kicker in the league.[27] Too bad we have decided that football is a boys' sport. If athletic programs encouraged girls to develop skills such as kicking or punting (and, when appropriate, blocking or tackling), would we still insist no female could be as good as a male? Unlikely. Rather, we don't even ask the question: Why aren't at least some women on the field as kickers—or referees or coaches?

As this book argues, the problem is that coercive sex segregation in sports is so taken for granted that it is all but invisible. However, when we take a look, we see six ways coercive sex-segregated sports policies are routinely institutionalized.

1. Different sports for males and females. Some sports are clas-sified as male or female to allow schools to balance gendered offer-ings in unrelated sports. For example, schools offer gymnastics for girls and wrestling for boys. This practice is a response to Title IX regulations that require schools to offer equitable sports options to both girls and boys. However, this is most often accomplished by gender-coding athletic pursuits. If football is for boys, then field hockey must be for girls, if equitable options are to be provided to both boys and girls—even though field hockey is popular among men outside the United States. Similarly, if baseball, our "national pastime," is offered for boys, then softball is offered for girls. Such sex typing creates conflicts for individual participants, including, for example, males who may wish to play volleyball, even when it is labeled a "feminine" sport.

2. Same sports, sex-segregated teams. Even when males and females do play the same sport, such as soccer, teams tend to be di-vided by sex. Though some females play on male club or recreational teams, it is not considered optimal. Usually school, college, Olym-pic, and professional teams—which set the standard—are male-only or female-only. Gender crossover—a boy on a girls' field hockey team, a girl on the boys' basketball team—becomes a notable exception with the individuals involved viewed as oddities, thereby further reinforcing the normalcy of sex-segregated sports.

3. Same sports, sex-segregated teams and/or sex-segregated rules. As Nancy Theberge notes, males and females who play the same sport often encounter male and female versions of rules, which reinforce prevailing norms that women are athletically inferior to men.[28] In professional basketball, for example, even as rule changes have made dramatic strides in recent years to bring the men's and women's game closer together, the NBA and WNBA still play for slightly different lengths of time (men: four 12-minute quarters; women: four 10-minute quarters).[29] In NCAA college play, there are rule differences completely unrelated to play. For example, men's games have three referees, one of whom must be present 30 minutes prior to the game while women have two referees, one of whom must be on the floor 15 minutes before game time.[30] Such differences—and there are many—create distinctions and preserve segregation, as players become accustomed to different rules even when they are irrelevant to the game itself.

Examples abound. In gymnastics, males and females compete on different equipment—and face different judging formulas. Athletes begin with a less than perfect score; women begin at 9.00 and men start at 8.60. Judges deduct for flaws in execution and missing elements in a routine. Gymnasts may earn bonus points, up to 1.0 for women and 1.40 for men. In some sports, the rule differences are silly. Women's singles games in badminton, for example, end at 11 points while men's play goes to 15. Is it possible female badminton players cannot physically endure four more points?

There are sex-based rule differences in nearly every sport. In tennis, of course, women have risen to prominence and have drawn higher TV ratings than the men at top tournaments, but matches are the best two out of three sets while men's events are the best three out of five. The lower limit for women was imposed in 1902 by the U.S. Lawn Tennis Association—over the objections of some women—because of Victorians' concern about females overexerting themselves.[31] Such concerns have fallen away, but the rules remain. Perhaps the women's two out of three makes for more entertaining play. Still, the different rules for males and females were used to discriminate against women's pay at Wimbledon, which in February 2007 announced equal prize money for male and female winners. Previously the women's champion was paid about 95 percent of the male champion's prize.[32]

Even recent sports preserve male-female distinctions. In mountain bike racing, introduced at the 1996 Olympics in Atlanta, the men's race covers between 40 and 50 kilometers while the women's course runs between 30 and 40 kilometers. The route, set the night before the race, aims to create a course that the top male can finish in 2 hours and 15 minutes—and the top woman can complete in two hours.[33] Why must highly trained female athletes race just 15 minutes less than males? Similar differences exist in bicycle road and track races, suggesting the goal is differentiation, not accommodation. Even in swimming events, where women have outperformed men in distance challenges, Olympic rules call for men to have a 1,500-meter race while the comparable women's race is 800 meters.[34]

In cross-country skiing, the Olympics have a 50-kilometer race for men, but no such comparable distance event for women. These kinds of bald distinctions exist in nearly every event (speed skating offers men a 10,000-meter race while the longest women's race is 5,000 meters). Such practices are odd, because, if anything, women ought to have a physical edge in endurance events—not a need for shorter race courses.

The institutionalized segregation of the sexes seems almost reflexive, established in some instances when males and females have successfully competed together. Rifle shooting, for example, has been part of the Olympics since 1896. In 1967, Margaret Murdock became the first woman to win a Gold Medal in an international match, besting male and female shooters from seven nations in the Pan American Games. She needed no accommodations—and there were none—when she and teammate Lanny Basham tied in the 50-meter three-position shooting event at the 1976 Olympics in Montreal. Judges broke the tie, awarding Basham the Gold and Murdoch the Silver, though they both stood atop the Gold Medal stand.[35] Murdoch recalls "there was more than one squabble" among international shooting officials after her impressive finish, and she contends it spurred officials to seek separate—and different—women's shooting events in the future. "Men didn't like having a woman beat them," she recalled in an interview.[36]

By 1996 in Atlanta, men's and women's shooting events were completely segregated, with seven events for women and ten events for men. In nearly all comparable events, men have more shots, more targets or—as in the pistol event—shoot from 50 meters while women shoot from 25 meters away from the target.[37] In some cases, they also use different equipment. Such allowances make little sense because women have no discernible disadvantage in shooting that would warrant segregation or differential treatment. A 2001 study of military rifle marksmanship, for example, examined the effects of sex, rifle stock length, and rifle weight on military marksmanship performance. Researchers studying marksmanship accuracy (proximity of shots to target center) and precision (proximity of shots to one another) found "no significant differences in either measure of marksmanship performance as a function of sex."[38] The only differences researchers found were that marksmanship was better with the shortest rifle stock and the lighter rifle—for both males and females.

While military training differs from the sport of rifle shooting, the notion of males and females performing comparably cuts across both disciplines. As opposed to the Olympics, college rifle teams are coed, with males and females competing with and against one another. In March 2005, University of Memphis junior Beth Tidmore won the NCAA individual air rifle championship, scoring 694.2, four points ahead of the University of Nebraska's Andrea Franzen, and ahead of Matt Rawlings of the University of Alaska–Fairbanks, who came in third. [39]

4. Same sports, sex-typed styles. The drive to present male and female athletes as utterly different, even within the same sport, supports formats designed to emphasize stereotypical "male" or "female" attributes. In gymnastics, for example, both men and women compete in the floor exercise and vault, but male and female performances are clearly differentiated. Women's floor routines must be 70 to 90 seconds and choreographed to music. Men's are 50 to 70 seconds and lack music. Routines are judged on different qualities as the entire effect of the floor exercise aims to be different. As USA Gymnastics guidelines observe for men, "The best gymnast will incorporate tumbling passes with substantial difficulty, performing multiple twists and flipping faltos at the end of their routines." Women, on the other hand, are instructed that "the best gymnast incorporates the quality of grace maybe disguised by movements of playful theatrics, but [judges] look for a dancer-like command of music, rhythm, and space."[40] Men are told be explosive; women, graceful. Such rules construct sex attributes by requiring men to perform in a masculine mode and women in a feminine one.

5. Same sport, required stereotyped sex role rules. In some sports, including couples skating, men and women perform together at the same time. However, they must adhere to stereotypical roles defined by their sex. The International Olympic Committee (IOC) describes figure skating events, for example, as consisting of "ladies' singles, men's singles, pairs, and ice dancing."[41] Right away, we are told it is not "women and men" but "ladies and men" who compete in Olympic figure skating. IOC rules further prescribe that in the "pairs event . . . the couple works as one unit, demonstrating overhead lifts, throw-jumps with the man launching his partner, and other manoeuvres."[42] Wouldn't it make more sense merely to require the stronger partner to launch the lighter one? That would allow women who are taller, heavier, and stronger than average for their female sex group to partner with men who are shorter and lighter than average for their male sex group.

Come to think of it, why should pairs figure skating require any sex difference at all, much less stereotyped sex difference? Why not let same-sex pairs compete in Olympic figure skating? If same-sex couples can get married, as they now can in the Netherlands, Belgium, Spain, Canada, South Africa, and in the state of Massachusetts, surely they should be allowed to compete with heterosexual couples in pairs sports events.

6. Sex-segregated structure. In some athletic events men and women compete in the same sport by the same rules at the same time, but the event is structured as two distinct contests. The Boston Marathon (like any number of marathons) has males and females compete in separate races that are run simultaneously. Elite male runners begin apart from elite female runners; races are covered by separate media trucks, and finishes are reported as different victories in distinctly different races.

The practice of framing these races as separate events perpetuates the widespread belief that males are always faster than females. At this point, the fastest man is speedier than the fastest woman in the marathon, but top male runners as a group do not outperform top female runners as a group. In the 2003 Boston Marathon, for example, results of the top 207 runners—those who finished the course in less than 2 hours and 50 minutes—show the first 15 runners to finish were men, but the next four were women. These four women outran all remaining top male performers. The mean running time for these top 207 runners shows women as a group turned in faster times than men. The mean time among top women was 2:36:55, while the mean among top men was 2:41:33, almost five minutes slower.[43]

Sex Segregation Constructs Sex Difference

The major argument justifying separate male and female teams is not merely that males and females are physically different, but that females are physically, if not emotionally and otherwise, inferior to males when it comes to sports. We will explore how physical sex differences relate to athletic performance, but not necessarily to female inferiority. However, for now, just consider the message that is so widely accepted: women are physically weaker and will get hurt if they "play with the boys." Or, if not physically injured, they will be badly beaten and emotionally crushed. Plus, the contest won't be worthwhile for the males. Segregating sports, the argument goes, reflects the fact of male physical superiority. Women shouldn't complain because sex segregation saves them from physical and emotional injury. But does it really?

Contact versus Noncontact Sports

The pervasive argument underlying coercive sex-segregating sports policies, however, is built on the faulty assumption that sports simply reflect what "is." In reality, sex-segregated policies *construct* sex difference, thereby articulating in athletic and public life the relative potency and status of what we mean by male and female. If sex segregation reflected actual sex-based physical differences, one would expect a connection between the degree of sex segregation and the specific physical demands of a sport. Plus, we would expect contact sports such as boxing, basketball, and football—in which attributes associated with males as a group (greater height, weight, upper-body strength) are advantageous—to be sex-segregated while noncontact sports or those less physically demanding (e.g., chess, billiards, duplicate bridge, table tennis, and bowling) to be sex-integrated.[44] Surely strength differences between men and women as groups don't bear on an individual's physical ability to shoot pool, play cards, or move chess pieces.

Yet the organization of Olympic sports reveals a peculiar pattern. Contact sports requiring physical attributes associated with men as a group, such as boxing, football, and wrestling, are sex-segregated. But so too are Olympic trial sports for which height, weight, and upper-body strength provide no advantage whatsoever, such as billiard sports, duplicate bridge (the card game), and chess.[45] Even these noncontact sports are organized into men's teams, women's teams, and, in some instances, mixed teams including males and females.[46] The belief that females cannot play card or board games with males is not rooted in physical group differences between the sexes. Rather, it comes from the pervasive assumption that women are just plain inferior to men in *any* sports competition, including card and board games.

The World Bridge Federation, which administers bridge competitions nationally and internationally, proudly proclaims, for example, that it "takes special care of particular groups of bridge players," which include "women, juniors and seniors."[47] Why must women—all women—be placed in a protected category? More importantly, what does it signify? Clearly it sends a message that being female is a handicap, much like being under- or overage.

A similarly artificial division exists in chess. Recall that the most powerful piece on a chess board is the queen. She can sweep across the board with more lateral and longitudinal scope than any other piece. Yet the queen was not introduced into the game of chess, which originated in India, until 500 years after people had begun playing. Interestingly, historian Marilyn Yalom argues that the introduction of the queen as the most powerful piece on the board reflected the growing recognition of female political authority in Europe during the Middle Ages, as living queens, empresses, and countesses wielded significant power.[48]

However, the organization of the Thirty-sixth Chess Olympiad, featuring International Chess Federation rules, belies any affirmation of female power. This chess competition featured team play with a separate women's division, "considered as separate competitions," and with rules that have women playing over three boards, while regular teams compete over four.[49] The positing of men as regular and women as exceptions should be familiar to students of feminist theory as it reflects a tendency, described by Simone de Beauvoir decades ago, for men to be the norm and women to be the "other," or the "second sex."[50]

Pocket billiards employs a similar organizational assumption: women are inherently inferior to men. Although billiards does not favor the strongest or tallest individuals, the BCA National 9-Ball Championships nevertheless feature men's and women's singles divisions (the men's division is limited to 256 participants and women's to 128) in which the men race to nine; women race to eight.[51] Why? Such well-worn practices of sex segregation in the organization of sports, regardless of a game's physical demands, do nothing more than reinforce sex role distinctions, thereby constructing and preserving images of male superiority rather than reflecting them.

Third-Party Exceptions

Not every sport, however, is segregated by sex. The exceptions tend to share one key quality: they involve a third party, such as an animal, car, boat, or airplane. Horse racing is sex-integrated with male and female jockeys competing side by side. Racing Hall of Fame jockey Julie Krone won the Belmont Stakes Race in 1993 riding Colonial Affair, has earned over $81 million in purses, and in 2004 was voted by *USA Today* as one of its "Ten Toughest Athletes."[52]

Other equestrian sports are also sex-integrated. At the Olympics, there are three main events—dressage, eventing, and jumping—which are sex-integrated, both for riders and horses (with male and female horses both competing). Dressage, often described as "horses performing ballet," focuses on the way horses respond to subtle aids and signals from their riders to perform complicated movements.[53] Perhaps given the delicacy of communication and response between horse and rider, we should not be surprised that dressage events are "mixed." Eventing, on the other hand, is a rigorous three-day event—a kind of equestrian triathlon encompassing dressage, jumping, and a demanding cross-country course which tests the endurance of horse and rider. Eventing is so challenging that only men who were commissioned military officers were originally allowed to compete. In 1956, it was opened to male contestants. Since 1964 women have participated, competing with men and, in the process, challenging stereotypical beliefs about female physical inferiority. In 1984 Karen Stives became the first woman to win an individual Olympic medal in the three-day event when she earned Silver.[54]

In addition, dogsled racing involves a third party and allows males and females to compete head-to-head. Perhaps the most demanding race is the Iditarod, which covers over 1,000 miles of rough Alaskan territory. Women have not only competed in but won the Iditarod. Clearly a jockey requires enormous strength to control a thoroughbred weighing perhaps a ton and jostling with other huge animals running at fast speeds in tight quarters. Dogsled racing, however, also demands enormous physical stamina, endurance, and strength, including the need to lift heavy sled equipment and bags of food for over a dozen dogs. Both of these sports demand more upper-body strength than billiards, bridge, or chess.

Why are sports like horse, dog, boat, and car racing sex-integrated while billiards, bridge, and chess are not? Possibly because when a woman bests a man in these racing sports there is a culturally acceptable explanation? That she had a better horse, car, boat, plane, or team of dogs? The guy has an out. Even if a woman wins, *she does not beat him.* Thus in third-party sports, women can win and not disturb social beliefs that she's a member of the weaker sex, triumphant only because of her animal or equipment.

Interestingly, there are exceptions to the tradition of gender segregation: some college and community club sports. Ultimate Frisbee, for example, produces hundreds of gender-integrated teams across the country, suggesting that males and females need not play apart.

Stereotyped Sex Roles

Sex segregation of sports makes instinctive sense to those who evoke a mental image of a hulking male athlete—our 350-pound NFL lineman—matched against a female athlete—perhaps a petite Olympic gymnast. But such thinking misses the tremendous physical variability that exists within each sex. Few people worried for her safety when female ice hockey player Angela Ruggiero, 5 feet 9 and 190 pounds, took the ice for the all-male Tulsa Oilers.[55] There was checking (no checking is allowed in women's ice hockey) but it was not a problem for Ruggiero. "Seconds after being checked on her third shift of the night, Ruggiero responded by slamming a Rio Grande Valley Killer Bees player into the boards," according to a press report.[56] Her physical strength, size, and skill made her perfectly matched for the competition, even though she was female.

Individual athletes have abilities that are not gender-specific. Could a female Olympic gymnast play nose tackle in the NFL? Unlikely. Could a male NFL nose tackle perform a bar routine? No. But male gymnast Paul Hamm sure can. There is much to consider about the nature and meaning of physical differences between and within genders relative to particular sports. Unfortunately, the practice of coercively segregating men's and women's play does not reflect carefully considered sex differences. Rather, it constructs and reproduces gender stereotypes.

Coercive Sex Segregation as an Instrumental Problem

Coercive Sex Segregation Is Not Helpful to Women

Organized sports suffuse every corner of our culture, from language and politics to school, recreation, and entertainment. Forced sex segregation in such an influential arena has a powerful impact on the construction of gender rules and roles. Segregating women from "playing with the boys" on the grounds that women, simply by virtue of being female, are inherently inferior to men reinforces women's exclusion from other sectors of American society. The practical reasons for challenging coercive sex segregation in sports, therefore, are instrumental as a means to promote women's greater equality with men not only in sports but in all areas of American society. Sex-integrated sports are an instrument for breaking down barriers, including stereotypical beliefs about a woman's "role" or "place." Sex integration of sports also challenges the belief that women as a group are inherently inferior to men as a group.

Some may disagree right off the bat that coercive sex-segregated sports instrumentally harm women. They will contend instead that without sex-segregated teams there would be no sports programs at all for women. As sports enthusiast Wade Woodson argues, "I fear that the surest way to destroy women's athletics would be to make the men's teams integrated."[57] He continues,

> As soon as you make the men's team a coed team, all other teams become "bush league." Women's sports struggle for recognition, funding and attention now. In an integrated world, the reasonable conclusion would be that any exceptionally talented and competitive woman would be playing on the integrated team. This would justify the claim that women's teams represent lower-quality athletics. Participation on the women's team would carry a greater stigma.

The question for those with such fears is, What do you think the *current coercive sex-segregated* sports policies mean? What they mean, obviously, is that women are so inferior that sex-integrated sports will hurt women, and that with the exception of a few athletically gifted females, women as a group are simply outclassed in competing with men as a group.

Let us suppose it's true: more men are athletically gifted in at least some sports, such as basketball, than women, if only because there are more men who are taller than women than women who are taller than men. But how does it help women as a group to hide the few women who are as talented as men by prohibiting qualified women from "playing with the boys"? Hiding the women who can compete with men reinforces the false assumption that no women can meet the challenge. Our position is that sex-segregated athletic policies have already established women's teams as the "bush league." Why perpetuate the image by prohibiting women who are better than bush league from "playing with boys"?

Our friend Wade also makes an oft-cited point that in the big-ticket sports, the "A-team will be mostly male." What is more, he says, "spectators won't want to watch anyone but the 'top' team. Sports are a meritocracy. The integrated A-team will justifiably get the glory, the viewership and the cash," leaving the "B-string and C-string males," who most likely would be left to "play with the girls," underfunded and undersupported by sports fans.

The problem is that sports are not truly a meritocracy, and coerced sex segregation is not limited to the big-ticket sports alone. To the contrary, coercive sex segregation in sports is the expected norm even in recreational settings, whether we are talking about four-year-olds playing T-ball or 55-year-olds playing club tennis. Even when a program is ostensibly coed, it is considered an exception to standard practice. In many places, T-ball is an ostensibly cogendered sport. According to the T-Ball USA Association, for example, T-ball is for children ages four through eight in which children hit the ball off a tee (there is no pitching).[58] However, a study in which researchers spent 22 hours observing YMCA kindergarten T-ball captured social pressure on girls who elected to play a "boys' sport." While coed YMCA kindergarten T-ball suggests equity and inclusion, the study showed instead the troubling and differentiated treatment of males and females by coaches, including differentiated access to learning new skills and improving play.

Researchers, for example, found top male players received the most coaching and attention, while female players were routinely ignored and sometimes embarrassed in front of peers. Consequently those who were good got better and those who most needed coaching were shunted to outfield positions (where kindergarten batters can't reach). Regarding female players, researchers observed that "coaches and peers convey traditional attitudes that girls do not fully belong in certain—traditionally male—sports."[59]

The study reported that the treatment of girls, which could be mistaken for harassment, unfolded in an organized setting in which participants, parents, and program administrators did not perceive that anything was amiss. It made no difference that one T-ball coach was female; social expectations ruled. In fact, Coach Carol told researchers that "none of the girls want to be here. Not one. If I put a coloring station in the corner, every girl would be there . . . dads take their sons outside to throw with. Girls stay inside and play dolls."

Such apparent lack of interest, researchers suggest, was no doubt influenced by a T-ball culture in which girls were frequently humiliated in front of peers. Even when boys made the same errors, girls were singled out for negative attention. In one instance, a boy, Richard, ran out onto the field doing cartwheels. When a girl, Helen, did the same thing a few minutes later, Coach Carol called her over, reprimanded her, and pulled her from the game. Richard was never spoken to. Girls who batted balls that were fielded for outs at first base were made to run around the bases twice as punishment—even as no punishment was applied to boys put out at first.

In addition, girls often were made to feel they shouldn't be participating. Coach Wayne dropped a ball he was trying to throw and said, "Look, I throw like a girl." "Before throwing it," researchers observed, "he contorted his arms and awkwardly threw the ball towards Helen, who was standing in front of him. This behavior both illustrated and created the image of girls as inferior, bringing one female player into the scene as a prop for depicting her own incompetence."

The girls also experienced other incidents of public humiliation, making it no surprise that three girls interviewed at the end of the season claimed not to have enjoyed playing T-ball, despite having the initial interest to sign up. If this study offers a window into a greater problem, is it possible to know how much of the male dominance in baseball is rooted in real biological, physical superiority—and how much in the heavy hand of social forces? Although this is one study, it narrates a problem we recognize extending beyond one program in one season. The athletic socialization that unfolds at beginning levels lays the foundation for future athletic interests. The message is ingrained that girls are not welcome in some sports. Never mind that they were technically allowed to sign up, the girls in this T-ball program were hardly treated with the encouragement and support we expect from those coaching this age group.

Coercive sex segregation remains the norm in elementary and middle school, even before reported sex differences triggered by puberty have yet to show. Sex-segregated policies are also the norm in high school, even when assumed physical disparities between males and females are belied by talented female athletes who outperform most or all male peers. Nonetheless, there is the phrase "you throw like a girl" to remind everyone that being like a girl means being athletically incompetent. Even girls don't like to be told they "throw like a girl."

Yet when researchers investigated the widespread cultural belief that males are inherently better throwers than females, they discovered no throwing gene attached to the Y chromosome. One study recorded the force of overarm throws with the *nondominant arm* in boys and girls aged seven to eight years old, nine to ten years old, and eleven to twelve years old. Results showed differences linked to age—not gender—in the power of throws. Sex differences, the authors noted, were only linked to throws with the dominant arm, suggesting "nonbiological factors are important in explaining the large gender differences in throwing noted in the literature."[60]

If coercive sex-segregated sports policies were limited to professional sports, we would still contend there is a problem for the talented woman athlete prohibited from "playing with the boys." However, coercive sex segregation pervades virtually all sports arenas. Worries that sex-integrated sports teams would create a hierarchy in which most women could not "play with the boys" and would be relegated to second- or third-tier play ignores the way current sex-segregated policies already do just that. Assumptions about female inferiority that serve as a rationale for coercively sex-segregated teams parallel the rationale for the Special Olympics, thereby reflecting the assumption that to be "female" is to be "disabled," while to be "male" is to be "abled."

In addition, when considering the implications of sex integration in sports, it is crucial to understand the value of role models to subordinate groups. There may be only one woman on the Supreme Court, but that does not discount her value to other women eager to establish credentials in the field of law. As long as at least "some" women excel in traditionally male fields, the claim that "all" women are unqualified—either by natural attributes or by virtue of socialization—is blatantly false.[61] Yes, it would be better to have four or five women on the Supreme Court, as it would be better to have at least 50 percent of the U.S. Congress composed of women instead of the 16 percent we have currently. However, while we wait for the perfect equality that most likely will never come, the few women who break barriers by entering and competing successfully in traditionally male fields provide tangible examples that coercive sex-segregated policies that would shut out *all* women are unfounded. Further, a separate Supreme Court for women only or a separate Congress for women only would merely reinforce the notion that women can't—or shouldn't—be integrated with men in the first place.

Coercive Sex Segregation
as a Normative Problem

Coercive Sex Segregation Is Not American

In 1960, a Harvard Law School dean recommended his brilliant student, Ruth Bader Ginsburg, to serve as clerk to Supreme Court Justice Felix Frankfurter. Six years earlier, Frankfurter had written the draft decree in *Brown v. Board of Education*, establishing that racially segregated public schools were unconstitutional on grounds that "separate is not equal." The decision, one of the most potent in American legal history, laid the foundation for civil rights legislation. The standard for equality would be guided not by tangible offerings but by actual inclusion. The mere existence of separate schools for blacks and whites, the court ruled, constituted inequality.

When it came time to apply that same principle to sex segregation, however, Frankfurter was far from a pioneer. Rather than welcome Harvard's star student, Frankfurter rejected her. Ginsburg obviously showed talent, including her work on the highly competitive *Harvard Law Review*, but Frankfurter balked. He stated publicly that he "was not ready to hire a woman."[62]

It is difficult to remember when it was acceptable to utter such a phrase, but for Ginsburg it was neither the first nor the last time she experienced sex discrimination. As one of only eight female students in her Harvard Law School class of 500, she and female classmates were chastised for taking spots from qualified males.[63]

Fortunately Ginsburg's story has a positive ending. Following Frankfurter's rejection, Ginsburg went to work for the American Civil Liberties Union, where she established a special unit to investigate and litigate cases of sex discrimination. Eleven years later, Ginsburg would argue before the Supreme Court—and win—the 1971 watershed case, *Reed v. Reed*,[64] which revolutionized how the Court evaluated claims of sex discrimination. It also set Ginsburg on a path that would earn her an appointment on the Supreme Court.

Although the case does not involve athletics, Ginsburg's argument in *Reed v. Reed* would be important to the rights of female athletes in the future as well as women's rights in general. In *Reed v. Reed* Ginsburg challenged gender bias that was reflected in policies enforcing distinct male and female domains. She argued against a state policy that, on the assumption that males as a group had more business experience than females, automatically gave preference to fathers over mothers as executors of children's estates. The Supreme Court agreed with Ginsburg's challenge, ruling gender could not serve as a proxy, or stand-in, for business experience. Just being male did not guarantee superior business acumen. The ruling extended the separate is not equal principle, previously applied only to race, to sex discrimination.

This was not the only case to question the fairness of practices based on gender stereotypes, but it marked a critical legal moment.[65] The decision brought the weight of the Fourteenth Amendment's Equal Protection Clause, crafted by Congress to prohibit discrimination based on race, to bear on cases involving discrimination based on sex. This case and the Supreme Court decision had far-reaching implications. It was no longer acceptable—indeed it was unconstitutional—in the eyes of the law to treat women according to group stereotypes. Individual women must be treated equally "in spite of," as the Court said, whatever group difference may exist between men and women.

The decision confirmed the nation's respect for an individual's rights, regardless of sex. Ginsburg recorded a key constitutional legacy with this win and proved again the power of America's founding ideals and liberal tradition to effect social and political change.

Individualism

From the start, this simple idea has been at the heart of the American system: individuals are equal in the eyes of the law.[66] Throughout history, constitutional amendments and court decisions prohibiting sex discrimination in pay, access to jobs, voting rights, and access to higher education, including all-male military institutions, have affirmed a national commitment to seeking equity through respect for individual rights under the law.

This root value stands in striking contrast to practices and policies of American organized sports. Institutionalized athletics have occupied a privileged space in our society, even encroaching on personal freedoms in the ordinary operation of programs, games, and events. Why have sports been given, in effect, a free pass when it comes to aligning with American values? In part, organized athletics are perceived as "wholesome" and as an important tool for bettering individuals and society. Sports are also intimately linked to our national cultural identity and embraced as the physical manifestation of American prowess and power.

Sports and American Values

The notion of sports as a positive American force is rooted in its creation. In the mid to late nineteenth century, when the nation was confronted with massive change, organized athletics provided a vehicle for teaching and sharing American values. To worried social architects who saw chaos in rapid industrialization (including fears of the consequences of man's loss of contact with nature) and large-scale immigration, sports provided a structure for managing this huge social shift. Organized sports offered new immigrants and migrants to cities the skills and the proper orientation to teamwork, discipline, and physical rigor essential to work and civic life. In 1907 a Protestant weekly, *The Independent*, echoed this belief when it argued the nation could "create a better race of manly beings, a better social state" through sports.[67]

Not surprisingly, the growth of organized sport coincided with the burgeoning parks movement. The movement pushed back against rapid urbanization and industrialization—and the stresses this new life brought—with the creation of pastoral and recreational landscapes in the middle of the city. These park spaces featured athletic facilities, including baseball fields and basketball courts. Yet even as recreation became something of a national focus, little consideration was given to the interests of women or blacks. Sport was about serving white males and clearly reflected class concerns. Although sport was idealized as a meritocracy, viewed as a force for mending social divisions, there were clear class distinctions. Some sports were for elites; some for the lower classes.

For some, sports had an urgent mission. Orchestrated physical exertion, some believed, was a critical antidote to an increasingly mechanized society. Some even saw organized sports in Darwinist terms as a savior of America's vigor and virility. Organized sports counteracted anxieties that the shift from farm to factory would trigger the physical and moral decline of a nation. This "new athletics," in the words of Luther Gulick, the prominent parks and recreation booster, was "a great new social agency" drafted by "the most fundamental needs of our time."[68] Note that Gulick minces no words; sports is a *social agency*.

By being cast as a solution to a social crisis, organized sports were immediately associated with a noble, civic-minded virtuosity. After all, they embodied the best American values, an alignment that even today provides athletics a protective sheen. Ironically, even as we embrace organized athletics as a force for civic unity and upbeat ideals, it conflicts with the American tradition of respect for individual rights and equal treatment under the law. Action on the field may be about winning and losing, but the structure which girds the play is more rooted in nostalgia than fairness. Courts have directed that people be considered as individuals, not judged by gender stereotypes. Organized sports, therefore, are precisely in conflict with such mandates.

Thus there are normative reasons for ending coercive sex segregation that arise from stated commitments to equality, fairness, and justice. More than half a century ago, the Supreme Court ruled in *Brown v. Board of Education* that "separate but equal" is "inherently unequal." Even if all schools get the same resources, racial segregation itself constitutes a harm to children in schools. The use of federal funds to support schools that enforce racial segregation is unconstitutional; equality and "liberty for all" are promised in our national creed.

Why should gender be any different? The fact of forced sex segregation in sports, aside from the practical considerations outlined above, also constitutes a harm to women.[69] If women are truly the equal of men in society, then the use of federal funds to support sex-segregated sports teams should also be unconstitutional. Such normative reasons for gender integration in sports rest on equality, liberty, and the interest in living up to the egalitarian principles as formalized by the U.S. Constitution.

Again, none of this should be construed to suggest that women should be forced to play on gender-integrated teams. As we explain in chapter 5, courts have supported voluntary segregation if it is requested by the historically less powerful group. Certain public schools, for instance, are experimenting with girls-only math classes, which have been held to be constitutional because they benefit women, historically the out-of-power sex.[70]

This book argues that coercive, or forced, sex segregation in sports should be called out for what it is: a violation of the Fourteenth Amendment's Equal Protection Clause. The policy premise in sports should be neutral as to sex classification, just as it is neutral on the issue of race classification. The only qualifications for playing sports, therefore, should be those related to an individual's abilities to play, not attributes stereotypically assigned to the sex or race group to which the individual belongs. Yes, African American men have excelled in professional basketball leagues, but this does not mean that an individual white man should be coerced to play on a race-segregated white basketball league on the grounds that white men as a group are less talented then black men as a group when it comes to playing professional basketball.

To the contrary, all sports competitions should be based on the abilities of the individuals who seek to play, not on stereotypical attributes of sex or race groups. The only exception, as we have pointed out, is voluntary segregation for a subordinate group in order to compensate for past discrimination.

Title IX's Impact on Women in Sports

Some ask, Didn't Title IX, passed by Congress in 1972, remove barriers to women's participation in athletics? Don't we see dramatic increases in the number of women excited about and participating in sports? Aren't we proud as a nation when our women's soccer team beats all others at the Olympic Games, something our men's soccer team could not do in 2004?

The answer, of course, is yes. Title IX has been a fabulous catalyst for introducing women into sports and onto athletic fields. The passage of Title IX in 1972 acknowledged the role of competitive sports in personal success. The law, though general in its language, drew attention to systematic gender inequality in educational policies in general, which later came to include disparities in educational sports programs. Although the law just applied to educational institutions receiving federal funding, Title IX has defined educational standards for fairness.

Title IX Is Not Enough

Ironically, however, although Title IX is generally viewed as having fixed the problem of gender equality in sports, we contend that nothing could be further from the truth. Even as the law drew more women into sports, the legislation codified a sex-segregated system of athletics within education contexts. The express purpose of Title IX was to prohibit sex discrimination in educational programs receiving federal support.[71] Nevertheless, it explicitly permitted sex segregation in contact sports. The regulation reads:

> A recipient may operate or sponsor separate teams for members of each sex where selection for such teams is based upon competitive skill or the activity involved is a contact sport. However, where a recipient operates or sponsors a team in a particular sport for members of one sex but operates or sponsors no such team for members of the other sex, and athletic opportunities for members of that sex have previously been limited, members of the excluded sex must be allowed to try-out for the team offered unless the sport is a contact sport. For purposes of this part, contact sports include boxing, wrestling, rugby, ice hockey, football, basketball and other sports where the purpose or major activity of which involves bodily contact.[72]

Although Title IX does not *require* sex segregation, the regulations explicitly *allow* it in contact sports. Critically, this mere permission has spurred the sex segregation of all sports, contact and noncontact alike. Schools typically offer a contact sport such as football on a sex-segregated basis, open only to males. Instead of offering a separate football team for females, as the law would suggest, schools offer alternative female-only sports. Football for males; field hockey for females. This practice has far-reaching results, including creation of separate boys' and girls' teams in sports that would not require such divisions. There are separate boys' and girls' teams in track, bowling, and tennis, among other sports in which there is no physical contact. In effect, Title IX reinforced, rather than challenged, assumptions of male superiority and female weakness.

Sports: A Gendered Battleground

From the moment female golfer Annika Sorenstam accepted a sponsor's exemption to play a PGA Tour event, the all-male Bank of America Colonial in Fort Worth, Texas, in May 2003, it started. Sports radio airwaves buzzed; golf chat sites were on fire: Could she or couldn't she?

"She doesn't belong out here," pro male golfer Vijay Singh said 11 days before the event. "She's the best woman golfer in the world, and I want to emphasize 'woman.' We have our tour for men, and they have their tour. She's taking the spot from someone in the field."[73]

This wasn't just the familiar claim a female was swiping food from the table of a male breadwinner. It reminded all that athletics is more than play. Stakes are high because organized sports offer men a means for demonstrating masculinity and displaying physical power. For Singh, Sorenstam's playing hit a nerve, the gut belief that it is *wrong*. Men are physically bigger, stronger, and faster and regardless of the challenge (the thinking goes) should win. Isn't that why women play with women and men play with men? There was no way, many assumed, Sorenstam could hit from the same tees as men and not be drubbed and embarrassed.

Singh's comment, though, reflected more than concern about an athletic mismatch. Men playing *with* women upset the social order. When Singh said Sorenstam didn't belong, he expressed a cultural view that *females should not compete with males*. For women, the game represented a struggle for equal status. No wonder Singh's remarks turned a sleepy PGA tour stop into a twenty-first-century battle of the sexes. Interest in Sorenstam's appearance had TV networks salivating. Singh decided not to play, but Sorenstam's opening round drew 1.5 million viewers, producing the best ever rating for USA Network's Thursday coverage of a PGA event.[74]

The battle of the sexes–style anticipation evoked memories of September 30, 1973, when Billie Jean King faced Bobby Riggs in a $100,000 winner-take-all tennis match. Riggs, an over-the-hill 1939 Wimbledon champion, appeared goofy as he baited King, paraded around with sexy young women, downed vitamins, and claimed men wrote him fan letters. "They want me to put her in her place," he boasted. He showed off a T-shirt with nipples cut out he planned to give King because he claimed she'd look better in it.[75] Despite the silliness, the event drew broad public interest. More than 30,000 spectators filled the Houston Astrodome. Some 50 million more watched on TV. Muscular men carried King onto the court like Cleopatra. Riggs arrived on a rickshaw pulled by "Bobby's bosom buddies," models in skin-tight garb.[76]

It was a promotional spectacle, but King focused and dispatched Riggs after three straight sets, beating him 6–4, 6–3, 6–3. To our eyes today, the match proved little about male and female athletic ability. Riggs was a 55-year-old former champion and King, at 29, was at the top of her game. (She would be ranked number 1 in the world for five years, and win six Wimbledon championships and four U.S. Open titles.) However, in 1973, when virtually any male was deemed superior to any female at virtually anything not domestic in nature, it was a symbolic event.

The world saw a talented, muscular, and competent young woman close out distractions to win in tennis, a game the nation saw could be a spectator sport. Viewers learned female tennis players were just as compelling as male players. And King had confronted that nagging Riggs prod. "Women," he'd insisted, "belong in the kitchen and the bedroom, not on the tennis court."[77]

The bluster about where female athletes belong is familiar but frustrating because it frames gender issues around social propriety, not physical ability. The struggle for women athletes is rooted as much in earning permission to play as in possessing the ability to compete. Clearly female athleticism speaks to more than sport. It matters, not just for the contest at hand, but for the bigger contest of women's equality. When a woman wins big, she pushes the boundaries a little, offering with each performance a revised vision of female social status, thereby challenging the presumption that sports is a male-only arena for defining masculinity in terms of men's physical—if not mental, emotion, and general—superiority over women.[78]

Riggs, embracing the "male chauvinist pig" label, echoed an era's taunt: women should be stationed at home, serving men. From the safety of a new century such assertions look ridiculous, but at the time, many women weren't sure that it wasn't true. When *Seventeen* magazine polled readers in 1975 and found that King was the most admired woman in the world, it was because her winning ways offered strength to other females.[79]

Singh's assertion that Sorenstam "didn't belong" on the men's tour was based on her sex, not her golfing ability. Ironically, Singh's remark clarified the stakes: Sorenstam didn't have to win; she merely had to prove she "belonged." It was still a big challenge. Unlike Riggs, PGA golfers are at the top of their game. Could Sorenstam compete?

Many expected her to cave under pressure. As the first round proceeded, however, a different story emerged: Sorenstam was playing well, more than holding her own. TV announcers were taken aback. "I'm ashamed to admit this, but I'm just getting started to know [Sorenstam]," said golf commentator David Feherty. "She has competed with an easy grace and dignity and with a childlike curiosity. Boy, can she play."[80] (This would not be the first or last time women would be compared with children.) CBS golf host Jim Nantz couldn't believe her focus. "She far exceeded anyone's estimates," he said. "I told a *Sports Illustrated* writer that you have the Sports Person of the Year now. It's over."[81]

When the first round finished, Sorenstam had scored a 71, one over par and tied for seventy-third among 114 players. The photo of Sorenstam pumping her right fist after a birdie on the thirteenth hole next to the headline on Kevin Paul Dupont's *Boston Globe* column the next morning said it all: "History Lesson: She Can Hang with the Boys."[82]

It was a huge moment. Sorenstam had showed in 18 holes that male and female golfers do not inhabit different universes, and that a woman can be in the mix with other top male golfers. Sorenstam did not perform as well the second day, shooting a 74 and missing by four strokes the cut that would have put her into the final rounds. She was understandably disappointed. Even though competing under what one writer called "the biggest media microscope the world could roll onto a golf course," she kept her poise and focus.[83] Her Thursday score beat 27 top male golfers, and even with her poor Friday round she still finished ahead of 10 men.[84]

Despite the second round letdown, no one who watched Sorenstam or wrote about her play had anything but praise. Sorenstam, however, was surprisingly apologetic. "I'm glad I did it, but I was in way over my head," she said. "I wasn't as tough as I thought I was." And then she said it, after beating some of the best male golfers in the world. She uttered the phrase that haunts women challenging the status quo.

"I've got to go back to my [LPGA] Tour where I belong," she said.[85] Sorenstam—even after a showing that quelled doubters who expected her to fold early, even despite Tiger Woods encouraging her to play more PGA events because the best have off-days— embraced the self-censorship so familiar to the female sex. The message must be stamped on our skin: *I don't really belong.*

Inferiority, Injury, Immorality

Women's Brains

The assumptions underlying coercive sex segregation in sports have haunted women's quest for equality since time immemorial. For example, the general public and experts of the day, including physicians, once embraced the belief that female physiology, including smaller brains and complicated reproductive systems, saddled women with stunning limitations. Educators contended that "because of" their physical differences, women are intellectually inferior. If women sought to "think with the boys," leading scientists and physicians warned, the immense demand of blood flow to the brain would sap female reproductive organs and leave them infertile. Prohibiting women from higher education, they argued, was for their own good, to protect them from such injuries. Even if women could and did "think with the boys," there was another problem: mixing the sexes was considered immoral. The powerful belief that males and females occupied distinct realms—hers the domestic, his the public—provided a necessary structure to society and protected the purity of the home. To mix the sexes, to breach the separate spheres, threatened the natural order.

Women's Brawn

Arguments advanced to prohibit women from engaging in the same higher education as men, therefore, turned on female physical differences and the three I's: inferiority, injury, and immorality. No one today dares suggest that a woman's reproductive organs "mean" she is unfit for sex-integrated academic studies, regardless of the intellectual rigor. Yet when it comes to athletics, the three I's prevail. Women's physical differences from men are interpreted to mean that females are athletically *inferior* to men, that women will be *injured* if they "play with the boys," and that sex-integrated sports programs, particularly in contact sports, such as wrestling, are *immoral* by virtue of the close physical contact required or simply by virtue of the damaging results some believe such policies portend for society in general.

The problem of coercive sex segregation is little more than the age-old problem of the three I's, transported from their nineteenth-century academic context as based on a physical analysis of women's brain size to their twenty-first-century athletic context as based on women's brawn size.

Stages of Desegregation

Just as policies based on the three I's did not instrumentally or normatively benefit women as applied to academic contexts, we argue that such policies also fail to instrumentally or normatively benefit women in athletic contexts. Now, as in the past, to challenge the three I's requires moving through a four-stage process. The first stage of sex desegregation requires challenging the initial stage of *prohibiting* women from participating in academic or sports activities in the first place. The second stage allows women to participate in academic or sports activities, but only on a *coercive sex-segregated* basis. The third stage allows women to participate in academic and sports programs on a *sex-integrated* basis. And the fourth stage permits women to choose whether they prefer a sex-integrated or sex-segregated context for their academic or sports activities, that is, *voluntary sex segregation.*

Academic programs in the United States traverse the full course of all four stages. While at first women were barred from academic contexts that required "male-like" intellectual work, coercively sex-segregated opportunities (the second stage) came with the birth of women-only colleges in the late nineteenth century. By the late 1970s, top universities became sex-integrated, marking the third stage of sex desegregation in higher education. Today, women choose whether to sex-segregate themselves voluntarily by attending women only colleges, such as Wellesley or Smith, or to attend sex-integrated colleges and universities, such as Amherst and Yale.

When we look at sports policies, however, it's obvious that we are far from desegregating sports on the basis of sex. Initially women were dissuaded from, limited in their access to, or prohibited from participating in athletics. Eventually passage of Title IX in 1972 moved sports policies to the second stage: coercive sex segregation. Women could play sports and were even encouraged to do so, but in coercively sex-segregated contexts. As in academic contexts, the move from prohibition to coercive sex segregation represented an important stride. But it is not the end point. Rather, the goal is to reach the stage where the subordinate group—women, in this case—can choose voluntary sex segregation in sports or sex-integrated sports.

Framing the Problem

Given this context, Sorenstam's apologetic stance was disappointing. Of course, it is disheartening to see someone who played so admirably embrace the language and belief of not belonging. But more critically, such behavior fits the historical pattern in which women denigrate their athletic achievements for fear of being perceived as "masculine" or to conform to gender-role expectations. Sorenstam was the first woman since Babe Didrickson in 1945 to play a PGA event, but she easily accepted her "place" as a woman, ignoring her accomplishments as a golfer.

To be fair, most female athletes are not politically minded and Sorenstam never viewed her PGA play as a gender breakthrough. She took it as a personal challenge, a means for improving her game. Her apologetic response is disheartening to feminists, but it illustrates the understanding female athletes have about their role in the sports world. They know the structure.

The way organized sports operate—at amateur, school, and professional levels—has been influenced by historical beliefs about the distinct "nature" of males and females. We assume boys throw balls better than girls. We assume males are physically superior so their races and contests should be longer or more challenging to make up for female limitations. Such accommodations are made without regard to physiological fact or abilities of individual athletes. The message is broadcast before the pistol sounds the start of the race: Men are better.

Actual performance of female athletes has been handicapped by cultural messages dissuading women from competing. Bold women have historically challenged barriers. They are the few, however. The tides shaping the landscape is the waves of females not comfortable competing against a hailstorm of negative messages. Females are taught from a young age to check their aggression, curb their passion to play hard, and, above all, not care about winning. Sports for women are supposed to be social, for fun and fitness—or so has been the message.

It is finally accepted that a male is not inherently a better lawyer or doctor than a female (although even now, men in high positions sometimes question women's biological abilities to engage in male-dominated fields, like math and science, as did former Harvard President Lawrence Summers in 2004). We now understand what we did not a generation or more ago, that individual abilities matter more than one's sex. Yet how do we begin to rewind knee-jerk gender presumptions in sports? How do we challenge gender bias?

There are different physical demands on athletes at all levels. There are different requirements of athletes competing in the Olympics versus, say, a club tennis tournament. And yet a sign of the depth of discrimination is the consistency with which patterns of gender bias exist. Too many male club tennis players believe they must be matched with a male player because a woman couldn't be challenging enough. Tennis may have a rating system in place, but it is generally applied within genders. Too many clubs offer competitions for men. And competitions for women. What does differentiation accomplish? Would any club make distinctions by race? A competition for white players and one for racial minorities?

Disentangling Sex from Athletic Abilities

The athletic expectations that are bound up with gender identity are as troublesome for the unathletic male as for the athletic female. Such expectations create anxieties for children at young ages. Parents of uncoordinated boys frantically search for a sport or sport-like activity at which their sons can appear competent and avoid social embarrassment. Parents of athletically gifted girls juggle pride in a daughter's prowess with worries she'll be too good and, therefore, alienated and whispered about. Is she gay? (Here as in other areas of society, "gay" is used as a code word for not fitting into established gender roles.) Not feminine enough? What's *wrong* with her?

The manner in which we structure sports in our society has consequences at once deeply personal and broadly political. It is tempting to view sports as millions of unrelated programs, clubs, and events. There are vast differences in physical demands and public attention, depending on sport, age, level of play. Yet there also exists a culture of sports. There are practices and patterns that persist, a mind-set replicated over and over. There is a belief system perpetuated, in part, because no one dares to challenge it. That, at the heart of it, is why we have written this book.

2

The Sex Difference Question

The Olympic Games must be reserved for men ... We must continue to try to achieve the following definition: the solemn and periodic exaltation of male athleticism, with internationalism as a base, loyalty as a means, art for its setting, and female applause as its reward.

—Pierre de Coubertin, founder of the modern Olympics[1]

Some boys cry when she beats them. One quit the sport after she pinned him in 15 seconds.

—Nikki Darrow, high school wrestler, and her mother,
Sandi Darrow, describing responses of male opponents
after losing to Nikki in competition

Playing "Like a Girl"

When NFL coach Bill Parcells was frustrated with receiver Terry Glenn for taking several weeks to recover from a hamstring injury when the two were with the New England Patriots in 1996, Parcells vented his displeasure with a single word. He referred to Glenn as "she."[2] Parcells was not the first to use the feminine pronoun to deride a male athlete. It has long been a motivational tool among coaches, and Parcells is known for his verbal zingers. The practice, however, reflects a troubling perception, not only that males and females are inherently different, but that the female difference is a lacking. To be "she" is to be less than "he."[3]

Male performance is the standard against which female performance is measured. Females may excel in "feminine" sports like dance, gymnastics, and figure skating. However, in other sports, particularly traditionally "male" sports like wrestling, baseball, or basketball, women are—sight unseen—presumed inherently, biologically, physically disadvantaged. If they do perform well, their femininity may be suspect.

The practice and power of gender marking in sports received special attention during the 2005 football season at the University of Iowa, where the visiting team's locker room was painted pink. In the late 1970s, former Iowa football coach Hayden Fry, a psychology buff, ordered the walls made pink to "weaken and debilitate opposing football players."[4] In 2005, when remodeling the locker room, team officials decided to extend the color to the carpet, urinals, and lockers as well. Feminists inside and outside the university complained that such an action and intent discriminated against women and homosexuals, igniting a national discussion in the sports pages. Said one Michigan player, "You're not in the locker room when you play. Just because I'm in a locker room that's pink doesn't mean I'm going on the field in a pink jersey."[5] Here, even as the player attempted to minimize the effects of a pink locker room, he still enforced gender stereotypes—and the power of the color pink to throw men off their game.[6]

Testing for Sex Difference

There is a general acceptance, therefore, that (1) not only are males and females physically different but (2) to be female is to be athletically inferior. Thus the color pink, because it is associated with girls, becomes a symbol for athletic inferiority. The assumption that females are athletically second-rate has been culturally embedded and legally enforced by mechanisms of coercive sex segregation. Until recently, women in international and Olympic competition were required to prove themselves female to compete in female-only events, although men were not asked to prove they were male. The logic for this asymmetry? Women competing in female-only events needed protection from males who might sneak into competition. The logic presumes males have a clear advantage and would beat all women. The reverse was not considered because women are presumed to be so inferior to men that a female sneaking into an all-male event would pose no real threat to any male athlete.

Thus the International Olympic Committee (IOC) and the International Amateur Athletic Federation (IAAF) policies did not monitor whether a female "passed" as a male. Rather, they only aimed to stop a man who might "pass" as female. As a result, the pressing question for women (but not men) seeking to compete in the Olympics and other international events was, How do I prove I am female?

Sex Tests

During the 1960s, Olympic officials answered that question by looking at women, literally. At the 1966 European Track and Field Championships in Budapest, Hungary, and the 1967 Pan American Games in Winnipeg, for example, female athletes paraded *naked* before a panel of doctors.[7] Judges visually inspected female athletes' genitalia looking for such abnormalities as no vaginal opening, an enlarged clitoris that could be a proto-penis, a penis, or testicles.[8] If the observant judges felt a woman "looked" female, then that woman "was" female.

Needless to say, women athletes complained. It was humiliating and degrading to be forced to display themselves before officials in this way. In response, the IOC and the IAAF found a new way to determine if women were female by replacing the eyeball test with a chromosome test. Then a funny thing happened. Women who looked female, felt female, and had always thought they were female—found out they weren't.

Polish sprinter Ewa Klobukowska was one such woman. In 1966, when she paraded naked under IAAF orders to participate in track meets, she passed as female. But one year later, when the chromosome test took effect, although Klobukowska easily agreed to have cells scraped from inside her cheek before the European Cup track meet in Kiev, she was stunned by test results. After all, the lithe 5 foot 7 blonde sprinter was, according to a press report, "sufficiently feminine to attract plenty of male dance partners in Warsaw night spots."[9] Her chromosome test, however, found she was not a woman as defined by international athletic competition rules.

This is because when her cell samples were subjected to a microscope, three Russian and three Hungarian doctors pronounced that Klobukowska was not female because she had "one chromosome too many."[10] They did not say which chromosome was extra. A woman has 22 pairs of nonsex chromosomes, the same as a man. In addition, females have two X chromosomes that determine sex, while males have one X and one Y, with the Y establishing maleness. It is possible, however, for individuals to have one chromosome too many by having an XXY combination, which yields external male genitalia and poor physical development, unlikely in a world-class athlete. More likely, as experts at the time suggested, Klobukowska was a mosaic, with some XXY cells and some with only X chromosomes. In such cases, individuals may be genetic males but have ambiguous or female-like genitalia. Most critically, however, athletes with sex-related abnormalities raised as females "have no unfair physical advantage," according to the Council on Scientific Affairs for the American Medical Association.[11]

The new chromosome testing that Klobukowska failed at the European Cup in 1967 and that was piloted for the 1968 Winter Olympics in Grenoble, France, was instituted for all Olympic Games beginning with the 1968 Mexico City Olympics.[12] Ostensibly, the testing sought to halt rumors of men masquerading as women and earning victories they did not deserve. Interestingly, however, only one man ever admitted to such a ruse. In 1957, Hermann Artjen of Bremen, Germany, said he was forced by the Nazis to enter the women's high jump in the 1936 Olympics. Despite the effective camouflage, being male hardly helped: he came in fourth.[13]

The Wrong Test

The real problem for women who appeared "too male" was not the result of male sex chromosomes, but of illegal performance-enhancing drugs, including the use of steroids. Although there later proved to be a very real doping problem, at the time, use of illegal performance-enhancing drugs seemed less important than enforcing the distinctions between male and female. This was done in the name of fair competition, but the method missed the mark by focusing on gender verification, not doping. In the end, sex testing was profoundly damaging to many female athletes who gained no competitive advantage from chromosomal abnormalities and yet felt exposed and humiliated. Most women who failed the female test quietly withdrew from competition. One, however, decided to fight.

Proving Herself Female

In 1985 Spain's top female hurdler, María José Martínez Patiño, found herself suddenly excluded from the World University Games in Kobe, Japan, when cheek cells revealed a Y chromosome. This caught Patiño by surprise. After all, she looked like a woman and had never considered herself as anything but a woman; but she was—according to IAAF rules—male. Patiño had only submitted to the tests because she had forgotten the certificate proving her female status at home. She was tested originally in 1983 in Helsinki, Finland, had passed, and had used the certificate from those results for entry at all subsequent competitions. It was revealed later that those Helsinki results were in error.[14]

Patiño, it turns out, was born with normal X and normal Y chromosomes, but because of a mutation elsewhere, she had androgen insensitivity and did not respond to male sex hormones.[15] She was born without ovaries or a uterus and had testes concealed in her labia. Even though the latter made testosterone, because her cells did not detect the hormone, her body never developed male characteristics. At puberty, her testes produced estrogen—as all testes do—and her waist narrowed, breasts grew, and hips widened. In other words, she developed as a woman and never suspected she wasn't genetically female.

It took Patiño nearly three years to win reinstatement to competition and to regain her place on the Spanish Olympic team. The key was a Finnish geneticist who in 1988 proved that her genetic status offered her no unfair athletic advantage. Despite the humiliation (she lost her university scholarship and her boyfriend, and faced tremendous personal stress), the IOC and the IAAF continued the practice of gender verification testing. Finally, in the early 1990s some physicians and athletic leaders—including the IAAF, which in 1992 recommended halting the tests—began questioning the value of gender verification testing. Increasingly, they found females with sex chromosome abnormalities being barred from competition—unfairly. In the most common of "intersex states," an individual possesses male genes but also a defect which prevents those genes from functioning, thereby bestowing to that individual no characteristics that are considered male or perceived to be advantageous in athletic competition.[16]

Yet sex verification testing continued. At the 1996 summer Olympics in Atlanta, for example, all female athletes—except those participating in equestrian events (which are mixed sex) and those who had been previously gender certified—appeared at the Olympic Village's Polyclinic to have cells scraped from the inside of their cheeks and sent to Emory University's Genetics Laboratory for testing.[17] Results showed eight female athletes—one in 423—failed sex tests, although further examination showed these were genetic abnormalities rather than men posing as women. All were permitted to compete. In fact, no sex tests in competition have uncovered any male posing as a female.[18] It wasn't until the 2000 Sydney Olympics that the IOC finally ended gender verification testing.[19]

Drugs versus Sex Difference

The end of gender verification testing was inevitable, if slow in coming. By the late 1990s, it became obvious that sex testing failed to address the real issue of unfair competition and was unacceptably traumatic for female athletes with chromosomal abnormalities. The real issue was the need for athletic organizers to stay ahead of those who would find other ways to cheat, specifically, by using illegal performance-enhancing drugs. This is a serious and constant challenge, whether the venue is the Tour de France, Major League Baseball, the Olympics, or college sports. There have been well-documented and disturbing stories of steroid abuses in Eastern European nations and, in the 1990s among Chinese athletes, including among female swimmers. (Officials were tipped off because a Chinese woman did not win an Olympic medal in swimming until 1988 and by 1994 they were dominating the sport, taking 12 of 16 gold medals at a world swim championship meet in Rome.)[20] In response to growing concerns, international athletics officials convened in Switzerland in February 1999 and accepted the Lausanne Declaration on Doping in Sport which established the International Anti-Doping Agency and created standards and testing policies.[21]

The use of illegal performance-enhancing drugs, particularly steroids, had attracted concern for years, even as officials focused on sex testing. Those concerns, however, tended in the case of female athletes to focus on how such drugs made women masculine, an apparently greater worry than performance-enhancing properties. Initial efforts, then, aimed to stop women from being male. In December 1980, for example, UCLA announced it would begin random testing of the 39 members of the women's track team. No such testing was planned for the men's team. The women's head track coach, Scott Chisam, said testing was meant to ensure the integrity of victories. "What we want is that when a United States athlete or a U.C.L.A. athlete is on the victory stand, we don't want anyone in second place to say that she beat her because of artificial means," he said. Ironically, Chisam said, the men's track team would not be tested because "a male athlete is a whole different story."[22]

Such bias reflects the narrow profile the female athlete is socially permitted to occupy. At the time, a *New York Times* article questioned Dr. Nell Jackson, assistant athletic director at Michigan State University, who said society hadn't given women athletes a chance to establish their identities. "If a male takes a steroid, and all the weightmen do," he said, "what's the connotation? If a woman takes it, she's taking drugs, she's not a woman."[23]

It is only recently that we have cared about the use of steroids by male athletes, while female athletes have faced such scrutiny for decades. This distinction reflects an underlying social bias. If a male takes steroids, he's just "more masculine," whereas steroid use by females blurs gender lines. Today we question the validity of some male athletes' record-setting performances. While steroids have no place in athletics, social pressures fuel an unfortunate double standard in which a male athlete artificially enhancing his body is wrong but understandable and natural, while a female athlete is considered unwomanly or grotesque.[24]

What Is Sex?

As Maria Patino and Ewa Klobukowska illustrate, nailing down what, biologically speaking, is female and what is male is more complicated than it first appears. Even when we consider sex organs, scientists do not always see a world divided in two. We assume XY male and XX female chromosomes, but as a 2001 Institute of Medicine report points out, "exceptions are more common than most people realize, resulting in chromosomal, gonadal, hormonal, or genital deviations from the chromosomal, gonadal, hormonal, or genital constitution of a 'typical' male or female."[25]

Although the number of babies born with mixed or nonmatching genitalia and sex organs or chromosomes of one sex and genitalia of another is considered rare, some experts argue such births are common enough—1.7 per 1,000, according to Brown University professor of biology Anne Fausto-Sterling. She suggests, provocatively, that social and cultural politics have created the male-female dichotomy where nature exhibits a sexual continuum.

"European and American culture is deeply devoted to the idea that there are only two sexes," observes Fausto-Sterling. "But if the state and legal system has an interest in maintaining only two sexes, our collective biological bodies do not. While male and female stand on extreme ends of a biological continuum, there are many other bodies . . . that evidently mix together anatomical components conventionally attributed to both males and females."[26]

Transsexual Athletes: Male or Female?

As we have seen, such mixtures have presented real controversy for athletic competitions which divide entrants dichotomously into only two sexes: male and female. While females with chromosomal abnormalities are no longer barred, the matter of assigning a sex to athletes has grown more complicated with the entrance of trans-sexuals into sports competitions. When Dr. Richard Raskind underwent a sex change operation in November 1975, becoming Dr. Renee Richards, it challenged the sports world in a new way. Before the operation, Raskind was an accomplished amateur tennis player, who in 1974 was ranked third in the East and thirteenth nationally in the men's 35-and-over division.[27] When Richards, now a woman, entered and was accepted to play in the Tennis Week Open by the tournament director, a longtime friend, 25 female players withdrew, arguing that despite the operation, Richards retained the genes of a man and some physical advantages, including height (6'2") and muscle structure. Even as these women protested, Richards earned support from Kathy Harter, the female tennis player Richards had defeated in a previous tournament. Harter argued that the Women's Tennis Association did not have the right to judge whether Richards was a man or a woman.[28]

When Is a Male a Male?

Transsexual athletes like Richards reveal how dependent organized athletics is on traditional gender constructions. Debate about allowing transsexuals to compete is ostensibly aimed at ensuring fair play, but it challenges our understanding of male and female. When, exactly, is a person male? And when does that actually bestow an advantage?[29]

Those questions are being vigorously debated. The challenge is this: just because the law recognizes an individual's sex, is that the sex he or she should adhere to for competition? As of 2007, there is not complete agreement on the participation of transsexual athletes. Individual sports federations such as the influential Federation Internationale de Volleyball (FIVB), require athletes to compete in the category of their birth sex, effectively restricting participation of transsexual athletes. However, before the 2004 Athens Olympics, the IOC decided to allow transsexual athletes to participate in their postsurgical sex category if they met certain criteria, including verifiable hormonal treatments.[30] In 2006, the IAAF's Medical and Anti-Doping Commission issued a policy supporting the IOC guidelines.

At the heart of the debate, of course, is the method of sex assignment and reassignment. While some transsexuals merely identify, dress, or live as the opposite sex, the focus for athletic organizing officials is on those who have undergone surgery to give themselves physical attributes of the opposite sex. In addition to surgery, these individuals follow up with hormone regimens. Female-to-male transsexuals are given doses of testosterone that research has shown to deepen their voices, atrophy breasts, halt menses, increase muscle mass, lead to weight gain and redistribution of fat, among other characteristics. Male-to-female transsexuals undergo regimens that include estrogen treatments that soften skin, decrease hair growth, enlarge breasts and nipples, and redistribute fat.[31]

Most of the athletic debate has focused on male-to-female transsexuals because some male characteristics such as muscle mass, height, and general size advantages are presumed to endure despite sex reassignment. This, however, depends on whether the surgery is pre- or post-puberty and on the extent of the hormone therapy. The IOC rules allow transsexuals who undergo surgery and hormone treatments before puberty to compete in their new sex category. Those who undergo surgery after puberty must undergo hormone therapy for at least two years before being permitted to compete. Ironically, there has been less concern about female-to-male transsexuals, although an individual receiving male hormone treatments could fail precompetition drug tests depending on the extent of testosterone treatments, effectively barring him from participation, creating a perhaps unintended bias against this group.

Debate around permitting male-to-female transsexuals to participate in sports competitions challenges the relative importance of birth sex characteristics and the effectiveness of hormone therapy. How important is the hormonal influence of puberty? Will muscle strength acquired during natural male puberty disappear? Diminish? While the IOC and IAAF require two years of hormone treatment before male-to-female transsexuals may compete, does the length of treatment needed vary for each individual? How do we know if the female hormonal treatment has been effective?[32] Arne Ljungqvist, the physician who headed the IOC committee that developed the policy on transsexual athletes, noted in a 2005 *Lancet* essay that while there is medical research on treating transsexuals, "there are little data relevant to the effects on athletic performance."[33]

As in earlier eras, attention to male-to-female transsexuals aims to halt the would-be male seeking athletic glory as a female. These individuals are not, however, the rumored posers of the pregender verification era. Rather, they suffer from gender dysphoria, estimated to be as high as 1 in 11,900 males and 1 in 30,400 females.[34] The notion of transsexuals undergoing sex reassignment therapy for athletic victory is absurd, particularly given the profound medical risks of high-dose hormone treatment. Plus, a male-to-female transsexual hungers to adopt social expectations of female behavior and most likely would not want to pass and still retain many male characteristics. And yet both the IOC and IAAF differentiate between male-to-female transsexuals who undergo sex reassignment treatment before puberty and those who do it afterward. Before puberty, there may be little—aside from a Y chromosome—to distinguish a transsexual boy-transforming-to-a-girl from a girl growing up to be a woman. After puberty, however, depending on the sport and the individual, residual male characteristics may matter a lot—or very little.[35]

What Is an Athletic Advantage?

The debate about admittance of transsexuals into athletic competition is important because it raises serious questions about what does—and does not—bestow a performance advantage on an individual athlete. How important, how relevant are male characteristics—or other enhancements—to competitive success? In a 2001 *New York Times* special report, sportswriter Jere Longman observed that in the future, the race by athletes to stay one step ahead of the World Anti-Doping Agency's ability to detect performance-enhancing substances will likely yield a new way of cheating, genetic engineering, by introducing into athletes' bodies genes aimed at enhancing performance.[36] The article, which reported on initial discussions by the World Anti-Doping Agency about the possibilities and challenges of gene manipulation in athletes, raises the possibility of breeding an athletic superstar by manipulating an egg or embryo.

What is a permissible edge? One might argue that top athletes are already physical outliers whose genetic advantages allow them to succeed above others. For example, during the 2004 Athens

Olympics, scientists observed that one reason swimmer Michael Phelps dominated was that he had a genetic advantage. He stands 6 feet 4 but has an elongated trunk, short legs (32-inch pants inseam), and double-jointed elbows, knees, and ankles which allow him to bend in the water as few other swimmers can. Plus, he has size 14 feet that are "like giant fins."[37]

Similarly, as Lance Armstrong rode to his seventh win in the Tour de France in 2005, allegations of doping were countered by Armstrong defenders who cited his superior physical gifts. The argument? He's just superhuman. Armstrong's doctor, Ed Coyle, who had been evaluating Armstrong at the Human Performance Laboratory at the University of Texas–Austin, noted that he possesses an oversize heart that can beat over 200 times a minute and can pump more blood, sending oxygen throughout his body at a rate most can't match.[38]

Is the playing field level when Armstrong competes? That is what we need to decide. What are the acceptable manipulations? In his article, Longman mentions a case in which a female basketball player from New York City asked her doctor to break both her arms and set them in a way that would make them longer, thereby aiding her play.[39] And what of those who have birth defects that give them elongated limbs? Flo Hyman, the superstar volleyball player who helped lead the U.S. Women's Volleyball Team to a Silver Medal in the 1984 Los Angeles Olympics, died suddenly at age 31 while playing volleyball in Japan in January 1986.[40] Only later was it discovered that the 6 foot 5 Hyman suffered from Marfan syndrome, a hereditary disease characterized by a tall stature, elongated fingers, and loose joints—qualities that also likely contributed to her success in volleyball.[41]

What, in short, is an acceptable genetic advantage? Should females who suffer from congenital adrenal hyperplasia—a condition which causes an oversupply of testosterone, resulting in extreme muscularity in women—be barred from competition? How does such a condition differ, from a policy-making vantage point, from some male-to-female transsexuals? Certainly to those athletes suffering from gender dysphoria, surgery and hormone therapy are a treatment—not an artificial means for gaining an athletic edge. (The 2006 IAAF policy identifies congenital adrenal hyperplasia, along with androgen producing tumors and anovulatory androgen excess as "conditions that may accord some advantages" but are nonetheless acceptable.)

Sex Group Differences

As Judith Lorber notes, until the 1700s, scientists and philosophers believed that there was only one sex and that "women's internal genitalia were the inverse of men's external genitalia: the womb and vagina were the penis and scrotum turned inside out." Of course, now, as she observes, "current Western thinking sees women and men as so different physically as to sometimes seem two species."[42] Thus the seemingly obvious statement that males and females are physically different often triggers stereotypes of male and female physical attributes and feeds a belief the sexes occupy opposite ends of the physical spectrum. To the contrary, the question, How different are males and females, is more to the point. And even more significant is the question, How do basic biological sex-group differences affect athletic performance? The answer depends on the sport. In some instances, female group differences give women an advantage, while male group differences offer advantages in other sports.[43]

What is key, therefore, when considering any advantage conferred by physical differences between men and women as groups is the particular sport in question. Yes, men as a group weigh more, are taller, and have more greater upper-body strength and more muscle mass than women as a group. But what constitutes a benefit in some sports (say, weighing 350 pounds playing on the offensive line in football, or being over 7 feet tall in basketball) may be a disadvantage in others (say, equestrian sports, car racing, boat racing, dogsled racing, airplane competitions, fencing, and gymnastics). Imagine, for example, putting a 350-pound lineman on a thoroughbred horse where the weight limit for jockey *and* saddle in the Triple Crown races is 130 pounds. Similarly, it would be ridiculous to cram a 7-foot basketball player into a tiny race car for the Indy 500.

At the same time, some physical attributes associated with women as a group—such as a lower center of gravity and a greater percentage of body fat—can be athletically advantageous. Might females (particularly those in middle and high school) have an edge in kicking field goals in which lower-body strength may help propel a ball over uprights? And what of wrestling, in which a lower center of gravity and stronger legs may help pin an opponent (particularly if a females' greater body fat percentages were accounted for in weight class divisions)? Or long-distance swimming, in which women's higher body fat provides more buoyancy and protection from frigid waters? Could females have an edge in superendurance running? There are clearly sports in which women's lower average weight and smaller average height may confer an advantage over males who possess a greater average height and weight.

It is simply flawed reasoning to assume that every female group difference represents a characteristic that makes women athletically inferior to men. To the contrary, whether a sex group difference is an advantage depends on the sport in question.

Men and Women as Groups

Weight and Height

Perhaps the most obvious group differences between men and women that impact sports are related to size and hormones. They affect athletic performance in terms of body metabolism, body composition, and size differences between male and female hearts and lungs. On average, as government and other data show, American men average 39.6 to 48.4 pounds more lean body mass, and 6.6 to 13.2 pounds less fat than women. American males as a group are 5.4 inches taller and 28 pounds heavier than American females as a group.[44] On average, men also have a wider upper-body frame.[45]

Testosterone

Obviously an essential physiological difference between males and females is hormonal. Both sexes have the same hormones, but women have higher levels of estrogen and men have higher levels of testosterone. Women, on average, have one-tenth the testosterone of men, although testosterone levels vary more greatly among women than men.[46] Testosterone is key to development of muscle. Research shows even when substances are used to amplify the effects of testosterone, responses to weightlifting are similar in males and females, suggesting testosterone is the greater variable in muscle development.[47] This means women with higher natural testosterone levels can achieve greater strength than women with lower levels.[48] Although men on average are capable of greater muscle mass than females on average, there is great variability among individuals, particularly women. Given cultural bias against women developing muscles, we may not yet know the physiological limits of female strength.[49]

Estrogen

Estrogen is responsible for women having a generally higher percentage of body fat than men while testosterone allows males generally greater muscle mass than females. This juxtaposition is typically seen as giving men an athletic advantage and women a disadvantage. However, the picture is more complex. For example, hormones play into differences in heat tolerance between males and females. Females have fewer functional sweat glands than males. As a result, women's body temperatures rise two or three degrees higher than men's before significant sweating begins the cooling process. Women record smaller body temperature changes than men when exerting themselves for long periods in heat or normal temperatures. Females cool down more quickly than males after exercise in hot weather.[50] In freezing temperatures, women's greater subcutaneous fat insulates the body. Consequently, even though women are more prone to heat stress, they lose less water than men and better compensate for exterior temperature effects.[51] Whether such attributes are a boon or a drag depends on the particular sport.

Lean Body Mass versus Fat

In general, more lean muscle mass offers an advantage in athletic performance because it influences an individual's strength and speed. It is not the only factor (as increasing coaching to improve individual athlete's biomechanics, for example, suggests), but it is significant. In the broadest sense, fat is the load to be hauled across a distance while muscle is the engine powering the body along that course. Men, on average, benefit because they have more lean body mass (or less body mass comprised of fat). Still, there is great variability within genders and between athletes in different sports. There are males with high percentages of body fat, just as there are women with little body fat. A trained male athlete's body fat may range from 7 percent of body mass for decathlon athletes to 20 percent among shot put throwers. Elite female runners may have body fat as low as 9 percent.[52] There is significant overlap in body fat percentages between male and female athletes.

Muscle Strength

Nonetheless, males have the potential to be, pound for pound, stronger than females. On average, females possess 40 to 60 percent of the average male's upper-body strength and 70 to 75 percent of the average male's lower-body strength.[53] These estimates, however, vary between trained and untrained individuals.[54] Increased opportunities for training and coaching for female athletes at all levels are narrowing gaps in absolute strength. Among highly trained power lifters, for example, one study found that performance differences between the sexes ranged from 0 to 8 percent.[55]

Males have the opportunity for more muscle than females, but male muscles are not stronger than female muscles. Measures, including strength relative to cross-sectional area of muscle, reveal that "the strength of men and women is nearly equal."[56] Males and females also have similar fast- and slow-twitch muscles. Still other research suggests when strength performance, including leg presses, bench presses, and grip strength are measured relative to lean body weight—correcting for differences in body mass composition—that "mean values of women and men did not differ significantly."[57]

A study of men and women in their twenties of leg-press performance relative to lean body mass showed that "the females were actually stronger than the men with respect to their lower body strength."[58] And a study of a smaller muscle, the *adductor pollicis*, which contributes to gripping, challenged males and females matched by strength to repeated exercise of the muscle. Results showed females had slower rates of fatigue and faster recovery between contractions.[59]

Oxygen

One key physical measure of an athlete's body functionality is the ability to take oxygen breathed in from the air and transport it to active muscles. Muscles use oxygen to produce ATP (adenosine triphosphate, a nucleotide), which fuels muscle contractions. The volume and speed of this process are referred to as aerobic power or VO2max. On average, a male's VO2max is 50 percent greater than a female's VO2max. This is because VO2max relies on three things: (1) the heart's capacity to pump blood, (2) the ability of the lungs to fully oxygenate blood returning from active muscles and other tissue, and (3) the oxygen-carrying capacity of the blood. Because males have generally larger hearts and lungs and higher hemoglobin levels, they are able to get more oxygen into the blood faster than females with generally smaller lungs and hearts.

Metabolism

This is a huge male athletic advantage, but it is not the whole story. Metabolic research suggests females have additional mechanisms for delivering oxygen to muscles or have more effective methods for shunting blood to active muscles.[60] While women have more body fat than men, this can be a boon in endurance events. Research shows females oxidize proportionately more fat and fewer carbohydrates than males in a fasted state. Because fat is a plentiful fuel (even lean athletes have good fat stores), carbohydrate or glycogen can be spared. When females consume carbohydrates during exercise, research suggests they also oxidize greater relative proportions of those carbohydrates than males do, which may spare endogenous fuel.[61] In other words, men's larger size may allow an advantage in powering muscle in some settings, but women's metabolic mechanisms may give females an edge in endurance.

The difference in the way males and females metabolize energy sources is an important but not fully explored area. Most research on muscle metabolism, nutrition, and exercise physiology has been conducted on males. The discovery that females have different mechanisms for fueling muscles affects nutritional and other training-related preparation. The lack of attention to female differences, metabolic experts argue, has put women at a historic disadvantage.

"There appears to have been a gender bias that has evolved in the area of muscle physiology with nutritional recommendations and programs developed with data derived primarily or exclusively from male subjects," said a metabolic researcher. "Misinformation and ignorance regarding female metabolism during exercise may have been factors in the exclusion of females from participating in the Olympic marathon until the Los Angeles games in 1984."[62]

Endurance

The story of female endurance has emerged in recent years. Studies matching equally trained male and female athletes reveal women's superiority in ultraendurance sports. A 1996 study, for example, showed equally trained males and females performed identically over 42 kilometers, but females outperformed males over 90 kilometers. Several studies yielded similar results, with a regression analysis showing a performance advantage for females over 66 kilometers.[63] Still, it is difficult to know if other factors—including training, experience, and the size of the female endurance athlete pool—shaped that 66-kilometer mark. Will females outperform males at even shorter distances in the future?

Estrogen seems to be the key to female advantage in ultraendurance events. The hormone appears to have a protective effect on muscles, minimizing skeletal muscle damage and soreness from exercise.[64] Other research shows estrogen may delay the onset of fatigue in part by spurring serotonin production, which increases energy and elevates mood. Estrogen may promote water retention, lessening dehydration in some settings, and may lessen free-radical damage, spurring quicker recovery of slow-twitch muscle.[65] More study is needed to fully understand estrogen's role, but early indications suggest it is a metabolic boon in endurance settings. Research shows, for example, mature female rats can run longer than mature male rats and use less muscle glycogen doing it. When male rats are administered estrogen, they too use less muscle glycogen and can run longer than untreated males.[66]

Lactate Tolerance

There is also the reality of lactate tolerance. During heavy exercise, lactate levels rise, which makes muscles tire. Lactate tolerance varies among individuals, marking differences in how long one continues at peak performance. Training also cannot be ignored. Differences in maximal oxygen uptake vary with training levels and suggest smaller sex differences among elite athletes.[67] In the end, it is not that males are built better than females. They are just built, on average, bigger, which in some—though certainly not all—instances provides a potential advantage.

And Last but Not Least: Genitals . . . Their Location, That Is

Freud is famous for asserting that men suffer from castration anxiety due to deep seated psychological dynamics, including the sight of girls whose "invisible" genitals proffer the image that men's might also disappear, that is, be destroyed. Not so. The invisibility of female genitalia does not signify the absence of genitalia much less their destruction, but simply their location inside, rather than outside, the body. What this means is that women's genitals are protected from external castrating injuries in contrast to men's genitalia that are not.

There is no sport where having one's genitalia located outside one's body provides an advantage. To the contrary, it is a disadvantage. It is such a disadvantage that in some sports there are rules that require players to wear a "cup"—a plastic covering for testicles to protect them from injury. In baseball, for example, catchers are required to wear cups in order to protect their testicles from injury resulting from pitches gone astray. An interesting question occurs, therefore, when a sport such as baseball becomes sex-integrated.[68] Should the requirement that a catcher wear a cup apply to a female catcher as well as a male catcher? The obvious answer would seem to be "no," since the location of female genitals inside the body protects them more than could any cup. However, not so, as 12-year-old Melissa Raglin found out in 1997 when she wanted to play baseball with the boys in The Babe Ruth League in Boca Raton, Florida.[69] This League required that all catchers must wear a cup. She protested that the rule was not necessary in her case since she had no genitals outside her body needing protection in the first place. So, too, did the National Organization for Women protest on her behalf, claiming that the rule was unnecessary for girls. Or, to put it another way, girls have an anatomical advantage over males when it comes to the location of their genitals such that girls do not need a cup protection.

Nevertheless, a Babe Ruth commissioner maintained that being hit by a baseball "in 'that region' could cause devastating long-term effects."[70] Assuming that what is meant by "that region" is one's genitals, Melissa and her supporters contended that this was only true for boys, but not for girls. The argument that girls had a physical advantage compared to boys, however, got nowhere. In the end, Melissa was required to wear a cup, if she wanted to be a catcher. She did, attaching the cup to her ankle.

The Female Physical Advantage

As scholars Shirley Castelnuovo and Sharon Guthrie analyze in their provocative book, *Feminism and the Female Body: Liberating the Amazon Within*, the icon of the Amazon stands for the cultural fear, if not hatred, that many women are "more powerful than many men."[71] Admitting the possibility, much less reality, of women's greater power than men's threatens established hierarchies of dominance constructed on exactly the opposite assumption that men are more powerful—mentally and physically—than women. Women who do achieve recognition as being superior to men, therefore, are routinely masculinized if not homosexualized, so that they are no longer "women," according to the social standards of a culture.[72]

It may be cultural habit to presume males superior athletes, but it is a habit that it is time to kick. As we have noted, there are plenty of examples in which women's biological attributes have yielded success in performance. The ultra marathon is one of them. In July 2003, for example, 42-year-old Pamela Reed of Arizona won the 135-mile Badwater Ultra Marathon, the sport's premier event, beating all men and women. Reed also won in 2002, setting a women's course record of 27:56:47 and beating her nearest competitor by nearly five hours. The grueling race begins in California's Death Valley and finishes halfway up Mount Whitney, the highest point in the United States. Interestingly, three of the top five finishers in 2003 were women.[73] Reed in March 2005 blazed a new trail by running 300 miles over 80 hours without sleeping. Reed decided to do the run after rival Dean Karnezes of California attempted a 300-mile run but only completed 262 miles.[74]

Women also appear physiologically suited to excel in sports in which the athlete is exposed to extreme temperatures. Their layer of subcutaneous fat, for example, appears to be a boon in the Iditarod, the challenging 1,200-mile dogsled race across Alaska's frozen terrain from Anchorage to Nome. Musher Susan Butcher, for example, won the race four times outright.[75] Libby Riddles, famous for being the first woman to win the Iditarod, did it in 1985, defying odds by, as the *Anchorage Daily News* put it, mushing 13 dogs out of Shaktoolik "and into the teeth of a blizzard that pinned every other racer" down.[76] By making this daring and courageous move, Riddles garnered a lead that none could overcome.

Women also have a physiological edge in distance swimming. Because in swimming the athlete's body is supported by water, "rather than being a problem, having a higher percentage of body fat may enhance performance," concluded researchers studying elite male and female swim performances. Greater percentages of body fat may enhance buoyancy and reduce drag in the water. In ultra long-distance swims, it may better insulate the body, slowing the rate of heat loss to cold water during long exposure.[77] And while some research suggests men have more absolute power in executing the crawl stroke, data in one comparison revealed that "despite arm length differences, females pulled deeper and narrower than males," making them "technically more efficient than males."[78]

Women have excelled in long-distance swimming. When American Gertrude Ederle became the first woman to swim the English Channel in 1926, she did it in 14 hours and 31 minutes, beating the records of the five men who had made the swim before her from 1875 to 1923.[79] Briton's Alison Streeter, the "queen of the channel," had made the 21-mile sea crossing 43 times by early 2005, more than any other person, male or female.[80] The accomplishment is impressive because each year only about half of the attempts to swim the Channel are successful.

In the United States, the Catalina Swim is a comparable distance, with 22 miles of open water between Santa Catalina Island and the California mainland. There are four course records (two one-way swims and two two-way swims, one each beginning on the mainland and the island), and three of those records are held by women.[81] Since the first race across the Catalina Channel was held in 1927, Penny Lee Dean, historian for the Catalina Channel Swimming Foundation and course record holder, observed that women have performed as well as men in the distance swims.

Even in dramatically shorter distance events in pool and open water, females have outperformed male counterparts. In records for seven races, from the one-hour swim to the two-mile race, statistics from long-distance championship events collected by the United States Masters Swimming organization show, among 19- to 24-year-old swimmers, for example, males hold records for distance or time in four events and females in three events.[82]

Women's bodies clearly do not handicap them in distance swimming, as Emily Watts discovered in 2002. Watts, mother of two, grew up in Potomac, Maryland, and swam at Walt Whitman High School in Bethesda until a shoulder injury curtailed her swim career. Years later, at age 26, Watts began swimming for exercise. "One thing led to another and I started doing shorter open water swims. I kind of got a bug in me," said Watts, in an interview.[83]

That "bug" drove Watts to race in—and win—the 2002 Manhattan Island Marathon Swim race, outpacing all other participants, including two men's relay teams in the 28.5-mile race around Manhattan. Watts, who turned pro in 2002, vividly recalls the reaction of bystanders when they realized she had won. "One gentleman came up and was bowing to me. A woman came up with her daughter and said, 'Look at that! A woman won!'" she recalled. "I don't think it shocked me. I don't know why it didn't. I do consider myself as an equal. Even in practice, even in other races, if I am swimming next to [men], I am just another competitor."

Watts came in third in the same race in 2004, behind first-place finisher Chris Derks and second-place finisher, Rendy Opdycke, a 20-year-old woman from Mercer Island, Washington. In that race, women were three of the top four finishers. Opdycke won the race outright in 2006.[84]

There are, in addition, sports in which women's physical differences as a group may not be handicaps. In sports as diverse as mountain climbing, fencing, and bowling, women may compete effectively with males. Concomitantly, there are sports in which men's greater height, weight, and upper-body mass not only fail to provide any benefit but are actually handicaps. As we have noted, such sports include horse racing and other equestrian sports, car racing, airplane competition, sailing, and some categories of gymnastics. Consider Danica Patrick, the 5-foot-1, 100-pound race car driver whose debut in the Indy Racing League has put her among the most successful competitors in the sport, even prompting an opponent to argue that her light weight was an unfair advantage. It should be no surprise that women can compete effectively in such sports on a sex-integrated basis. The surprise has come in Patrick's case because even as she has what may turn out to be a physical advantage, car racing has been long considered "a man's sport." We must recognize that such performances are not a fluke, and that women, based on sex group differences, may be equally or better suited for such sports than men.

Wrestling

There are also sports in which males and females might (and in some instances do) compete equally, particularly at certain ages. Wrestling is a fundamental physical contest. While some aspects of wrestling appear clearly to favor males because of their greater average upper-body strength and higher percentage of muscle, females' generally lower center of gravity can aid in pinning an opponent. What most handicaps women, however, is not related to the technique of the sport itself, but rather to the manner in which this sport is structured: Wrestlers must compete in weight categories that do not account for variations in lean muscle mass between genders. Females who compete with males (usually in high school matches) have a decided disadvantage because a male will have more muscle mass than a female at the same weight class. Females also face the social hurdle of competing, because wrestling has long been thought of as a "man's sport." Still, females are excelling in this sport, in some cases against male opponents.

Take Nikki Darrow.

All summer long, as a Mount Greylock Regional High School sophomore, she received e-mails from guys with the same question: How much did she weigh? More accurately, they wanted to know how much she'd weigh come wrestling season. The importance of the question from prospective opponents became clear when Darrow, blond ponytail pulled tight, bounced up the carpeted stairs of her family's western Massachusetts home to her room—decorated in her favorite colors, purple and intense pink. Female-cut wrestling uniforms called singlets were looped over a bedpost, and a long shelf boasted trophies and medals from years of Little League and seasons as a member of the otherwise all-male high school wrestling team. Tacked to the wall were three invitational wrestling tournament brackets with her name on the champion's line. A notation on the 2003 Mount Greylock Invitational said she pinned her male opponent in 51 seconds. No wonder guys wanted a heads-up before Darrow entered their weight class.[85]

While Darrow was dedicated—she lifted weights daily, ran cross-country in the fall, trained several times a week at a well-known wrestling center an hour from her home, and attended national and international girls' wrestling tournaments—she was dogged by the old perception that wrestling is for boys. The idea of girls wrestling—or worse, girls wrestling against boys—jars the sensibilities of some who find such physical competition inappropriate.

Nonetheless, the sport is growing nationally among girls, and 2004 marked the first time women's freestyle wrestling was included in the Olympics. For girls like Darrow, who in 2005 was ranked first in the 114-pound weight class by the United States Girls Wrestling Association, competing on a boys' team was the only choice at the high school level.[86] However, the notion so bothers some that a state representative in Minnesota in 2002 filed a bill to ban mixed-sex school wrestling there.[87]

The measure died, but it ignited a debate about femininity and masculinity—and the differences between them. Not surprisingly, some concern focused on physical contact between teen boys and girls. The heart of the matter, however, was the presumption that vast natural differences between males and females made mixed-gender contact troubling and athletically unfair. In fact, as noted above, the real problem is that weight classifications fail to consider the relative proportions of muscle mass versus body fat that contribute to a wrestler's overall weight. It may be time to consider other factors in creating categories for competition. Currently, however, the use of total weight only for classifying wrestlers disadvantages females because males will have more muscle mass than females even when weighing the same.

Nonetheless, wrestlers like Darrow offer evidence countering the belief that every sex group characteristic gives male athletes the edge over females. Female flexibility and lower center of gravity may be overlooked as advantages that perhaps can compensate for the muscle mass/body fat ratio that favors males. Plus, some females are simply more skilled wrestlers. In 2006, for example,

Michaela Hutchinson won the Alaska state wrestling title in the 103-pound division, beating all comers, male and female. When she beat wrestler Aaron Boss, he remarked simply, "I don't look at it as a loss to a girl. I look at it as a loss to a wrestler."[88]

Rock Climbing

Rock climbing may favor the long of limb, but one of the top climbers in the world is a petite 5-foot, 100-pound woman named Lynn Hill. Hill was the first person—male or female—to free climb the treacherous nose of El Capitan in Yosemite National Park in September 1993, when she was 32. She advanced up the face of the rock, using her finger strength, her grasp, and her flexibility to scale, with ropes used only for safety purposes.[89] Hill not only accomplished the feat but did so twice.

When Hill made her first climb of El Capitan, she was accompanied by British climber Simon Nadin, whose exhaustion and swollen hands kept him from completing the free climb. Hill too was suffering but determined. In a first-person account, she describes being "prepared to commit myself entirely to realize the dream" of a free climb.[90] She described making her way up "the lower crack, feeling relaxed and smooth. I continued with a bit less authority on the first series of moves as I felt my strength waning." But even when tired, Hill was clear: "These observations did not penetrate my will to persevere," illustrating that sports success entails more than biological group characteristics. It also involves motivation and training by *individuals*.

Motivation and Training

Motivation Has No Gender

Why do some win and others lose? What allows one person to observe pain and push past it while another gives in? Great athletic achievements require the raw material of physical gift, but much more is involved in success, including training, conditioning, and practice. There is also another critical variable: mental toughness and determination. This characteristic describes the person who steps up and performs, who does not allow for defeat—and it is not sex-linked. It is up for grabs and provides the ultimate athletic edge.

Individual Variability and Social Factors

As already noted, males as a group, on average, have more muscle mass and less body fat do than females as a group. But individual characteristics ultimately matter more than group characteristics. Some women are not only mentally tougher than some men, but physically or athletically tougher as well. Some women have less body fat than some men and may be stronger, faster, more coordinated or agile, thereby making the business of gender-related group averages irrelevant. Individual variability, in other words, may trump gender-linked characteristics, perhaps as a result of individual body makeup, training, conditioning, diet, experience—or the physical challenge at hand.

Gender-based comparisons are also subject to social bias. Researchers, for example, found in power lifting that the smallest performance differences between males and females (10 to 30 percent) were at the lightest weight classes. This may suggest lighter women have more lean body mass for their weight than heavier female lifters. Or it may reflect the fact that there aren't many female power lifters in higher weight classes.[91] For decades, women have been conditioned to train and work out less rigorously than males. They have worried about gaining "unfeminine" muscle mass. As social tastes change, will gaps between male and female absolute strength close as more women train harder?

Biology or Training?

Because physiology can be influenced by social factors, researchers are still trying to understand what constitutes a biological factor and what is the result of social experience. The historic taboo on women's athletic training leaves a clear legacy. Females for years, even generations, followed workout regimens which assumed they were physically weaker than male counterparts. We had "girls' push-ups" in which the knees, not the toes, made contact with the floor. Girls did the "flexed arm hang" instead of pull-ups. One study reports that from 1976 to 1978 female air force cadets performed a flexed arm hang instead of the pull-ups required of men, study authors said, "because of the belief many of the women would not be able to perform even one pull-up."[92]

This worry turned out to be unwarranted. In 1979, the air force made tests for males and females similar, including requirements for standing long jumps, push-ups, two-minute sit-ups, and 600-yard runs. Not surprisingly, between 1977 and 1987 women increased the number of push-ups performed by 111 percent, while men increased them by 42 percent, on average. Women's sit-ups also improved. When first admitted to the academy, females performed an average of seven fewer sit-ups than male colleagues. Eleven years later, however, females averaged seven more sit-ups than males during the two-minute drill.[93]

Women can build strength and improve performance when challenged and provided with the opportunity. Research shows women have the same ability as men to increase strength with training. And training makes a tremendous difference in athletic performance and body composition. Research shows athletes' bodies make functional and structural adaptations to skeletal muscle reflecting the sport for which they train.[94] For example, a study comparing female college field hockey players and untrained females revealed dramatically more fast- and slow-twitch muscle fiber among players than non-athletes. Athletes possessed, on average, 64.5 percent fast-twitch fiber where nonathletes had 15.5 percent, resulting from changes in body composition with training.[95] Such differences are apparent to even casual observers who can see that the female college athlete today (name the sport) bears little resemblance physically to her counterpart of 20 or 30 years ago.

Women athletes today look like athletes, not girls in uniforms. Still, the troubling increase in female athletes suffering from anterior cruciate ligament (ACL) injuries, debilitating tears to the knee ligament, has spurred the suggestion that females are not made for certain sports, or are not as physically tough as males. While ACL injuries in males are associated with contact sports like football, females typically injure the ACL in noncontact settings, often in basketball or soccer, sports which demand quick changes in direction. Female athletes who participate in jumping and cutting-type sports have a four- to sixfold higher incidence of serious knee injuries, compared with males in the same sports.[96] Researchers

are seeking an explanation and question whether it is anatomical, hormonal, or neuromuscular. There is a lot of focus on how
females land after jumping and whether the problem arises from
a difference in protective muscle tissue that could lessen the pressure on the ACL of landing. One study suggested that "females
displayed muscle synchrony less protective of the ACL than
males, possibly increasing their susceptibility to non-contact ACL
injuries."[97]

Dr. Bertram Zarins, chief of sports medicine at Massachusetts
General Hospital in Boston, believes the male-female injury differences are structural. Zarins, an orthopedic surgeon, said women
have lighter bones and a different relationship of the pelvis to the
knee, which he argues is a source of trouble. "When a man lands, he
lands straight," said Zarins, emphasizing his point during an interview by standing and jumping in his office.[98] When a woman
lands, he said, jumping a second time and showing a wobble of his
leg, "there is an inward thrust of the knee."

While women are more prone to ACL tears, males also experience the injury; many learn ways of preventing reinjury in the
future. Zarins noted that women trained to land straight suffer
fewer ACL injuries. Data reported at a 2000 conference on prevention of noncontact ACL injuries showed that designing a knee injury prevention program decreased ACL injuries by 89 percent over
a two-year period among Division I college basketball players.[99]

At Harvard, Dr. Arthur Boland, head physician for the university's athletic department, said they now train female athletes in
better ways to jump and land. "These are learned things," said
Boland. "With these exercises, we reduce [players'] injuries and give
them greater vertical height jump. They become essentially better
basketball players."[100] Boland, who has worked with Harvard athletic teams since 1969, said female athletes have made such huge
strides that the women he sees today bear little resemblance physically to the female athletes, even of the recent past. "What I have
seen more than anything over the last decade is the [very high]
level of training and conditioning," said Boland. As a result, he said,
the types of injuries he sees vary more by sport than by gender.
Male and female athletes from comparable teams tend to suffer the
same sorts of injuries. One exception is ice hockey, in which the
men's game (which allows checking) yields different injuries than
the women's game (which does not allow checking).

Interplay of Biology and Social Influences

What appear to be absolute biological responses, therefore, are often colored by social practices. That is not to negate biological differences between the sexes. Traditionally, the chief differences were presumed to be the visible ones, rooted in reproductive function. Biology, however, does not operate independent of other factors. "There is no such thing as a pure biological effect, just as there is no such thing as a null environment (one devoid of any influence)," observed Institute of Medicine researchers. "The 'biology' of any given individual therefore includes genetic, physiological, and hormonal effects as well as environmental, behavioral, and societal influences that shape that individual."[101]

New research embraces an expanded picture in which hormone-responsive genes are influenced differently by male and female hormones throughout the life span. Other research shows genes on X and Y sex chromosomes expressed differently by males and females, encoding proteins that affect biological or physiological pathways.[102]

In still other cases, gender-based social practices or environmental factors may be mistaken for sex-based differences. For example, researchers said, many variables influence bone mass, including genes, hormones, and societal factors. Exercise and body weight affect development of bone formation. Researchers note that social conventions in the United States have favored thinness in females, and consequently it is less common for girls and young women than for boys and young men to perform vigorous weight-bearing exercises, which build bone mass. Such social realities may contribute to observed sex differences in the development of bone mass. "In other words," they write, "culture and behavior (gender) become contributing causes to differences in bone mass between males and females (sex)."[103] One has only to observe the changing fashion of female muscularity over recent decades to see the power of societal practice to literally reshape the female athletic ideal from, say, a slender and girlish Chris Evert to a blatantly muscular Serena Williams.

There are two issues here: the "purity" of the male and female sexes (as suggested by Fausto-Sterling and others) and the "purity" of biological differences between the sexes. Both are muddy, however, not pure. Although popular sports trade in sex and gender stereotypes, such practices do not reflect reality. The variety and spectrum of human physical attributes more closely reflect a matrix in which individuals occupy different intersections than the traditional image of a world split in half, divided according to sex and/or sex group differences. Even biologically based study conclusions may reflect social bias. Comparing male and female lower-body strength may yield an absolute, though inaccurate figure. What if the study had been done in 1967 instead of 2007? We would expect women to be stronger in 2007 simply based on the fact that it is more socially acceptable for women to lift weights and develop muscles now than it was 40 years ago. Observed physiological differences between males and females, then, may reflect biologically based factors or reflect athletic practices and conventions. For years, conventional wisdom held females were not physiologically capable of breaking a 2:20 marathon. Then that record was shattered three times in 18 months.

When we talk about what is biologically "male" and what is "female," therefore, we must remember that "pure" mental images are colored by social influences. The female athletes who perform today are physically and athletically a universe apart from the women who played a few decades ago. Imagine if today's female athletes could travel back in time to the 1960s or 1970s. The rapid evolution is frankly stunning—and instructive.

Can, or Should, Women Be Big and Strong?

It is one thing to see NFL players on television, or even from the stands of a game, and quite another to see them in person. One August afternoon in 2003, three massive men entered the waiting room of Dr. Bert Zarins, chief of the hospital's sports medicine service at Massachusetts General Hospital. The one wearing mirrored sunglasses, a silver hoop in each ear, and a large bejeweled cross suspended from a chain around his neck had to crouch to fit through the door (of normal dimensions), making it appear as if he were slipping into a dollhouse. The three were pro football players—linemen—in town to try out with the New England Patriots and have their physicals with Zarins, one of the official team doctors. The men were so huge that their very existence would seem to shatter any argument that male and female athletes could stand shoulder to shoulder in play.

But then who *could* stand with these guys? Zarins observed that athletes today are getting larger. He pointed out that he—a

Lafayette College soccer player from 1959 to 1963—couldn't make his old team were he a kid today. "People are much bigger," he said. "If you look at the NFL, the size of players is much, much bigger than it used to be."[104] Data support Zarins's point. One analysis shows the 1936 Packers offensive line averaged 6-foot-1 and 221 pounds, puny compared with the 1996 Cowboys offensive line, which averaged 6-foot-4 and 319 pounds.[105]

Bigger Females

Male athletes are not the only ones getting larger. A 2004 *USA Today* profile of University of Minnesota basketball player Janel McCarville (she is 6'2" and 220 pounds) described her as "a new breed of player in the women's game: a wide-bodied star who not only rebounds but can run, catch and shoot."[106] The writer observed that McCarville "wears men's size-14 sneakers but moves her feet with a dancer's grace." While college women's basketball programs do not list women's weights, Minnesota coach Pam Borton noted that large, agile female players have become increasingly common. "We have seen a shift in the last five years to more players with more bulk, more size, and more strength," said Borton.[107]

In weightlifting, Cheryl Ann Haworth, member of the 2000 and 2004 Olympic teams, was 5 feet 10 and 300 pounds as a 17-year-old high school senior in 2000. As a high school softball player, Haworth was so good teammates called her "The Arm." When her father took her to meet a weightlifting coach in 1996, and she heaved a bar with 100 pounds on it "like it was a loaf of bread," the teen embarked on what has already been an impressive career.[108] In June 2006 she moved to Colorado Springs to live at the U.S. Olympic Training Center and prepare for the 2008 games. As a recent USA Weightlifting bio observed, "She is currently the youngest lifter to ever hold Senior American records, and holds all school, age, junior and senior records for her weight class."[109]

The addition of women's weightlifting and pole vault events in the 2000 Olympic Games acknowledged the changing size and strength of female athletes, as does the rising interest in women's professional football. The WPFL, for example, boasts two divisions and 15 teams. The expansion of sports for women that champion traditionally male qualities of strength and power, suggests increasing respect for female athletes of all sizes. In the fall of 2006, Holley Mangold, a 5-foot-9, 310-pound guard on her high school football team, made history by advancing with her team, Archbishop Alter High School, to the Ohio Division III championships.[110] It is difficult to know if there are more large females or whether we are simply seeing—at long last—the emergence of legitimate athletic opportunities for large, strong females. The social pressure on females to be slim is widely considered responsible for eating disorders among female athletes, whose very training puts them at odds with social gender images.

Even McCarville, who lost 50 pounds in college, said that gender norms cut deep for large female athletes. "A lot of girls don't like to talk about their weight," she commented.[111] McCarville was teased about her weight growing up but turned her size into a positive attribute. "The way I see it is, that's what got me here. Why not be proud of it?" While McCarville capitalized on her size, many others have not embraced athletics as a vehicle to accept their bodies.

Social Pressures on Females Conflict with Sports

Dr. Carol Otis, renowned women's sports doctor, coauthor of *The Athletic Woman's Survival Guide* and consultant to the Women's Tennis Association Tour, insists lingering social pressures on females to be slender hampers athleticism. In the past, Otis said, it was believed that a woman was in top shape if she stopped menstruating. Now researchers and physicians see amenorrhea as evidence of trouble. "It is a sign that you are overtraining or have an underlying medical problem," she said in an interview.[112] Not menstruating, said Otis, signals an energy imbalance, that a woman is exerting more than she is taking in or suffering from an eating disorder, common among competitive female athletes.

Otis noted troubling social pressures while surveying young women at elite junior tennis camps. She asked these top female players to name their athletic role models and they repeatedly mentioned glamour girl Anna Kournikova and not more muscular and accomplished athletes like Serena Williams, Justine Henin-Hardin, Martina Hingis, or Kim Clijsters. Otis blames cultural pressures, even on top female athletes, for driving girls in training to pursue unrealistic and unhealthy model-like thinness. "The biggest issue for women is fitting in with the cultural notion of attractiveness," observed Otis. Girls, she said, still believe being an athlete is socially risky and consequently pursue sports with a nervous eye on their attractiveness.[113]

Being Big Is Socially Acceptable for Males

On the other hand, it is fine for males to be large. In fact, size may be a ticket to athletic success. Males from a young age embrace their physical size as an advantage. That is not true for large females, whose size is often perceived as a barrier to athletics and a mark of shame, the excuse for sitting on the sidelines instead of reaching for iron. Large, muscular women must also fight the presumption they are necessarily lesbian or "butch." And we all must fight against biases that mark being lesbian questionable in the first place. Yes, males are larger than females, on average. However, the social pressures faced by *smaller* than average males and *larger* than average females set the sexes on very different paths unrelated to individual physical athletic potential. Truth is, being large and female can be a gift, just as it is for males, where those characteristics enhance one's performance. However, getting females—and society—to view physical size as an athletic attribute—rather than as a sexual attribute—will take time. Consider that when supersize NBA star Shaquille O'Neal was chided for falling into the obese range after the Associated Press applied the body mass index (BMI) to athletes, the 7 foot 1 player who weighs 325 pounds brushed aside any concern with a quip. "I've read that same formula, but as an athlete, I'm classified as phenomenal," said O'Neal. "You can look it up."[114] In contests where size matters, males have a twofold advantage: They are, on average, physically larger, and their size is socially accepted.

Closing the Performance Gap

On a chilly March day in 2003, the Reggie Lewis Track and Athletic Center in Boston was the site—as it has been in recent years—of the USA Indoor Track and Field Championships. Spectators sat on aluminum risers as events unfolded on the track and inner oval.

There were men's events and then women's events, often alternated, but always set apart in time. Several women's world and U.S. records were broken during this meet.

The men were faster. However, if you watched the women's 60-meter hurdles, a curious thing happened: Gail Devers finished one heat in 7.74 seconds, the time posted on the screen at one end of the track center, setting a new American record. During the initial men's 60-meter hurdle heats, only three out of 23 men ran faster than Devers. Does it matter that the men's hurdles were higher? Of course. (Never mind that the men tended to knock over more hurdles than the women.) However, to see official times displayed in which men's and women's times overlapped in a sprinting event was striking. A few weeks later, the 2003 USA Masters Indoor Track and Field Championships were held at the same track. Joan Benoit Samuelson ran 3,000 meters, finishing more than a second faster than running legend Bill Rodgers. They ran the same race, but not at the same time. Some who may object to such comparisons will observe that Bill Rodgers is older. However, why not have Samuelson and Rodgers, both Master's division runners, compete on the same track at the same time? Certainly not all of Rodgers's male competitors were exactly his age, either.

Women are closing the gender gap in sports. If you think of athletic performances of both sexes as distinct bell-shaped curves, one beside the other, along the same axis, you see that "as women have gained access to better facilities and better training, the bell curves have moved closer together," Lynda Ransdell, chair of the Department of Kinesiology at Boise State University in Idaho, pointed out in an interview.[115] Like the old myth that female brains weren't wired to excel at math even though test scores show most girls and most boys earn roughly the same scores, the iron-clad belief that males are universally better athletes now looks suspect. More than sex, raw athletic skill matters more.

"There is a significant level of overlap between the average female competitor and the average male competitor," said Ransdell. "When you get to the higher-level male and higher-level female, there are few who can compete with them." Top female athletes, she said, outperform average males, something evident to anyone standing along a marathon route. While very top men still outperform very top women, very elite women today beat even very good male competitors. British marathoner Paula Radcliffe has outrun all her countrymen.

Women's sports are in their relative infancy compared with men's sports. How can we truly physically compare the sexes when women are far from their athletic potential? How much faster, how much stronger, how much better will women get? It will be years before we know. Still, there are signs of a changing dynamic as women record firsts in competitive sports.

In January 2002, Mission Betty became the first all-female team to play in the Pee Wee International hockey tournament in Quebec, making it to the quarterfinals.[116] In December 2002, college junior Katie Hnida became the first woman to play in a Division 1-A college football game when she attempted an extra point for New Mexico in the Las Vegas Bowl.[117] The kick was blocked, but on August 30, 2003, Hnida scored two field goals for New Mexico against Texas State, becoming the first woman to score in a Division 1-A football game.[118]

In February 2002, Canadian Olympic star Hayley Wickenheiser became the first woman to score a goal in a men's pro hockey game. She played for the leading Finnish team, Salamat, with whom she landed a season contract.[119] Of course, in January 2005, Angela Ruggiero became the first woman to play a position other than goalie in a U.S. men's pro hockey game when she took the ice for the Tulsa Oilers.[120] In 2002, free diver Tanya Streeter broke the men's no limit world diving record, reaching a depth of 525 feet off the Turks and Caicos Islands.

In August 2003, Team Challenge US became the first all-female squad to win sailing's small keel boat Yngling World Championships in Warnemunde, Germany.[121] As of February 2005, a female sailor, Ellen MacArthur, owned the around-the-world sailing record.[122] And in March 2004, high school basketball star Candace Parker became the first woman to win a major slam dunk contest, beating five men in an event that was part of McDonald's All-American game in Oklahoma City.[123] During the 2005–2006 season, as a member of the University of Tennessee women's basketball team, she became the first female player to dunk in a women's college game.

In March 2005, bowler Liz Johnson became the first woman to reach the championship round of the Pro Bowler's Association

Banquet Open tournament since the PBA began in 1958. Johnson, who made it to the final round, losing to Tommy Jones, 219–192, took home a check for $20,000—and changed many minds (including her own) about female bowling ability. "I was always curious how women would do," Jack Jurek, a pro from Lancaster, New York, told *Sports Illustrated*. "[Liz] has proven they can play with us." Most telling, however, was that until she actually competed, Johnson presumed males were much better than she was. "Honestly," she said, "I didn't think I was good enough to bowl on the men's tour."[124]

This listing of firsts and bests by women is not exhaustive but a snapshot of accomplishments. It is only now that women are, with frequency, performing at world class competitive levels that put them on par with men. This is a beginning, a sign of what is physically possible for female athletes given training, conditioning, determination, and support. The physical differences between males and females will produce advantages for each sex in particular competitions. These impressive performances underscore the overlap in physical abilities between males and females and the potency of individual athletic ability.

Competitive Drive Does Not Have a Sex

The decision by star golfer Annika Sorenstam to compete with the men at the Colonial was a beginning. Although Sorenstam did not make it into the final rounds, she showed that she could play with the boys. She may compete again in a PGA event, but seems to have focused on winning on the women's tour. She had a spectacular 2006 season, winning several tournaments including the U.S. Women's Open in Newport so that by mid-September her lifetime earnings had surpassed the $20 million mark, the most ever for a female golfer.[125] But if Sorenstam has stated her intention to play where she "belongs," a younger golf talent—Michelle Wie—believes that, ultimately, where she belongs is playing against the men. Wie, who is 6 feet tall and averages 290 yards off the tee, already outdrives many male professional golfers. In 2003, she became the youngest golfer to take an adult national title when she won the Women's Amateur Public Links event. Most telling, however, is Wie's vision: She wants to win the Masters, the males-only tournament no woman has played in, much less won. Tiger Woods won three times. As B. J. Wie, Michelle Wie's father observed, "Tiger is her benchmark. Not women—Tiger."[126]

Wie has garnered media attention, praise, and criticism as she has pursued that goal, playing in men's PGA events and women's events as well. In 2006, she won a local qualifying tournament for the men's U.S. Open but failed to win at sectionals. Still, her performance drew widespread praise and she was invited to play in the men's European Masters. Wie told reporters that she likes competing with men. "Playing with the men, I get to learn so much more and when I do well, it feels really good," she said.[127] Wie demonstrates a fundamental athletic truth: the best want to compete with the best and not be restricted by their gender into sex-segregated competitions. The belief that women are, by dint of sex, unable to play as well as men is an outdated assumption. Some venues more than others advantage male or female biology, but social barriers—often passed over as all but invisible pressures—are strikingly powerful.

Thus the very notion of dividing athletics coercively—and "solely" on the basis of sex on the grounds that women are inherently physically inferior to men—ignores that some female group differences *advantage* women athletes. It also ignores how individual motivation, training, and distinct personal characteristics play into the outcome of an athletic contest.

Title IX: Old Norms in New Forms

Today, education is perhaps the most important function of state and local governments. Compulsory school attendance laws and the great expenditures for education both demonstrate our recognition of the importance of education to our democratic society. . . It is the very foundation of good citizenship . . . it is doubtful that any child may reasonably be expected to succeed in life if he is denied the opportunity of an education. Such an opportunity, where the state has undertaken to provide it, is a right which must be made available to all on equal terms.

—*Brown v. Board of Education, 1954*

Prejudice against women is the last socially accepted bigotry.
—Senator George McGovern, 1971[1]

Donna's Dream

By the time she was five years old, Donna Lopiano wanted to pitch for the New York Yankees. Far from an idle dream, Lopiano recalled growing up in Stamford, Connecticut, "on a street with 15 boys and one girl" where she prepared for her imagined future, throwing 500 pitches a day against the side of her parents' garage.[2] "By the time I was 10, I had developed a rising fastball and an impressive curve that would drop off the table, and I was hard at work on a Bob Turley drop," noted Lopiano.[3] So when it came time for Lopiano to take the ritual first step for an aspiring young baseball player—joining a Little League team—she was more than ready.

Lopiano remembers well the Saturday morning she and her friends, all of them boys, went to tryouts. Everyone was nervous, but Lopiano had anticipated this day for years. She was enormously talented, and it soon became apparent that she was the most skilled player in tryouts. She was drafted the number one player. This didn't surprise her because she knew—as did everyone else—that she was the best.

Then, as she excitedly punched her hand into her glove, waiting for practice to start, a tall father approached and her world stopped. He held a rule book and was pointing to page 14, where three words altered her life forever: "No Girls Allowed."[4] Lopiano cried for months. The prohibition was devastating to a girl who had dedicated the time and energy of her youth to a game at which she so clearly excelled. And it happened solely because she was female.

Title IX: Does It Solve the Problem?

Many will say Donna's problem was not that her dream was impossible, but that she was ahead of her time. If she had just been born a little later, she would have benefited from passage of Title IX, landmark legislation that opened doors for women in sports. Or would she?

Title IX has changed the way people think about women's sports and female athletes. Strictly speaking, however, Title IX does not address organizations like Little League because the law—never envisioned as addressing athletics in the first place—targets only educational institutions receiving federal funds, not nonscholastic sports organizations. Ultimately it was not Title IX but rules passed by Congress and signed by President Gerald Ford in December 1974 that secured for girls the right to play Little League.[5]

However, Title IX is today generally viewed as having fixed the problem of gender inequality in sports, at least in educational settings. Yet the law never identified coercive sex segregation as a form of sex discrimination in athletics. In fact, right from the start and still today, Title IX explicitly permits coercive sex segregation in contact sports. Thus Title IX doesn't help female athletes seeking to "play with the boys," since it permits barring girls from such settings solely because of their sex.

In part, this is the result of the history of sex discrimination in education and the manner in which the legislation came about. Thanks to a long legacy in which female students were barred from equal educational opportunities solely because of their sex, Title IX was not conceived with athletics in mind. Rather, when the law was passed in 1972, Congress sought to end pervasive sex discrimination and sex stereotyping in admission to colleges and universities and in academic subjects—discriminatory practices that were commonplace in educational institutions, from public to private schools, from elementary to college levels of education, and in professional schools, such as medicine, business, and law. Girls were routinely steered away from top math classes, barred from shop courses, deemed unable to operate slide or movie projectors, and pressed into "female" career paths.[6] Prior to Title IX, women also faced overt discrimination in admissions policies, academic scholarships, and in the hiring and retention of women faculty in higher education.[7]

The first priority of Title IX, then, was to address the legacy of prejudice and discrimination against women that denied them educational opportunities, which in turn affected workplace opportunities and women's social and economic status. Women had been barred from whole fields on grounds that they couldn't handle the educational rigors or, alternately, because it wasn't a female's role to train for careers as lawyers or physicians, which required advanced schooling. Woman's role was as wife and mother, not professional.

This combination of pressures—beliefs that females couldn't and shouldn't participate in competitive activities—kept women from advancing not only in sports but also in academics and the professions. Thus Congress's first concern in passing Title IX was not athletics but equal academic and educational access. Sports were an all but invisible component of that concern—and an unintended one at that. Secretary of Health, Education, and Welfare Caspar W. Weinberger was not alone in expressing surprise when sports leapt to the fore of the Title IX debate. "I had not realized until the comment period [for Title IX regulations] that athletics is the single most important thing in the United States," Weinberger quipped during a Senate subcommittee hearing in June 1975.[8] He was responding to NCAA worries the law would bankrupt men's college sports programs. Many were unhappy about the prospect of girls in auto body class, but fully opening athletics to females was a pointed threat to masculinity.[9] As a result, male-centered organizations like the NCAA fought hard to limit Title IX's application to sports.

Women's Brains

To understand the context of Title IX's passage—and its goal of correcting women's lack of access to academic opportunities—we must realize that the law sought to confront cultural beliefs about female intellectual weakness that had lingered since the late nineteenth and early twentieth centuries. Leading physicians and scientists proclaimed higher education for women a useless endeavor because women's brains are second-rate. They warned the rigors of higher education would injure females, who were burdened with delicate and complex reproductive systems. Consequently the norm was to prohibit women from obtaining college and professional degrees. What now appear to have been sex-based educational barriers were previously considered protections for women.

As already noted, there are four stages to desegregating policies for subordinate groups. The first *prohibits* a subordinate group from participating in an activity altogether. The second stage allows the subordinate group to participate, but only on a *coercive sex-segregated* basis. The third allows the subordinate group to participate in the activity on a *sex-integrated* principle. And the fourth permits the subordinate group to choose participation on either a *sex-integrated or voluntary sex-segregated basis*. In the case of women seeking access to advanced education, the first stage—prohibition—was justified by a bizarre energy conservation principle that categorized female brains as inherently inferior to male brains. But this was not the last time women would face imposed classification.

The First Stage: No Higher Education for Women

Energy Conservation Principle

Nineteenth-century scientists used an energy conservation principle to explain the workings of the human body. As Victorian psychiatrist Henry Maudsley intoned, "When nature spends it in one direction, she must economize in another direction."[10] In 1847 German scientist Hermann Helmholtz published a paper on "The Conservation of Force," later described as the conservation of energy, which applied rules of physics to biology. The body was a zero-sum container of fixed energy. Energy spent on one organ necessarily limited energy available for use in another organ.[11]

Prominent scientists of the day, including Harvard physician Dr. Edward H. Clarke, elaborated on the conservation of energy principle by explaining that the human body possesses three major systems: the nutritive, the nervous, and the reproductive. Clarke, author of the influential 1873 book *Sex in Education*, argued that men's and women's bodies were the same in respect to the first two systems but not the third. That is, women were distinguished by their complicated and demanding reproductive system.[12] Scientists reasoned that women who enrolled in college and therefore faced demanding intellectual work would draw energy to their brains, thereby leaving none for reproduction. Scientists hypothesized that women would develop reproductive illnesses and diseases, including amenorrhea, dysmenorrhea, chronic and acute ovaritis, prolapsus uteri, hysteria, and neuralgia. If a woman used too much energy for studying, in other words, her uterus could shrivel up, leaving her infertile. This was an injury not only to women but also to society.[13]

The notion that women must choose between using their brains or their uteruses persisted well into the twentieth century. In the 1970s, former congresswoman Patricia Schroeder famously defended her ability to be both lawmaker and mother, saying "I have a brain and a uterus, and I use them both."[14]

Smaller Heads and Smaller Brains

Feminine limitations extended beyond reproductive organs. Nineteenth-century scientists also found a mental inferiority in women because as a group they were seen to have smaller heads than men and thus smaller brains. At this time, craniometry, the study of the cranial measurements as a means for classifying people, was widely researched and practiced. This discipline linked skull characteristics to race, intelligence, and criminal temperament, with craniometry even used to justify racist policies. The British claimed skulls of Irish and black Africans bore similarities to Cro-Magnon man. This "evidence" fed specious arguments that Irish and Africans had brains closer to apes than British citizens, a claim used to justify British imperial domination of the Irish and Africans.[15]

Some prominent scientists voiced doubts and failed to validate connections between racial types and cranial measurements. But others conducted research to support the notion of ranked races and sexes.[16] Women fared poorly in these analyses. To some scientists, women's allegedly smaller head size explained the "vague 'imperfections' of the female brain."[17] Scientist George Romanes in 1877 observed "secondary sex characteristics," revealing that a woman's smaller brain "displays itself most conspicuously in a comparative absence of originality, and this more especially in the higher levels of intellectual work."[18]

During this era, French scientist Paul Broca studied male and female brains from corpses, proving conclusively, according to him, that women had smaller craniums and hence were inferior to men. Gustave le Bon used Broca's "evidence" to conclude that even "in the most intelligent races, as among the Parisians, there are a large number of women whose brains are closer in size to those of gorillas than to the most developed male brains."[19] Those studying women's intelligence, he noted, "recognize today that they represent the most inferior forms of human evolution and that they are closer to children and savages than to an adult, civilized man."[20]

Absurd as this now sounds, in the nineteenth century it merely fed prevailing scientific and popular beliefs. German physiologist Paul Mobius in 1901 argued women could not think independently, were predisposed to be mean and untrustworthy, and were fundamentally emotionally imbalanced. "If woman was not physically and mentally weak, if she was not as a rule rendered harmless by circumstances, she would be extremely dangerous," he concluded. Sexologist and social philosopher Havelock Ellis found female limitations in concert with her social role, explaining that "woman is biologically nearer to nature and nearer to the child than is man. Nature has made women more like children in order that they may better understand and care for children."[21] Female inferiority, in other words, was the catch-all explanation for myriad observations, including an absurd belief that women prefer passive methods of death (suicide), because it requires little physical exertion to, say, give themselves up to elemental forces (gravity) by throwing themselves from heights.[22]

Men, these thinkers and scientists argued, have larger brains because evolution required it, creating over time stark differences between the sexes. "The man who fights for two or more in the struggle for existence" and "who is constantly active in combating the environment and human rivals, needs more brain than the woman, whom he must protect and nourish," argued Broca disciple anthropologist Paul Topinard. In contrast, Topinard stated, the "sedentary woman, lacking any interior occupation, whose role is to raise children, love, and be passive" had far less need for brain or brawn than the male.[23] Charles Darwin too classified women as having "faculties [that] are characteristic of the lower races, and, therefore of a past and lower state of civilization." In *The Descent of Man*, Darwin observes that "the chief distinction and intellectual powers of the two sexes is shown by man attaining to a higher eminence in whatever he takes up than woman can attain, whether requiring deep thought, reason, or imagination, or merely the use of the senses and hands."[24]

The "evidence" was overwhelming: women are intellectually, plainly, baldly, inferior. No wonder women were chastised for blurting out ill-informed ideas, the intellectual equivalent of "throwing like a girl." The stereotype of women being "illogical" persisted for decades. However, no thought was given to the fact that females were barred from learning or developing intellectual skills at the same level as males. And placing women in a social hierarchy with children and animals fed the notion of males as unquestionably physically and mentally superior.

Naturalizing Social Construction

The first stage, which involved prohibiting women from "thinking with the boys," presented a conundrum. Policies that denied women access to higher education gave them no way to demonstrate their intellectual capabilities—and such lack of opportunity to demonstrate smarts was taken as "evidence" that women had none in the first place. Thus female failure to display stunning brain power was chalked up to *natural differences* between male and female brains, not to socially constructed policies giving men access to educational opportunities while barring women.

The Second Stage: Coercive Sex-Segregated Education

Female Education

The notion of female physical and intellectual inferiority dovetailed with the conviction that society depends on women and men to operate in separate spheres. Women couldn't and shouldn't compete with men intellectually or physically. Critically, females should not do anything to endanger their reproductive health, heterosexual attractiveness, or domestic identities as wives and mothers.[25] This nineteenth-century belief that women are (1) too weak to handle higher education, (2) don't need higher education (or shouldn't need it), and (3) shouldn't have higher education gave way eventually to the idea that women could have some higher education as long as it was tailored to women's difference from men and did not require direct intellectual competition with men. As a result, women's access to higher education moved from the first stage, prohibitions against any higher education, to the second stage, namely, coercively sex-segregated education that was explicitly designed to reflect (socially construct) women's presumed difference from men. The result was the establishment of women-only colleges.

This second stage of desegregation for subordinate groups to some degree constitutes "progress" because it opened up previously prohibited opportunities, albeit on a coercively sex-segregated basis. Women-only colleges provided curriculum considered appropriate only to women. Strikingly, even nineteenth-century advocates of women's education were careful *not* to seek for females the same schooling considered appropriate for males. Such tactics were espoused by Mary Wollstonecraft, who wrote *A Vindication on the Rights of Women* in mid-eighteenth century England and was a renowned advocate of women's education. She couched her radical demands for women's rights in a conservative approach, arguing women needed education in order to be better mothers.[26] In other words, women could be educated, but it had to suit their social roles, not put them in competition with men. This reinforced the belief that women *could not*—and for women's and society's sake, *should not*—handle the same intellectual challenges as men.

As a former Wellesley College president, Lt. Commander Mildred McAfee, explained, "Women's colleges started because women could not get an education in existing institutions. Thus, women's colleges were developed by those who were determined to prove that women could acquire education without losing health or feminine virtue."[27] Founders of women's colleges reflected a tone of determination tempered by the times: " 'They' say women's minds aren't good enough to stand intellectual effort. 'They' say it will make them unwomanly and that they cannot stand the physical strain of higher education. All right, we'll show 'them'!"[28]

Such advances, made as they were without establishing women's intellectual equality with men, became vulnerable to setbacks, particularly after World War II.

Gendering Education with the GI Bill

World War II engaged all of American society. Political scientist Suzanne Mettler notes that citizen soldiers—the vast majority of whom were men—defended the country through military service. Less often noted is that most American women contributed to the war effort, also including some in the armed forces. Females, for example, made up 60 percent of workers in defense industries, a field critical to military success. Women also strengthened the U.S. domestic position by planting Victory gardens to lessen dependence on food imports and by ensuring retailers adhered to price controls.[29]

When the time came to reward contributions by thousands of citizens, however, it was only those who served in the military who counted, more specifically, only the men who served in the military. In 1944, President Franklin Roosevelt signed the Servicemen's Readjustment Act of 1944, known as the GI Bill of Rights,[30] which was originally set to expire in 1956.[31] Benefits included in the GI Bill have since become perks used to attract citizens to military service. At the time, however, the GI Bill was the primary vehicle for rewarding military service in World War II by offering veterans access to educational and vocational training in relation to their length of service.

For example, veterans who served at least 90 days after September 16, 1940, earned one year of training under the GI Bill, and an additional month for every additional month of military service. Amendments to the law permitted veterans to get up to four years of free schooling, depending on length of service.[32] The maximum tuition and fees paid to a veteran in any one year was $500, but $500 was more than any school charged at the time. The GI Bill also provided monthly subsistence payments to veterans and dependents, supported housing loans, and health care.

Not surprisingly, more than 2.3 million veterans used the GI Bill to attend college, while 3.5 million used it to attend other schools. Some 1.6 million gained on-the-job training, and another 760,000 underwent farm training.[33] The cost was staggering. By 1955, the federal government had contributed $14.5 billion to the GI Bill for education and training alone (by 2002, that figure had reached $108 billion).[34] In 1947, the year use of the GI Bill peaked, a stunning 49 percent of all students at American colleges were veterans.[35] However, the students who were benefiting—almost to a person—were men, not women.

War Is for Men Only

Strikingly, the vast majority of women were left out of the veteran benefits provided by the GI Bill, in part because women were not drafted in the first place. War has long been considered a man's job, and it's only recently that public discomfort with women warriors has begun to abate. Today females comprise 15 percent of the armed forces. But it wasn't until 1976 that Congress opened officer training academies to women. In 1994, women earned the right to fly combat aircraft and serve on surface warships. However, they still may not serve on submarines, in the Special Forces, or in direct combat, including infantry, armor, and some artillery units.[36] As in the past, arguments about women's military service have been subject to the familiar notion that women should be protected and not be the protectors. Only now does the debate about women's access to combat-related duties acknowledge the desire for military women to gain access to the same career advancement opportunities as their male colleagues.

In May 2005, debate erupted in Congress after House Republicans sought to restrict women's military roles. The measure, it turns out, would have barred women from serving in some 22,000 positions they already held, spurring an awkward confrontation between military leaders and Republicans. Certainly the characteristics of war, such as the borders between noncombat and combat roles, have blurred. Rules bar women from "direct combat," defined as engaging the enemy "well forward on the battlefield." Yet such definitions are almost academic in places like Iraq, where there is no clear front line. Failure to integrate women fully into the military has supported the constitutionality of an all-male draft. As the Supreme Court ruled in 1971 in *Rostker,* if women are not assigned the same military combat tasks as men, then it is constitutional to draft only men for combat duty.[37]

Women Volunteers

If the Court in 1971 could uphold the constitutionality of an all-male draft, one can be certain that in the 1940s the idea of drafting women wasn't even considered. Naturally, the only women in the military then were volunteers. As a result, there were only 332,000 female World War II veterans compared with more than 16 million men, due to the fact that men, not women, were drafted.[38] As is the case today, although female military volunteers in World War II held noncombatant positions, they were official and critical players in battle who faced the full gamut of war's ugliness and sacrifice.

In 1942, Congress established a Women's Army Auxiliary Corps (WAAC), which in 1943 was changed to Women's Auxiliary Corps (WAC). Similarly, the navy authorized a Women's Naval Reserve, and the Marine Corps created the Marine Corps Women's Reserve. The Coast Guard established the Women Accepted for Volunteer Emergency Service (WAVES), whose first director was Lt. Commander Mildred McAfee, president of Wellesley College. (McAfee held both posts simultaneously). By 1944, WACs were serving in North Africa and the Pacific, and landing on the beaches at Normandy.

In 1945 alone, more than 2,000 WACs were stationed in North Africa. By the end of World War II, more than 8,000 WACs were stationed with military personnel in the European Theater. These military women faced combat danger while working as nurses aboard hospital ships, while aiding air evacuations, and while simply being present as war raged around them. Six nurses were killed, for example, when a Japanese suicide plane bombed the hospital ship USS *Comfort*, anchored off Leyte Island. Four other nurses were wounded.[39]

Military women were captured and taken as prisoners of war. Clara Gordon Main became one of the first POWs, captured while serving as a stewardess aboard a ship rescuing U.S. Marines from China.[40] In 1941, two days after Pearl Harbor was bombed, Japanese soldiers took five navy nurses prisoner, transporting them to Japan, where they were held until 1942. For three years, the Japanese held 67 army nurses and 16 navy nurses as prisoners of war. On May 6, 1942, when Corregidor fell, women were captured and brought to internment camps in Manila. They were not liberated until 1945.[41]

Sex Bias and Veterans Benefits

After World War II, however, women found that their efforts—from direct war involvement to work "manning" defense and other industries at home—counted for little. When President Roosevelt signed the GI Bill of Rights on June 22, 1944, the official text of his public statement embraced both "service men and women" in the opportunity to resume "their education or technical training after discharge."[42] However, reality looked quite different. Trouble arose around definitions. Even when women engaged in military activities, such as flying B-26 Marauder medium bombers on "tow target" and other service missions, they could be declared nonveterans and therefore ineligible for veteran's benefits. The women's air force service pilots (WASPs) experienced this fate. Thirty-eight WASPs flying military aircraft died in the line of duty but none received a burial with military honors, nor were their surviving female colleagues eligible for GI Bill benefits, including education and training funding, low interest housing loans, or Veteran's Administration health benefits. Despite their clear contributions and sacrifice, they were not legally recognized as veterans until 1979.[43]

Similarly, Congress did not officially recognize women who had served in the Women's Auxiliary Corps (WAC) as veterans legally eligible for benefits until after 1980.[44] Long after the expiration of their GI Bill benefits, these courageous women received the military honors they were due, but not the educational and economic benefits they deserved. Each WASP was awarded the Victory Medal in 1984, and those who had served more than one year also received the American Theater medal.[45]

The problem of sex bias in accessing military benefits continued long after World War II. One government report acknowledged that "even women serving as nurses at combat hospitals in Vietnam have experienced problems in gaining recognition as veterans."[46] A 1982 Government Accounting Office report revealed a disturbing pattern of substandard treatment of female veterans seeking legally mandated health care through veterans hospitals. The report cited the case of 10 women at a San Francisco medical facility who were denied care for gynecological problems, including some described as serious, because the problems were non–service connected—even though, as the report notes, "virtually all outpatient medical needs of non-service-connected male veterans were treated."[47] Thus Ann Bertini, who served as a World War II army nurse, said the GI Bill was viewed as "a policy for the men. I mean, they really created it with the men in mind, didn't they?"[48] Clearly they did. It was not until the 1980 census that American women were asked if they had ever served in the armed forces. To the government's surprise, 1.2 million indicated they had.[49]

Return to Domestic Roles

Women were also perceived as not being in need of the GI Bill benefits because, as Mettler notes, women, whether World War II veterans or not, "were expected to be at home raising children, and this was not viewed as requiring higher education."[50] In the post-war era, marriage rates skyrocketed to include 96.4 percent of all women and 94.1 percent of all men; fertility rates increased, and the baby boom generation arrived.[51] Women who were eligible for GI Bill benefits and knew about them still failed to use them, citing reasons involving "family obligations, such as caring for children or supporting a husband's breadwinning role."[52]

Finally, women faced serious hurdles, namely, employment discrimination. The GI Bill did not do for eligible female veterans what it did for male veterans, in part because women faced a limited range of school and work opportunities. It was common, for example, for medical schools to limit admission of women to 5 percent of an incoming class. So even a woman who had access to government support for education had to find an institution that would have her. As a result, only 132,000 of the 332,000 female veterans received benefits compared with 8.3 million men who used the GI Bill.[53] In the end, the GI Bill flung open doors of opportunity to a generation of men, providing a particular boost to the economically disadvantaged, but provided no comparable educational lift to a generation of women. With university admissions policies giving preference to veterans (who were mostly male), women faced a double barrier as they were often denied admission to provide enough space for the men. Cornell restricted female enrollments to ensure spots for veterans. At Penn State, freshmen women were not even admitted to the main campus until enough veterans (virtually all males) had graduated, which happened by 1949.[54] Veterans' preferences extended to employment. Women who sought civil service positions quickly learned that even if they scored as high as or higher than men on qualifying tests, if those men were veterans, the veteran would get the job.

Gendered Education in the 1964 Civil Rights Acts

Some have raised questions about how much blacks benefited from the GI Bill, but there is no such debate about the Civil Rights Act of 1964, which was passed to aid African Americans.[55] This landmark legislation was the culmination of executive and congressional policies seeking color-blind standards for societal activities, including housing, employment, public accommodations, and education.[56] In 1954, the Supreme Court ruled in *Brown vs. Board of Education* that in the context of public education, "separate was not equal." As the Court stated, "We conclude that, in the field of public education, the doctrine of 'separate but equal' has no place. Separate educational facilities are inherently unequal . . . segregation . . . deprive[s] [people] of the equal protection of the laws guaranteed by the Fourteenth Amendment."[57]

The Civil Rights Act of 1964 reinforced the *Brown* decision in education and extended the ban on coercive racial segregation to other sectors of American life. Title II of the law (see Table 3.1) specifically prohibited racial discrimination or segregation in public accommodations. Title III required the desegregation of public facilities on the basis of race. Title IV concerned public education and specifically invoked prohibitions against segregation in public schools on the basis of race. While the law plainly focused on racial discrimination, Title VII of the act famously prohibited race *or* sex discrimination in employment. Not surprisingly, the inclusion of "sex" in Title VII has been the focus of tremendous policy interest. As a result, attention to Title VII of the 1964 Civil Rights Act often overshadows attention to Title IV that refers to educational policies. Such lack of attention is unfortunate because Title VII did nothing to promote women's equality in academic educational policies. Rather, it would take a special piece of legislation to address this: Title IX.

Employment (Title VII)

The only place in the Civil Rights Act of 1964 where one finds protection against sex discrimination is in Title VII of the law, which prohibits such bias in employment practices. Title VII applied to employers in industry affecting interstate commerce which have 15 or more employees; employment agencies, labor unions, and joint labor-management committees which control apprenticeship and other training programs.[58] Title VII, however, does not apply to federal, state, or local government employers, or to educational institutions.[59] Nevertheless, Title VII did force the creation of new employment policies for women. As a 1970 summary of Title VII in the *Duke Law Review* so quaintly put it, "Title VII extends not only to black people but to those individuals who may be denied

TABLE 3.1   Provisions of the Civil Rights Act of 1964[a]

Title I. Voting Rights	No literacy test as a qualification for voting in any Federal election
Title II. Injunctive Relief Against Discrimination in Places of Public Accommodation	Race and Religion: No "discrimination or segregation on the ground of race, color, religion, or national origin"
Title III. Desegregation of Public Facilities	Race and Religion: Protects any "individual...[who] is being deprived of or threatened with the loss of his right to the equal protection of the laws, on account of his race, color, religion, or national origin, by being denied equal utilization of any public facility, which is owned, operated or managed by or on behalf of any State or subdivision thereof..."
Title IV. Desegregation of Public Education	Race and Religion: " 'Desegregation' means the assignment of students to public schools and within such schools without regard to their race, color, religion, or national origin..."
Title V. Commission on Civil Rights	Race and Religion: Duties of the Commission: 1. "Investigate allegations...that... citizens...are being deprived of their right to vote...by reason of their color, race, religion, or national origin..." 2. "Study...legal developments constituting a denial of equal protection of the laws under the Constitution because of race, color, religion or national origin..." 3. "Appraise the laws and policies of the Federal Government with respect to denials of equal protection of the laws under the Constitution because of race, color, religion or national origin..."

TABLE 3.1 (*continued*)

	4. "Serve as a national clearinghouse for information in respect to denials of equal protection of the laws because of race, color, religion or national origin, including but not limited to the fields of voting, education, housing, employment, the use of public facilities, and transportation . . ."
Title VI. Nondiscrimination in Federally Assisted Programs	Race and Religion: "No person in the United States shall, on the ground of race, color, or national origin, be subjected to discrimination under any program or activity receiving Federal financial assistance. . ."
Title VII. Equal Employment Opportunity	Race, Religion, Sex: "It shall be an unlawful employment practice for an employer . . . employment agency . . . labor organization . . . [or] on-the-job training program . . . to fail or refuse to hire or to discharge any individual or otherwise to discriminate against any individual with respect to his compensation, terms, conditions, or privileges of employment . . . to limit, segregate, or classify his employees in any way which would deprive . . . any individual of employment opportunities . . . because of such individual's race, color, religion, sex, or national origin . . ." Bona fide occupational qualification (bfoq) exception: "It shall not be an unlawful employment practice . . . to employ any individual . . . on the basis of his religion, sex, or national origin in those certain instances where religion, sex, or national origin is a bona fide occupation qualification reasonably [and] necessary to the normal operation of that particular business or enterprise . . ."

a. *Document PL 88-352; July 2, 1964; 88th Congress, HR 7152* employment because they are...members of the *fairer sex.*"[60] When the law passed, officials predicted there would be as many as 2,000 complaints of sex discrimination filed. They were shocked when 8,852 charges were registered in the first year alone.[61]

Of course, the Civil Rights Act of 1964 aimed to "eliminate *racial* discrimination," not sex discrimination.[62] President Lyndon Johnson, before signing the bill into law on July 2, 1964, addressed the nation in a television broadcast from the White House. Tellingly, his remarks focused on racial discrimination as a historical problem. (Sex discrimination didn't merit mention because it wasn't a "problem," but merely reflected "natural" differences.) Johnson said:

> We believe that all men are created equal—yet many are denied equal treatment. We believe that all men have certain inalienable rights. We believe that all men are entitled to the blessings of liberty—yet millions are being deprived of those blessings, not because of their own failures, but because of the *color of their skins.*
>
> The reasons are deeply embedded in history and tradition and the nature of man. We can understand without rancor or hatred how all this happens. But it cannot continue. Our Constitution, the foundation of our Republic, forbids it. The principles of our freedom forbid it. Morality forbids it. And the law I sign tonight forbids it.[63]

Most analysts consider inclusion of "sex" in Title VII of the Civil Rights Act of 1964 to be a historical accident—or perhaps the result of a joke. Why a joke? Because the proposal to include sex in Title VII was made by Rep. Howard Smith (D-VA), who vehemently opposed passage of *any* titles included in the 1964 act. He considered it so preposterous to think employment could be organized without regard to sex, that he believed adding "sex" to the language would trigger the bill's doom. Despite the laughter and derision his proposal caused among representatives in attendance, a few courageous female House members—who had been thinking along the same lines, albeit with seriousness—stood and defended with great force the idea of banning sex discrimination in employment.[64] To everyone's surprise, the amendment survived votes in the House and Senate, and was included in the Civil Rights Act of 1964.[65]

Quirk or Quest for Employment Equality

It is difficult now to find anything laughable about women seeking equal work opportunities. However, employment practices in the 1960s and early 1970s reflected rigid sex stereotypes, fully embraced by the public and schoolchildren whose textbooks kept "female jobs" distinct from "male jobs." Most girls didn't dare consider entering a male field.

Thus the ban on sex discrimination in the workplace in the context of Title VII came when women still lacked equal access to education and training. Without competitive skills, the value of banning sex discrimination in the workplace was limited. Certainly, Congress in 1963 had passed the Equal Pay Act, which demanded women receive the same wage for the same work as a man. However, that didn't guarantee that a woman would be hired for the same job as a man in the first place. Nor did it guarantee that once hired, terms of employment would be the same for a woman as a man. Nor did it guarantee women the same educational opportunities as men, which were necessary prerequisites, of course, for eligibility for the same jobs. In short, there were many ways to avoid giving women equal pay or equal access to jobs.

One of the most devious was the common practice of advertising jobs on a sex-segregated basis. Newspapers listed jobs by "help wanted—female" and "help wanted—male." Even the Equal Employment Opportunity Commission (EEOC), created to enforce Title VII, at first saw nothing wrong with this advertising.[66] Why? While race discrimination appeared clear, sex discrimination was vague and somewhat incomprehensible to EEOC officials charged with defining and administering Title VII regulations. In 1965, for example, at a White House conference to discuss what was meant by "equal employment opportunity," EEOC officials weren't sure if Title VII prohibited or permitted a hamburger stand to hire "pretty girls...to increase sales." Yet challenging such deep-rooted bias was considered a waste of time. Not the *real* problem. One EEOC commissioner said the agency should go after the "most flagrant [sex] discrimination," but that it was not EEOC's task to get "on our charger to overturn patterns."[67]

Yet it was precisely the problem of patterns that blocked women's social, work, and educational opportunities. Airlines routinely fired stewardesses when they reached their early to mid thirties, and/or were married, because they no longer fit the job. Female public school teachers were commonly fired when they became pregnant, for fear it would shock students' sensibilities to see a teacher who presumably had engaged in sexual intercourse.[68] In one case, Cindy Judd Hill, a music teacher, managed while on sabbatical to finish her master's degree, fulfill all requirements of her leave, and take off a week to have a baby. The Pennsylvania school district promptly rescinded her sabbatical pay and fired her.[69]

Sex-Segregated Help Wanted Ads

Because the EEOC at first found nothing wrong with sex-segregated employment advertisements, the American Newspaper Publishers Association in 1966 sought official approval to continue the practice. The EEOC officially pronounced sex segregation acceptable:

> Advertisers covered by [Title VII] may place advertisements for jobs open to both sexes in columns classified by publishers under "Male" or "Female" headings to indicate that some occupations are considered more *attractive* to persons of one sex than the other.[70]

The commission's cavalier attitude toward sex segregation in employment angered feminists, and some identify this treatment by a federal agency as a key impetus for the founding of the National Organization for Women (NOW) in 1966. Although it may seem far-fetched today to care about, much less seek to remove, sex segregation in sports policies, in the 1960s the same sentiment prevailed, as most saw no reason to halt sex segregation in employment practices. Initial feminist demands to desegregate employment were met with ridicule, as articles and editorials in major newspapers derided the idea. An August 1965 *New York Times* headline quips, "For Instance, Can She Pitch for the Mets?"[71] The article reports on government leaders gathering to tackle "the bunny problem"—how to handle under Title VII the prospect of a male applying to work as a Playboy bunny. This bunny problem, as it became known, was popularized in a 1965 *Wall Street Journal* article evoking the image of a "shapeless knobby-kneed male 'bunny' serving drinks to a group of stunned businessmen in a

Playboy Club." Stories also offered the image of "a matronly vice president gleefully participating in an old office sport by chasing a male secretary around a big leather-topped desk."[72]

As the tone suggests, the notion that sex segregation (or sex discrimination, depending on how you viewed it) should be eradicated was not taken seriously. Even the civil rights officials charged with enforcing Title VII played into stereotypes, responding at one gathering to those "men who might find a male secretary disturbing."[73] The *Washington Post* reported that EEOC Executive Director Herman Edelsberg said to reporters that "there are those on this Commission who think that no man should be required to have a male secretary—and I am one of them."[74] When EEOC Chairman Franklin Delano Roosevelt Jr. was asked by reporters on the day Title VII became effective, "What about sex?" he quipped, "Don't get me started, I'm all for it."[75]

The National Organization for Women, however, found sex-segregated job advertising discriminatory and in 1967 picketed the *New York Times* offices to protest the practice.[76] In 1968, the EEOC finally declared sex-segregated help wanted ads illegal. The Supreme Court confirmed the constitutionality of the EEOC ruling in 1973.[77] From that point on, employers were required to state that they "recruit employees of both sexes for all positions, except where sex is a bona fide occupation qualification . . . [and they] offer employees of both sexes an equal opportunity for any jobs they are qualified to perform, except when sex is a bona fide occupational qualification."[78]

Bona Fide Occupational Qualification (BFOQ)

If the EEOC's ruling seemed to fix the problem, the exception made for "bona fide occupational qualification" opened another loophole. Note that Title VII refers to "individuals" and not "groups," and prohibits employment discrimination solely because of sex or race even if there are "valid factual data" about "intrinsic differences" between sexes or races. At first blush, then, Title VII seemed to provide parallel protection for racial minorities and for women. However, the regulations allowed exceptions to a ban on sex segregation on the basis of what was termed bona fide occupational qualifications

(BFOQ). In other words, if an employer demonstrated that being a man or a woman was an essential job qualification, that employer was free to discriminate solely on the basis of sex.[79] No parallel exception was made for race.

Fulfilling the Customer's Psychological Needs

Employers soon attempted to stretch the BFOQ to include sex stereotypes. Some airlines tried to justify a requirement for female flight attendants by insisting women were more soothing and sexually appealing to airline passengers (who were presumably heterosexual males).[80] As Southwest Airlines argued in a case as late as 1981, they were in the business of selling "love" in the air. The airline used Dallas's Love Field as its hub and claimed sexy, female flight attendants were central to their marketing strategy.

The Court carefully considered this argument. While noting that sexy, female flight attendants might have an impact on the economic prospects of the airline, which was facing bankruptcy, the Court nevertheless ruled the major work of an airline was transporting people from one place to another. The Court ruled it was not "essential" that flight attendants be female rather than male. As for the assertion that women were better at soothing airline passengers, the Court said that even if it accepted this doubtful premise, *some men* could better reassure anxious passengers than *some women*. The Court said airlines should hire males sensitive to passenger needs rather than hire no men at all.[81] Thus the Court established that a person's sex was not a BFOQ for being a flight attendant.

Sex Authenticity

On the other hand, courts recognized instances in which customers require authenticity as a component of service they receive. Shakespeare fared well using boys to represent females in play performances, but audiences today want real women in the part. Courts have ruled that when roles demand a particular sex as an "essential component," such as in acting or modeling positions, it is acceptable to use a person's sex as a criterion for employment. That is to say, "though Title VII attempts to correct misapprehensions and stereotypes based on sex, it does not attempt to further the proposition that men and women are interchangeable for other, non-employment purposes."[82]

Some employers claimed women were not physically strong enough for some occupations, such as telephone repair work, and argued they should be allowed to hire only men for such jobs.[83] This approach did not hold up in court. Courts denounced "employers' reliance on 'class stereotypes' to deny women who were otherwise perfectly capable of performing the duties involved the opportunity to obtain desirable positions."[84] Courts established that employers may not base job opportunities on paternalistic attitudes about the weakness of women compared with men. Such attitudes, courts said, merely lock women "in golden cages."[85]

This rule holds even when there are statistically significant differences between the sexes. Even if women as a group have better driving safety records than men, it is not permissible to hire only women as truck drivers or chauffeurs. Employers must rely on safety records of the *individual* driver in making employment decisions, regardless of the driver's sex.

The Inseparability and Dominance of Sex-Based Aspects of the Job

Courts recognize there are some jobs that may only be done by members of one sex. Defined as "sex essentiality," it describes jobs such as wet nurse, actress, or model, in which the sex of the person is directly required for employment. When the sex of a person may appear to be essential to the job, such as dean of women at a college, courts have directed employers to separate the "sexual from the nonsexual aspects of the job."[86] Thus, even if a school could effectively show that "only a woman could adequately counsel female students," that fact alone does not qualify as a BFOQ. Rather, the courts said, the school must separate counseling and administrative components of the dean's position. If counseling female students requires a female dean, fine, but the rest of the dean's tasks must be open to both men and women.[87]

Some jobs make it tough to separate sexual and nonsexual components, particularly work that requires sex appeal and the ability to attract members of the opposite sex. In those cases (say, the job of topless waitress) courts have narrowly allowed sex to be used as a requirement for employment. This allowance, however, is distinguished from jobs in which sex appeal may be "useful" in attracting customers but is not central to the job. Hence, being a wait person in general cannot be defined in terms of a person's sex. Interestingly, it is perfectly okay for an employer to include "sexual attractiveness" in a job description, as long as the employer requires both male and female employees meet that criterion.[88]

Unalterable Conditions

Lastly, courts allow sex as a BFOQ when an employee's sex is an essential characteristic to performing the job. By this, courts mean jobs such as restroom or locker room attendants, in which the sex-segregated nature of the facility would make presence of the opposite sex disturbing. Courts also recognize that business dealings with some countries which impose strict prohibitions against women's participation in business arenas could render "sex" an essential criterion for doing business with those countries.[89] Courts have ruled that men's prisons, for example, possess unalterable conditions and an atmosphere that make it too dangerous to hire women as prison guards. In addition, the presence of female guards at communal showers and toilets could well violate male prisoners' rights to privacy. As one state public safety official put it, "The presence of women in a confined environment 'where there are no heterosexual outlets would unnecessarily arouse and possibly even incite the inmates.'"[90] Here officials take the paternalistic view that sex segregation is protection for women.

Sex Segregation in Employment: The Exception, Not the Rule

Title VII sought to protect individual women from work-based sex discrimination, but the BFOQ allowed some sex segregation to continue. Still, it represented progress as employers could not use stereotypical notions of women's strength or weakness, sexual attractiveness, or factual statistics about group differences as employment criteria. While not a complete ban on using sex as a qualification for employment, it did dramatically change the workforce. In the end, Title VII was most notable not for adding great numbers of women to the workforce (in 1964 women already comprised more than one-third of paid workers) but for challenging the sex-segregated principle of women's employment.[91] It altered attitudes, the law, institutional practice, and the very notion of women's work and men's work.

Title IX of the Educational Amendments of 1972

Where Title VII altered women's employment opportunities, Title IV of the 1964 Civil Rights Act did nothing to challenge sex discrimination in education. Any discussion of Title IX, then, begins with the Civil Rights Act of 1964 and the omission of "sex" in Title IV. It was that glaring absence that the Educational Amendments, including Title IX, sought to correct in 1972.[92] The major purpose of Title IX was to gain for women the educational access that the GI Bill paid for and secured for economically disadvantaged men and that Title IV of the Civil Rights Act of 1964 guaranteed successfully to African American men.

Today women serve as presidents of major universities, including formerly male-only institutions. It may be difficult to evoke the furor ignited when women merely sought admission to colleges and universities on an equal basis with men. But furor there was. Harvard University vehemently objected to eliminating sex discrimination in admissions policies, asserting that the institution not only had the right but the duty to discriminate on the basis of sex to ensure the university's financial health "because men alumni contribute more generously than women alumnae." Harvard insisted that "having a non-discriminatory [sex] policy would impair the financial condition" of Harvard.[93]

This was, however, about more than endowments. Any change in roles or opportunities between dominant and subordinate groups alters power structures, whether the groups are identified in terms of class, race, or gender. Representative Bella Abzug of Manhattan saw this clearly in 1971, asserting, "Certainly we cannot expect that the men who head these institutions [colleges and universities] . . . will look favorably upon women...seeking admission to their institutions. Unbiased admissions policies would threaten the male power structures which presently control these institutions...Their fears are not unfounded. As women gain equal access to institutions of higher learning, they will also gain greater access to the other facets of the power structure of the country—political, social, economic."[94]

In 1972, the burning issue at the center of Title IX was not sports but women's equal entry into educational institutions as students, scholarship recipients, and faculty. Female students were not to be denied access to the same educational settings and opportunities as male students, a straightforward goal made clear in the wording of Title IX, a subsection of the Educational Amendments of 1972. The simple text of Title IX reads:

> No person in the United States shall, on the basis of sex, be excluded from participation in, be denied the benefits of, or be subjected to discrimination under any educational program or activity receiving Federal financial assistance.[95]

From the start, Title IX was a weak, even meek tool. Regulations accompanying Title IX allowed a number of exemptions, in contrast to Title IV of the Civil Rights Act of 1964, which offers no such parallel exemptions from enforcing racial equality in education. For example, Title IX allowed religious organizations with "contrary religious tenets" to discriminate on the basis of sex. Title IX exempted the military services, the merchant marine, and any "educational institution whose *primary purpose* is the training of individuals for the military services of the United States," which would include secondary military training schools. Oddly, Title IX also exempted "any public institution of undergraduate higher education which is an institution that *traditionally* and continually from its establishment has had a policy of admitting only students of one sex." Social fraternities and sororities need not comply with Title IX; neither did "any program or activity of any secondary school or education institution specifically [organized] for the promotion of" boys or girls, such as Boys Nation conference and Girls Nation conference. Regulations exempted beauty pageants in educational programs and exempted them from Title IX, noting they "shall not apply...to any scholarship or other financial assistance awarded by an institution of higher education to any individual because such individual has received such award in any pageant in which the attainment of such award is based upon a combination of factors related to the personal appearance, poise, and talent of such individual and in which participation is limited to individuals of one sex only."

Thus, even as Title IX purported to guarantee equal educational access to women, it also ensured that society remained properly "sexed." It was fine for religious institutions to teach that men and women were inherently different and could not attend school together, though no such permission was accorded these institutions when it came to race. Military schools could continue to bar women without even offering separate educational opportunities, whereas no such permission was granted for race. Yes, Title IX and Title IV did address sex discrimination and racial discrimination, respectively, in educational settings. Yet where Title IV cited coercive segregation as a culprit in racial inequality, Title IX found no parallel problem with coercive sex segregation. On the contrary, Congress endorsed traditional sex segregation, even when it meant (as in the case of military institutions) leaving females without comparable opportunities.

Title IX and Sports

"Segregation" is not the only word missing from the original Title IX legislation; the word "sports" is too. Clearly the main purpose of Title IX was not seeking inclusion for women in school sports programs but ending everyday sex bias at institutions receiving federal funding (which includes most public schools and colleges). When sports came up at all in Congress, references generally took the form of assurances that Title IX would *not* affect athletics. Sports programs, for some, were peculiar and unique extracurricular activities, like "classes for pregnant girls or emotionally disturbed children" for which Title IX "would allow enforcing agencies to permit differential treatment by sex only."[96]

Thus many were surprised when sports became the focus of Title IX debate. Some organizations, like the male-dominated NCAA, lobbied hard to protect male sports programs. The reason was obvious: schools, with the help of groups like the NCAA, had spent decades building men's sports programs, garnering both financial support and public recognition. By contrast, women's sports programs enjoyed neither. Men didn't want their prized programs hurt by the new law. Lobbyists and members of Congress tried to get sports exempted from Title IX. When such efforts failed, they tried other tactics. In 1974, Sen. John G. Tower proposed exempting "revenue-producing sports." His amendment was rejected in favor of the Javits Amendment, which more vaguely allowed the Department of Health, Education and Welfare (HEW) to issue Title IX regulations "with respect to intercollegiate athletic activities" that would allow "reasonable provision considering the nature of particular sports."[97] That language left a lot of wiggle room.

Sports: Integrate or Segregate?

Even after Title IX was passed and even after its vital link to athletics emerged, it was still not clear what school athletic programs should look like. Title IX offered the obvious opportunity to give girls access to the same athletic experiences as boys. It also offered a less obvious opening to extend sports opportunities to the less athletic (whether girls or boys), thus addressing a persistent criticism of male sports programs, which emphasized stars. Unfortunately, that opportunity vanished between the law's passage in 1972 and 1975 when HEW issued Title IX regulations. Writer Dan Wakefield observed in the *New York Times* that both sides suffer when there is social inequality. "There is no way of making a whole lot of little girls miserable by segregating sports according to sex without also making a whole lot of little boys miserable," he wrote.[98]

Wakefield's point applies precisely to the unathletic boy routinely called out in a sports culture in which every male is expected to aspire to top athletic performance. He described physical-education class softball games in which he and another boy volunteered to play the outfield. He played so far back he was "nearly hidden among a grove of trees behind the diamond." One day, as he edged into the foliage, he asked the other boy what he was doing back there too. " 'Same thing you are—trying to avoid the ball,' " the boy replied. "In high school, that was a hard thing for a boy to admit," noted Wakefield, who advocated an end to "the notion that 'manhood' is equivalent to athletic prowess . . . [and] getting rid of the notion that women who enjoy and excel at sport and who want to make it a pastime or even a profession are not somehow deficient in 'femininity' or aberrant in their behavior."

In other words, there was recognition, even at the time, that the debate about Title IX was about more than sports programs. It was about gender identity and gender relations. A recast system that was less rigid, Wakefield and others saw, was possible in the unisex 1970s and could benefit not only girls (as was the focus) but boys who didn't want to (or couldn't) fulfill social expectations that they be talented athletes. Youth sports could be a coed venture, with exceptions in some settings for single-sex play when it was warranted. The National Organization for Women, among others, saw in mixed-sex teams a means to improve working relationships between the sexes. "We expect adult men and women to be able to work and function together on a cooperative basis. Yet all their growing up years they are separated and the differences between them are pointed out," Judy Wenning, NOW national task force coordinator, argued in 1974.[99]

Instead, of course, Title IX regulations replicated existing sex bias and never demanded equality for women's programs. As Margaret Dunkle, associate director of the project on the status and education of women for the Association of American Colleges, observed in 1976, "If when Title IX was passed in 1972, opportunities for women were terrible, now they've improved to bad—and that's certainly progress."[100]

Enforcing Sex-Segregated Sports

Title IX is celebrated for opening the door to organized athletics for women. Yet Title IX opened a sex-segregated door, a type of door the federal government would have prohibited if it were a matter of race. Title IX regulations, as clarified by Congress, explicitly permit separate teams for each sex when team selection is based on competitive skill or for contact sports.[101] This means that when a school has a team for boys but no such team for girls, regulations require that "members of the excluded sex must be allowed to try-out for the team *unless the sport is a contact sport.*" Contact sports, according to the regulations, included boxing, wrestling, rugby, ice hockey, football, basketball, "and other sports the purpose or major activity of which involves bodily contact."[102]

This rule merely acts as a warning to schools: create a girls-only team to match every boys-only team.[103] In 1970s America the stipulation sounded reasonable. After all, girls had little access to athletics and it seemed possible some could get hurt if they played contact sports against well-trained boys. Unfortunately this approach failed to consider abilities of individual girls and failed to address the real matter, which was sex discrimination. More profoundly, explicitly allowing sex segregation in contact sports has had the far-reaching effect of sex segregating not only contact sports but virtually all sports. One effect of the way Title IX permits sex-segregated teams, as law scholar Deborah Brake notes, is to solidify "the connection between sport and male dominance."

Such fallout from the regulations is even more striking when you consider that before Dan Wakefield and NOW praised the opportunities of mixed-sex sports, schools in 1971 and 1972 had begun allowing girls to play on boys' golf, tennis, track, and swim teams (noncontact sports).[104] That halted with implementation of Title IX regulations, spurring sports programs to be divided based on gender ahead of skill. Instead of encouraging mixed-sex teams by competition level (similar to college Divisions I, II, and III), Title IX effectively preserved male teams intact, creating junior sports programs for females that were intended not to challenge male programs.[105] Granted, it may not have appeared that way at the time, particularly to some feminists who favored sex-separate sports. However, failure to think creatively cemented a system in which women's sports are still playing catch-up. This is not to deny that females may benefit from being able to develop athletic skills apart from males, but Title IX's implementation quashed any notion of using sex segregation as an exception, rather than the rule.

The regulations, however, needed to answer a key question: What should equality (such as it was) look like? The answer is hardly satisfying. Enforcement provisions of Title IX aim to get percentages of women playing sports comparable to percentages of female enrollments at educational institutions. Regulations sought access to coaching and equipment for women athletes comparable with men. They sought comparable sports schedules for both sexes. And, if all this wasn't happening, regulations just wanted some assurance that institutions were moving in the right direction.

When we examine all the regulations created by HEW to implement Title IX, there is not a word about sex segregation. As a result, Title IX and its implementing regulations allow, if not blatantly support, a separate is equal doctrine for male and female athletes, an approach clearly prohibited for racial differences by Title IV of the Civil Rights Act of 1964, not to mention *Brown v. Board of Education*.

Implementation of Title IX

Even after Title IX was passed in 1972, and even after it took three years to create regulations, educational institutions were given another three years—until 1978—to comply with the law. There was no rush to get girls on the field. By comparison, the sweeping No Child Left Behind law signed by President George W. Bush in 2002 called on educational institutions to become accountable immediately with schools required to show improvements on standardized test scores virtually overnight. Compliance for sports programs was far more relaxed, demanding that athletic departments meet *one* of three requirements: (1) The proportionality rule. An educational institution must provide athletic opportunities to females and males substantially proportionate to their respective enrollments. For example, if a college has 55 percent men and 45 percent women as undergraduates, athletic participation should reflect a 55:45 mix.[106]

(2) The gender equity rule. The educational institution must show that it "fully and effectively" meets the interest of the gender that is underrepresented.[107] Since historically women have been the gender underrepresented in sports programs, this means the only excuse for not providing proportionate opportunities for men and women is proving that all athletic interests of all women have been completely and fully met. In March 2005, the U.S. Department of Education issued a controversial "clarification" placing the burden of addressing such interest on students and government investigators,

not colleges. Under the redefined rules, a college only has to send out an Internet survey to judge student interest or lack of it. Failure to respond to the survey is accepted as evidence of low or no interest.[108]

(3) The historical progress rule. The only other excuse for not providing proportionate opportunities for men and women is the ability to show a continuing effort to expand opportunities over time for the underrepresented gender.

Impact of Title IX: Changing Quantities, Not Principles

On a positive note, these rules—what law scholar Jessica Jay categorizes as a form of formal equality law—ushered in a new era in women's sports, attracting huge numbers of females to join athletic teams.[109] Female high school sports participation rose 800 percent, from 300,000 to 2.7 million young women between 1971 and 2000.[110] Sports participation among college women has risen 372 percent over that time, from 32,000 to more than 150,000 women. Athletic participation among women of color in high school and college rose 955 percent over those years.[111]

Notably, although male participation in high school sports has stalled over the past decade, holding steady at 47 percent of male students, female participation has increased steadily to 33.5 percent of female students.[112] The gender gap is closing, suggesting an expanding pool of female athletic talent and the promise of more parity in college numbers.[113] It also bodes well for the continued emergence of supertalented female athletes.[114]

As well as providing more athletic opportunities for women, Title IX also set the stage for a new kind of celebrity, offering women for the first time a mainstream vision of athletic success. While female athletes can now dream of playing on an Olympic team, the promise of a professional career, while increasingly possible, remains largely elusive. The landscape is improving, but too few female athletes have opportunities beyond college, particularly to earn a living even remotely akin to comparable male athletes, for whom big-money careers provide an incentive for hard work.

Women athletes receive greater respect today but relatively skimpy media attention. Still, credit Title IX for providing hard-working young women the opportunity to develop skills and to link "female" with "athlete." Thank Title IX for making Venus and Serena Williams household names, for HBO's decision to make the *Dare to Dream* film chronicling the U.S. Women's Soccer team, and for the growing visibility of women's college basketball that has *USA Today* producing a pullout section for the women's NCAA March Madness tournament.[115]

Title IX: Still Not Well Enforced

Not everyone greeted Title IX with enthusiasm. It remains a controversial policy whose thirtieth anniversary in 2002 spurred heated discussions, debate, a lawsuit—and little change. In 2007, as the law turned 35, the same heated attacks and debates continued. From the feminist perspective, Title IX does not do enough. An important first step, the law has not been well enough enforced to be effective. In 1997, 25 years after the law's passage, the Office of Civil Rights, charged with implementing Title IX, received 700 complaints alleging sex discrimination,[116] including 83 related to sports programs at elementary and secondary schools.[117] Despite federal mandates, many institutions still are not meeting requirements.

Likewise, a 2004 *Annual Report on Gender Equity* published by the *Chronicle of Higher Education* noted, "Reports submitted to the U.S. Department of Education also show that many colleges, large and small, do not appear to have gotten the message about gender equity in sports."[118] Data show females comprise 54 percent of college enrollments but only 42 percent of college athletes. The *Chronicle* report shows at 707 institutions, the proportion of women playing sports lagged behind proportions of women in the student body by more than 20 percent.

Financing has also lagged for women's sports. The *Chronicle* report shows that at more than 230 institutions, women's sports received less than 30 percent of the operating budget for all athletic teams. Among Division I schools in 2002–2003, the average budget for men's sports was $6.1 million while the average budget for women's sports was $3.2 million. The report also notes an investigation by the California Postsecondary Education Commission found 84 percent of California community colleges out of compliance with Title IX, as were 43 percent of four-year colleges. And this isn't the only public system with such problems.

The news is not all bad. Gender equity advocates applauded in 2006 when University of Tennessee women's basketball coach Pat Summitt surpassed the million-dollar salary mark, and as women's sports (especially softball) have earned more television coverage on ESPN. But there is increasing concern about the large disparity between post-season high-profile play for male and female athletes. During the 2004-5 academic year, 1,000 more male athletes than female athletes had opportunities to participate in post-season play, a gap that has widened in recent years. "There's a glaring inequity that exists in the NCAA championships program," Jean Lenti Ponsetto, athletics director at DePaul University and former chair of the NCAA championships cabinet, told the *Chronicle*.[119]

Title IX: Opportunity, Not Equity

Title IX, heralded as creating new opportunities for female athletes, hasn't yielded equity. As a 2002 report by the National Women's Law Center observes, "Because of Title IX, women have gone from being almost totally excluded from intercollegiate athletics to having a disproportionately small but important share of athletic opportunities."[120] The federal Office for Civil Rights publicized "successes" that offered a window on slow progress and piecemeal enforcement: a brand-new high school featured a state-of-the-art baseball facility for boys, "including dugouts, generous seating, lockers, a storage room and PA system."[121]

Meanwhile, the girls had no softball field. The school instead made arrangements with a church to share its field. OCR rightly trumpets the results of its intervention, which produced a comparable softball facility for the girls. But the very fact that a high school today could be constructed with such blatantly unequal facilities for males and females reveals the unfortunate truth: Title IX has not been effective enough in changing societal practices and cultural bias.

And chief among the sex stereotyping and sex difference myths that we must overcome is the assumption that women as a group are so different—inferior—that sports require coercive sex segregation.[122] Yes, as a second step in challenging sex discrimination that prohibited women from "playing at all," sex segregated sports is improvement. However, it is time to move on to the third stage of breaking down sex discrimination barriers by embracing the sex-integrated principle that women can—and should—not only play, but "play with the boys."

4

Sex-Segregated Sports on Trial

Athletic competition builds character in boys. We don't need that kind of character in our girls, the women of tomorrow.
    —Hollander v. Connecticut Interscholastic
    Athletic Conference (1971)[1]

Scarcely any political question arises in the United States which is not resolved, sooner or later, into a judicial one.
    —Alexis de Tocqueville[2]

"Don't Forget to Be a Good Boy..."

The scene on August 18, 1920, was a dramatic one. For over 70 years, suffrage reformers had been trying to win for women the right to vote. Finally, on June 4, 1919, both Houses of Congress passed with a two-thirds majority the Nineteenth Amendment to the Constitution prohibiting states from disqualifying women from the franchise solely because of their sex. The notion of women voting, however, was still so controversial that getting the required thirty-six states to ratify the amendment was by no means a foregone conclusion. All southern states had voted no, but thirty-five states had voted yes. Tennessee was the final, thirty-sixth state, on which the fate of woman suffrage rested.

Lobbying in the Tennessee legislature for and against the woman suffrage amendment on that fateful day was intense. Forces on both sides of the issue had swarmed to Nashville, each intent on victory. Anti-suffrage legislators wore red roses in their lapels to indicate how they would cast their votes and pro-suffrage supporters wore yellow ones. The problem was that right before the roll call vote, the red roses outnumbered the yellow ones on the floor of the Tennessee legislature 49 to 47.[3] Gasping for air, however, woman suffrage reformers were given a lifeline when one legislator switched his vote from nay to yea. Now the votes for and against woman suffrage were tied at 48 to 48. Another roll call vote would have to be taken, and another legislator wearing a red rose would have to switch and vote yea, if woman suffrage was to succeed. However, on the next roll call vote, there were no switches, requiring yet another roll call vote.[4]

What happened next is history. The youngest member of the Tennessee legislature, Harry Burn, wearing a red rose, changed his vote from a no to a yes on the third roll call vote, handing to woman suffrage advocates the thirty-sixth state they needed. Later, asked why he changed his vote, he said that his mother, who lived in east Tennessee, had sent him a telegram in which she had written, "Don't forget to be a good boy," Harry, and "vote for suffrage." He had placed the telegram in his breast pocket, where he felt its weight.[5] On August 26, 1920, President Woodrow Wilson signed the Nineteenth Amendment into law.

Social Policies Make Citizens

Of course, some would decry that the Nineteenth Amendment constitutes nothing more than "formal equality," that is, simply a piece of paper that purports to achieve equality between men and women when it comes to their political citizenship.[6] Formal law alone does not equality make; it is also true that formal law not only is a vital first step, but as more and more scholars argue, formal laws impact public opinion by virtue of defining who is in and who is out of the civic community. In this respect, the Nineteenth Amendment is an example of how laws make citizens. This is true not only in terms of the formal rights of citizens but also in terms of the new ways the public views people who have been declared, by virtue of a law not to mention an amendment to the Constitution to be citizens equal to others. Of course, most women in the United States were citizens before gaining the right to vote, but they were citizens without power to participate in politics on the same basis as men and without the regard from the public as having that power. The Nineteenth Amendment changed the *meaning* of being female, from one signifying political exclusion to one signifying political inclusion. We continue to feel its impact today, every time we talk about women and politics, observe Rep. Nancy Pelosi's historic ascension to Speaker of the House, and appreciate the viability of a woman candidate for president.

What is true of the Nineteenth Amendment is also true of other social policies, as a growing number of scholars demonstrate how institutions and social policies in a wide range of areas have the power to make people citizens—or not. Political scientist Andrea Campbell, for example, shows how public policies (who gets benefits and how benefits are administered) can spur beneficiaries to increase participation in American society. She observes that the substantial transfer of federal benefits to senior citizens via Social Security and Medicare policies, for example, makes this group the "Über-citizens of the American polity" whose voting and campaign contribution rates are higher than any other age-group's.[7] Political scientists Suzanne Mettler and Eric Welch argue that public policies are interpretative mechanisms for citizens, shaping "their sense of their role, status and identity within the polity."[8] Mettler notes that the GI Bill was a social policy that marked beneficiaries as having made particularly valuable contributions to American society, which in turn stimulated citizen participation rates among those GI Bill recipients. Robert Lieberman and Jacob Hacker argue persuasively that the content and administration of the state's social policies affect the recipients' degree of civic engagement.[9]

Thus institutions and public policies matter not merely for the instrumental benefits they bestow, but for the symbolic meaning benefits have to recipients and nonrecipients. Receiving a benefit because of one's war service or because one has reached a certain age communicates to recipients—and all of society—that those defending the nation through military service and those who are elderly are valued by the government and the people. To the extent that citizenship means inclusion, beneficiaries of social policies acquire a particularly salient citizenship status.

Educational Policies Make Citizens

Of the institutions and public policies in a democracy that convey citizenship status, education is among the most important. As philosopher John Dewey said in 1936, education involves more than preparing students for a life of private fulfillment and professional accomplishments. Rather, he claimed, the ultimate rationale of education in a democratic society is to make society work democratically. This means that educational institutions and policies "must model the qualities of citizenship they hope to inculcate in their students."[10]

We can apply this principle to Title IX by asking what type of civic inclusion this law provides for women. The answer is that Title IX created sports inclusion for women, but it did so on the basis of reinforcing the sex stereotypes responsible for women's exclusion in the first place. In other words, the interpretative message conveyed by Title IX as an educational policy is that girls/women couldn't and shouldn't play with boys/men.

Congress and the Courts

Social policies come about in two major ways: Congress legislates them and courts adjudicate them.[11] Clearly the sports part of educational policies legislated by Congress was skewed toward preserving antiquated views of sex differences. For this reason, girls and women who sought to challenge stereotypes that they were, solely by dint of their sex, athletically inferior to males—or shouldn't be allowed to play with males—turned to the courts to seek equal rights. This provoked a number of court decisions whose net effect was to redesign the legislation originally passed by Congress.[12] While Title IX permits sex-segregated sports, courts suggested that the U.S. Constitution did not.

Segregation and the Equal Protection Clause

Race and the Equal Protection Clause

The Equal Protection Clause of the Fourteenth Amendment, as initially intended by Congress, mandates that the state treat people equally in spite of their racial group differences. The question is, How to define equal treatment? In 1896, the Supreme Court considered this question in *Plessy v. Ferguson* in the context of a railroad policy that separated riders into two racial groups, black and white, and provided separate passenger cars for each. In *Plessy*, the Court ruled that the state treated people equally if facilities provided to each racial group were equal. Hence "separate but equal" was constitutional if separate passenger cars for blacks and white were comparable.

Then, in 1954, the Supreme Court overruled *Plessy* in the landmark case *Brown v. Board of Education.*[13] In *Brown*, the Court redefined the meaning of equality established in *Plessy*. *Brown* affirmed earlier Supreme Court decisions that required consideration of both tangible and intangible factors when evaluating equality. Intangible factors included the "reputation, administrative experience, position and influence of alumni, standing in the community, traditions, and prestige" of educational institutions.[14] In addition, the Court established in *Brown* that equality and inequality are not defined by whether facilities provided different racial groups are equal, but rather, *by the very fact of separating people into racial groups* in the first place.

Thus *Brown* ruled that whether railroad passenger cars—or schools—are comparable on tangible and intangible criteria for each racial group was irrelevant. The very act of separating individuals into groups based solely on race is what makes treatment unequal and hence unconstitutional. It is the coercive segregation on the basis of race, therefore, that defines unequal and unconstitutional treatment. As the Court wrote in its unanimous opinion, "separate but equal" was itself *"inherently unequal."*[15]

The *Brown* decision made it virtually impossible for the state to discriminate against an individual solely because of that person's race. The Court categorized race as a suspect classification, which means the Court uses strict scrutiny when evaluating legislative and state policies that invoke race. As a result, it is only constitutional for a state to segregate people on the basis of race if there is a compelling state interest for doing so. A compelling state interest includes matters such as threats to public health, public safety, or national security. Even when there is a compelling state interest, however, the Court requires government to use the narrowest means to implement its goals.[16] State policies targeting individuals not engaged in criminal behavior but belonging to racial groups that disproportionately engage in criminal behavior—racial profiling—are illegal and unconstitutional. Courts have ruled that all individuals have the right to be treated equally by the state in spite of racial group difference and despite correlations between racial groups and regulated behavior, such as criminal behavior.

Sex and the Equal Protection Clause

In 1971, the Supreme Court in *Reed v. Reed* extended the "separate is *not* equal" principle of the Equal Protection Clause to sex discrimination.[17] Although the Court ruled that different treatment of males and females by the state does not trigger strict scrutiny, as for race discrimination, the Court did establish that sex discrimination triggers intermediate scrutiny.[18] This means the state must have a legitimate goal for coercive sex segregation, and that coercive sex segregation must be an efficient and narrowly tailored means for achieving that goal.

Reed involved a state policy that gave preference to fathers over mothers as executors of children's estates on the grounds that men as a group had more business experience than women as a group. By designating the sex with the more likely business experience, the policy aimed to cut the administrative load in courts, which would otherwise hold hearings to decide which parent should be executor. The Court struck down this policy, finding it an unconstitutional use of sex as a proxy for business experience. As the Court stated, the Equal Protection Clause requires that a classification on the basis of sex "must be reasonable, not arbitrary, and must rest upon some ground of difference having a fair and substantial relation to the object of the legislation, so that all persons similarly circumstanced shall be treated alike."[19] The Court ruled that eliminating one sex was arbitrary and doing so discriminated against women similarly situated to men in their ability to be executors of estates.

In later cases, the Court ruled that for the state to treat individuals differently solely because of their sex, it was not enough to show that sex group differences simply correlate with traits or behaviors the state seeks to regulate. Instead, the state must show that the sex difference and the traits or behaviors in question correlate strongly enough to warrant using an individual's sex group as a surrogate for the trait or behavior. An interesting case testing what qualified as "strongly enough" was *Craig v. Boren*.[20]

In 1976, the Court considered in *Craig* an Oklahoma law that allowed women aged 18 to 20 years to buy beer containing 3.2 percent alcohol, but prohibited males from making the same purchases until age 21. The state of Oklahoma justified this law by arguing it was needed to provide for traffic safety. Oklahoma officials documented that the state arrested 11 times as many 18- to 20-year-old males as females for drunk driving, and about 10 times more males than females for public drunkenness. A survey also showed more male than female drivers preferred beer to other alcoholic beverages (84 percent to 77 percent, respectively). Thus the state believed it was perfectly legitimate to promote public safety by treating 18- to 20-year-old males and females differently where it involved the legal purchase of beer.

The Supreme Court ruled otherwise, reiterating in *Craig* the principle established in *Reed*, stating that for gender to serve as a "proxy for other, more germane bases of classification ... [there must be a strong] congruence between gender and the characteristic or trait that gender [is] purported to represent."[21] As the Court stated, "In light of the weak congruence between gender and the characteristic or trait ... it was necessary that the legislatures choose either to realign their substantive laws in a gender-neutral fashion, or to adopt procedures for identifying those instances where the sex-centered generalization actually comported to fact."[22]

As this standard suggests, the key issue in *Craig* was not whether there was a correlation between gender and drunk driving among 18- to 20-year-olds—the state documented that there clearly was— but whether or not this correlation was *strong enough* to justify using gender as a "classifying device" for promoting traffic safety. The Court decided in *Craig* that although a correlation existed between gender and drunk-driving arrests, it was not strong enough to justify using gender as a "classifying device." As the Court stated in *Craig*:

> The statistics broadly establish that .18 percent of females and 2 percent of males in that age group were arrested for that offense. While such a disparity is not trivial in a statistical sense, it hardly can form the basis for employment of a gender line as a classifying device. Certainly if maleness is to serve as a proxy for drinking and driving, a correlation [sic] of 2 percent must be considered an unduly tenuous "fit."[23]

In two separate cases, the Court even ruled that sex *cannot* be used as a proxy for the capacity to be pregnant or vice versa. As the Court put it in *Geduldig v. Aiello* in 1974, pregnancy is not a characteristic that divides people into males and females, but rather into two groups, "pregnant women and nonpregnant persons.[24] While the first group is exclusively female, the second includes members of both sexes."[25] Hence the Court found a "lack of identity" between pregnancy and gender.[26] Although there is obviously a correlation between gender and pregnancy, the Court established that it was not strong enough to justify using one's sex as a proxy for pregnancy or vise versa.

The Court took the same stance two years later in *General Electric v. Gilbert*.[27] The Court reiterated, "While it is true that only women can become pregnant, it does not follow that every legislative classification concerning pregnancy is a sex-based classification."[28] To say a person is "female" does not mean that person is, ever will be, or can be pregnant. To say a person is not pregnant does not reveal whether that person is male or female. That is, the correlation between pregnancy and sex is not strong enough to use sex as a surrogate for pregnancy.

Sex Segregation and Education in Court

The Court's findings in *Geduldig* and *Gilbert* came in the context of plaintiffs arguing that policies excluding pregnancy from insurance disability coverage constituted sex discrimination. The Court ruled that the policies did not, and in the process observed that pregnancy was not a proxy for sex nor sex a proxy for pregnancy. But the question remained: When is it permissible to segregate on the basis of sex?

Not often, as it turns out. In 1982, the Supreme Court ruled in *Mississippi University for Women v. Hogan* that a male applicant denied admission to a university-level school for women solely because of his sex had the right under Title IX to pursue a private cause of action against the school.[29] The university was the state's oldest publicly supported all-female college in the United States. Joe Hogan was a registered nurse but did not have a B.A. in nursing, and wanted to enroll and earn one. The university said Hogan could audit courses, but it would not allow him to earn credit. In *Hogan*, the Court established a heightened standard for evaluating discrimination on the basis of sex, one that required an "exceedingly persuasive" justification.

In *Brown*, the Court had ruled that tangible and intangible factors must be considered when evaluating equal educational opportunities. While in *Hogan* the Court did not stipulate tangible and intangible factors be considered in sex-segregated educational institutions, it did establish that although Title IX exempts single-sex institutions from sex discrimination policies, the law does not—and cannot—exempt any institution from "constitutional obligation."[30]

In *Hogan*, the state's primary justification for the all-female school was to compensate for past discrimination against women. The Court found this argument unpersuasive. As the Court noted, "Rather than compensate for discriminatory barriers faced by women, MUW's policy of excluding males from admission to the School of Nursing tends to perpetuate the stereotyped view of nursing as an exclusively woman's job."[31] The Court also found fault with the state's claim that admitting men to MUW's nursing program would disrupt the women's education. The Court ruled, "MUW's policy of denying males the right to enroll for credit in its School of Nursing violates the Equal Protection Clause of the Fourteenth Amendment."[32]

In 1996, *United States v. Virginia* built on the higher standard for sex discrimination as established by the Court in *Hogan*.[33] The Virginia Military Institute (VMI) prided itself on its "adversative" educational model. Living quarters are designed to be stark, uncomfortable, and lacking in privacy (all doors and windows are kept open at all times). Peer pressure is used to instill discipline and school values. The educational program aims to "reduce all cadets to the lowest level,"[34] by employing "physical and mental stress in order to break down the confidences of a cadet so as to make him acutely aware of his limits."[35] In other words, VMI forces students to find out how much abuse they can take before breaking down.[36] It was the opinion of VMI administrators that admitting women would destroy its adversative model because women could not endure the "intense mental and physical stress" used by staff "to train students to perform successfully under adverse conditions and to teach them to recognize and cope with their individual limitations."[37] Thus VMI simply ignored the applications from 347 women it had received since 1980. In 1990, however, one female applicant filed a complaint with the U.S. attorney general.

Eventually the Supreme Court decided the fate of coeducation at VMI. Although it is constitutional to establish single-sex schools for the sex that has historically been excluded from educational opportunities, such as female-only educational institutions, it is not permissible to do so for the sex, males, which has historically benefited from educational opportunities, unless the institution in question can show that a single-sex policy is necessary to accomplish its educational goals.[38] In a 7–1 decision (Justice Clarence Thomas recused himself because his son attended VMI), the Court held that VMI failed to show how a male-only environment was necessary to fulfill its educational goals.

Thus, by excluding women, VMI violated the Equal Protection Clause of the Constitution. As the Court put it, the judicial system must take "a hard look" at "fixed notions concerning the roles and abilities of males and females," such as generalizations about women's physical and mental inferiority compared to men. The "notion that admission of women would downgrade VMI's stature, destroy the adversative system, and, with it, even the school, is a judgment hardly proved, a prediction hardly different from other 'self-fulfilling prophe[cies] . . . once routinely used to deny rights or opportunities. Women's successful entry into the federal military academies, and their participation in the Nation's military forces, indicate that Virginia's fears for VMI's future may not be solidly grounded."[39]

The ruling raises the question, If women can "play with the boys" at adversative educational institutions such as VMI, why not in athletic programs in middle school, high school, college, and recreational contexts, if not professional leagues too?

Sports and Courts

Over the past 30-plus years, courts across the country have considered sex discrimination in general and coercive sex segregation in particular in athletic educational policies. A search reveals over 500 cases heard at the state, district, and Supreme Court levels of the American judicial system. An analysis of cases reveals that the largest percentage (32 percent) involve sex discrimination targeting students. These include gender disparities in scholarship availability, teams, facilities, and scheduling patterns. The second most litigated issue relates to coaching. One-fifth of cases (20 percent) brought to trial involve issues such as hiring and promotion of male and female coaches, salary differences, and resources available to male versus female coaches. The third most litigated issue is sex segregation.[40] Nearly one-fifth of cases (18 percent) involve girls wanting to "play with the boys," or boys wanting to "play with the girls."

These suits involving sex segregation specifically consider the legal disconnect between a Title IX that permits coercive sex segregation in contact sports and an Equal Protection Clause of the Constitution that courts have ruled generally does not.[41] No case involving coercive sex segregation in sports has reached the Supreme Court, so we cannot point to a definitive judicial ruling about the constitutionality of such policies. However, the pattern indicates that courts across the country at state appellate and federal district levels are more prone than not to find it unconstitutional to prohibit qualified females from "playing with the boys" solely because of their sex. The embrace of lower courts' use of Equal Protection analysis in the context of overturning sex-segregated sports policies along with the Supreme Court's recognition that sex discrimination violates the Equal Protection Clause leads some law scholars, such as Patricia Lamar, to project that the Court may in the future endorse a "policy with respect to sex discrimination as far-reaching as that propounded in Brown."[42] Legal scholar Lee Schottenfeld concurs, noting that "gender segregation schemes are increasingly being invalidated" by means of court decisions.[43]

The Equal Protection Clause
and Other Legal Entitlements

Clearly Title IX seems to allow females to be excluded from male contact sports teams. However, as legal scholar Dana Robinson argues, there are at least "two lines along which sports and gender are evaluated," Title IX and the Fourteenth Amendment.[44] Consequently, courts have considered sex-segregated policies not only in terms of Title IX, but also in terms of the Equal Protection Clause of the Fourteenth Amendment of the Constitution, as well as state-level Equal Rights Amendments (ERA) to state constitutions, and state-level legislation proscribing sex discrimination.[45] The Equal Protection Clause demands that all similarly situated individuals receive "the equal protection of the laws." The Supreme Court has interpreted this to mean "all persons in similar circumstances shall be treated alike."[46] Thus policies that treat individuals differently *solely* because of their sex are subject to intermediate scrutiny as to whether such policies are constitutional.

In addition, 19 states have state-level Equal Rights Amendments (ERAs) that specifically prohibit sex discrimination. Many other states have statutes prohibiting sex discrimination in general, and still other states have statutes prohibiting sex discrimination in public accommodations, which would apply to publicly sponsored recreational sports programs. Thus sex-segregated sports policies are also subject to state-level review.[47]

Some issues related to sex discrimination and athletics have reached the Supreme Court. Notably, the same year that the Supreme Court ruled in *Reed* that the Equal Protection Clause of the Fourteenth Amendment covered sex discrimination, the Court also ruled in another case, *Swann v. Charlotte-Mecklenburg Bd. Of Educ.*, that it was critical to eliminate vestiges of state-imposed segregation in the context of gender as well as race, and not only in academic educational contexts, but also educational contexts involving athletics.[48] However, no case explicitly involving the issue of sex-segregated sports, where sex segregation is defined by a prohibition against girls/women playing on the same team with boys/men "solely" because of an individual's female sex classification, has reached the Supreme Court. However, the issue about whether it is permissible to prohibit girls/women from playing with the boys has been the subject of court cases at the state and federal appellate levels. Since the passage of Title IX, there have been forty such cases. In general, and certainly over time, courts clearly have been reluctant to allow coercive sex segregation in sports programs, even when they involve contact sports. Of the forty court cases involving sex-segregated, male-only teams (in educational or recreational settings) on which qualified girls/women wished to participate, in 85% of these cases, courts ruled that such sex-segregated policies are not permissible, as indicated in Table 4.1. In the six cases (5%) where courts ruled otherwise, the vast majority of these cases (four out of six) were decided in the 1972–73 time period just after the 1971 *Reed v. Reed* Supreme Court decision that ruling that the Equal Protection Clause did prohibit sex discrimination (discussed above), only one case was so decided after the *Craig v. Boren* that affirmed the power of the Equal Protection Clause for prohibiting sex discrimination (discussed above), and no case was so decided since the 1996 *VMI* case that offered additional proof that the Equal Protection Clause prohibits sex segregated educational policies that disadvantage women, even if Title IX permits such policies (discussed above). Hence, as Table 4.1 reports, there is reason to conclude that "playing with the boys" is a legal, if not constitutional, right that courts will affirm, if and when the stalwart and courageous girls and women come forward to stake their claim in judicial arenas. To appreciate just how stalwart and courageous such challengers must be, let us consider a few who had the energy, resources, and commitment to demand—and to get legal affirmation of—their *right* to play with the boys.

Playing Football with the Boys

Football is obviously a contact sport and one traditionally played by males. This makes football a good litmus test for the legality and/or constitutionality of coercively sex-segregated sports. Some contact sports, such as wrestling, involve contact, but not contact likely to be injurious. Football, however, involves direct contact between players that can be extremely dangerous. Thus if coercive sex segregation is unconstitutional in football, surely it should be unconstitutional to sex-segregate wrestling, basketball, soccer, baseball,

TABLE 4.1   Court Decisions in Sex-Segregation Law Cases since
Title IX (1972), Female Plaintiffs[a]

Supreme Court Cases	Include[b] Girls/Women	Exclude[c] Girls/Women
1971 *Reed v. Reed* Swann (sex discrimination in athletic educational policies)		
	1972 Golf: *Reed** Noncontact sports: *Haas**	*1972* Swimming: *Bucha** Noncontact sports: *Hollander** **All sports: Gregoria[d]***
	1973 Tennis: *Morris** Tennis, cross-country: *Brenden** Swimming: *Kelly*^ *1974* Swimming: *Kelly** Cross-country: *Gilpin** **Football: Clinton**+ Baseball: *NOW*+	*1973* Tennis: *Ritacco**
	1975 **Football: Darrin*** **All sports: Packel*** Baseball: *Fortin*^ General: *Penn*#*^	*1975* Tennis: *Ruman**

TABLE 4.1 *(continued)*

Supreme Court Cases	Include[b] Girls/Women	Exclude[c] Girls/Women
1976 *Craig v. Boren*	*1976* Cross-country: *Bednar** Baseball: *Carnes** *1977* Basketball: *Lavin** Soccer: *Hoover** **Football: *Muscare*+** **Contact sports:** 　　***Opinion of Justices, MA*#*^** *1978* Swimming: *Leffel** *1979* Basketball: *Dodson** *1980* General: *Pavey*^ 1981 **General:** 　　***Yellow Springs*#**	
		1982 Basketball: 　　*O'Connor*#
	1983 **Football: *Force*#** Basketball: *Forton*+ Soccer: *Simpson*+ Boating: *Power* 　　*Squadrons*+ *1985* **Football: *Lantz*#** *1988* **Wrestling: *Saint*** 1989 Baseball: *Israel** *1992* Ice Hockey: *Cook*^	

(continued)

TABLE 4.1 *(continued)*

Supreme Court Cases	Include[b] Girls/Women	Exclude[c] Girls/Women
1996 *VMI*	1996 **Wrestling:** *Adams** *1999* **Football:** *Mercer*^ Officiate: *Kemether** 2002 General: *Beal*^	

a) *Does not include cases that were dismissed without a finding pertaining to the legality or constitutionality of sex-segregation policies, female plaintiffs. Does not include cases that focus on rules of play. Does not include cases that involve professional sports. For a complete citation of the cases, see Appendix 4.*

b) *Cases in which the final ruling of a court was that girls/women must be included on/in male-only teams/sports.*

c) *Cases in which the final ruling of a court was that it is permissible to exclude girls/women from male-only teams/sports.*

d) *Cases involving contact sports are in bold type.*

+ *Recreational*

Middle school, junior high

* *High School*

^ *College*

or any other sport. Between 1974 and 1999, courts reviewed five prominent cases focusing directly on the exclusion of females from football teams solely because of their sex.[49] These cases included recreational town sports as well as middle school, high school, and college football teams. While recognizing that Title IX permits sex segregation of contact sports, in all five cases courts ruled that other constitutional principles do not permit sex segregation, even in contact sports. Thus in all five cases, courts ruled that qualified girls/women must be allowed the opportunity to try out for male-only football teams.

Middle School Football

In 1983, Nicole Force, an eighth grader at Pierce City Middle School in Missouri, put the principle of coercive sex segregation in football to the test. She was an avid athlete who participated in swimming, diving, organized softball, basketball, and elementary school football. In eighth grade, when she decided to try out for the football team, she faced an immediate problem. There was no mixed competition in football. Instead, she was offered the alternative "female" sport of volleyball. School officials all agreed Nicole would be a good football player and have no problems playing. Yet if they let Nicole play, school officials argued, they would have to let other girls play too. Officials worried that if girls started playing on the middle school boys' football team that "high-school girls might wish to play on the high-school football team," and fretted about the "potential safety risk to a female competing in a contact sport with males."[50] The argument was familiar: sex-segregated sports protected girls from injury. School officials also offered a second argument, worrying that if girls could play football, that meant the "possibility that boys would wish to participate on the girls' volleyball team," which would limit athletic opportunities for girls because the boys presumably would beat out girls for team spots.

A federal district court in Missouri addressed the conflict with Title IX and the Equal Protection Clause head on, noting the school's blatant "gender-based classification" may be allowed under Title IX's acceptance of sex segregation for contact sports. However, the court said, the Equal Protection Clause prohibits such gender-based classifications unless they serve "important governmental objectives" and "the discriminatory means employed are substantially related to the achievement of those objectives."[51] Critically, the court said the test for determining the validity of a gender-based classification has to be "free of fixed notions concerning the roles and abilities of males and females." The court said classifications must not reflect "archaic and stereotypic notions." However, the ruling clearly instructed that if the "objective is to exclude or 'protect' members of one gender because they are presumed to suffer from an inherent handicap or to be innately inferior, the objective itself is illegitimate."[52]

The court agreed that ensuring sports programs are "as safe for participants as possible" was an "important governmental objective," but so was "maximizing the participation of both sexes in interscholastic athletic events."[53] The court acknowledged that "the average male, even at 13, will to some extent outperform the average female of that age in most athletic events." (Interestingly, what seemed an acceptable acknowledgment of across-the-board male athletic superiority in 1983 is less so today.) Still, in keeping with the court's reasoning, the point was not to debate relative athletic ability between males and females in general, but to consider the specific case of Nicole Force. While the court said separate male and female sports teams were "a constitutionally permissible way of dealing with the problem of potential male dominance," the court saw no reason to exclude Nicole Force from playing. "There is no evidence, or even any suggestion that [she] . . . could not safely participate in [the] . . . football program," the court ruled.[54]

In addition, the court noted that the school system did not apply the "safety factor" to males. There was no screening for males as to their qualifications for playing football. In the end, the court found an "insufficient relationship between the defendants' announced goal of 'safety' and a rule which automatically excludes all eighth grade females from competing with eighth grade males for a place on the football team."[55]

The ruling made the plain point that if the goal was to maximize educational athletic opportunities for all students, regardless of gender, then it made no sense to deny all females a chance to try out for the football team. The court found that even though Title IX allowed girls to be excluded from football, the Equal Protection Clause did not.

High School Football

This was not the only case involving a girl who wanted to try out for an all-male football team. Two years later, in October 1985, 16-year-old Jacqueline Lantz filed suit, challenging rules barring her from trying out for the high school football team in Yonkers, New York. Her suit specifically challenged New York State regulations prohibiting males and females from playing together in six contact sports: football, boxing, ice hockey, rugby, wrestling, and basketball.[56]

Lantz claimed the state prohibition violated Title IX and her right to equal treatment under the Equal Protection Clause of the Constitution. The Southern District Court of New York addressed Lantz's Equal Protection claim, noting the only argument for discrimination on the basis of gender was in cases in which there is "'exceedingly persuasive justification' showing at least that the classification serves important governmental objectives and that the discriminatory means employed are substantially related to the achievement of those objectives."[57] The message was this: You could discriminate on the basis of sex, but only if you could prove that the reason for doing so was critical for achieving larger "governmental objectives." Not surprisingly, the school—as in other cases—argued that it was trying to achieve a key governmental objective: protecting the health and safety of female students.[58]

The court found "no quarrel with the importance of that objective," but did object to the use of coercive sex segregation to achieve female safety. The court acknowledged data presented by school officials establishing that "as a general rule, [male] senior high school students (aged 15 through 18) are more physically developed, stronger, more agile, faster, and have greater muscle endurance than their female counterparts." It also acknowledged medical opposition to females playing on male contact sports teams, including football. The state attorney general filed a brief asserting that "it makes no difference that there might be a few girls who wish to play football who are more physically fit than some of the boys on the team."[59]

The court, however, disagreed and emphasized that it *does* make a difference if even one girl wishes to try out for football and is prohibited from doing so by New York State regulations. The court also observed that assertions about male physical superiority were "averages and generalities" and did not consider the particular abilities of girls as individuals.

As a result, the court ruled the state prohibition had no "reasonable relation" to the governmental objective of female safety because—and this was key—the effect of the regulation was to exclude "qualified members of one gender" simply on the assumption that they "suffer from an inherent handicap" or are "innately inferior." Thus, the court ruled, sex-segregation policies prohibiting Jacqueline Lantz from trying out for the football team violated the

Equal Protection Clause of the Constitution—regardless of what Title IX or state regulations said. It was not a difficult decision, as the court noted in its ruling that "every court which has considered questions like the one facing the court in this case [in the past 13 years] has reached the same result" and cited 10 cases between 1972 and 1983.[60]

While Jacqueline Lantz won the right to try out for the Lincoln High School football team, the junior, who was 4 feet 10 and 116 pounds, conceded that by the time the ruling came down she wasn't in top physical condition. "I know personally I'm not ready for it," she said, noting that her legal victory cleared the way so "other girls can play without having to go through this court stuff."[61] Lantz nonetheless worked out with the team, though by the time she was permitted to play in late October she had missed much of the season and training.

"She's right where everyone else was the first day, but it's not the first day," Coach Tony Arrichiello noted after Lantz looked tired and lagged behind boys during a two-mile run.[62]

The difficulty for girls challenging the right to play with boys in contact sports is the expectation, at least initially, that the girls will be athletically gifted. There is a pervasive notion in organized sports that boys are better than girls, but there are a few gifted, or athletically exceptional, girls. There is little mention or thought to unathletic boys who are nonetheless presumed to outperform female counterparts in sports. What is striking about these legal cases is how consistently courts confront cultural presumptions head-on. Jacqueline Lantz may not have fit anyone's physical image of a high school football player, but the court ruled she had *the right* to try out. The right, in essence, to test one's individual skills cannot be terminated. Rulings in both *Force* and *Lantz* (and others) acknowledge cultural presumptions of male athletic superiority. As females have become more experienced athletes and competitors, however, such presumptions appear gratuitous.

College Football

Eight years after Jacqueline Lantz became the first female allowed to try out for a New York football team, Heather Sue Mercer decided she too wanted to play. Mercer was running around the track at Yorktown High School when she saw the football team's place-kicker boot a ball between the uprights.[63]

"I thought, 'Man that looks like fun,'" Mercer, a high school varsity soccer player, told a reporter later.[64] The school's athletic director arranged for Mercer to meet football coach Ron Santavicca. The coach brought her out to the field where she promptly put 20 out of 20 balls through the uprights—from 40 yards out. Santavicca was impressed. Mercer went to football camp over the summer and returned in the fall as a senior, the only girl among 65 boys on the team. She became the team's placekicker, replacing the previous kicker who had triggered her interest and who had graduated the previous spring.

Mercer had a fabulous season. She led her male counterparts in Westchester County in scoring, with 34 points. A news report at the time notes Mercer "outscored her competition despite missing three games during the regular season with strained ligaments in her left leg."[65] Mercer had the support of the coach and teammates. Even the school's cheerleaders enjoyed rooting for her. "We think she's great; we're really proud of her," Monica Curtis, the cheerleading captain said. "If she can get us points, I'm all for it. It's not your sex; it's your ability. If I could do that, I'd be out there."[66]

Unfortunately Mercer did not find the same support when she arrived at Duke University in the fall of 1994. She tried out for the football team as a walk-on kicker. She didn't make the team but was allowed to be team manager and participate in practices and conditioning drills. The next year, the Duke senior football players selected Mercer to be their kicker in a traditional intrasquad scrimmage held each spring. In this game, she kicked the winning 28-yard field goal. The kick was shown on ESPN and the football coach, when interviewed by the media, said Mercer was on the Duke football team. The Duke kicking coach also told Mercer that "she had made the team."[67] She was "officially listed by Duke as a member of the Duke football team on the team roster filed with the NCAA and was pictured in the Duke football yearbook."[68]

Soon, however, Heather Sue Mercer began to experience discriminatory treatment from head football coach Fred Goldsmith. She claims Goldsmith "did not permit her to attend summer camp, refused to allow her to dress for games or sit on sidelines during games and gave her fewer opportunities to participate in practices than other walk-on kickers." She also claimed Goldsmith "made a number of offensive comments to her, including asking her why she was interested in football, wondering why she did not prefer beauty pageants rather than football, and suggesting she sit in the stand with her boyfriend rather than on the sidelines" with the team. Finally, he informed Mercer he "was dropping her from the team" altogether.[69]

Mercer protested. She argued she was more qualified than some male walk-on kickers and filed suit. In her case, Mercer argued she experienced sex discrimination in violation of Title IX. Interestingly, even though Title IX permits sex segregation in contact sports, once a team has been integrated and contains both male and female members, the court ruled that Title IX does not allow discrimination based on sex.[70] The Fourth Circuit federal court ruled that since Duke had made Mercer a member of the football team, football at Duke could no longer be considered a single-sex sport. As a coed sport, football coaches were required to treat players equally, regardless of sex. The court supported Mercer's contention that she had faced discriminatory treatment solely because of her sex.[71] In October 2000—long after Mercer had graduated—a jury awarded her $2 million in punitive damages, money Mercer's lawyer said was planned to finance scholarships for female placekickers. The jury took just over two hours to find that the school had discriminated against Mercer solely because of her gender.[72]

Thus we have three cases involving the right of girls to play with the boys in the contact sport of football—one at the middle school level (Force), one at the high school level (Lantz), and one at the college level (Mercer). None of these cases reached the Supreme Court, but they are examples of how different courts have reached the same conclusion: even in a contact sport such as football, prohibiting females from playing with the boys solely because of their sex violates the Equal Protection Clause. In the case of Mercer, the courts ruled that according to Title IX, once a contact sport has been sex-integrated, women and men must be allowed to compete together.[73]

Wrestling with the Boys

If it is unconstitutional to sex-segregate football, then it must be unconstitutional to sex-segregate wrestling. This is a particularly relevant issue because female interest in wrestling has exploded in recent years. In many schools, there are girls' wrestling teams, but in many other schools female wrestlers compete on teams with males and against male opponents. Some regularly beat male opponents. Even as more girls appear on previously all-male wrestling teams, the notion strikes some as improper. Some male wrestlers still forfeit matches rather than compete against females, and some school and athletic officials have lobbied state legislators to stop girls and boys from wrestling together.

Consequently some female wrestlers have been forced to fight to participate in their sport. Since the passage of Title IX, courts have reviewed three cases in which girls sought to wrestle with the boys.[74] In two of these cases, courts said that even though Title IX permits sex segregation in contact sports, schools must allow qualified girls to wrestle with the boys. Although Title IX permits sex segregation solely on the basis of one's sex, the Equal Protection Clause of the Fourteenth Amendment does not. We can see this constitutional reasoning at work by taking a look at what happened to Tiffany Adams when she sought to wrestle with the boys.

Tiffany Adams lived in suburban Wichita, Kansas. As an eighth grader, she wrestled on her school team without controversy. However, when she entered Valley Center High School in 1996 and wanted to join the wrestling team, she faced conflict because wrestling was designated a sport for boys, not girls.[75] Under Title IX, her school contended, wrestling was a contact sport, and it violated school policy for girls to wrestle on the boys' team.

As in other cases, the school argued it was concerned for Tiffany Adams's safety. The school observed that the average high school boy weighed 145 pounds and could bench press over 200 pounds, more than the average high school girl.[76] Thus school officials defended sex segregation in wrestling to protect (physically inferior) girls from being injured by (physically superior) boys. The school also noted Title IX "does not require coed participation in contact sports."[77]

The court again agreed that student safety was an important governmental objective, but pointed out that Congress cannot "substantively limit constitutional rights."[78] The court stated that Title IX can provide remedies, including equity policies, but Title IX *cannot provide remedies that limit a constitutional right.*[79] The court was making a key point. If sex segregation limited a constitutional right, the fact that Title IX permits sex segregation in contact sports is irrelevant. As in other cases, the court acknowledged that while student safety is an important governmental objective, schools may not use coercive sex segregation to achieve it.

The court also made a key point about the argument that sex-segregated sports protect girls from injury. The court said there was no evidence that Tiffany Adams was more at risk than any other student who wanted to wrestle. The only evidence of a safety risk, after all, was based on general group differences between boys and girls and not on Adams's qualifications as a wrestler. The court said that while it was reasonable for schools to consider sex differences in size, strength, and experiences when setting sports policies, it was not acceptable to use a student's sex as a surrogate for those qualities.[80] The notion of protecting qualified girls from wrestling injuries while not protecting qualified boys, the court said, "suggests the very sort of well meaning but overly paternalistic attitude about females which the Supreme Court has viewed with such concern."[81]

The most pointed statement, however, was the court's contention that instead of protecting Adams, sex-segregated sports policies actually *caused her injury.* The court said depriving Tiffany Adams of a constitutional right represented "irreparable harm" because she missed opportunities to develop her talents as a wrestler.[82] Not being allowed "to compete, practice, or learn the sport of wrestling," the court stated, led her to fall behind in her development as an athlete, "and as a practical matter she would most likely be prevented from being able to compete in the future."[83] The court was clear: the sex-segregated sports policies that prohibited Tiffany Adams from wrestling did not serve any "substantial governmental interest" and, therefore, violated the Equal Protection Clause.

Some may look at Tiffany Adams's case and ask, So what? One girl is deemed eligible to wrestle with the boys. Yet the decision was far-reaching. When this case was heard in 1996, some 800 girls competed in wrestling in the United States and many male teams had female members. In May 2005, officials for USA Wrestling estimated 7,000 to 10,000 girls were wrestling, including 5,000 at the high school level—and most on male teams.[84] This case validates the principle that girls have a right to wrestle with the boys.

The case also highlights the problematic nature of sports policies that segregate based on sex. The court made a critical point: sex-segregated sports policies that prohibit females from playing with males on grounds that females as a group are inferior to males as a group have the effect of *constructing* sex differences—*not reflecting* them. Such policies, they assert, create and insist on notions of male and female not rooted in the matter at hand. Tiffany Adams had even furnished evidence of her qualifications to compete on the boys' team, providing a middle school record showing she had beat boys in wrestling. The notion that she was physically inferior and might be injured didn't jibe with experience. It merely fit and reinforced stereotypes.

Tiffany won her case and was allowed to join the boys' high school wrestling team, but she wasn't welcomed eagerly. "A lot of my friends backed away from me, and guys on the team tried to bully me out of wrestling," Adams said.[85] However, Adams wrestled, even against other girls, including twin sisters Marilyn and Sharilyn White from Derby, Kansas. Sharilyn White, who beat Tiffany Adams in a close match, noted that Adams was "tough, better than a lot of boys I've wrestled against."[86]

Playing Baseball with the Boys

For more than 100 years, baseball was the preeminent sport in the United States, one that defined American culture. Walt Whitman said about baseball,

> It's our game: that's the chief fact in connection with it: America's game; it has the snap, go, fling of the American atmosphere; it belongs as much to our institutions, fits into them as significantly as our Constitution's laws; is just as important in the sum total of our historic life.[87]

Baseball also has been viewed as a sport for men—for fathers and sons, not mothers and daughters. Culturally that may still be true, but legally Title IX and the Equal Protection Clause changed all that. Girls have every right to play baseball with boys. Yet the deep male tradition has made it historically difficult for females. As a result, many have been forced to go to court to fight their way onto the diamond as players.[88]

Title IX may permit sex segregation in contact sports, but is baseball a contact sport? Legally, a major purpose of contact sports involves contact, such as shoving, pushing, blocking, tackling, or punching.[89] By this standard, basketball and baseball would not be contact sports, since it is not a major purpose in these games to punch and otherwise physically contact opposing players. Certainly contact happens, but no more so than in a sport like soccer, not considered a contact sport. In basketball, it is a foul to make contact with another player, and punching—in any sport except boxing—is grounds for ejection. There may be physical contact between players in baseball—particularly between a base runner and catcher at home plate—but this would be the same as for softball (which is *not* a contact sport).

When it comes to basketball and baseball, therefore, some might wonder if they should be classified as contact sports in the first place. When we seek guidance from Title IX, however, we find not so much a rationale based on whether "contact" is a purpose of sport as we find lack of clarity—and an opening for politics. According to Title IX's precise language, "contact sports include boxing, wrestling, rugby, ice hockey, football, basketball and other sports the purpose or major activity of which involves bodily contact."[90] Anyone who wonders why basketball is included in that list should recall ferocious lobbying by the NCAA—and widespread sympathy among legislators—to preserve intact its two largest men's sports dynasties: football and basketball. Including both as contact sports, some believed, would excuse them from aspects of Title IX that many initially feared would require women be allowed to compete with men.

NCAA Lobbying

From the outset, there was worry about what Title IX would do to male sports programs. The NCAA argued to Congress and the White House (President Gerald Ford, a former college football player, was sympathetic to concerns about threats to football programs) that Title IX would destroy intercollegiate sports, announcing when regulations were issued in 1975 that "this may well signal the end of intercollegiate programs as we have known them for decades."[91] Debate around Title IX regulations, then, was more outwardly concerned with protecting male programs than ensuring real access or equality for female athletes. Consider that the NCAA at first succeeded in getting the House to exempt altogether "revenue-producing" men's sports—football and basketball—from Title IX regulations, before reversing itself 10 days later.[92] The law also gave schools a long time to comply and included the provision that Congress review Title IX regulations and make changes *after* President Ford signed them. Ford even wrote to Senate and House committee leaders in July 1975 saying he welcomed hearings on the law.[93] The law's lack of clarity allows debate and reinterpretation of regulations that continue to this day. In 2002, the Bush administration's Commission on Opportunity in Athletics suggested changes that would have vastly undermined Title IX's power. These were mostly withdrawn following public outcry and protests by feminist groups such as NOW.[94]

Baseball: Contact Sport or Not

While baseball at the college level was more Olympic sport than revenue producer, it represented a symbolic encroachment of females into a male domain. Although baseball is not named as a contact sport in Title IX regulations, it became classified as a contact sport by virtue of lower court decisions issued after Title IX was passed and before regulations were written. Amateur baseball organizers—such as Little League—wanted baseball treated as a contact sport, a move that appeared to be a tool for prohibiting girls from playing. At the time, some judges were all too happy to comply.

In 1973, U.S. District Court Judge Barron P. McCune in Pittsburgh ruled that the Avonworth Baseball Conference had every right to bar 10-year-old Pamela Magill from playing baseball because it was a contact sport. The Avonworth Baseball Conference argued that Magill's admission to the league would downgrade her team talent-wise, inhibit play, complicate the task of fathers who volunteered to coach, and greatly embarrass the boys who had to sit on the bench while a girl was on the playing field. "I doubt if there's any unconstitutional discrimination in this instance or discrimination of any kind, for that matter," said the judge.[95]

Likewise, in May 1974, Judge Edward Day in the U.S. District Court in Providence ruled that a 10-year-old girl, Allison "Pookie" Fortin, was not discriminated against by Darlington Little League when she was barred from playing because she was female. In his opinion, Day said barring Fortin from baseball because of her sex was permitted "where a contact sport is involved."[96] The court found the "material physical differences between boys and girls in the 8–12 age bracket are sufficient to warrant excluding girls on the basis of protecting them from injury."[97] The case was overturned on appeal.

However, not all courts found baseball a contact sport, or one from which girls could be excluded. In 1976, the Eastern District Court of Tennessee ruled the Tennessee Secondary School Athletic Association must allow a high school girl to play baseball with the boys on the grounds that there was no baseball team for girls and that baseball is not a contact sport.[98] Yet later, in 1978, Linda Williams was a senior at Wheatley High School in Houston, Texas, when she was barred from playing on the boys' baseball team. The University Interscholastic League, which governed Texas high school sports, had separated all girls' and boys' sports. Williams, described as "a hard-hitting right fielder," was told her team would forfeit any game in which she played.[99] She quit the team after a month of practice and filed suit. "It is wrong to tell us we can't play baseball, I know that," said Williams at the time. "Now whether all girls and boys should be on the same teams, I don't know. However, at least girls ought to have the opportunity."[100]

Fortunately for Williams, the case was heard quickly. Federal District Judge Woodrow Seals ruled less than a month later that Williams had been denied her rights under the Equal Protection Clause of the Fourteenth Amendment. "There really is no rational reason why she should not play baseball at this time," Seals ruled.

Williams's teammates and coach were thrilled. "They're overjoyed Linda is coming back," Coach Eugene Jones said of his players. He said Williams was "one of my best three or four outfielders and one of my better hitters."[101]

Court Consistency

As courts considered cases in which girls wanted to play on male contact sports teams, the message was remarkably consistent. Title IX's blessing on sex-segregated teams was not the last word; the Constitution was. Thus most, but not all, court cases have been decided in favor of overriding gender stereotypes that form the basis for sex segregation as indicated in Table 4.1. When athletic policies seek to exclude females, courts require proof that an important governmental objective requires coercive sex segregation as a means to achieve that goal. Courts have generally rejected claims that females are inherently weaker than males or that sex-segregated sports are the way to protect females in fulfilling this "important governmental objective" of player safety. Put another way, courts agree that protecting students, including women, from injury is an important governmental objective, but they reject the notion that coercive sex segregation is the way to do it.

Can Boys Play with the Girls?

During these years the courts clarified another area of confusion. Some schools resisted mixed-sex sports because they feared that if girls were allowed on boys' teams, then boys would be allowed on girls' teams. They worried that boys' greater athletic experience at that point in history meant boys would effectively take over girls' sports teams. The legal term for this is "encroachment." Courts have established that qualified girls may try out for boys' teams. But what about the reverse? Can a boy who is qualified play a sport for which there is only a girls' team, like field hockey or gymnastics?

The common rationale for prohibiting boys from playing on girls' teams is that schools must guarantee athletic opportunities to females to make up for past sex discrimination in sports. One method for doing this is to reserve teams for only girls. But is sex segregation a constitutional method for advancing athletic opportunities to women as a way of compensating for past discrimination? In other words, does the Constitution support a kind of sports affirmative action for females?[102]

According to most court decisions, the answer is yes.

Consider the case of John Williams, a student at Liberty High School in Bethlehem, Pennsylvania. In 1992 he wanted to play field hockey, even though his school only offered it as a sport for girls. Field hockey, a popular male sport in many parts of the world, is not designated as a contact sport so the law does not explicitly permit sex segregation for field hockey. In court, John Williams argued that the school's sex-segregation policy in field hockey violated Title IX and his rights under the Equal Protection Clause.[103] Williams had played on a mixed-sex field hockey team in eighth grade and when he entered high school, he made the girls' team as a goalie.[104] The school later removed him from the team, saying the policy did not allow boys to play a girls' sport. In 1992, a federal trial judge ruled that Williams had a right to participate. He played on the team as it compiled a 4–11–4 record. Later, however, the U.S. Court of Appeals, Third Circuit decided the case.[105]

The case prompted a debate in which the court concluded that field hockey indeed was not a contact sport. Although it involves contact, the court ruled that contact was not a major purpose of the sport. The court ruled that Title IX did not permit sex segregation in field hockey, but that the law does allow sex segregation as a means to provide athletic opportunities to members of a sex that have been excluded in the past.[106]

In the case of sports opportunities, the court interpreted that to mean not a particular sport, such as field hockey, but rather athletic opportunities in general. Even though males might have been excluded from playing field hockey, males have not experienced a lack of opportunity to play sports in general. However, the court ruled, women have experienced that lack of opportunity. "Although Title IX ... [applies] equally to boys as well as girls, it would require blinders to ignore that the motivation for promulgation of the regulation on athletics was the historic emphasis on boys' athletic programs to the exclusion of girls' athletic programs in high schools as well as colleges."[107] The court said that redressing "the effect of prior discrimination" would "entail the development of athletic programs that substantially expand opportunities for women to participate and compete at all levels."

In other words, the court decided that Congress intended Title IX to serve as a remedy for past discrimination against women in sports programs. At the time, the court also noted what others had before—that females couldn't compete physically. The differences between males and females were so great, the court stated, that "it takes little imagination to realize that were play and competition not separated by sex, the great bulk of the females would quickly be eliminated from participation and denied any meaningful opportunity for athletic involvement." The court also said that "boys, as a class, are undoubted[ly] better physiologically equipped to play field hockey than are girls."[108]

The Williams case was not the first or only one to seek access for a boy to a girls' athletic team. In 1978, when Christopher Mularadelis was a sophomore at Haldale High School in Cold Spring, New York, he tried out for and earned a spot on the girls' tennis team. The school had been unable to field a boys' team and Mularadelis was ranked as the number two singles player.

At the start of the spring season in his junior year, however, the school board said Mularadelis could not play, citing a new policy banning boys from girls' teams because, they said, "the opportunities for girls to participate are more limited than for boys."[109] The school offered 11 boys' sports teams with more than 180 positions for male athletes and six girls' teams and only 74 positions for female athletes—in a school that was half girls and half boys. Mularadelis, with his father Constantine acting as his attorney, made two arguments, both unsuccessful. He contended that keeping Mulardelis from the team was not in the "letter or spirit of Title IX" and that the gender-based classification system excluding him from the girls' tennis team violated the Equal Protection Clause. The court decided that precluding males like Mularadelis from the girls' tennis team was "a discernible and permissible means toward redressing the disparate treatment of female students in scholastic athletic programs."[110]

This finding was consistent with similar cases, including that of an Arizona high school volleyball player, Gregory Clark, who had played on an Amateur Athletic Union national championship team but found no boys' volleyball team at his high school. He was denied the opportunity to join the girls' team on the same grounds as Mularadelis. Similarly, another male volleyball player, Trent Petrie, was denied access to the girls' team. The court argued there need not be a reciprocal and symmetrical relationship between girls' and boys' teams in that girls could play on boys' teams, but boys could not play on girls' teams.[111] In Trent Petrie's case, for example, the court noted boys were excluded "not because they were not likely to be good enough but because they were likely to be too good to permit adequate opportunity for girls." The court said in the case of boys' being denied access to the team, the "exclusion here carried no stigma of unworthiness to the excluded class."[112]

The courts were generally consistent in their rulings. Even if Title IX permitted it, the Constitution insisted girls be allowed to try out for male sports teams, even for contact sports. The courts also observed the power of Title IX to work as an affirmative action tool. Individual boys could be denied specific rights to play on girls' teams because females historically and still today have fewer athletic opportunities than males as a group. Thus, as legal scholar Jamal Greene, notes, the asymmetry between athletic opportunities historically offered to males versus females is the best justification for the "one-way ratchet that allows women to participate in male-only sports without extending the same opportunity to males who wish to participate in female-only sports."[113]

Individuals, Not Groups

Nonetheless, in the case of girls "playing with the boys," courts did affirm an essential, critical fact: sports are not played by group averages but by individual athletes. From the standpoint of law, court decisions reveal a pattern suggesting it is unconstitutional to bar an individual woman from "playing with the boys" solely because of her sex. Individual females who are qualified to play sports, even contact sports, may play with whomever they choose, including males. Given the long history of female exclusion from sports, courts have also made it clear that girls can play on all-female teams or on male teams. That is not true for males (although some boys do in fact participate on female teams in some places, often in high school field hockey or volleyball, if challenged legally they may have difficulty). Thus courts have ruled that women may voluntarily segregate themselves, but it is unconstitutional to segregate them coercively.

Sex-Segregated Sports as the Disability Model

The Melody Lingers On

Despite the courageous corps of females who have challenged their exclusion from playing with the boys in court, doubts remain about whether men and women can—or should—compete with each other. Much more often than not, the predictable, knee-jerk reaction is NO! The reason, equally predictable, is the belief that women are so inferior to men that they will always lose.

Yet when we believe women will almost always get beaten by men, we are talking about women as if they constitute a disabled group: being female is the condition of being physically (if not also psychologically) handicapped compared to men. We are suggesting women don't have the physical strength to compete with men and lack other qualities too, including plain old aggressiveness. Males become the athletically "abled" group and females the athletically "disabled" group. Following this logic for a moment, we might suggest that the descriptors—abled and disabled—help explain why females are segregated from males in sports in the first place.

Same-Sex Special Olympics?

This mode of thinking suggests that women must be segregated from men in order to find arenas where they can compete "at the same level" by competing only with other females, that is, with similarly disabled athletes. This way of thinking also assumes women require modified rules, which call for them to score fewer points, run shorter distances, and otherwise lessen the challenge to make it manageable for "disabled" athletes. Thus we can consider coercively sex-segregated sports policies as a kind of same-sex Special Olympics. Same-sex sports with same-sex rules allow "disabled" females to learn about competition and winning, teamwork, hard work, and the thrill of participation in a manner parallel to the experience for "able" males without suffering the inevitable defeat females would experience if they tried to compete directly with males. Unfortunately, that type of reasoning about coercively sex-segregated sports policies looks too much like outmoded coercively segregated education policies for disabled children of by-gone days.

In the past, educational policies segregated disabled from abled children, but that is no longer the norm. Today, the resounding message of voluminous research on special education points to the importance of including disabled students alongside abled ones. The consistent message is that what serves special needs children—whether developmental delay, hearing impairment, blindness, emotional disorders, attention deficits, or other conditions—is mainstreaming. Segregating disabled (a term not typically used any longer) children is beneficial only when segregation occurs in a limited and voluntary manner. What does not help special needs children is coerced segregation. Education research also points out a key benefit of mainstreaming not only for special needs children but also for regular education peers. Integration in educational policies—mainstreaming—is good for everyone.[114]

One key problem for any subordinate group is that coercive segregation enforces a second-class citizenship. This was certainly true in the past for special needs students. Much as those coaching women's sports teams complained about inferior equipment and resources, lower budgets, less desirable scheduling of practice times and games, and so on, so too did those teaching special needs children make similar complaints. They had the least desirable classrooms, fewer resources, and less money than did the teachers of other students. In addition, much as the rules for female versions of sports are unnecessarily watered down, so too educators in the 1930s and 1940s found curriculum for special needs students unnecessarily watered down.

Mainstreaming

Mainstreaming and inclusion refer to the "integration, for educational purposes, of children with disabilities into classes that contain primarily children who are developing normally."[115] The term "mainstreaming" also connotes that a disabled child will be placed in the least restrictive environment (LRE), a requirement that was mandated by the Individuals with Disabilities Education Act Amendments of 1997 (IDEA).[116] Although mainstreaming and inclusion have not been precisely defined by federal legislation, there is general agreement on what is intended. Special needs children, when appropriate, should be placed in the class in which they would be if they were not disabled. Put another way, the goal of mainstreaming is to bring the services to the child, not the child to the services, that is, to leave the disabled child in an integrated educational setting with abled children as much as possible.[117]

If we were to apply the mainstreaming principle to athletic programs, this would mean (disabled) females would be encouraged to play with (abled) boys as much as possible. In other words, mainstreaming in athletic programs would establish integration between the sexes as the rule, not the exception. This would hold for all sports—as mainstreaming holds for all educational policies.

Of course, some might find that some boys are more "disabled" than girls when it comes to athletic prowess. But that is precisely the point. The assumption that females cannot play with males is flawed because it assumes that females are a disabled class, when, in fact, they are not. There are many boys who are less athletically gifted than many girls. Thus the first step in mainstreaming is to determine who belongs to the abled and disabled groups. In the case of sports, one's sex is not an accurate surrogate for how fast individual boys and girls can run, how strong or coordinated individual boys and girls are, and so on.

The Social Construction of Disability

One giant problem with dividing individuals into groups of abled and disabled, whether in athletics or education, is that the very concept of "disabled" is socially constructed. Schools, in fact, struggle to classify which students are actually "special needs" and which are not.[118] Testing repeatedly reveals such large overlaps between children believed to be regular education and special education that it can be impossible to define two distinct populations.[119] Education experts estimate that "on any given day more than 80 percent of a school's student body could be classified as learning disabled."[120] According to educational specialists, "when test results do not produce the desired outcome, evaluators often change the yardstick: 'If the test scores indicate the child is ineligible, but the teacher really feels the child needs help, we try to select other tests that might make the child eligible . . .' The tests then become 'a means of corroborating referral decisions. Testing, therefore, does not drive decisions, but is driven by decisions.' "[121] Research even shows that on a wide variety of tests, students already identified as having a learning disability did not differ from other low achievers considered "abled."[122]

The trouble with such classifications is the same trouble that exists in effectively labeling female athletes as less able than male athletes. If we were to administer a "sports test," objective measures of oxygen intake, upper-body strength, coordination, height, weight, muscle mass, and so on, the results might—or might not—be useful in differentiating able athletes from disabled ones. Some athletes will measure off the charts, as some students score off the charts. But if we aim to classify, as well as create fair policies, for those in the great middle ground, we will find a great deal of overlap of athletic aptitude between males and females.

The Importance of Inclusion

Some believe that inclusion is a form of social justice as basic to American society as the Constitution. Such thinking considers that the "categorical segregation of any subgroup of people is simply a violation of civil rights and the principle of equal citizenship."[123] Chief Justice Earl Warren established inclusion as the constitutional norm in the landmark *Brown*, remarking that separateness in education can "generate a feeling of inferiority as to [children's] status in the community that may affect their hearts and minds in a way unlikely ever to be undone. This sense of inferiority...affects the motivation of a child to learn...[and] has a tendency to retard...educational and mental development."[124]

Advocates of educational inclusion note the parallels between efforts to integrate disabled children into the regular classroom with struggles to integrate blacks into white classrooms. Many parents and children found that "in far too many communities...[the same] administrators, teachers, and other school personnel (e.g. social workers, school psychologists)" who had blocked the school doors to African Americans in the 1950s were the ones blocking the school doors to disabled children in the 1960s.[125] Educator and author Jonathan Kozol has pointed out a racist aspect to classification, noting gross overrepresentation of minorities in special education.[126]

Others observe that African American students are much more likely to be categorized as needing special education services than whites, making them subject to less demanding schoolwork, more restrictive classrooms and isolation from their peers, as well as being less likely to be placed in advanced or gifted educational programs.[127]

Sports policies that put all females into special needs athletic programs, so to speak, without basing such classifications on clinical criteria or objective testing, are blatantly sexist. In this sense, integrating disabled students with the abled—or female athletes with male athletes—speaks to what we mean by democracy, that is, equality of opportunity for all.[128]

More than democratic philosophy, we have federal legislation mandating integration of regular and special needs children. In addition to the Individuals with Disabilities in Education Act (IDEA), Congress in 1973 passed the Vocational Rehabilitation Act, requiring that "children with disabilities cannot be discriminated against based on their disability."[129] In 1990, the Americans with Disabilities Act became law, ensuring that "no qualified individual with a disability shall, by reason of such disability, be excluded from participation in or be denied the benefits of the services, programs or activities of a public entity, or be subjected to discrimination by any such entity."[130] The act also recognizes the harm of segregation and requires any public entity *not* "provide different or separate aids, benefits or services to individuals with disabilities or to any class of individuals with disabilities than is [sic] provided to others."[131] Congress makes clear that children with disabilities should share the educational environment with abled children.[132]

The courts have supported Congress in this effort. Beginning in 1975, the pattern in court decisions favors integration whenever possible.[133] The U.S. Court of Appeals for the Third Circuit ruled in 1993 that a boy with Down's syndrome had a right, on the basis of IDEA, to receive an education "in his neighborhood regular school with adequate and necessary supports," thereby "placing the burden of proof for compliance . . . squarely upon the school district and the state rather than the family."[134] The assumption that mainstreaming is the premise, not an option, when it comes to educating disabled students was explicitly stated in the ruling of the U.S. Court of Appeals for the Ninth Circuit in 1994 in *Holland v.*

Sacramento Unified School District. Here, the judge held that "when school districts place students with disabilities, the presumption and *starting point is the mainstream.*"[135]

Benefits of Inclusion

Based on analyses of 11 studies conducted from 1975 to 1984, which included 264 students, researchers found disabled students who were mainstreamed consistently outperformed comparable disabled students who were not mainstreamed. The evaluators concluded that mainstreaming is effective "in improving performance, attitudinal, and process outcomes for handicapped students."[136] Researchers report the most dramatically positive outcomes in students' communication and social skills. The presence of regular students fosters development of language and social competence for disabled students more reliably than a segregated classroom with only disabled students, which researchers found actually impeded development of language and social capacities among disabled students.[137]

Thus there are real benefits to mainstreaming in education, as there are real benefits to mainstreaming in sports. The gains are not all one-sided. Research shows mainstreaming allows friendship to flourish between special needs and regular students—something impossible in a segregated setting.[138] In a study of Midwestern communities, for example, researchers found mainstreaming benefited general educators, special education personnel, and students categorized as having no disabilities, particularly in the area of perceived social competence. Fears that disabled students would be rejected or stigmatized by regular education peers proved unfounded. Abled classmates accepted disabled counterparts, and educators said these integrated classrooms were good for them, their teachers, and all students.[139]

In classrooms, as on the playing field, relationships are built in the process of the act, whether learning or playing, which carry value beyond the sum of the academic or athletic challenge. Mainstreaming makes schools better learning communities and integrated sports teams can make us a better society. Same-sex sports teams for female athletes, like segregated special needs educational classrooms, certainly have a place. But these same-sex teams should be the exception, not the norm, and based on consent, not coercion.

Educational institutions need to redress a long history of excluding women from sports programs. Same sex teams for females is one, but not the only, way to do that. We must also consider presenting students, parents, teachers, coaches, and the public an integrated image of females and males playing together, whenever and wherever possible.

5

INVENTING BARRIERS

The basic discovery about any people is the discovery of the relationship between its men and its women.
— Pearl S. Buck, *Of Men and Women*

The pedestal upon which women have been placed has all too often, upon closer inspection, been revealed as a cage.
— Brenden no. 11, 1297

"Facts" versus "Meanings"

How many times have you gotten into a cab, met a friend for dinner, or had a drink with colleagues after work, and found yourself opening the conversation with an observation about sports? Sports facts figure into speech patterns designed to connect strangers or set the scene for greetings among friends, much as do facts about the weather. Even those who eschew an interest in sports get drawn into the fray. When one author's son moved from Boston to New York, he reported that people constantly observed, "Gee, it must be hard to be a Red Sox fan and live in New York." The assumption was that the most salient difference between living in Boston and the Big Apple must be sports loyalties (even if it wasn't). The power of sports talk is nowhere more evident than on sports radio, where fans tune in to confirm their allegiance to the home team, express their views on the decisions of management or player performance, and boost their commonality. Discussions are often detailed, including talk of salary caps, draft pick strategies, and injury reports. Nonetheless, there is a remarkable myopia to these conversations, which utterly fail to acknowledge the meaning of sports. Sports policies can be used to construct—and deconstruct—race and sex hierarchies. As such, sports is much more than facts; it is also an arena for establishing—or challenging—the meanings associated with race and sex differences.[1]

The Social Construction of Sports

In C. L. R. James's classic *Beyond a Boundary*, he explores the way a sports competition is a microcosm of the racial, class, and power structures of society, a site that reflects and reinforces the powers that be, but also provides opportunities to challenge prevailing myths about which people and what groups are superior versus inferior. Sociologist Douglas Hartmann points out that knowing involves both facts and ideas. Any sport may be understood as a set of facts—rules of play, strategies of the game, particular equipment used, particular playing fields or arenas of play, types of clothing worn, regulations for spectators, and so on. However, sports never exist in the abstract. Rather, all games are embedded in larger social and political situations in which the meaning of a game is defined by historical contexts and the racial, class, and gender identities of players and spectators.[2] Who wins a game (and who cares who wins) has a more significant meaning than merely who gets the most points according to the facts—rules—of the game. Who wins a game reflects, reinforces, or challenges who is viewed as winning in society if not the world; who cares about the outcomes of games also is meaningful to people on the basis of their own racial, class, gender, and national identities.[3]

Sports as Drama

Despite understanding that facts and ideas are embedded in athletic competition, intellectual historians and social critics don't generally view sports in this way, preferring to apply such interpretations to performing arts, which more overtly encompass facts and ideas. The facts of a play are clear. There are specific words actors must say, stage directions, specifications of who plays the characters (their ages, class, race, gender, relationships to each other, and so on). In many plays it's also possible to discern who wins and who loses in the unfolding drama. However, dramatic art forms also contain ideas. They dramatize conflict, competitions, and tensions, which reflect, reinforce, or challenge the social and political world to which they belong. It is the social embeddedness of theater productions—plays as ideas—that keeps social critics engaged, not plays as facts.[4]

One could also direct the same analysis toward sports. In *The Real Thing*, Tom Stoppard does just this when his main character, Henry, a writer, compares good writing to playing cricket well. Henry's wife likes a particular writer that Henry despises. In trying to explain why this writer is bad, Henry employs a sports example. He picks up a cricket bat and says to his wife:

> If you get it right, the cricket ball will travel 200 yards in four seconds . . . What we're trying to do is to write cricket bats, so that when we throw up an idea and give it a little knock it might travel. Now, what we have here [the bad writer's play] is a lump of wood . . . trying to be a cricket bat, and if you hit a ball with it, the ball will travel about 10 feet.[5]

Stoppard's insight about the parallel constructions of art and sports is an exception, not the rule. Why are art and sport so rarely analyzed in parallel? Hartmann blames the paradox that plagues sports, which arises because "those who know the most about sport tend not to have the inclination or ability to realize its broader social connections and significance, while, on the other hand, those who have the requisite skill to understand the broader social dimensions tend to ignore or dismiss sport as a phenomenon worthy of social scientific investigation or serious political consideration."[6] Sport hasn't attracted much serious intellectual analysis, Hartmann says, "despite its manifest importance in people's lives." He says sport "tends to be left out of the history books, the political tracts and philosophical treatises on the meaning of human life."[7] He argues that the manner in which sport is generally practiced and experienced is "a social form that is both serious and non-serious, at once trivial and insignificant and yet also weighty and deeply meaningful."[8]

We may not think about performance theater as games, but we must think about sports as performance theater. Consider sports as a form of theater that millions in the United States follow on a daily basis (more than any theater production can boast). Hartmann interprets both sports and theater as dramatic spectacles that highlight "glorious uncertainty." Both feature the "centrality of the body: its sheer physical form and visual sensuality, the movement and motion that is inherent" to both field and stage. Sports and theater both demand immense skill, training, and experience to execute well. Both offer viewers "timeless tensions such as those between the universal and the particular, innovation and conformity, or, perhaps above all else, the individual and the society."[9] The essential point: sports is not like drama but *is* drama.[10] Consider that participation in sports is not limited to players in the game but includes spectators as well. Hartmann suggests that for engaged spectators, the players and the game itself "come to represent and embody specific social groups and cultural values. Witnessing them, identifying with them and rooting for them provides an opportunity to reinforce and even reflect upon one's own (often implicit) place in and understanding of the social world."[11] James further suggests that cricket (and other sports) offer a better vehicle for transformative social change than film, dance, drama, or music because the very organization of sports contains moral norms corresponding to a democratic society. Sports can be a "progressive social force" because of the "moral structure" of games, which includes acceptance of the principles of meritocracy, self-discipline, hard work, cooperation with others, competition with others, respect for the rules, loyalty, and civility, including being a good loser or a generous winner.[12] Requisites for playing the game mirror good citizenship in American democracy, and, as Robert Simon notes, are based on principles of "fair play."[13]

Sports may yearn to be Lady Justice, dressed in male garb. The notion of sport as the epitome of egalitarian ideals is marred by the glaring fact that it doesn't include women as equals.[14] Organized sport has unfolded instead with a consistent underlying intention: to draw sharp distinctions between the sexes. Athletics have defined the social understanding of masculinity, while women seeking access to athletics have faced barriers, including many invented merely to separate male and female.

The Beginning of Organized Sport in America

Made for Men

The rise of organized sport in America came, like so many enduring cultural structures, from a need. The mid to late 1800s saw a nation in the midst of rapid industrialization, immigration, and urbanization. Athletics offered a vehicle for addressing worrisome social problems that accompanied rapid and profound change. It was no mistake that organized sport blossomed at precisely the moment it became aligned with larger social goals and needs. Athletics offered more than amusement. Play was not for play's sake; it was the engine for a greater mission.[15]

Athletics and America's Mission

The marriage between sports and social goals set the stage for athletics to be viewed (1) not as trivial play, which could be derided as wasteful, but as a productive vehicle for teaching skills and values that could be applied elsewhere, and (2) as a force for modernization that could shape cultural attitudes. The history of sport, then, is not a string of rule changes, statistics, and the bios of exceptional players. It is a force whose very appeal as leisure—both for the masses and, separately, for the elites—offered those influential in governing organized sports the power to shape not just a game but a society.[16]

The key to the birth of structured, organized athletics was the changed attitude of religious leaders in the mid to late 1800s. In early America, sport-like activities, including boxing and cockfighting, were popular, but the betting, drinking, and brawling that accompanied contests, coupled with the Puritan suspicion of play, made sports unpopular with religious leaders and pious governors. Aligned with steamy "joys of the flesh," sports were suspect and laws were passed to limit athletic play. Some early Americans did embrace athletics but were careful to put them in proper context: the belief that work could rightly be leavened with play. President John Adams, for example, sailed, wrestled, swam, skated, flew kites, and enjoyed shooting.[17]

Stabilizing Industrial Society

However, it was the nineteenth century and America's transformation from an agrarian nation to an industrial society rife with new immigrants and a new ethos of capitalism that saw the massive organization and acceptance of sports. Instead of being relegated to a conflicted place in society, religious, political, and moral leaders believed sports could address social and cultural problems. Athletics were redefined as a means for practicing self-discipline and ingraining principles of ethical conduct. By the 1850s this "muscular Christianity" was the new gospel. The flesh was no longer the enemy of the pious spirit but its very vessel.[18] The playing field was not a place to escape duty but a site to demonstrate the honor and morality expected of a Christian gentleman—but not, of course, a lady.

Sports, then, provided real and legitimate social utility.[19] Rapid industrialization fed anxiety about the movement away from a rural society to an urban one, from a society in which people toiled in isolation to one in which they were required to work (in factories) in groups. Athletics helped provide a new paradigm for human interaction. As social reformer Luther Gulick notes, "the mass, the team, the gang, the institution" were the new social and labor structures.[20] Sports could train men for modern life, offering skills relevant to the workplace and to neighborhood civic demands. In cities, where social workers grappled with huge influxes of new immigrants (and overcrowded and unsanitary tenements), athletics taught cooperative values and the "American way." Sports, in other words, provided stabilizing principles and practices at the very moment the nation needed them.[21] But, again, largely for men.

Nation Building and Immigrants

"Strength, courage, and a wholesome spirit of emulation, are among the best characteristics of all really great nations; and the presence of these noble attributes in the Man depends largely upon his training as a Boy," reads the preface to the 1864 edition of *The American Boy's Book of Sports and Games*. "Though the pursuit of simple and healthy amusements may not actually *make* heroes, it may certainly cultivate and develop all the heroic elements that may be inherent."[22]

The handbook reflects the era's mind-set in explicitly fusing athletics with national identity, nationalism, and masculinity. The book carefully announces that where different versions of rules for sports and games exist, "our American method of playing them has been strictly adhered to in every case." The book also assures that "many purely national amusements, unknown abroad, such as Base-ball, etc., have been accorded a prominent place." The message in these and similar handbooks was obvious: organized sports went hand in hand with nation building. By providing boys and young men—but not girls and young women—the means to learn American values and masculine mettle, sports were not only a healthy diversion but also a key for founding modernization in America on a principle of sex segregation.

Urbanization

One reality of modern society was its increasing diversity. As immigrants came to America from around the world and as country dwellers moved to cities, the need to forge a sense of commonality was pressing.[23] Athletics addressed this urgent demand. The Young Men's Christian Association (YMCA), founded in England and brought to America in 1851, steered poor and immigrant youth into safe activities. Such service, however, was not merely for fun but aimed to make a boy's body into a worthy spiritual vessel and able servant of Christ. The gospel was spread in gymnasiums as youth learned the Christian approach in which mind, body, and spirit worked in unison.

To keep young men interested, 25-year-old Luther Gulick, then the superintendent of the Springfield, Massachusetts, School for Christian Workers (later the Young Men's Christian Association

Training School), in 1891 gave one of his workers, James Naismith, the task to "supply for the winter season a game that would have the same interest for the young man that football has in the fall and baseball in the spring."[24] This assignment produced the game of basketball. While the sport immediately caught on and provided an outlet for rambunctious youth, it was used as a vehicle to instill Christian virtues of self-restraint, fairness, and honor.

The burgeoning parks movement, which saw creation of public spaces and playgrounds, helped popularize basketball among immigrant groups, including Jewish youth, who several decades later would dominate professional basketball. Critically, however, the parks movement legitimized the need for recreational spaces as integral to public and civic life. Intellectuals who argued man was losing touch with nature and, as a result, to a vital "energy source" essential to man's survival, pressed for creation of natural oases in cities. Gulick and other influential thinkers argued that urban parks provided an antidote to anxieties of overindustrialization. Public parks and sports facilities, they argued, were critical for humans to preserve their physical vigor in an increasingly mechanized world.

Some of those concerns today seem far-fetched, but the shift from farmwork to factory work, from an agrarian to an industrial economy, removed many individuals from the everyday physical labor to which they were accustomed. Ralph Waldo Emerson worried that "civilized man has built a coach, but has lost the use of his feet."[25] To ease anxieties that industrialization would be man's ruin, sports preserved elements of nature in daily life. Public parks, with their playgrounds and fields, helped resolve the seeming conflict between the rapidly modernized landscape and the Darwinist belief that man's survival rested on remaining physically vigorous. At the same time, increasing scientific knowledge, growing interest in sanitation, cleanliness, and sexual health, along with support for cultivating and enjoying the body, all supported the widespread popular commitment to athletic pursuits. Primarily for men.

It's Natural: Physically Strong Man

The social construction of the "naturally" strong man as an a priori assumption to the development of sports programs, however, ran into trouble in the late nineteenth century. With the attendant luxuries of city life for those who could afford them, some intellectuals worried men were being transformed into genteel dandies, losing their "naturally" masculine physical vigor and fighting character. Some feared urban social life, with its offerings of theater, museums, fine dining, and articulate conversation—instead of manly activities such as hunting, harvesting, and physical labor—were making men soft. They saw the worrisome feminization of society. Oliver Wendell Holmes, writing in the *Atlantic Monthly* in 1858, fretted about the "black-coated, stiff-jointed, soft-muscled, paste-complexioned youth... [that] never before sprang from the loins of Anglo-Saxon lineage."[26] Such softness, thinkers argued, was best countered with vigorous athletic challenges to reconnect men with nature and their manliness.

Football to the Rescue

Football offered one clear and obvious answer to the era's apprehensions. No sport is considered more masculine than football (even today despite growing numbers of programs for women and girls). The game possesses overtly militaristic qualities, with the use of strategy and brute force to take an opponent's territory. As in combat, teammates protect one another from hits and make coordinated attacks. With long passes we now call "bombs" and with the wearing of helmets, much like soldiers in combat, football has long evoked the language, symbolism, and ethos of war. It was no mistake, for example, in 1890 that Henry Lee Higginson contributed money to build Harvard's Soldier's Field in memory of young Brahmins killed years earlier in the Civil War. Football was—and is—the sport of combat and heroics, male camaraderie, masculine initiation, and self-sacrifice.[27]

The very toughness of football, many believed, was just what a society of soft males needed. If bloody Civil War battlefields had once initiated their fathers and grandfathers into manhood, the football gridiron would be the proving ground for a new generation. This was where sons would be tested and trained, where they would learn lessons of vigor and leadership and, at the end of it all, become men.[28]

The rules have been altered considerably over the years, but football remains a game of male public aggression whose warlike qualities appeal to America's bellicose character. It is the football team, and its attendant image of hypermasculinity, which typically determines a high school's rivalry. Hitting is an integral part of play. Should we be surprised that a high school team's preplay preparation today may include warlike explosions of emotion? The Kahuka High School football team in Hawaii performs a haka, a Polynesian war dance, before games.[29]

Football, with its ethos of battle, also created a social structure through its network of fans and alumni. Even in the late nineteenth and early twentieth centuries these structures reproduced existing social and power relationships. The football game gathered society's powerful to celebrate the coming-of-age of young male players. The Yale and Princeton rivalries were so intense and celebrated that an annual Thanksgiving game drew wealthy men who bet hundreds of thousands of dollars on the outcome. Women dressed in furs and jewels marked the game as a debutante ball of another sort, in which the manhood of players was the focus of presentation and celebration.

While some athletic events attracted public interest on their own, the growing media industry fueled the exploding interest in spectator sports. The rise of sports newspapers and magazines, along with sports sections in daily newspapers, brought news of contests and results to audiences that otherwise would miss the athletic drama. Although sports publications first appeared in the 1820s, and the reporting of scores and results attracted broad audiences for baseball and boxing, among other pursuits, this did not happen without controversy. Then as now, interest in sports information was tied to gambling; the more news, the more wagering. As a result, some women saw sports newspapers as a threat to the moral sanctity of the home and made a show of not allowing sports pages in their houses. This only pushed men to gather in barbershops, bars, and social clubs, cementing them as sites of sports talk.[30]

Sports and American Consumerism

Despite—or perhaps because of—the racy cast of sporting news, interest grew, fueling athletic consumerism among fans (called cranks or fanatics) and feeding a burgeoning American mass culture. Sports offered a way to "be American." Even as Jewish immigrant parents took a dim view of their sons playing baseball, an editor of the *Jewish Daily Forward* encouraged a father to let his son play and become competent at the sport. "Mainly, let us not raise the children that they should grow up foreigners in their own birthplace," he advised.[31] However, even as sports appeared to offer a unifying effect, drawing together people of different classes, races, and genders (baseball promoters held ladies' days to attract women), the sports themselves hardly promoted egalitarian values. In fact, evolving rules did the opposite, codifying the means for segregating and excluding individuals.

Sports: Class and Race Segregation

While athletic clubs sprang up to promote play, venues for rowing, yachting, tennis, croquet, golf, and even horse racing were private spaces, providing a protected environment where leaders of business and industry could socialize and recreate apart from the masses. In turn-of-the-century America, the Newport Country Club was favored by Astors, Vanderbilts, and Stillmans while Whitneys, Harrimans, and Belmonts gathered at racing stables, and Rockefellers, Carnegies, and Tafts golfed at private clubs.[32]

Organized sports also enforced racial segregation, even when it served a competitive disadvantage. In the 1890s black baseball players, once routinely included on white teams, were banned from professional play as racial segregation practices spread. This came as scientists during the late 1800s through the 1930s perpetuated beliefs that people of European decent (particularly northern Europeans) were the most intellectually—and athletically—gifted, a notion which supported a broader assertion about white racial superiority. By the time black runners like Jesse Owens challenged Nazi racial ideology with their athletic successes (he won four Gold Medals at the 1936 "Hitler Olympics"), a new explanation had emerged: African Americans were closer to nature and excelled in unthinking competitions against more intellectually endowed whites. Even Owens's coach, Dean Cromwell, argued that Owens and other African Americans triumphed because "he is closer to the primitive than the white man."[33]

Overt racial bias was also enforced as football moved from college campuses to a national audience. Although professional football was officially reintegrated in 1946, black players in the 1950s faced slurs and harassment on the field and were barred from staying with teammates during away games at hotels in segregated cities. Washington Redskins owner George Preston Marshall even made a display of refusing to allow black players on his team, which was not integrated until 1962, when John F. Kennedy's administration pressured Marshall to comply with federal antidiscrimination laws, using as leverage the fact that the new Redskins stadium was built on federal land.[34] Aside from the political pressure, it was certainly clear by this time that refusing to sign black football players put any team at a competitive disadvantage.

Sports and Sex Segregation

The exclusion and abuses of black athletes are disturbing and well documented. On the other hand, the treatment of women has received relatively little notice in the annals of sports history. We lack a broad awareness that the very creation of organized sport in America is based on the practice of sex segregation and an overriding belief in female weakness. Women's athletic opportunities have been hard won, but have come with a caveat: female athletes must conform to, rather than challenge, standards of femininity.

It's Natural: Physically Weak Woman

Women's bodies may be their own, but they are also highly charged cultural symbols. Throughout history, women's bodies have been the subject of powerful interpretations that have shaped social roles and myths about female limitations. The most obvious physical differences between males and females have served as the basis for controlling female activities, including athletic, workplace, and political participation.

Women's Weak Bodies

Victorians presumed that women were morally strong but physically weak. Men were the opposite: physically strong but needing female influence to keep their moral compass in check. Even before reproductive biology was understood, women's recurring cycles were used to portray women as frail, unstable, faulty, and imperfect. Aristotle declared menstruation a sign of female inferiority, arguing that women had a passive role in reproduction, merely providing nourishment while males created heat which transformed matter into semen—and life. The cold female was the container; her monthly discharge was useless nourishment.[35] Others were convinced menstruation represented fluids accumulated from leading an idle life. While men and women both generated surplus matter, women eliminated theirs as menses while men applied theirs to athletics.[36]

Seventeenth-century physicians viewed menstrual discharge as a literal leak and evidence that the uterus is the weakest part of the female body since it fails to hold its contents. Dr. Regnier de Graaf actually compared menstrual blood leaving the uterus to wine or beer seeping out of a defective barrel.[37] Still others theorized that any problem a woman experienced—whether physical or emotional—would flow to the weakest part of the system, the uterus. This image of female weakness set the stage for later restrictions placed on women under the guise of "protecting" delicate organs—or protecting society from the tainted female.

By locating feminine weakness in the womb, men (who had no such equivalent body part) were exempt from faults that, biologically speaking, could only belong to a woman. The belief that menstruating women were unclean and contaminated—a notion dating to biblical times—fed conventional wisdom that a woman could not cure meat while menstruating.[38]

In what today appears to be an absurd exchange of views, an 1878 issue of the *British Medical Journal* published letters on the question of whether or not a menstruating woman could contaminate food and how that might relate to her ability to perform professional medical tasks. One writer suggested that because dead meat couldn't cure during a woman's period, then "what would result, under similar conditions, from her attempt to cure live flesh in her midwifery or surgical practice?"[39] It was a woman's physical nature that made her an unsuitable physician.

Institutionalizing Barriers

One way to ensure that "natural" differences remained undisturbed was to prohibit deviance from socially established norms. Football prevented the feminization of the male. Women, on the other hand, could only engage in athletic activities that emphasized their femininity and acknowledged their reproductive capacities. Medical and health experts, based on faulty understanding of women's bodies, radically limited female exertion for fear that too much activity might "dislodge" the uterus, "robbing future generations." Even pioneering female doctors echoed the mantra of restricted activity. Dr. Elizabeth Scovil, in her popular *Preparation for Motherhood Manual,* advised that "most women are able to get enough exercise just moving around the household, and a long walk doesn't bring sufficient compensation for the fatigue it causes."[40] An 1879 medical text tells girls to "spend the year before and two years after puberty at rest," and to endure menstrual periods "in the recumbent position."[41]

This was the era of the "rest cure" for nearly any ailment, and the concern that, as one 1874 text warned, "a single ride on horseback, a single wetting of the feet . . . may entail lifelong misery."[42] Such missives had the powerful and tangible result of casting female weakness as natural and an inescapable characteristic of the sex. It was a simple leap, then, to move from protecting women from physical exertion to protecting them from mental exertion as well. In 1873 the eminent Dr. Edward Clarke, professor at Harvard Medical School and author of the classic *Sex in Education* (so reviled by suffragists), argued that studying diverted blood and energy vital to reproductive organs and directed it to the brain. If a girl "puts as much force in her brain education as a boy . . . the special apparatus will suffer," warned Clarke.[43] Others cautioned that overstimulating the female brain would result in stunted growth, nervousness, hysteria, and even insanity.

The connection between socially approved femininity and physical weakness persisted well into the twentieth century, even if messages grew more subtle and were couched in common sense. Medical experts conceded that women needed *some* exercise to be fit enough for childbearing and child-rearing. But what form should that exercise take? Competing beliefs about how women should engage in athletics—calisthenics or competition—were embedded in a broader set of contradictory messages to women about their bodies. Even as girls were assured that menstruation would not disable them, they were advised to severely curb activities during menses. The notion of periodic invalidism was ingrained as "natural" to females and conveniently explained why women were un-suitable for certain jobs. (Even into the 1970s, for example, some argued that if a woman were in the White House she could acci-dentally set off a nuclear war if she went berserk during her period.) It was, in other words, difficult to know where fact ended and pre-vailing social beliefs began.

The impulse to preserve female social difference through in-terpretation of female physical difference was a clear subtext in advice for girls approaching puberty. Despite findings by some physicians, including Dr. E. H. Arnold, that suggested activity during one's menstrual period actually reduced pain and fatigue, many others argued persuasively that menstruation was in-capacitating.[44] In the 1940s, girls given the *As One Girl to Another* pamphlet by Kotex received stern warning: "Don't get your dates mixed." They were told that "if you're fairly regular, you can count ahead twenty-eight days and know . . . in advance whether to let the team count on you for the big basketball game or not."[45] Even if girls didn't feel constrained by their periods, they were warned to "Think Twice!" of vague physical damage they might cause to their bodies because "dashing around violently brandishing a weapon of sport jiggles you up." At dances, menstruating girls were urged to "sit down now and then" while "tennis, basketball, and other stren-uous sports should be postponed."

The Right Kind of Play—for Ladies

Separate Sports Spheres

The private, protective confines of country clubs offered women the greatest athletic opportunities. Females could exert themselves away from public view, in effect participating athletically without encountering the "wrong" sort of people or, alternatively, overtly challenging male athletic dominance. Women's demonstrations could remain essentially private; they most definitely would not perspire in public. Even as they took up genteel sports like tennis, golf, and croquet, however, they encountered rules about dress, comportment, and play. This would not be a replication of battle, but a pageant of gentility.

For women, then, sport was not a means to demonstrate strength and ferocity, but to appear fashionable and ladylike. Sports such as tennis and croquet, for example, called on females to wear long, heavy dresses that hampered movement but preserved feminine appearance. Rules reinforced the belief that female sport was about socializing. In 1902, for example, the U.S. Lawn Tennis Association restricted women's play to two out of three sets instead of three out of five for fear women would overexert themselves.[46]

Ladylike Croquet

Victorian women confronted restrictions in athletics with varying success. In croquet, men and women played together because it was not very athletic and the garden-like setting was suitable for courtship. Nonetheless, croquet provided women a venue for challenging traditional roles, as they shed their passive demeanor to dominate and even humiliate male players. Some of the humiliation was highly symbolic, as when women lined up two balls together, lifted their long, heavy skirts, placed a delicate foot on their own ball, and swung their mallet to send the male opponent's ball skittering off course. In an era of repressed sexual mores in which the foot was a displaced symbol of the genitals, the raised skirt constituted an erotic act, and the thwacking of a male opponent's ball symbolic castration—and female dominance. Women also humiliated men by simply beating them, which happened often enough that women were said to benefit from steadier nerves and a greater opportunity to practice.

The croquet craze that gripped polite society in the mid to late nineteenth century reveals both women's athletic skill and the pleasure they took in aggressive and successful performances, whether in leisure or championship play. At the time, there was widespread attention given to accusations of women cheating. An 1868 *Harper's Bazaar* article on croquet made light of cheating strategies, including some women's habit of allegedly repositioning balls by discreetly dragging them with the hems of their heavy skirts. Another writer, more serious in tone, noted the skirt-dragging trick and begged, "Ladies, be honorable, and reform this trick altogether, for in most cases you do not need these little helps: you are generally better players than men."[47] If women did indeed cheat at croquet, their desire to beat men by any means necessary offers tantalizing evidence of women's interest in winning—and in countering social expectations.

The Right Clothes

Feminine Attire

From the start, clothing was a problem for women athletes. If male athletes replicated the soldier on the battlefield, women remained bound to the boudoir. Sports, then, should not interfere with the need to remain at all times physically pleasing. So for women athletes, appearance mattered as much as performance. This meant women wore corsets and heavy skirts, which severely restricted their movement. Females were so inculcated with the belief that such clothing was proper, however, that when Clara Gregory Baer introduced bloomers as required gym class wear at Newcomb College in 1894, "the young women who came to class in long dresses, bustles, hats, gloves, and heels balked at this perceived immodesty."[48] In the end, Baer worked to "sweat off" corsets, persuading students to don lighter, less restrictive bloomers. The discussion about female attire was (and is) central to debate about women's sports. In the 1930s and 1940s, short shorts and shiny fabric used for uniforms in industrial sports leagues struck female physical education instructors as racy and immodest. During the 1950s, a desire to please male spectators spurred the Amateur Athletic Union at national girls' basketball tournaments to have females parade around the court at halftime so fans could select a beauty "Queen of the Court." Such pageants sent an unmistakable message that a girl's physical appearance is just as important as her basketball ability.[49]

Sexy Attire

Even today, female athletic talent competes with female sex appeal. Some sports industry leaders have suggested the key to increasing public following of women's professional basketball and soccer is to demand players to wear more revealing uniforms. Sepp Blatter, the president of FIFA, soccer's international governing body, said women should wear "more feminine" uniforms to attract spectators. One online sports columnist insisted the success of the WNBA could rest with skimpier garb. "Maybe sex appeal IS the way to sell the sport," columnist Pete DeWolf wrote. "Essentially it is going to take shorter rims or shorter shorts to get me to watch."[50] He's not the first to make the point. Itty bitty swimsuits are credited for making women's beach volleyball a hit in the 2004 Summer Olympics.

Alas, we have not traveled far enough away from Victorian social structures. Rather than provide a means for breaking down traditional roles, attention on physical appearance and dress has females athletes still judged for their sex appeal, not their athletic zeal. Women have been appreciated for their athletic talent (think beach volleyball duo Misty Mae and Kerry Walsh), but their physical appearance is never far from the discussion. Even top female athletes are viewed within sex roles before they are considered as athletes. Meanwhile, male counterparts routinely see their performance on the field translated by sports analysts into evidence of leadership ability.

The Meaning of Attire

Dress itself is not the chief matter but how it defines female athletic participation, symbolically and literally. Dress signals social standing and political power, leading feminists to use garments to visibly articulate a political agenda. Just as bra burning in the 1960s sent one message of female liberation, in the late 1800s, bloomers sent another. Women's desire to have greater range of movement for activities including bicycling and basketball prompted Amelia Bloomer to popularize loose-fitting Turkish pantaloons as an alternative to uncomfortable, restrictive stays (so tightly laced women could hardly breathe) and as many as 12 pounds of skirts.[51]

Not surprisingly, the physical freedom bloomers offered made them symbolic of female political and social freedom as well. Bloomers were the favored dress of suffragists, including Elizabeth Cady Stanton, Susan B. Anthony, and Lucy Stone. (Women's rights activists were known as "bloomers.") The dress was so controversial and revolutionary, however, that it initially drew public ire, driving Stanton to write Anthony to say she was abandoning the style to avoid alienating those who might otherwise support woman suffrage. "We put the dress on for greater freedom, but what is physical freedom compared with mental bondage?" Stanton concluded.[52]

Bloomers and less restrictive clothing did catch on. The turn of the twentieth century brought the "New Woman" whose slender athletic physique was epitomized by the Gibson Girl, first introduced to Victorian readers in 1890 by illustrator Charles Dana Gibson. The Gibson Girl, with her golf club or tennis racquet in hand, broadened acceptance of women in individual elite sports, but she remained unquestionably feminine. The focus was on healthy, attractive appearance, not athletic prowess, making the Gibson Girl more a fashion image than trailblazer for female athleticism. The translation of female sport into a style rather than an activity reflects a stubborn truth: society is most comfortable with the female body when it is not challenging gender ideals but embracing them. In the *Sports Illustrated* swimsuit issue, the sole connection between female models and sports is a focus on the human body.

And yet confusion persists. Men's media outlets like ESPN are on the prowl for candidates to fill lists of sexiest female athletes. Some women sports stars, including tennis players Anna Kournikova and Maria Sharapova, swimmer Amanda Beard and race car driver Danica Patrick have used their trim, muscular bodies to model. Most women understand that fitness promotes health, but the more pervasive message is that the real benefit of women's sports—even the motivation for women at the gym—is to make female bodies pleasing to men. Men get the message that they should play to win; women that they should play to please. This sexualization and objectification is double-edged. While it offers a muscular image which idealizes female strength over Twiggy- or Kate Moss–like physical frailty, it is singularly focused on the posed, motionless female body, and not the feats that body can perform.

The dual faces of organized athletics—the female side and the male side—were enforced from the start. Even advocates for women's sports embraced a sex-typed ideology, as evident in a 1965 directive from Mabel Locke, officer for the National Section for Girls' and Women's Sports (NSGWS), a governing body for women's sports, to college physical education professors. Locke, who later advocated for gender equity in pay, nonetheless called on instructors to keep talented female athletes from dominating play and programs. Instructors, she advised, should "direct those students with high-level capacity into channels where her ability will be used to serve others first, themselves second." The gifted female athlete was to "use [her] talent as a service to others rather than to bring glory to self or to school."[53] It didn't matter if a female had stunning skills; she would not be recognized or rewarded for those abilities. On the contrary, she would have to hide them.

Keeping Feminine

All the fuss about women's sports attire ensured their adherence to the proper feminine image while playing a sport. But eventually this grew more complicated. Trouble surfaced as women sought to play sports that looked a lot like boys' games. Women's sports advocates then worked overtime to control the manner in which females played and the reason for which they played. Women's sports emphasized athletics as a vehicle, not an end in itself. Women's sports were not about winning but about developing social skills, which dovetailed perfectly with female roles as wives, mothers, and community members. Even when women appeared to play the same game as men, approaches and rule differences enforced distinctions. Women's games were, in effect, declawed of any possibility of aggression or competition, designing for females softer versions of boys' sports.[54]

Women's sports were clearly differentiated from male games in several ways, including rule changes that restricted exertion, length of play, or physical contact. Women's teams might be limited to a few games in a season. At the college level, the push to eliminate interscholastic competition yielded play days, meetings in which home and visiting players were scrambled to remove any team identity and emphasize fun and socializing.[55] This obviously minimized the value of team practices or strategies. Women's games also included refreshments at the end of play as a reminder that it was ultimately a social event, a practice that continues in some arenas to this day. In recreational tennis, for example, women's leagues typically expect the home team to provide a buffet for players, not the case in men's leagues. The 2005 Dorothy Bruno Hills

Indoor Tennis League rules state that "the home team Captain is responsible for arranging refreshments."[56]

At the turn of the twentieth century, women internalized so many messages about female weakness and sex-based limitations, it seems now remarkable that they even got out of bed in the morning, much less found their way onto playing fields. For those women who did play, it happened despite—not because of—cultural norms. Given so many restrictions, advocates and athletes worked hard to unlock gym doors. But note that they didn't break any doors down. Careful, accommodating advocacy made sense at the time but slowed the evolution of female athletes and women's athletics. Instead of challenging gender dictates, they accommodated them. The female physical educators who worked so tirelessly to expand sports opportunities for women ultimately employed an approach that effectively marginalized women's athletics for much of the twentieth century.

Basketball

The development of women's basketball is an effective model for viewing challenges facing the fledgling women's sports movement. By the early 1900s, basketball was the most popular sport in America among girls and women. Its popularity drove female physical education instructors—who at the time controlled women's athletics—to formulate and execute a philosophy of athletic participation that would set the tone for all women's sports. Anxieties about women's sports being too competitive, too male, or unladylike would influence programs for decades.

The story of "bloomer basketball" captures the tension between feminine ideals and concerns about the perceived masculinity of athletics. Female physical educators recognized the social, health, and even economic value of team sports like basketball, but labored to keep the game within their definitions of propriety. The rise of women's colleges in the late 1800s and early 1900s provided a natural forum for team sports and an alternative to elite individual sports like golf and tennis. Almost as soon as basketball was invented in Springfield, Massachusetts, in 1891 by James Naismith, Smith College physical education director Senda Berenson introduced a modified version to her students. Like others, Berenson saw basketball not just as a game but as the vehicle for a broader mission. Berenson understood the link between athletics and economic power, and suggested the game "came on at the right moment in history...One of the strong arguments in the economic world against giving women as high salaries as men for similar work is that women are more prone to illness than men. They need, therefore, all the more to develop health and endurance if they desire to become candidates for equal wages."[57]

Berenson pressed for more rigorous exercise for females than was advocated in the past, but remained mindful of prevailing views—and expectations of Smith administrators and parents. She made clear that "the aim in athletics for women should above all things be health—physical health and moral health."[58] While Berenson saw the political and economic benefits of fitness, she did not view sports competition—winning—as a desirable goal. Her modified basketball rules emphasized cooperation and socialization.

Berenson thought it critical to restrict players' movement. Her rules, first published by Spalding in 1901, limited exertion by dividing the court into thirds and requiring players stay in assigned sections. Players were prohibited from physical contact and interfering with the shooter. They could not grab the ball and were limited to one and later to three dribbles. Berenson would regularly publish revisions of the rules until 1917.

The experience of modifying basketball for college women positioned female physical educators as the "experts" on women's sports, and convinced Berenson and others to establish a structure for cooperation and communication within the women's interscholastic sports world. In 1899, they founded the Women's Basketball Committee, which would be the first of many successive governing bodies for women's sports, including the Committee on Women's Athletics (CWA), the National Section on Women's Athletics (NSWA), the National Association for Girls and Women in Sport (NAGWS), the National Association for the Physical Education of College Women (NAPECW), and the Women's Division of the National Amateur Athletic Federation (WD NAAF).[59] Basketball may have triggered the creation of these governing bodies, but administrators quickly expanded their oversight to other sports as well. In 1916, the National Council of the American Physical

Education Association set up rules committees for women's field hockey, track and field, and swimming.

A postplay reception was a regular part of many games and in keeping with the "milk and cookies" approach to women's sports that emphasized socializing over competition. Still, despite news stories mentioning players' social graces and reporting on the receptions, sometimes given by coaches, faculty, schools administrators, townspeople—and even occasionally by college men—basketball was a successful competitive college sport for women, particularly in certain regions. When Berkeley and Stanford women's basketball teams played each other in May 1896, the event drew "700 women of fashion," according to a news report, which noted that police had "great difficulty" keeping men (who were not allowed to attend at that time) from passageways and the roof of the Page Street Armory, where the game was held.[60] Interestingly, after two 20-minute halves in which Stanford won 2–1, players from both teams were greeted with rousing celebrations and honors at their respective colleges. The two teams split the gate receipts, with Stanford using their take to build "a cinder track for women," the news report states, while "the Berkeley money will go toward defraying the expenses of the athletic team (male) on its approaching Eastern tour." Ohio was also home to a lively women's basketball rivalry among colleges, including Ohio State University, which attracted a large fan base and news coverage. But this suddenly ended in 1907 when Ohio State's director of physical education, Dr. H. Shindle Wingert, banned women's basketball. He proclaimed public sports contests "morally and physically detrimental to women."[61] This abrupt reversal was part of a pattern repeated at colleges and universities—and in states and communities—across the country. At the very moment women's athletic success approached men's programming in stature and following, it was derailed.

As Robin Bell Markels observes, "From 1904 through 1907, women's basketball in central Ohio, led by teams from Ohio State, exploded onto the sport scene and enjoyed a public exposure, popularity, and institutionalization that was not seen again in Ohio until the 1980s, when women at Ohio State began playing in the Big Ten under NCAA auspices."[62] It was, ironically, the popularity of women's basketball—not the lack of interest—that made it a public target for suppression. Their success challenged gender norms, the feminizing aftergame receptions notwithstanding, and ultimately brought about their demise.

Growing discomfort with females playing basketball on college campuses was no doubt influenced by the Amateur Athletic Union's approach to the women's game. The AAU, a male-run organization founded in 1888, favored high-level competition for the best players and attracted lower-class women who were not college educated. The lack of a college education was not all that set the AAU at odds with the physical education instructors. The AAU tournaments (only for white teams until the mid-1950s) attracted disdain because events emphasized players' sex appeal. Those who ran the AAU tournaments, in other words, made an end run around the physical educators' approach to preserving femininity by redefining it as baldly and boldly sexy, not as virtuous motherhood.

Players in AAU tournaments did not have to worry about being overly aggressive. They could be as ferocious as they wanted, as long as they wore makeup and dressed in an appealing fashion. Tournament organizers ensured there would be no confusion and no accusations that players were mannish. Tournaments often featured halftime beauty pageants and had a bawdy atmosphere that attracted sponsors and appalled groups like the National Section on Women's Athletics. Some AAU basketball events, for example, featured motorboat and airplane rides, free throw contests, and postgame dances. Despite cries of outrage by female physical educators, women's basketball thrived through teams organized by the AAU, by YMCAs, YWCAs, and churches. The relative popularity of industrial teams, for example, was evident in cities like Oakland, where some 80 plants participated in a women's basketball league that featured 144 players in 1936 and drew more than 4,000 spectators.[63]

The face-off between female physical educators and the AAU was rooted, of course, in conflicting beliefs about femininity. Where the AAU reveled in titillation and physical abandon (but maintained male control over the women), the NSWA wanted to see females in control. Unfortunately neither banishing women's competition nor using basketball games as beauty pageants offered an ideal model for the development of women's sports. Both had their flaws. The first defined women as weak; the second as sex objects.

Fitness and Socializing but Not Competition

The antics of AAU women's basketball make it apparent why female physical education instructors wanted control of women's sports. As a result, despite AAU success, female physical educators managed to define the cultural parameters of appropriate athletic participation for girls and women. Their mantra of noncompetition, coupled with the belief that sports should teach females social skills and help them get fit for motherhood, came to dominate and limit women's sports. In the introduction to a 1928 volume, *Field Hockey and Soccer for Women*, for example, author Ethel Perrin, assistant director of health education for the Detroit Public Schools, extols play for girls but underscores the real aim: "We are training for good citizenship."[64] Perrin encourages cooperation with the opposing team, noting that "the dominant idea of the coach in making arrangements for the game is to 'take' every advantage that the law allows, when a little 'give' would be of real social significance to the players."[65] The message is not merely about sportsmanship but downgrading competition. Perrin also points out the role of soccer in preparing for childbearing. "Our women need strong, healthy bodies," she proclaims. Although "kicking a ball is as natural for a girl as for a boy," Perrin notes, "the resultant strengthening of the abdominal muscles is more important in her life than in his."[66]

The message meshed with old Victorian beliefs that males and females need to operate in distinct spheres. Women may have cast off constricting nineteenth-century dress, but mandates about the separation of masculinity and femininity still held sway in the early twentieth century. So even as sports grew in popularity and colleges offered instruction in basketball, swimming, baseball, and field hockey for girls, many still emphasized Swedish gymnastics and calisthenics. Classes used wands, Indian clubs, and music to teach lessons on posture, maternal health, even ways to enhance feminine beauty and curves. Sports were available, but many physical educators opposed competition in favor of low-impact activities including folk dancing, balancing stunts, and "posture parades."[67] Exercise was merely a tool to restore feminine beauty and energy sapped by taxing college studies. Sports, in other words, helped a girl prepare for "vigorous womanhood," but only if done properly, following girls' rules. Instructors believed women's play should be "a sheltered refuge from a competitive and male-dominated society."[68]

Girls were directed to be sportswomen and not athletes, by women's sports governing bodies which called on colleges to emphasize intramurals over varsity play. By 1930, "play days" were the preferred practice for half the colleges in the country, according to a survey by the National Amateur Athletic Federation, which embraced the goal of "play for play's sake."[69] This principle endured into the 1960s. The low value placed on women's competition is evidenced in a 1950s anecdote about the University of North Carolina field hockey team. Because the team had no outdoor facilities of its own, games took place on the football field, when it was not being used by the men. They could not put markings on the field and were only permitted to use the end zone. In her book, feminist historian Mary Jo Festle reports the UNC field hockey team actually had to quit in the middle of an intercollegiate game when the marching band stormed onto the field for practice.[70] The obvious message: women's play didn't really matter. Such attitudes fit the social mandate that women not compete too rigorously or take themselves too seriously as athletes.

Class and Race

The conflict between female physical educators and the AAU also reflects the schism in women's sports around issues of class and race. The same cult of invalidism that had upper-class Victorian women embracing weakness as a sign of social status continued in a different vein into the twentieth century. Women who sweat, played too hard, or ran too fast challenged class codes. Even for Babe Didrikson, an unruly Texas girl who caused trouble in school, her athletic success was accompanied by criticism of her brusque manner and her masculine dress (that is, until she started wearing makeup and skirts). Nonetheless, for lower-class women less concerned about being tomboyish, sports offered a venue for recognition and success. Still, this was tricky territory to negotiate. The crusade against competition by educated white women (the physical education instructors) in effect narrowed the range of acceptable athletic practices that fit with notions of the right kind of play. This opened up opportunities for black female athletes, especially when physical education instructors deemed track and field inappropriate for females.

Track and Field

In track and field, the ghost of the 1928 Olympics loomed large. When several women collapsed after running the 800-meter race, organizers limited women's distance running for future games, a move which had a domino effect in limiting all women's distance running (women would not be allowed to compete in the Olympic Marathon until 1984), and serving as hard evidence (or so many insisted) for worries about female frailty. Frederick Rand Rogers penned a 1929 paper warning of dire health risks inherent in women's track and field competition. He warned it was "profoundly unnatural" for women and would interfere with reproductive functions.[71] At the same time, Lou Henry Hoover, President Herbert Hoover's wife, spearheaded an effort within the Women's Division of the National Amateur Athletic Federation (NAAF), to petition the International Olympic Committee to eliminate women's track and field altogether.[72] Female physical educators agreed that running "subjected women to debilitating physical, emotional, and sexual strains."[73]

Some (most notably the AAU) continued to encourage females to run track, but others pressed for its elimination. In the late 1950s female physical educators attacked the AAU, charging that high-level training in preparation for Olympic competition in 1956 was "exploiting our girls."[74] Colleges were urged to drop track programs. One NSGWS (National Section on Girls and Women's Sports, a predecessor of the NAGWS) leader proclaimed, "We no longer feel track and field meets the needs, socially or psychologically, of the modern college girl."[75] The message became even more sharply defined: Girls should not compete, period. "Sports for girls and women in this country should be conducted toward the complete development of the individual for the place she probably will occupy in American society as a wife, mother, or career woman," one physical education professor argued.[76]

As many schools ended their track programs, one notable program was born at the Tuskegee Institute in Alabama. Under coach Cleve Abbott, successive teams of African American women runners dominated track and field from 1937 to 1948. During Abbott's tenure from 1936 to 1955, Tuskegee athletes won 49 indoor and outdoor track individual titles and as a team won 14 national championships.[77] Among Abbott's six Olympic Gold Medalists were Alice Coachman and Mildred McDaniel, both inducted into the USA Track & Field Hall of Fame. Despite their tremendous accomplishments, news accounts—in both black and white press—marginalized these athletes. They presented particular challenges, not only because of their race and gender but because they participated in a male sport. Particularly in the white press, this led to the female runners being viewed as mannish.[78]

As a result, even as these runners produced a clear and enviable model of female strength, they confirmed derogatory beliefs about what it means to be black and a female athlete.[79] Even the black press criticized successful black female athletes, dismissing talent as "tomboyism" as did Sam Lacy, a sportswriter for the *Baltimore Afro-American*. In writing about tennis star Althea Gisbon in 1957, although she played an acceptably feminine sport, he argued that her success could be explained because she was a tomboy, "not only the best girl athlete in her community, but as good as most of the boys as well." This, he went on to say, was a problem. "In later life, the 'tomboy' finds herself victimized by complexes. Miss Gibson is no exception."[80]

Among black colleges and community organizations, there was also sensitivity to prevailing views of femininity, which were felt even more keenly than in white colleges. Some anxiety in the black community arose out of concern that overly aggressive black female athletes would be viewed as "immoral" or "uncivilized," labels that would stigmatize all African Americans.[81] In the end, the drive to ensure that African American women athletes were feminine prompted schools to drop women's basketball and track programs and to remind women that playing sports wouldn't help them find husbands. The threat that women of any race who were good at sports might not be marriageable persisted into the 1960s and 1970s.

Title IX and the 1970s

What is significant about the 1970s, however, is its legacy as the heyday of sameness feminism. A host of congressional legislation and court cases established that federal law and/or the Constitution required that men and women who were similarly situated be treated the same "in spite of" their sex. Granted, the Supreme Court never adopted the highest level of scrutiny when ruling on the constitutionality of treating people differently solely because of their sex, but the Court's adoption of intermediate scrutiny made it nearly impossible to defend policies that implemented sex discrimination. Consequently the 1970s witnessed the sex integration of academic opportunities, employment opportunities, and sex-integrated views of how men and women should be equal in the eyes of the law in spite of their group differences. It's striking that this sex-integrated model prevailed in every arena of American life, save one: sports.

The policy goal of Title IX was to open up admissions, scholarships, and other benefits of academic institutions of higher learning to men and women on an equal basis, as if men and women are the same in spite of their sex group difference. In the context of academic programs, Title IX did that. At the same time, the 1970s saw landmark legislation and Supreme Court decisions on issues as diverse as rape and equal access to credit, all rooted in the underlying belief that males and females should be treated the same legally. When it came to sports, however, Title IX diverged from the prevailing view and practice, treating females differently under the law. Sports, in other words, presented a special problem.

Inferiority

Women Are Not Worthy

Title IX, as many observe, opened doors. But the law came at a time when men's high school and college sports were ascending to new heights of popularity and commercial success. By comparison, historically dismal female athletics made the notion of true equality seem absurd. Many presumed women were not worthy of equality and were being given what they did not deserve, a point underscored in the male-run NCAA's 1975 newsletter, accusing the AIAW of seeking to finance women's athletics by "living on big brother's credit card" using income-oriented male athletic programs "to finance the females in the style to which they feel they should become accustomed."[82] Such a condescending rant ignored the fact that women contributed the federal tax dollars that benefited these same educational institutions now balking at sharing what had in the past belonged almost exclusively to male athletes.

A key problem with Title IX was that the law was not scheduled to be enforced until December 1978, six years after its passage. This invited debate about the wording of regulations and it fueled political maneuvering by male athletic directors, including the NCAA, which complained the cost of Title IX would cut into men's sports programs. There was also foot dragging by schools, which simply put off compliance, arguing they needed to wait for final regulations. Even after 1978, some still ignored the new rules, knowing full well of uncertainty at HEW about how to enforce them.

And yet Title IX is widely supported despite its compromising tone because it recognized sports were not just for males. Women could play too, and Title IX gave them ammunition to fight for that right. In March 1976, 19 members of the Yale women's crew team (and a *New York Times* reporter), emboldened by the law, charged into the athletic director's office. The women had been forced, after working out on the river, to wait, shivering, on the bus parked at the boathouse while the men's team took hot showers before the ride back to campus. The women stripped off shirts to reveal "Title IX" penned in blue marker on their breasts and backs. News traveled the world. Within a week, the women's crew team had showers.

Compliant Sex Discrimination

Such displays drew publicity, but disparity between sports offerings for males and females persisted. " 'Compliance' is not a synonym for 'equality,' " sports advocate Christine Grant of the University of Iowa observed at the time. "In reality, compliance could well be a synonym for 'continued discriminatory treatment.' "[83] She said policy interpretations of Title IX permitted her university to spend $3.5 million on men's sports and only $850,000 on women's.

The discrimination that continued seems stunning today because it underscores the belief that female athletes were simply less than male athletes. At a 1974 women's basketball game at the

University of Cincinnati, for example, officials cleared the women from court with five minutes remaining in a close game because the men's team wanted to warm up.[84] At the University of Minnesota, the women's swim team coach was paid less than minimum wage and swimmers practiced in a smaller pool than the men, which was available for fewer and inconvenient hours. Each male swimmer had a locker while 38 women shared two lockers. Women had no access to amenities men took for granted like parking spaces, hair dryers, and letter jackets. Women who needed athletic tape used the men's leftovers.[85]

Injury

Women also have been hampered by the presumption that they are more frail than males and need protection. This protective impulse is embedded in Title IX regulations barring females from male contact sports teams—a stance courts have ruled violates the Equal Protection Clause. Still, even as courts rejected the idea that females required special protection, schools and organizations kept making the argument, in part because it is rooted in cultural practice. Today, we still debate how close to danger female soldiers may be sent, even when danger is ill defined and has a way of seeking soldiers out, whether or not they intend to put themselves in harm's way. We see protectionist instincts in sports rules (Why should males who play ice hockey face the dangers inherent in checking while females are sheltered from hits?) and in slow acceptance of women participating in sports like wrestling and boxing.[86]

The idea of females engaging in dangerous activities is one set of concerns. The other set involves worries about the risk to females of playing with or against males, regardless of the danger of the activity itself. When Little League officials and their lawyers sought to bar girls, their argument focused on the presumption that eight- to twelve-year-old boys were stronger than eight- to twelve-year-old girls and that girls would be injured in mixed-sex play— arguments that were rejected in a November 1973 ruling by New Jersey civil rights examination officer Sylvia Pressler. And yet the worry that girls could get hurt has stuck.

History of Female Protection

Protectionist attitudes toward women are rooted in beliefs about feminine weakness and vulnerability that have been emphasized to various degrees throughout history. Ironically, measures meant to keep females safe have typically handicapped or injured them, whether financially, socially, or economically. When daredevil performances were popular in the late 1800s (think Houdini-like public exhibitions), an Englishwoman referred to in print only as "Miss Cove" fell to her death when her parachute failed to open during a stunt. The event triggered a call to expand the Children's Dangerous Performances Act of 1874 to include females, thereby imposing restrictive protections on adult women. At least one newspaper reporter wondered "whether it is just and logical to permit men and youths just over age to continue dangerous exhibitions in which children and women are forbidden to participate." Barring female performers from activities for their own good effectively denied these women a job and a livelihood.[87]

In the 1930s, American cowgirls faced a similar crisis. Until this time, several highly skilled female bronco riders earned more in yearly prize money than their male counterparts. But in 1929, popular cowgirl Bonnie McCarroll was thrown and trampled to death while competing as a bronco rider at the prestigious Pendleton Roundup. The public was horrified by her death, triggering a movement to halt female bronco riding altogether. By the 1940s, authentic cowgirls had been driven from the sport of bronco riding, replaced by more socially acceptable glamour girls on horseback who entertained audiences as costumed cowgirls but did not perform alongside cowboys. Ironically, McCarroll's fatal—and fateful—accident was the result of hobbled stirrups, which were considered more feminine (and acceptable) than the traditional slick riding she was known for.[88]

The public doesn't like to see anyone injured, particularly not children or women. This is true whether we speak of soldiers in a war zone or players on a field. Yet how much right or responsibility the state has to protect females is a matter of debate. Why, for example, should women be protected from injury when men are not? Shouldn't women be allowed to make up their own minds about how much risk of injury they are willing to tolerate on the same basis as men do? In the end, the question about female protection entails more than personal safety. It also involves propriety and the belief that women simply shouldn't engage in some activities.

Immorality

Couldn't and Shouldn't

The notion of males and females competing together also causes anxiety because *it feels wrong*. Some believe sex-segregated sports protect girls from the awful trauma of being beaten by boys; others offer that if or when girls beat boys the entire social order will collapse. One aspect of argument for sex segregation in sports, then, has been the belief that girls simply shouldn't play with boys. Even today, opinions differ about using male practice teams to help women's college basketball teams prepare for competition. In New Jersey, a girls' basketball team lost game after game to male opponents in a YMCA league during the 2006–2007 season, but accepted the losses as part of a learning curve that ultimately would make them better players.[89] Yet many debate whether such a strategy is appropriate.

In the early 1970s, before Title IX was fully vetted and regulated, it seemed all right. In the spring of 1972, the New Jersey State Athletic Association, which makes rules for high school sports, said schools could petition to allow girls on male sports teams. Between the March 23 announcement and April 30, 17 girls completed paperwork and were trying out or officially competing on formerly all-male sports teams while "many more girls are working out unofficially with boys' squads," the *New York Times* reported.[90] For many girls, playing with boys was not a big deal. Joann Eufemia, described in a news report as "a shy, pretty junior at Highstown High School," made her school's golf team. "I like it," she said. "We play nearly every day and we get to play on lots of different courses. I don't mind playing on a team with boys. I'm used to playing with my father and his friends. Somebody said it bothers some of the boys, and that surprised me. Maybe they're afraid I'll beat them."[91]

Before Title IX regulations were even drafted, a number of schools interpreted the law as meaning females had to be invited onto male teams. In September 1972, the Eastern College Athletic Conference announced females were eligible for all varsity teams at its 214 member institutions.[92] The rule change came about because Karen Wise, a junior at Windham College in Putney, Vermont, threatened legal action after being told her inclusion on the basketball team violated conference rules. Opening up conference play to females, however, was mostly a legal maneuver. As Eastern College Athletic Conference legal counsel George Bisacca made clear, "All we're doing is opening it up so you can use women. You don't have to."[93] But some did. Maurice Zarchen, University of Rhode Island athletic director, was more than happy to invite Patt Cooke, Rhode Island women's amateur golf champion, to join the school's varsity team.[94]

Despite such cases of forced and voluntary inclusion, many other sports governing bodies simply couldn't conceive of a place for females in the male universe of competitive athletics. A June 1973 report by the Pennsylvania Education Committee provided to the National Organization for Women, for example, offered budget allotment figures for several school districts showing gross inequities between budgets and athletic offerings for boys and girls. In Pittsburgh, high school boys could choose from 10 sports and had an annual athletic allocation of $323,868. Girls had zero—no sports, no dollars. In the much smaller Monaca School District, high school boys had four sports and $20,700, junior high school boys had two sports and $3,750. Girls in junior high and high school had zero—no sports, no dollars.[95]

Authors of the report saw the problem plainly. The Pennsylvania Interscholastic Athletic Board had 19 men and no women and included in its bylaws a problematic rule in Article 19. Section B states, "Girls shall not compete or practice against boys in any athletic contest." This was the practice and control one feminist activist pinpointed when she observed that "these state athletic associations are bastions of sexism."[96]

Interestingly, there was no objection to another stipulation in Article 19 demanding schools "encourage ladylike qualities in girls' sports participation" and that females wear clothing "which is clean and so designed and worn as not to be objectionable or sensational."[97] Such stipulations reveal the bias and the fears of men in charge of athletic programs at the time. To them, female athletes were a socially disruptive threat and an incursion into male territory. This was not about sports ability or even about protecting females from injury. Rather, it was about gender and power, about moral codes and cultural mores. Girls could play, but they had to be feminine so that real sports for males could remain celebrated displays of masculinity. To do otherwise would constitute an immoral disturbance of society.

The "Mannish" Woman

Female physical educators' drive to keep play feminine, like AAU efforts to make athletes appear sexy, were not mere reflections of those organizational cultures. They addressed worries about homosexuality. There was plenty of ordinary concern that female athletes might behave in a manner unbecoming their gender. But increasingly, beginning in the early 1900s, many feared females with man-like athletic prowess might become manlike in their sexual preference. From 1896 to 1916 there were 566 articles published on female sexual "perversions," "inversions," and "disorders."[98] Despite such concerns, actual talk about homosexuality remained below the surface. "Had nature intended for her to compete in man's sports she would have been differently constructed anatomically," observed Harvard President Charles W. Elliot in a 1904 newspaper story questioning the appropriateness of women playing basketball.[99] His comments were part of a public debate about "the extent, if any, to which basketball and athletics made women masculine."[100] While proper female sports such as field hockey, dance, and tennis did not challenge gender roles or require gender-inappropriate behavior, basketball, baseball, and track did.

This was initially more of a point of caution, given women's growing independence in many areas of society. By the 1920s, after all, flappers had brought a coy sexuality and freedom to women's public behavior, a sort of gender liberation coming after women first filled male responsibilities at home during World War I and earned the right to vote in 1920. World War II saw women assuming male jobs and roles on an even larger scale. However, the end of the war signaled an about-face, and by the late 1940s and into the 1950s and 1960s there was a fervent, almost frenetic return to traditional gender roles.

The 1930s, however, marked a key shift. Athletics moved from symbolizing the New Woman to becoming a suspect activity. Women athletes who in the past were thought to develop ugly masculine muscles, now might, owing to the passion that sports stirred, develop masculine sexual interests as well. Experts asked, if the excitement of sports drove females into a state of hysteria in which their feminine quality of control gave way to masculine fervor, might they eschew heterosexuality for female love? Could sports transform ordinary women into deviant Amazons?[101]

There was no shortage of warnings. One expert in the 1930s intoned that "girls trained in physical education to-day may find it more difficult to attract the most worthy fathers for their children."[102] The suspicions didn't fade. In 1960, a *New York Times Magazine* headline asked, "Do Men Make Passes At Athletic Lasses?"[103] The answer, the reader learns, is no. The warning that athletic women would fail to attract dates and husbands did little to lure females to sports.

From Mannish to Lesbian

This connection between athletic play and heterosexuality was a new calculus in the male-female dichotomy that had ruled social views of sports. Athletics always involved asserting one's virility. Yet that quality was not so much sexual as symbolic of masculinity in its broadest form. In other words, sports were a means for demonstrating strength, aggressiveness, leadership, and other male characteristics. Now there arose a more explicit connection between male athletics and sexual power. Being a successful male athlete now included the presumption of male heterosexual potency. This created problems for women and gays. "Normal" women were not aggressive and athletic. Women who were good at sports, the thinking went, must be lesbians.

The reverse was also true: male athletes weren't gay. The stigma of being abnormal in an aggressively heterosexual culture of men's sports is to blame for the secrecy around gay male athletes.[104] The public and media responses to athletes' revelations of exposure to the HIV virus underscore the degree to which athletics—particularly on the professional level—are a highly sexualized and heterosexual environment.

When two heterosexuals, basketball great Magic Johnson and boxer Tommy Morrison, revealed they had been exposed to the HIV virus, news coverage emphasized their sexual potency and masculinity. It cast them as making innocent mistakes while trying to accommodate the women clamoring for sex, just red-blooded men unable to resist temptation.[105] In contrast, when openly gay swimmer Greg Louganis announced his HIV-positive status, some suggested that the disease was a "natural and expected part of the gay life course." Coverage was more concerned with the hetero-sexual people working at the 1988 Olympics who may have come in contact with Louganis's blood than possible risk to the swimmer's sexual partners.[106]

The connection between athletic females and homosexuality has some basis in reality. Sports have traditionally provided a safe place for lesbians to connect, and a site in which gay women can eschew ultrafeminine expectations in dress and grooming without attracting individual attention.[107] At the same time, however, the overplayed stereotype of female athletes as mannish lesbians has suppressed the popularity of women's sports, support for female athletes, and the recruitment of straight females into sport. Such cultural pressures had a clear result, particularly in the 1940s and 1950s: females simply didn't play as hard, if they played at all. Those talented female athletes who did play well developed an apologetic stance, trying to compensate for their athletic ability by overemphasizing feminine dress, makeup, or mannerisms.

In other words, the sense that athletics are male has colored and complicated women's entry into sports, erecting barriers with long histories and deep roots. The false assumption of female physical inferiority and the social mandate to protect women from injury (even when the protection *is* the injury) have formed the basis for arguments—in courts and in conversations—for why females and males should have sex-segregated athletics. When those arguments fail, another potent barrier appears: the cultural belief that girls just plain shouldn't play with boys.

Croquet was a popular sport among men and women while courting, though women (known as skilled players) were widely accused of cheating. This 1875 engraving shows four men and three women playing croquet indoors during a Saratoga, New York, storm. Schlesinger Library, Radcliffe Institute, Harvard University.

This 1877 depiction of "muscular womanhood" illustrates the sort of gentle exercise designed to enhance female roles, making women fit to bear and raise children, but not to overexert themselves. Sally Fox Collection, Schlesinger Library, Radcliffe Institute, Harvard University.

Celebrated as the first college women's basketball game on the West Coast, the May 1896 contest between Berkeley and Stanford attracted "700 women of fashion" and required police to keep males (who were barred from attending) off the roof and out of passageways leading to the Page Street armory. Stanford won, 2–1. Sally Fox Collection, Schlesinger Library, Radcliffe Institute, Harvard University.

This postcard from the early 1900s relayed a message that has been directed at women for generations in different forms: playing sports threatens one's feminine appeal (or as a 1960s *New York Times Magazine* headline put it, "Do Men Make Passes at Athletic Lasses?"). Sally Fox Collection, Schlesinger Library, Radcliffe Institute, Harvard University.

HER CURVES CONFUSED THE MIGHTY BABE

While other girls her age were thinking of parties, dances and dates, Miss Jackie Mitchell, newest recruit of the Chattanooga Lookouts' baseball team of the Southern association, dreamed of a career with an organized baseball team. Her present chance, she confides, is an answer to that dream. The layout above present three characteristic views of the pretty high school girl. At the left she is shown with her father, Dr. Joe Mitchell, an ardent baseball fan, who encouraged her love for the game. Below, in the inset she is shown stirring a cake batter in the kitchen of the Mitchell home. On the right she is the southpaw wonder.

After Chattanooga Lookout left-handed pitcher Jackie Mitchell struck out Babe Ruth and Lou Gehrig on April 5, 1931, a newspaper photo montage carefully emphasized her feminine side by showing her "stirring a cake batter in the kitchen." *Helena Daily Independent.*

Helene Mayer (right) fences against Olympic gold medalist Nedo Nadi of Italy in this 1935 photo, the same year Mayer beat out all male competitors and became the men's fencing champion of the San Francisco division of the Amateur Fencer's League of America—until fencing officials passed new rules and revoked her title. Bettmann/CORBIS.

Girls were instructed not to overexert themselves physically during menstruation, as in this 1940 Kotex pamphlet *As One Girl to Another*. Image courtesy of Harry Finley, Museum of Menstruation (www.mum.org).

Members of the Women's Army Auxiliary Corps took part in physical training exercises (this one in 1943) to prepare for assignments during World War II. Schlesinger Library, Radcliffe Institute, Harvard University.

Tennis star Althea Gibson (shown in this June 1957 photo at Wimbledon) was such a superior athlete that Sam Lacy, sportswriter for the *Baltimore Afro-American,* declared her "not only the best girl athlete in her community, but as good as most of the boys as well," which, he emphasized, was not necessarily a good thing. Bettmann/CORBIS.

One year after Bobbi Gibb (disguised in her brother's shorts and hooded sweatshirt) sneaked onto the course to become the first woman to unofficially run the Boston Marathon, Kathy Switzer registered without revealing her sex. During the marathon on April 19, 1967, trainer Jock Semple (in street clothes) tried to pull Switzer from the race, but male runners surrounded her and Semple was wedged off the race course. Donald L. Robinson/Bettmann /CORBIS.

On September 30, 1973, Billie Jean King vs. Bobby Riggs was billed as the "Battle of the Sexes." Before 30,472 spectators in the Houston Astrodome—and 50 million more on TV—King dispatched Riggs in three straight sets, 6–4, 6–3, 6–3. Focus on Sport/Getty Images.

After twelve-year-old Maria Pepe was removed from her Hoboken, New Jersey, Little League team in the spring of 1973 because of her sex, the National Organization for Women successfully challenged the "no girls" rule on her behalf. The decision spurred protests but eventually forced Little League to admit girls. Bettmann/CORBIS.

Rifle shooter Margaret Murdock competed alongside male teammates and competitors before international and Olympic events were divided by gender. At the 1976 Olympics in Montreal, Murdock and teammate Lanny Basham tied for first place in the 50 meter three-position event, until judges broke the tie and awarded Basham the gold medal and Murdock the silver. Basham invited Murdock to share the gold medal platform. Photo courtesy of Margaret Murdock.

The packed stadiums and huge fan following for the 1999 U.S. women's soccer team caught the media off guard, but was powerful enough to trigger the launch of a professional women's soccer league. Rose Bowl Stadium spectators went wild on July 10 as the United States beat China in a 5–4 shootout to win the World Cup Final. Tore Bergsaker/Sygma/CORBIS.

After scoring the winning penalty kick, U.S. women's soccer team midfielder Brandi Chastain ripped off her jersey revealing her sports bra and her buff physique in what became one of the most talked about images of the 1999 Women's World Cup win. Mike Blake/Reuters/CORBIS.

When British marathoner Paula Radcliffe crossed the finish line of the London Marathon on April 13, 2003, in 2:15:25, she set a women's record that has yet to be broken and became the fastest British marathoner, male or female. Warren Little/2003 Getty Images.

Annika Sorenstam clenched her fist as she birdied the 13th hole during the first round of the Colonial PGA golf tournament in Fort Worth, Texas, on May 22, 2003. She became the first women in fifty-eight years (since Babe Didrickson) to play in a men's PGA event. Although she wowed spectators in the first round, she performed less well in the second round and failed to make the cut. Kevin Lamarque/Reuters/CORBIS.

When former Presidents George Bush and Bill Clinton set out to raise money and awareness for tsunami victims in Southeast Asia, they chose the biggest stage in America: the Super Bowl. The easy comfort between political and athletic power is on display February 6, 2005, at the Super Bowl XXXIX Fox Sports desk as broadcaster (and former NFL quarterback) Terry Bradshaw chums it up before the game with Bush and Clinton. Frank Micelotta/2005 Getty Images.

Candace Parker, who is 6'4", dunks the ball against Lateefah Joyce of West Virginia on December 20, 2006, more than a year after she became the first female player to dunk in a college game. In high school, she was the first female to win a slam dunk contest, beating out male contenders in the 2004 McDonald's All-American event. In April 2007, she led the University of Tennessee to the NCAA Division I Championship and was named the tournament's Most Outstanding Player.

BREAKING BARRIERS

Joe, we're depending on those muscles for America.
> —Franklin Roosevelt, speaking to Joe Louis
> before the 1938 World Heavyweight boxing match.[1]

No one can make you feel inferior without your consent.
> —Eleanor Roosevelt[2]

Sports as a Political Tool

So far we have argued that sports are more than entertainment, that they represent a site which reflects, reinforces, and constructs the meaning of race, class, and sex differences in American society. Beyond that, athletics can also be used to challenge inequalities and injustices that are inconsistent with the egalitarian promise of American society. We often see sports used as a conservative tool to maintain social, economic, and political inequalities and injustices. But sports can just as well be a transformative tool for deconstructing social norms that perpetuate old hierarchies and stereotypes of racial, class, and gender groups, thus producing what some refer to as the paradox of sports.[3]

What is critical to the culture of a democratic society is not so much what sports are played as how they are played. Sports were once segregated by race, thereby reflecting racial inequalities, injustices, and tensions in American society. Such policies mirrored assumptions that African Americans were inferior to whites in general, a flawed belief then extended to sports. The racial segregation of sports competitions reflected and reinforced racial segregation as an operating principle in the American state. This, in turn, supported underlying assumptions about the racial inferiority of African Americans and the social impropriety of whites and blacks interacting, which included playing sports together.

Challenging race barriers in sports has taken years. Despite important watersheds (including the first meeting in the Super Bowl between two African American head coaches on February 4, 2007) blacks are still seeking representative access to key power positions in sports. And yet these are active debates and crusades. Sports are an active site for social and political transformation.[4] Many sporting events are charged with racial significance, but one compelling example remains the boxing matches between American Joe Louis, known as "the Brown Bomber," and German Max Schmeling, idealized and celebrated by the Nazis as a symbol of Aryan supremacy. When the two met for the first time on June 19, 1936, tension ran so high that the Associated Press the next day reported officials attributed 12 deaths to excitement over the radio broadcast of the Louis-Schmeling fight.[5] After Schmeling knocked out Louis in the twelfth round to win the match, street fights broke out in Harlem.[6] In Germany, Joseph Goebbels, Hitler's propaganda minister, cabled congratulations to Schmeling: "I know you fought for Germany; that it's a German victory. We are proud of you. Heil Hitler. Regards."[7] Hitler soon added his congratulations,[8] along with flowers and, later, an invitation to lunch with the *Führer*.[9] Although boxing was not very popular in Germany at the time, Schmeling was a national hero. This was not just a sporting event but a many-layered political bout.

Two years later, when Louis and Schmeling met again on June 22, 1938, the stage had been set. This boxing match was weighted with meaning far beyond the two individual men. A member of the German Boxing Commission described Schmeling as our "Sport Soldier No. 1."[10] Louis, however, was ready for the rematch. Anticipation before the fight was so great that when Louis was visiting

Washington, D.C., for the Negro Elks Convention, President Franklin Delano Roosevelt heard about him being in an Elks parade and sent a car to bring him to the White House. As Louis described it a decade later, "The President had me lean over so he could feel my muscles. He said, 'Joe, we need muscles like yours to beat Germany.' "[11] Louis said he knew that "the whole damned country was depending on me." No wonder sports analysts, like Dave Kindred of the *Sporting News*, argued that no fight ever "carried more symbolic weight than the Louis-Schmeling" fight of 1938. Needless to say, Louis was determined to win. As he sat the night before the match with his friend, sportswriter Jimmy Cannon, Cannon surmised Louis was aiming for a knock-out victory, which had been his calling card in past fights. Cannon estimated aloud that it would take six rounds. "No," Louis said, "one."[12]

Louis was right. He defeated Schmeling in the first round in two minutes and four seconds before 80,000 spectators.[13] The victory set off celebrations around the country. Newspapers reported street dancing and firecrackers going off in Chicago's black neighborhoods and elsewhere.[14] The lesson of the Louis victory was unmistakably resonant. As American sportswriter Heywood Broun wrote at the time in the *New York World-Telegram*, "One hundred years from now some historian may theorize, in a footnote at least, that the decline of the Nazi prestige began with a left hook delivered by a former unskilled automotive worker who had never studied the policies of Neville Chamberlain and had no opinion whatever in regard to the situation in Czechoslovakia."[15] Clearly, however, this sports competition had a potent meaning within American society. It is safe to say that by opening the door to black boxers, Louis led the way for African Americans in other sports to break racial barriers.

Integrating Baseball and Football

When the Brooklyn Dodgers and their farm club, the Montreal Royals, signed Jackie Robinson in 1946, it was widely seen as the beginning of racial integration in modern professional sports in America. Although players "believed to have some Negro blood" had played in professional baseball, it was done by designating them as Cuban, Mexican, or Indian, thus skirting political controversy. However, in Robinson's case, the *New York Times* noted in 1946,

"No attempt has been made to disguise Robinson's racial heritage. He is a test case."[16]

He was not, however, the first or only black athlete to compete on a public stage. Many high schools and colleges (particularly in the North) had black athletes on football, baseball, and track teams, but the status of baseball in America at the time made his inclusion symbolically significant. Meanwhile, a similar drama of integration was playing out in professional football, adding weight to the political resonance of athletic integration. In 1946, pro football was in its twelfth straight season as an all-white league, not by rule but by custom. And yet it was increasingly clear that ignoring talented black college football players made no competitive sense. In 1946, Cleveland's Paul Brown (they would join the NFL a few years later as the Cleveland Browns), signed Marion Motley and Bill Willis[17] and the Los Angeles Rams signed black players Kenny Washington (Jackie Robinson's classmate at UCLA) and Woody Strode, who later became a film star.[18]

Such action was important to the cause of racial integration. For Washington, who languished in low-level pro football for a decade before joining the Rams, his signing was symbolic because his best years of playing had been lost to a segregated system. And yet his star power (he was considered the best player in the 1930s at UCLA) helped break down the race barrier in pro football. The situation arose because the Rams needed to use the Los Angeles Coliseum, and Leonard Roach, Coliseum Commission chairman, made it clear he was "against Jim Crow, not only in football, but in all other forms."[19] To get access to the facility, the team signed Washington and Strode.

Despite the inclusion of black players on professional baseball and football teams, it would be years before civil rights laws took effect. And yet these black athletes—difficult as it was individually—made sports a site for displaying the absurdity of racial segregation. When Jackie Robinson's farm team, the Montreal Royals, were to play the Giants' Jersey City farm team, the Little Giants, in Jacksonville, Florida, reporters covered his exclusion.

The City of Jacksonville owned the public park where the two teams were to play in March 1946, and recreational park rules specified that, according to playground executive secretary George G. Robinson, "Negroes and whites cannot compete against each other on a city-owned playground." Dodger President Branch Rickey said he would not send Robinson or black teammate John Wright to Florida but said he was not pleased: "We will not take the onus for this thing. Let there be no misunderstanding about that."[20]

Sports, then, became a vehicle for challenging assumptions about racial segregation, based on wrongheaded notions of black inferiority and the sense that integration wasn't socially appropriate. It became clear to spectators, fans, fellow players, and team coaches and owners that they needed black players to compete. Barring them was unfair and foolish. That doesn't mean these players didn't suffer personal attacks (including unfair and illegal hitting and physical attacks in football) and hurtful exclusions.[21] But the highly visible challenges being made to race segregation in sports aided parallel arguments about the ills of race segregation in society and helped propel the issue into the courts. In 1954, the critical Supreme Court ruling that "separate is not equal" in the context of public education launched the civil rights movement. So by 1962, when Washington Redskins owner George Preston Marshall continued to bar black players from his team, President John F. Kennedy was able to challenge him on legal and not just social grounds, using anti-discrimination laws that made it illegal to deny blacks a place on a team that played in a stadium built on federal land.[22]

What about Women?

While women have faced similar presumptions about their lack of fitness as athletes and the propriety of their inclusion in sports, they have been less successful than African Americans in using the athletic field as a tool for political gain. While the Anglo-American psyche was able to overcome myths of white athletic supremacy to appreciate and accept the black athlete, women have made no such strides. Women have beaten or out performed men, but rather than yielding recognition of female power, such results have spurred suppression.

Baseball: Striking out Babe Ruth

In 1931, 17-year-old pitcher Virne "Jackie" Mitchell became the second woman in history to sign a professional baseball contract when she was recruited to play for the all-male AA Chattanooga

Lookouts by owner Joe Engel. On April 2, 1931, Mitchell pitched in an exhibition game against the Yankees, playing before a crowd of 4,000, including press. After Mitchell struck out both Babe Ruth and Lou Gehrig, she was pulled from the game. A few days later the baseball commissioner, Kennesaw Mountain Landis, voided Mitchell's contract, saying baseball was "too strenuous for a woman."[23] Judge Landis's reasoning appeared to embrace general concerns about female physical frailty, but it's hard not to read the greater worry. How does it look when a 17-year-old girl strikes out two future Hall of Fame hitters?

Interestingly, one newspaper account minimizes Mitchell's skills, saying that "Babe politely lifted his hat to the first woman ever to crash what hitherto has been considered a purely stag affair," and suggesting in the subhead that "Babe and Lou ... Didn't Try Very Hard."[24] By contrast, another newspaper account acknowledges her skill with the headline "Her Curves Confused The Mighty Babe," but emphasizes her femininity by juxtaposing a photo of Mitchell as "a southpaw wonder" beside two other photos, including one in which "she is shown stirring a cake batter in the kitchen of the Mitchell home."[25]

A similar contract-canceling fate befell shortstop Eleanor Engle in June 1952, though she was ultimately excluded with the blunt argument that women simply should not play baseball. Two days after Engle signed a minor league contract with the AA Harrisburg Senators, Minor League head George Trautman voided it, saying "such travesties will not be tolerated."[26]

At the recreational level, teen baseball player Margaret Gisolo had a similar experience after she created a national furor in 1928. Gisolo, 14, played second base for the Blanford, Indiana, American Legion team, batting .455 and helping her team win the Indiana state title.[27] Like other females, Gisolo became the target of protests, not because she wasn't able to compete with the boys but because she was too good. While the Legion program was intended for boys only, the rules did not explicitly state this. Tension boiled over after a game on June 18, 1928, in which Gisolo's team played against a Clinton, Indiana, team to see who would advance in the American Legion tournament. After 12 innings, the score was tied 7-7. When Gisolo came to bat and singled, driving in the run that would win the game 8-7, she had already stolen three bases and handled 10 plays in the field. The Clinton coach was furious and protested the game, arguing that, as one newspaper account put it, "the rules did not provide for girls to compete with boys and that by playing Margaret, Blanford had used an ineligible player."[28] The league commissioner (ironically, after consulting with Commissioner Landis) ruled Gisolo eligible because rules did not exclude female players.[29] After the season, the rules were changed to explicitly prohibit girls from playing.[30]

Fencing

Helene Mayer was a phenomenal fencer. However, because she was female, her impressive talent created "a unique problem in national sportsdom," according to a February 1935 news article whose headline reveals the conflict: "Blonde German Girl Threatens To Win Men's Fencing Title."[31] The story describes how 24-year-old Mayer, a 5 foot 10, 150-pound woman who had fenced since she was 11 years old, beat out all male contenders to earn the men's fencing champion title of the San Francisco division of the Amateur Fencers' League of America.[32] Mayer, a naturalized German émigré who was an instructor at Mills College, was qualified to compete for the Pacific Coast men's championship as a result of her San Francisco win. That is, until New York fencing officials objected, quickly passing a ruling and revoking her title.[33] A 1938 article notes Mayer's championship status was revoked "after she held the title for a day or two" on the grounds that "fencing involved a form of bodily contact, even though it was just with the tip of a foil, and that a chivalrous man found it difficult to do his worst when he faced a woman."[34]

Swimming

From the afternoon in 1918 when Sybil Bauer was noticed by a swim coach at the Illinois Athletic Club (which had just begun allowing females into the pool), it was clear she had exceptional athletic talent.[35] Bauer would have a brief (she died at age 23) but stunning swim career. By the time she died in 1927, she held 23 world records. During an October 1922 swim meet in Bermuda, Bauer broke three world records in the backstroke, including the men's world record in the 440-yard event. Bauer cut four seconds off the record previously held by Harold Krueger of Honolulu. The *New York Times* buried the story on page 19, but the headline relayed the magnitude of the feat: "Woman Breaks Man's Record For First Time in Swim History."[36] She later beat even that record, bettering her time by another second to 6:23.

Bauer was such a dominant backstroke swimmer that she sought to compete with men at the 1924 Olympics. As a February 1924 editorial in *The Nation* noted, "No man in the annals of sport has finished the quarter-mile back-stroke swim within five seconds of Miss Sybil Bauer's time, and naturally Miss Bauer wants to enter the regular event in the Olympic games."[37] Bauer, described by the writer as "a woman who can outclass all the women in her field and all the men as well," simply wanted to compete at an appropriate level during an era when women's events were not taken seriously. After all, the writer noted, "women of today have had only a few years of participation in sport," and few pursued athletic competition with any rigor.[38]

A *New York Times* writer framed the matter on many minds: "Is it conceivable that a woman shall be allowed to compete against men?"[39] The answer would be no. The Olympic rules committee quickly turned down her request. Bauer would not be allowed to defend her record against male challengers.[40] The problem was evident: Bauer upset the gender order and news accounts said so, describing her request as "a modest invasion of men's rights"[41] and suggesting the problem with her competing against males was that keeping sexes separate had "ages of precedent behind it, and therefore is not to be sneezed at."[42]

By the time Bauer died in a Chicago hospital from an illness described as a cold, her accomplishments were cast as impressive but unnatural. She was referred to in news accounts as a "mermaid," suggesting she was not fully human.[43] Some reports blamed Bauer's death on the physical strain of competitive swimming. "Sybil Bauer's Death Caused by Exertions," was the headline of one newspaper article.[44] The writer noted Bauer "died in a Chicago hospital the other day but she really killed herself a year ago," referring to a 1926 AAU swim meet in St. Augustine, Florida, at which Bauer broke two of her own world records.[45]

Victorian Pedestrians

The rise and fall of the walking craze that gripped America and England from the 1850s to the turn of the twentieth century reveal the difficulty that ensues when females outperform males. The craze highlights a fascinating conflict between the Victorian image of female physical frailty and the spectacle of women "pedestriennes" walking with impressive speed and endurance. It also reveals the perceived connection between physical vigor and political power.

There was not a single format for what were known as walking matches, but the proliferation of contests offered a stage on which women could (in some instances) compete directly with men. News accounts of the time reported that at some contests thousands of paying spectators (some even bought season tickets to walking events) gathered to watch both male and female walkers either in separate matches or against one another. Walking matches took different forms, comprising either a preset distance with walkers making laps of a track to see who could complete the distance most quickly or a time-limited event in which whoever covered the most ground in the time allotted was the winner. Still other matches were mere efforts of endurance. Pedestrians might walk around a track, a course, or between cities.

Distances varied radically, with one Ohio match for women over 75 lasting a mere four miles, while others spanned hundreds of miles.[46] One *New York Times* report heralded Chicago pedestrian May Marshall, who in Washington, D.C., broke a record held by Ada Anderson, who had popularized walking events as entertainment. Marshall also beat male challengers. In November 1876, she out walked pedestrian Peter Van Ness in Central Park Garden, turning in a better time for 20 miles and earning a $500 purse.[47] Marshall also beat Van Ness in a February 1876 walking match.[48] Marshall competed in a hundred-mile walking match in Jamestown, New York, against Daniel Carroll, beating him to earn $400. A local newspaper said that Marshall "kept one lap ahead from the 53rd mile."[49] Female pedestrians also appeared as celebrity guests to spur on male contestants in hometown fund-raisers.

In his study of the walking craze, historian Dahn Shaulis observes the tension between women's impressive physical feats and Victorian moral codes.[50] News accounts express this conflict, at some points reporting walking feats as laudable examples of "physical culture," and at others betraying disgust. One 1879 news report disdainfully reported, "the pitiful spectacle of 18 women starting on a six days' walk for money prizes was witnessed by about 1,000 spectators in Gilmore's Garden last evening." The writer notes approvingly that one woman "was withdrawn from the contest by her husband."[51] A later report on the same contest, in which several contestants had dropped out, is interpreted as all the evidence needed to "show the disastrous effect of such a terrible strain upon the constitution of the average woman." The subhead plays up the point, noting that "one of those who retired [was] seriously injured, and another insane."[52]

It may be difficult today to appreciate the appeal of walking contests, but clearly these female pedestrians displayed striking, even riveting physical strength and endurance. Their feats were so impressive that suffragists pointed to female walkers to counter arguments that women were too weak to handle the responsibilities of full citizenship, including the vote. Pedestrian Bertha Von Hillern, who drew thousands of spectators to days-long walking contests, was not interested in challenging Victorian moral codes, but others were quick to see political value in her physical vigor. As one suffrage newspaper writer argued, Von Hillern's walking 350 miles in six consecutive days and nights "seems to me the most effective answer to Dr. Clarke's 'Sex in Education,' ... She would certainly convince the strongest men who might undertake to walk with her, that the human female ... is quite as enduring as the male."[53]

Physical accomplishments, many wise women saw, were tools to refute political limitations, including those opposed to woman suffrage. As one writer observed, "To-day it is the walking match; next it will be the coveted entrance to the Bar. After that, who shall tell how soon the ballot will come."[54] The conflict inherent in the act of "frail" women walking hundreds of miles—even beating men in some cases—fed the collapse of the walking craze, as editorial opinion turned, casting walking as dangerous to women's health, disgusting, and immoral. One tabloid writer charged contests were fronts for thieves and prostitutes. Soon walking contests were sneered at or prohibited altogether. What had been a glorious example of female physical vigor and victory became unseemly and illegitimate, quashed the moment it was interpreted as a threat to male power. This would be a pattern repeated in the future.

Women Opposed to Women's Equality

Men were not the only ones concerned about how women's athletic accomplishments might upstage the old gender order. Plenty of women were unhappy as well. This resistance to women's progress by other women is a familiar subtext in the evolution of women's quest for equal rights. One obvious example is the woman suffrage movement in which support and opposition did not fall along gender lines. In addition to local antisuffrage organizations, in 1911 the National Association Opposed to Woman Suffrage was organized in New York.[55] These groups framed woman suffrage as destructive to women's best interests. As Helen Kendrick Johnson put it in a 1913 publication, it was foolish for women to seek "the most horrible of conflicts—that of Sex. So far from the 'taking of the ballot' being 'trivial,' it is the most serious and dangerous business in which a woman can engage. The home is not a natural institution unless it is maintained by natural means, and woman suffrage and the home are incompatible."[56]

The Eagle Forum

Today, of course, we have Phyllis Schlafly and her Eagle Forum, a platform she uses to advance traditional views of women as domestic beings who should stay home and care for children, in contrast to men, whose masculinity is needed in the military and in the workplace. Schlafly condemns feminists for seeking government-supported day care facilities so that women can participate more equally in the workforce with men. As she puts it, "The daycare issue . . . [is] the heart of feminist ideology . . . Feminist ideology teaches that equality for women depends on the government relieving women of the burden of child care so they can advance in the labor force."[57] Similarly, it is the masculinity of men upon which the nation depends in times of domestic and international crisis. As she states,

> One of the unintended consequences of the terrorist attack on the World Trade Center on September 11, 2001, was the dashing of feminist hopes to make America a gender-neutral or androgynous society. New York City's firemen dared to charge up the stairs of the burning Twin Towers, and the firefighters' death tally was: men 343, women 0. . . .

The feminists had made repeated attempts to sex-integrate New York's fire department through litigation, even though the women could not pass the physical tests. They even persuaded a judge to rule that upper body strength is largely irrelevant to firefighting. But September 11th called for all the masculine strength that strong men could muster. Firefighting is clearly a job for real men to do the heavy-lifting, not affirmative-action women.[58]

Similarly, Schlafly proclaims,

President George W. Bush sent our Special Forces to the rugged and remote Afghan hills and caves to get the terrorists, dead or alive. Fighting the Taliban is a job for real men. When the national media interviewed some of our Marines, one of our guys said, "There's no place I'd rather be than here." America is fortunate that the warrior culture has survived 30 years of feminist fantasies and that some men are still macho enough to relish the opportunity to engage and kill the bad guys of the world. . . .[the goal of feminists] has always been careerism for female officers at the expense of combat readiness. With a real war going on, this is no time to try to appease the unappeasable feminists in their perennial pursuit of an androgynous military.[59]

Not All Differences Are the Same

The point to remember, therefore, when addressing the issue of women's equality with men in American society, from both historical and contemporary perspectives, and on all issues—from suffrage, to the military, to the workplace, to abortion rights, to sports—is that support for women's equality does not split down gender lines. Some men and, of course, some women support sameness feminism, namely, they support policy goals that give to women who have the same abilities as men the same opportunities in society to exercise and develop those abilities.

Also, as we would expect, some men deplore sameness feminism. However, what is unique when it comes to women as a subordinate group is that so too do many women.[60] This is because sex is such a different attribute than all other ascriptive group differences we acquire accidentally at birth: race, economic background, religious background, linguistic heritage, and what country, as well as which historical period we are born in. The difference is that when subordinate groups such as African Americans use sameness arguments to advance their equality in American society, despite many in the dominant racial group (whites) opposing such change, there is no segment of the African American population that formally organizes itself to oppose changes that confer on them equal rights in relation to whites.

Both women and blacks have advocacy groups to advance their equality in American society. Indeed, the National Organization for Women was established in 1968 as a counterpart to the NAACP, which was founded in 1909. However, blacks have no counterpart to Phyllis Schlafly's Eagle Forum, nor did blacks have any organizational counterpart to antisuffrage leagues that women established to oppose their *own* enfranchisement.

What is significant about sex as an ascriptive group difference and about women as a subordinate group in American society compared to men, therefore, is that the couldn't and shouldn't mantra based on concerns related to women's inferiority, women's injury, and women's immorality is not limited to male concerns about changing the gender order, but also to female concerns. Consequently, when we examine the history of how sports policies became so gendered—and the tenacity of that gendering even today—we see that coercively sex-segregated sports policies are a product not only of male bias that views women as inferior but of female bias that aligns with those male beliefs. We can see this in the "feminine bargain" that was struck in the 1950s.

The "Feminine Bargain"

A Rude Awakening

President Dwight D. Eisenhower, an avid sports fan, observed after watching a US-USSR track meet that "athletic competition can perhaps, in the end, prove more effective than the most skilled diplomatic maneuver."[61] Eisenhower in 1956 launched the President's Council on Youth Fitness whose research concluded Americans were growing physically "soft." Meanwhile, citizens read about studies in which American children were less fit than foreign peers, including one showing British girls outscoring American boys.[62] Concern about poor fitness fed displeasure with America's athletic showing in world competition, spurring the council's executive director to argue that in getting America "off its seat and onto its feet, the victories in the field of international competition will inevitably follow."[63]

The problem, of course, was that while the United States had dominated most Olympic Games held before the 1950s, that dominance faded when the Soviet Union joined the Olympics in 1952. Suddenly, communist Russia was surpassing U.S. medal counts by wide margins. In 1956, the Soviets won 98 medals to the Americans' 74; in 1960, 103 to 71.[64]

America was losing the athletic cold war and one big reason, political leaders concluded, was because U.S. females were being soundly beaten by their Soviet rivals. At the 1960 Olympic Games, for example, Soviet women earned more than twice as many medals as American women, 28 to 12. A 1963 *Sports Illustrated* article asked, "Why Can't We Beat This Girl?" and featured a full-page photo of "a beautiful young [Russian] girl . . . with auburn hair [who] not only looks better than the girl next door, she most certainly can run much faster."[65] The article said the reason American girls can't run faster is that "most will not even try."

Competitive Women Athletes

To improve America's competitive showing, government leaders wanted to encourage more females not just to take up sports but also to become more competitive. Messages, however, were carefully crafted. Instead of emphasizing how sport would improve character or build muscles, messages sought to persuade girls that athletics would make them more appealing to boys. One physical educator cast athletic competition as useful training because "competition for boyfriends, for jobs, for husbands, for advancement will all enter into the future of any girl."[66]

Still, as historian Mary Jo Festle observes, the urging of girls to take up competitive sports was not unbridled encouragement, but what she calls "the feminine bargain." As long as women worked to display their femininity (one track coach boasted about requiring runners to wear makeup while competing) and played by girl's rules (clearly differentiating their efforts from "real" male competition) they would be exempt from unflattering stereotypes of female athletes. They must, in other words, be females first and athletes second.[67]

Little League Lockout

Donna Lopiano found out the hard way that Little League Baseball was no mere sporting opportunity but a tenaciously guarded male tradition. Little League is the only youth sports group to operate under federal charter, granted by Congress July 16, 1964. At that time, Congress recognized the organization's role in helping boys develop skills for "manhood." The recognition echoes long-held beliefs in the power of sport to shape society and groom males for leadership roles in political, business, and social realms.

Lopiano was neither the first nor the last girl who wanted to play Little League Baseball. Passage of Title IX offered females ammunition to try out, but Little League did not give in easily. It was not surprising that the organization battled the admission of girls, but it was surprising how little the actual fight had to do with athletic ability and how much it had to do with preserving male power and tradition.

Little League beginnings date back to 1925 when the American Legion in Milbank, South Dakota, created a baseball league for teenage boys, including a tournament structure.[68] This format was picked up and established for preteen boys in 1938 by Carl Stotz, an oil company clerk, and his friends, who lived in Williamsport, Pennsylvania. They won sponsorship from local companies, and in 1939 the first Little League, Inc., game was played. By 1947, Little League held a World Series; one year later Little League had grown to 307 leagues in the United States; by 1951, Little League included as many as 776 programs. In 1952, Little League got its first full-time president, Peter J. McGovern, and comprised more than 1,500 programs. In 1953, the Little League World Series was televised on CBS and announced by Jim McKay; Howard Cosell announced the play-by-play for ABC radio. By 1956, there were 3,300 Little Leagues. In 1957, the first non-U.S. team, from Monterrey, Mexico, won the Little League World Series.[69] In 1964, Congress granted Little League Baseball a charter of federal incorporation.[70]

Little League, significantly, embraced a policy of racial integration. In 1955, these policies were tested when 61 all-white teams from South Carolina refused to play with the single African American league in the state. Little League promptly disqualified all 61 teams.[71] When it came to sex integration, however, Little League fought it every step of the way.

The notion of Little League as a male institution began with Stotz. He started the organization expressly to teach boys the values of sportsmanship, fair play, and teamwork. Even while recognizing the importance of these values to all children, regardless of sex, the organization excluded girls from the start. In fact, "boy" was written into the Rules of Little League in 1941: "Any boy who will not attain the age of 13 years before September 1st, of a given calendar year shall be eligible to active membership in the League."[72]

In 1950, Kathryn Johnston was the first girl to break the all-boys rule, using the same approach Bobbi Gibb would use in 1966 when she ran the Boston Marathon by disguising herself as a male. As Kathryn recalled, she tried out for the team in Corning, New York, along with her brother, Tommy. She had short hair, which she tucked under her cap to pass as a boy, used the name "Tubby" Johnston, and earned a spot on the King's Dairy team. Once in the dugout, as Kathryn relates, "I talked to the coach . . . and told him I was a girl." This particular coach responded in an enlightened manner, saying, "Well, you're good enough to make the team." So she could stay.[73]

The Little League Corporation, however, had a different opinion. Whether the two are related is unclear, but in 1951, Little League regulations added the clarification that "girls are not eligible under any conditions."[74] Nonetheless, girls kept turning up on other boys' baseball teams. In May 1963, for example, *Life* magazine featured the accomplishments of Nancy Lotsey, an eight-year-old girl who played in the New Jersey Small-Fry League. In her debut with an all-boys team, a news report states, the young pitcher "hit a home run, struck out three opposing batsmen and was the winning pitcher. And thanks to Nancy's fastball, the team went on to chalk up a 10-1 record for the season and, with it, the league championship."[75]

Little League, however, was determined not to see girls on boys' teams and warned teams with girls that they would lose their charters. The corporation claimed that "baseball is traditionally a boy's game" and that "to admit girls would certainly cripple the program."[76] One of the first confrontations took place in 1973 in Michigan. A suit was filed on behalf of 12-year-old center fielder Carolyn King challenging the no-girls rule.[77] She was joined in the suit by the Ypsilanti Little League and the City of Ypsilanti, whose city officials threatened to bar Little League from using city ballparks if the national organization didn't let King play. The national Little League office fired back, threatening to revoke Ypsilanti's Little League charter if King remained on a team.[78] The suit was eventually dismissed "for lack of jurisdiction," as was a similar case in Rockingham, North Carolina. But it spurred others to consider legal action.[79]

While the Michigan case was pending, the Little League battle flared up on the East Coast. The organization heard of an 11-year-old girl, Maria Pepe, playing on the Young Democrats Little League team in Hoboken, New Jersey. As Maria recalls, she was in sixth grade when boys were signing up for Little League tryouts. "I just loved baseball and I wanted to play," she recalled.[80] She went with several boys to sign up but didn't go inside. The boys told coach Jimmy Farina that "there's a girl outside and she can play. She's good, she does this, she pitches, she hits, she catches." Farina said to "bring her in." After talking with Pepe, Farina recalled, "I said, 'Why don't you play,' and she was jumping up and down." She was the starting pitcher in the team's first game.[81]

Maria's team sponsor and teammates were very supportive. Not so, however, parents and coaches of boys on opposing teams, who lodged a protest, forcing the league to decide what to do. Quickly the corporation warned the Hoboken Little League that it would revoke its charter if Maria continued to play. While Farina refused to make her quit, a league official went to the Pepe home and announced that her playing days were over. "I was stripped of my uniform because I was a girl, not because of an inability to play," recalled Pepe. "As a 12-year-old, I couldn't stand up for myself and that really hurt."[82]

Maria Pepe wasn't the only girl facing such challenges. Sharon Poole, a freckle-faced 12-year-old in Haverhill, Massachusetts, was a talented player for the Indians but faced taunts. "We don't want girls invading our league," boys on bicycles jeered from behind the backstop during a game in 1971. Teammates supported her, but parents didn't like a girl on the team. After two games she was ordered to quit, and the games she had played in were nullified.[83]

Both Pepe and Poole felt they had no choice but to bow to Little League policy. The story might have ended there for Pepe (as it did for Poole), if not for the National Organization for Women, which filed a grievance on Pepe's behalf with the New Jersey Division on Civil Rights in May 1973. Suddenly Pepe's plight won public attention. The New York Yankees arranged a day in Maria's honor, invited her family to Yankee Stadium, gave them seats close to the dugout, and presented Maria with a Yankee jersey and players' autographs. When the *New York Times* polled 50 players on the Yankees and Mets, 61 percent of Yankees and 70 percent of Mets agreed girls should be allowed in Little League. Yankee pitcher George Medich asserted, "The question isn't why should girls be allowed to play with the boys; it's why shouldn't they?"[84]

Pepe's case was heard in November 1973. After six days of testimony, the New Jersey Division on Civil Rights ruled that Little League's prohibition against female players violated state and federal antidiscrimination laws. "The institution of Little League is as American as the hot dog and apple pie," said state civil rights examination officer Sylvia Pressler. "There's no reason why that part of Americana should be withheld from girls."[85]

As Pressler's comment suggests, there was more at stake than letting girls like Maria Pepe pitch some games and take her at-bats. Little League, as Pressler noted, was an American institution and battling for girls' rights to play was huge. Pepe was too old to play Little League by the time the case was resolved. But the battle was bigger than one girl. It mattered to groups like NOW that were interested in gender equality and to traditionalists who saw a threat to Norman Rockwell-like clarity around gender roles. Little League was a test case, not just in legal terms but for male-female roles in the world of athletics.

During testimony, Little League lawyers and officials argued girls should not play with boys because baseball was a male sport and because girls would be injured. Dr. Creighton J. Hale, physiologist and Little League executive vice president, argued that girls' reaction times were not as fast as boys, a point refuted by Dr. Arthur Honuth of Trenton State College. Hale also, according to a summary of his remarks, warned that "the possibility of cosmetic injury is much more 'socially damaging' for a girl than it is for a boy."[86] Little League medical experts said females had lighter bones, were more frail and vulnerable to injury, which was refuted by Dr. Joseph Torg, pediatric orthopedic surgeon and consultant to the Philadelphia 76ers basketball team who said disparity in bone strength between boys and girls was negligible and that, if anything, girls' bones were more resistant to fracture than boys' bones.[87]

Interestingly, Dr. Thomas Johnson, a San Diego psychiatrist, argued that forced integration of the sexes was bad for children's mental development. "Boys like to be with boys and girls like to be with girls," he said.[88] But Dr. Antonio Giancotti, a psychiatrist at Hackensack (N.J.) Hospital and University of Rome professor, said it was abnormal to segregate the sexes. Pressler's response revealed how much the integration of Little League mattered to the larger issue of gender equality. "I have no doubt that there are many reputable psychologists who would agree with the 'birds of a feather' theory," Pressler stated. "But the extension of that is whites like to be with whites, blacks like to be with blacks and Jews like to be with Jews; and that whole theory is a contradiction to the laws of this state and this country."

Pressler argued that "the sooner little boys begin to realize that little girls are equal and that there will be many opportunities for a boy to be bested by a girl, the closer they will be to better mental health." Pressler was "satisfied that children between the ages of eight and 12 perform differently on an individual basis, not on a sexual class basis. Just as Little League protects weak boys, they can protect weak girls." Further, she said, "while there are boys who are stronger than girls, there is a great overlap of girls who are stronger than boys."[89]

The ruling created an uproar. Little League officials appealed the order to integrate, and parent groups with names like the Committee to Save Little League in New Jersey gathered signatures. In March 1974, after courts three times refused to stay the Division of Civil Rights order, the case went before a three-judge panel. Meanwhile, most of the 2,000 Little League teams in the state suspended operations rather than include girls. One notable exception was in Hoboken, where local league officials held tryouts that drew 50 girls and 175 boys.[90]

The March appeal hearing drew throngs to the New Jersey capital, where "some 800 Little League boys and their coaches, mothers and fathers jammed the State House in Trenton to present petitions bearing 50,000 signatures and asking for postponement of the Civil Rights Division's order."[91] Robert H. Stirrat, a Little League vice president, said he was surprised anyone wanted girls and boys to play baseball together. "We always assumed baseball was a boys' sport," he said. "We think most people always have felt that way. We assume they've accepted baseball as a male prerogative of some sort."[92]

The hearing featured predictable arguments. The old saw that boys are bigger and stronger than girls at this age may seem reasonable—until you see them. One *New York Times* photo showed nine-year-old Amy Dickinson standing beside four male teammates from Tenafly; she is a full head taller. Dickinson was voted the number-one draft choice by coaches and managers from among 150 youths aged eight to nine. "She was superior to all the boys," said a Tenafly Little League manager who refused to be identified in print, given the emotionally charged climate at the time.[93]

Ultimately, of course, Little League lost its appeal. In December 1974, President Gerald Ford signed legislation passed by Congress that officially opened Little League baseball to girls. Congress also amended Little League's federal charter to refer to "young people" instead of "boys" and deleted the reference to the organization's promotion of "manhood."[94] In response, Little League moved quickly in 1974 to create a softball program, effectively attracting girls to fast-pitch play and away from Little League baseball.

The opening of Little League Baseball to girls marked a new era. Symbolically, at least, girls were now part of an American and formerly all-male institution. People could now see some girls playing alongside boys on spring and summer evenings. It was not always easy for the girls. Just because the law said they could be there, didn't mean they were welcomed then—or even today. Still, the image showed those who cared to notice that some girls could play effectively with boys. The integration of Little League, like the passage of Title IX, provided an opening to think anew about youth and amateur sports. But attention turned to practical matters, including abiding by the law. Title IX regulations would take more than a decade to be sorted out, but change was coming. The question was, How to comply?

Feminist Protests on Both Sides

"SEPARATE IS NEVER EQUAL!!!!!" It was precisely the link between athletics, masculinity, and power that mobilized feminists in the early 1970s.[95] Activists in Pennsylvania were clear about what they wanted: "Equal numbers of sports, equal amount of expenditures, and equal facility and equipment availability." They wanted women to make up half of "all governing and administering bodies of the PIAA [Pennsylvania Interscholastic Athletic Association]." They also recognized the need for affirmative recruitment to increase the numbers of women coaches and officials.[96] Here they acknowledged two important facts: women needed help getting up to speed athletically and they needed clout to shape policy.

Across the country and at different institutional levels, similar battles were being waged. In Minnesota, the Twin Cities NOW chapter proposed a plan for integrating girls' and boys' high school sports that was published in the *Minneapolis Tribune* and endorsed by the newspaper and a local TV station.[97] NOW members spurred reforms, filing suit against the school district after a personnel director wrote a job description for the St. Paul supervisor of athletics post intended to exclude female applicants. ("We don't want a woman for this job," the personnel director stated in explaining why prospective hires needed "evidence of successful experience in organization of boys' physical education, coaching, and athletics.")[98]

At the University of Michigan, a woman named Marcia Federbush formed a group called the Committee to Bring About Equal Opportunity in Athletics for Women and Men at the University of Michigan and filed a 58-page discrimination complaint with the Department of Health, Education, and Welfare under Title IX. In her press release detailing the complaint, Federbush states that the University of Michigan, "a giant educational institution with nearly 25,000 full-time undergraduate students, currently has NO official intercollegiate athletics program for women." Federbush said that during the 1971–1972 academic year, the budget for men's intercollegiate athletics was $2,611,196 while for women it was $0.[99]

In addition to her focus on "the gross discrimination in athletics against women," Federbush raised thoughtful questions about how a publicly funded university should structure its competitive sports program. "May the publicly funded university offer athletic programs with distinctly separate philosophical orientations, stresses, and rules of conduct for the two sexes, or should the university administration formulate a set of goals and acceptable practices that will pertain to all members of the university community, male and female?" she asked. Federbush touched on problems that both public and private schools still struggle with today, namely the role of athletics in the broader mission of the university:

> May a public educational facility be guided in its athletic programs by outside organizations, more or less controlling intercollegiate athletics for men and women, which set and enforce arbitrarily different standards, emphases, or values for the conduct of athletics for the two sexes possibly without due regard for the range of individual abilities, interests, and needs existing within each group or for the well-being of students of both sexes?[100]

Federbush recognized the power of sports as well as the easy vulnerability of institutional athletics to outside manipulation. Not only did Title IX mark an opportunity for rethinking sports along lines of gender equality, it provided a moment to set down clear goals for school-based sports that might have halted the athletic arms race now underway and offered a more sane approach to college sports that could serve a broader group of talented athletes.

Even as women's sports advocates were content with the increased access to programming that Title IX promised, feminists mapped out a strategy that recognized broader implications. In 1973, Eleanor Smeal (who would later become national president of NOW) headed up the organization's Pennsylvania chapter and in a November 14 letter urged fellow activists to adopt the group's demands for school athletic programs, including the "immediate integration of all publicly supported play, sports, and physical education activities from preschool, nursery school and kindergarten ages and moving upward."[101] Smeal also demanded females be treated "as individuals in their participation in sports," and insisted on "the immediate and energetic promotion and development of sports and physical education programs and scholarships for girls and women on the principle of affirmative action and reparation for past inequities."

Throughout her letter—sent as the state attorney general sued the PIAA to end the ban on interscholastic sports for girls—Smeal included the message, typed in all caps: "SEPARATE IS NEVER EQUAL!!!!!" It is a problem, she warned, when men "are listed as qualified to officiate in girls' sports, [but] women are not listed as qualified to officiate in boys' sports." It is a problem, she said, when girls are given sports with "flexible seasons," presented as means for allowing them freedom, when in fact, Smeal argued it "masks the reality that with flexible seasons for girls, girls are given the courts and the fields in the off-season and undesirable times. SEPARATE IS NEVER EQUAL!!!!!"

The separate is never equal principle was also a key point in the Twin Cities proposal. "To overcome both the actual and implied inferiority of separate athletic programs for girls, the athletic programs of the schools should be integrated with respect to sex in all of those aspects in which this can be accomplished consistent with the goals of athletic competition," insisted authors of the Twin Cities plan.[102]

Benefits of Sex-Integrated Sports

There were two key arguments for mixed-sex sports in the 1970s. One was that athletics was political currency. The second was that putting boys and girls together, particularly in sports and at levels of play in which physical differences between the sexes mattered little, offered males and females a basis for building stronger personal relations. As one news report summarized the NOW position, "Mixing in athletics is an important part of building a foundation for well-adjusted adult relationships between men and women."[103]

Today's conventional wisdom about the power of shared sports experiences to forge relationships and key leadership skills was present in the early 1970s. Women's advocates, including Anne Grant West of NOW, saw that girls needed "in" on the ground floor of these experiences. This was not mere utility that said, "Open teams to girls because the government says you've got to." This was an intelligent and strategic position.

Key opinion leaders at NOW were not the only ones who saw value in mixed-sex sports. Ed Hudson, director of the Washington, D.C., branch of the Boys' Clubs of America told the *New York Times* that coed sports programs helped alleviate social awkwardness among teens. He also opened Boys' Club membership to girls.[104] In Los Angeles, school board member Georgiana Hardy was a strong supporter of integrated athletics. She argued that one reason the United States "has done so badly in the Olympic games is because we haven't allowed girls into the really tough competition."

Segregated or Integrated?

Still, some prominent female athletes, including Olympic Gold Medalist swimmer Donna deVarona, opposed women being matched against men. Australian track star Jean Roberts, who in 1974 was assistant director of women's intercollegiate athletics at Temple University, supported integrated sports programs but single-sex competition.[105] By 1975, when Jan Cunningham, national coordinator for NOW's national Women in Sport Task Force, wrote to committee members, it was clear that feminists were divided. Cunningham referred to it as "the separatists vs. integrationists controversy."

"N.O.W. has no official position on this question," she wrote. "However, in our Title IX comments filed with HEW in 1974, N.O.W. took the position that no female may be legally barred from participation in a male team on account of her sex. The future may call for total integration." Cunningham stated she was "aware of the policy arguments favoring both separatist and integrationist positions. The integrationist argument that we've had separate but equal in the past and it hasn't worked is valid. On the other hand, the separatist argument that women are not physically capable of competing with men (in some sports) and aren't ready to compete with men is valid."[106]

The debate was a fair one. Would women, could women, win and gain enough glory if they played with men? Would women, could women, win enough attention and support if they built their own empire? On the one hand, athletic directors and supporters of male sports wanted nothing more than to create separate teams for girls (as fast as they could) to keep girls from elbowing in on the good things they had for the boys. As a practical matter, many school districts had offered no interscholastic sports for girls for years (as in Pittsburgh) putting females at a clear disadvantage in competition. On the other hand, some athletically talented girls were determined not to be pushed aside.

Participation versus Competition

Historically, women's sports has paid less attention to offering high level competition in favor of letting more girls play. The emphasis on participation over competition was the central philosophy that shaped development of women's athletics.

Competition is king in American amateur sport, but the women's model also embraces valuable messages of sportsmanship, inclusion, and participation. Welch Suggs, in *A Place on the Team: The Triumph and Tragedy of Title IX*, praises the value-laden, social approach to sport historically embraced by women's athletics.[107] While it is tempting to flee this past and embrace competition, it is important to recognize the worth of the character-based approach to sports. The majority of youth, middle school, high school, or college athletes never go on to professional sports careers. Making sure kids take away lessons about character and teamwork imparted by athletics is more useful in the long run than being regional champs.

On the other hand, making the mission of women's sports social development and men's pure competition simply reproduces traditional gender role divisions and unequal power dynamics. There is value to some of both, but not as gender-labeled approaches. After all, some female athletes crave high-stakes competition. And some male athletes would benefit from and enjoy more emphasis on team spirit and participation.

In the 1970s, however, feminists worried that decades of ignoring competition would effectively sideline girls who lacked the training to compete with boys. And this was a reasonable concern. While baseball player Sharon Poole in Haverhill, Massachusetts, was, as her coach asserted, "better than 75 percent of the league," he also noted that she had been handicapped by the lack of organized athletics for girls: "There is nothing for them, not even a softball league."[108] Those girls who did have access to organized athletics were drilled with the message that their job was to support the team, not seek personal glory. So the gifted female athlete was largely adrift. Suddenly, however, feminists needed these gifted female athletes. It was the girl who knew how to compete with boys who made possible the political demand that females be given access to previously closed sporting opportunities.

These talented female athletes provided compelling evidence for expanding women's access to sports by being allowed on boys' teams. This was not a selfless mission. Skilled female athletes desired the challenge of competing with males. Phyllis Graber, a 16-year-old Jamaica High School tennis player in New York City, said playing with boys would make her better. "I was looking for competition so I could improve my game," she said, explaining why she wanted to join the all-male tennis team.[109]

Coed Can Be Good

Sex Integration in the 1970s

Before the passage of Title IX in 1972, events were set in motion suggesting that the old practice of sex-segregating sports could be recast into new sports policies that supported sex integration. The question of whether girls could—or should—be allowed to play on boys' sports teams, therefore, did not begin with Title IX. Rather, the notion of sex-integrated teams had attracted particular attention in the late 1960s and 1970s, when Title IX regulations were still being formulated. Today we mark the passage of Title IX as a historic moment, but it was not the sole call for rethinking gender relations.

Rather, Title IX's passage in 1972 came amid the larger feminist drive to gain equality for women in American society, and specifically as the women's liberation movement made gender equality and social roles subjects of public debate. People were thinking anew about male-female relations in every area of daily life. The emphasis was on sameness feminism, on gaining opportunities for women to participate in education, in employment, in politics, and in life in general on the principle that women were equal to men in spite of their sex group differences.

Title IX merely confirmed the direction of social change. Margaret Dunkle of the Association of American Colleges noted at the time that the new anti–sex bias law was only a single factor in the shifting gender equation. "Title IX has given it a push," Dunkle said, "but God forbid, if it were ever repealed, we could not turn back the tide. There has simply been too much pressure from women athletics [sic], women in the professions, women's organizations, even parents."[110] As previously all-male colleges like Harvard and Yale and all-female colleges like Sarah Lawrence and Vassar opened their doors to the opposite sex, they integrated physical education classes. Such classes were later dropped as requirements, but in 1969 males and females played coed sports, including field hockey, tennis, track, dance, and swimming.

Coed Is Good

Aside from some "male" athletic territories into which women could not venture (notably the Harvard and Yale squash courts), there was a striking coed spirit in the air. One *New York Times* article noted that "a dozen Harvard men are taking modern dance classes at Radcliffe, while another 10 are registered in ballet and jazz classes. Last year, a number of Yale men requested ballet instruction, which will probably be given next year." The story reported, "this year 39 Harvard men and 38 Radcliffe women are playing field hockey together on Tuesday and Thursday afternoons."[111] The article featured two photos, one of men doing ballet alongside women at Harvard and another of males and females spotting one another in a coed gymnastics class at Yale.[112]

At the high school level, before passage of Title IX, some schools experimented with mixed-sex interscholastic sports teams. In February 1969, New York State's education commissioner, James E. Allen, announced an experimental program to allow high schools to have mixed-sex teams in noncontact sports, including swimming, golf, tennis, bowling, and riflery. In announcing coed teams, the Education Department asserted that there was little argument for *not* integrating teams: "In a limited number of experiences that have come to our attention wherein girls competed on boys' teams, the only negative feature is that it is not yet socially acceptable for a girl to defeat a boy in athletic competition," the department stated. Even after consulting state medical personnel, the department letter asserted that "there were no medical reasons to prohibit such activity."[113]

The experiment, which grew to include 100 high schools (all outside of New York City), was viewed as a success. "The experiment reportedly met with considerable favor from the participating school officials, coaches, and boy and girl athletes," the *New York Times* reported in February 1971. "The department now is considering recommending a change in state policy to permit mixed teams and has indicated it would allow the city schools to introduce such a practice as an extension of the 1969–70 experiment."[114]

In March 1971, the New York State Board of Regents voted to let girls compete with boys in noncontact sports, including archery, badminton, bowling, fencing, golf, gymnastics, riflery, shuffleboard, skiing, swimming and diving, table tennis, and track and field. Rules stipulated girls could compete on boys' teams "if their school does not have a girls' team in the sport." However—and this is key—rules also said girls could participate on boys' teams "if the principal or chief executive of the school feels that an athletically talented girl should be allowed to compete on the boys' team in order to meet her needs, even though the school has a girls' team."[115] Thus the policy supported coed play even when schools had separate single-sex teams.

In New York City, public schools chancellor Harvey B. Scribner in February 1971, noting the success of the state experiment and appeals by Phyllis Graber, the Jamaica High School tennis player, recommended that girls be allowed to compete with boys in noncontact sports. Graber had tried to join the school's all-male tennis team the previous spring but was denied a spot because of her sex. It certainly wasn't a matter of ability, as Graber defeated two boys in practice who later made the team. The coach wrote in a letter to the New York Civil Liberties Union (which would handle Graber's appeal) in which he stated, "Phyllis has the ability and the skill to qualify for the team, and I am sure she would do well in competition."[116]

The recognition that girls were capable of playing with boys was shared by students themselves. In a May 1971 issue of *Senior Scholastic*, results of a National Institute of Student Opinion Poll of 27,800 high school students showed one-third of boys would welcome girls into sports activities. Only 7 percent of respondents of either sex opposed coed sports teams in school. One-third or more of boys favored coed teams for tennis, swimming, and track.[117]

Title IX Confusion

It was clear that some girls were as good as some boys. It was also clear that Title IX was coming and could reshape the athletic landscape. However, ambiguous regulations and delays in implementation and enforcement fueled confusion (even after regulations were issued in 1975, compliance was delayed until 1978 and then interrupted again because of the Grove City case). Institutions and states created policies intended to comply with Title IX, but there was enough uncertainty that policies were grossly different at different institutions. Some even conflicted with one another, suggesting no clear notion of the law's real intention.

On July 1, 1974, UCLA became the first university in the country to open all athletic activities to women, including varsity football.[118] Just three years later, however, all 49 Los Angeles city high schools were suspended from sports competition for one full year by the California Interscholastic Federation because girls had been permitted to play on boys' teams when separate girls' teams existed, a violation of its federation rules.[119] Meanwhile, less than a year later, in January 1978, a federal judge in Dayton, Ohio, ruled that regulations outlawing coed sports teams were unconstitutional, even in contact sports.

In his Ohio ruling, U.S. District Court Judge Carl Rubin said the question of whether a high school girl competed alongside boys was a matter of personal choice, not sex. His ruling, the result of a lawsuit filed on behalf of two seventh grade girls barred from the middle school boys' basketball team, went further than Title IX had. Rubin stated girls "must be given the opportunity to compete with boys in interscholastic contact sports if they are physically qualified." He said separate teams "cannot serve as an excuse to deprive qualified girls positions on previously all-boy teams, regardless of the sport. It may well be that there is a student today in an Ohio high school who lacks only the proper coaching and training to become the greatest quarterback in professional football history. Of course, the odds are astronomical against her, but isn't she entitled to a fair chance to try?"[120]

Rubin's ruling framed the issue in terms of personal choice, recognizing constitutional support for individual rights in spite of membership in a subordinate group. This was just the beginning of tension between Title IX regulations (which allowed exclusion by sex in contact sports) and constitutional demands that similarly situated individuals be treated similarly under the law.

In 1974, the Nebraska School Activities Association voted to create state tournaments for girls in basketball, tennis, golf, and gymnastics, thereby effectively requiring them to be single-sex sports throughout the state. The association also voted against letting girls compete on boys' teams, even in noncontact sports.[121] Like Little League's immediate creation of a girls' softball program, creating female-only sports was viewed as a way of keeping girls out of boys' sports. Or so many hoped.

Girls Want to Play on Boys' Teams, Even in Contact Sports

Even as male athletic directors and some female physical education teachers favored sex-separate sports, some females still wanted to play on male teams. Girls showed up for tryouts, including for sports like football, soccer, track, and wrestling. In 1974 in Oakdale, Minnesota, DeAnn Locren tried out for 10- to 12-year-old Trojan Cup football. At first, boys resented her. "But after they found out she could really play, they forgot she was a girl," said Ted Burth, a community athletic official. In Montgomery County, Maryland, 11-year-old Dina Lauricella became a star on the previously all-male football team. Montgomery County sports coordinator James J. Wilshire told a reporter that Lauricella "was a little larger, a little quicker, and could throw as well as the rest of them."[122]

Bona Fide Athletic Qualification (BFAQ)?

If many institutions were unsure how sports should be understood— as a sex-specific activity or an activity based on individual skill— Title IX settled the question, coming down on the side of defining sports as a sex-specific activity. This happened, however, in a rather obtuse manner. Because the law permitted sex segregation in contact sports, it effectively fostered policies that led to sex segregation in all sports. If a school, for example, designated football as a sport only open to males, football became a male sport. To balance its offerings under Title IX, schools established female-only sports such as field hockey and gymnastics. In other instances, schools provided sex-segregated teams in the same sport, such as basketball and soccer. The bottom line was that Title IX's permission to sex-segregate contact sports effectively led to universal sex segregation in virtually all sports. The model became clear and was adopted across the country. Athletic departments would have girls' teams and boys' teams. They wouldn't play together.

This was the same struggle Congress and federal agencies faced in the 1960s when required to enforce legislation banning sex discrimination in the workplace. They had to decipher when it was permissible for a job to be "male" and when "female." In the case of employment and sex segregation, congressional agencies tried to probe beneath the surface of ad hoc sex-segregated employment to discern the reason (if any) a job required a person to be male or female to do the work. Thus in the implementation of Title VII, officials recognized some work (e.g., sperm donor, ova donor; exotic dancer or topless waitress; or male/female models and actors) did indeed require sex-specific attributes. In that case, therefore, Congress permitted a person's sex to be a bona fide occupational qualification (BFOQ). Sex could be a BFOQ when only one sex had the requisite attribute required for the job (as in sperm/ova donors), when sex difference was the primary purpose of the job (exotic dancer, topless waitress), or where a person's sex was a component for establishing authenticity (male/female models or actors).

But Title VII did not allow claims based on statistical differences between males and females, suggestions that it might improve revenue to hire only male or female employees, arguments that an employer needed to protect women from injury possibly incurred at work, or claims that customers would be more comfortable with members of one sex.

The problem with sex segregation, as initially permitted by Title IX, however, is that it was never based on how *attributes of particular sports* corresponded to *attributes of being male or female*. Presumably most contact sports advantage individuals of greater than average height and weight, assuming they have appropriate athletic skills. Males and females do differ on average in these areas, but there is considerable variability among both. Clearly height and weight are not sex attributes that correspond to contact sports in the same way that, say, sex attributes do for the capacity to be sperm or ova donors.

Rather, if sports had particular size requirements, those qualifications, but not their sex, could define the pool of eligible participants.

Similarly, if contact sports are considered to be dangerous sports, then the danger exists for everyone who participates, whatever their sex. On what grounds, therefore, should women be protected from injury and not men? In employment, sex is not a BFOQ for dangerous jobs.

If the problem with contact sports is that they involve contact between the sexes, what is it about being male and female that prohibits contact? Surely we do not want to live in a country where a male physician cannot examine a female patient, a male dentist cannot work on the teeth of a female patient, a male surgeon cannot operate on a female patient. Any sexually based contact in sports is inappropriate, whether between two men, two women, or a man and a woman. However, contact in sports should have no more to do with sexual contact than the contact between physician and patient. If it does, that is a serious matter, but equally problematic whether the parties are same sex or mixed sex.

How—or Why—Does Title IX Allow Men's Sports and Women's Sports?

If Title VII effectively banned the notion of male and female work, how do we have the American social, cultural, and business institution known as organized athletics practiced on a sex-segregated basis? Why do we have men's sports and women's sports? Many people make the obvious point about physical differences between males as a group and females as a group. But so what?

As Title VII regulations specify, statistical group differences cannot be used as employment criteria. What matters is the individual's strength and physical characteristics in relation to employment qualifications, not their sex. If a woman is strong enough to lift the weight required for a job, she is qualified to hold that job. End of discussion.

Why doesn't the same principle apply to sports? If a 17-year-old girl can strike out Babe Ruth, why can't she keep her minor league contract instead of being fired? If a woman wins a fencing match against a man, why can't she keep her title? If Donna Lopiano was, at 10 years old, the biggest and best Little League player in town, why exclude her from the team? If Michelle Wie or Annika Sorenstam are among the nation's top golfers, why should they need a sponsor's exemption or special invitation to play PGA events? Why do sports remain the most sex-segregated secular institution in American society, exceeding even the military? And why do people barely notice, much less fail to complain?

There are several ways to approach such questions. It is important to see that these issues are inseparable from cultural beliefs about masculinity and femininity, as well as a historic understanding of sex roles. But we must also consider the role of legislative logic, which not only influenced the structure of organized athletics but also aided the course of men's and women's sports as distinct entities excused from ordinary expectations of sex equity.

Protecting Males

If the reason Title IX permits sex segregation in contact sports is to protect boys' masculinity from the injury of losing to or even competing with girls, even that would not be recognized as an acceptable BFOQ under Title VII. Thus what was (and still is) missing from Title IX is anything comparable to a BFOQ that would specify when and where sex segregation is legitimate in sports. That is, there is no bona fide athletic qualification (BFAQ) for sports, and if Congress wishes to permit sex segregation in sports, there must be.

Title IX was important, even critical. But it unfortunately reinforced—rather than challenged—the belief that women are inherently inferior to men. The law also failed to challenge cultural norms of propriety when it comes to direct physical contact between men and women in athletics. Yes, football is a contact sport, but why does that warrant excluding women from playing with the boys? Surely, at some levels and in some settings, females can play football as successfully as males. Doug Flutie was allowed to prove wrong those who would write off a quarterback generously listed at 5 foot 10 on the basis of height alone.

What we must do (which was never done when establishing Title IX as the law of the land) is look again at the foundation. We must consider what, if anything, would constitute a BFAQ for sex-segregated sports. Aside from any sex group differences we may link to athletic competition, we must remember that sports come down to a challenge between individuals, and the Equal Protection Clause of the Fourteenth Amendment requires government treat similarly situated individuals equally in spite of their race or sex, even if Title IX doesn't.

Sameness and Difference

The policy objective here is to combine sameness and difference in sports programs for women. We seek sex-integrated sports policies that not only allow but also encourage females to "play with the boys." We advocate programs for girls that promote their involvement in traditionally male sports, much as there are programs for girls to promote their involvement in traditionally male educational subjects, such as math and science. Girls should be encouraged to play football if they are interested, instead of believing their only proper role is cheering on the sidelines. In fact, the vast majority of boys who play youth football lack the skills necessary for high school teams, making it particularly troubling that most girls feel they can't participate in what has become the most popular spectator sport in America. Why should girls feel that "they don't belong" in pads and helmets when their playing ability differs little from that of the boys who do suit up? The overarching goal of sameness feminism in this setting is to actively encourage and promote sex-integrated athletic programs wherever possible. On the other hand, there are virtues in difference feminism. Those women who, as the traditionally subordinated group in sports programs, wish to play only on same-sex teams or within same-sex sports arenas should be able to do so. But this should be voluntary (rather than coercive) sex segregation. Women who eschew math for literature in college, thereby affirming intellectual interests traditionally associated with women, may do so. The problem exists when educational policies coercively restrict women from taking math classes with boys, even if there are same-sex math classes for women. Women may self-segregate when they find themselves in traditionally male fields, but it must be their choice. More to the point, however, women should not merely be allowed to enroll in male-dominated math programs, they should be urged to do so. Likewise, females who want to play traditionally male sports ought not to be merely tolerated but actively encouraged.[123]

PASS THE BALL

"We ain't what we oughta be,

We ain't what we wanna be,

We ain't what we gonna be,

but thank God,

We ain't what we was."

—Anonymous African American woman,
quoted by Dr. Martin Luther King[1]

Sports Matter to Social Equality

When former (and 2007 fill-in) Yankees pitcher and frequent Cy Young Award recipient Roger Clemens earned career victory 300 on June 13, 2003, he won kudos not only from sports fans but also political figures. Two weeks after the win, a *New York Times* reporter spotted two congratulatory letters atop a black case near Clemens's locker—one from U.S. Senator Kay Bailey Hutchinson and one from President George W. Bush, who praised Clemens as a "positive role model."[2] Left unsaid was exactly what kind of positive role model Bush thought Clemens was, but that was hardly the point. Praise was message enough. Athletic feats are more than play and athletes more than players.

Sports matter in American society, and not only for the personal pleasure provided to participants or the entertainment value to fans. Sports represent power. From small-town life to the national stage, from the boardroom to Capitol Hill, the drama of athletic contests and admiration for winning athletes (and those involved in sports at a variety of levels from coaching to the media) define what we mean in America by "success."[3]

There is no mistaking the value of having a winning team, or even a major team, to a nation, city, region, or school. It bestows status in a way little else can. That some 70 teams in four major professional men's sports have built new stadiums in the past two decades—with more under construction or in planning stages—is as much a reflection of community desires to gain elevated national profile as it is about providing teams a venue to play and fans to watch.[4] Despite research showing stadiums provide few economic advantages, most continue to be publicly subsidized, sold by politicians who strike a tender nerve: community egos. Is this city a third-rate locale or a first-rate happening place with a major sports team?

Proponents argue that the social power of sport is a vehicle for building community and, critically, the ticket to becoming a class-A city.[5] One study noted advocates seeking new football and baseball stadiums in Cincinnati targeted the public psyche, urging from T-shirts, ads, and bumper stickers to "keep Cincinnati a major-league city." In Cleveland, new stadium advocates warned that without the facility, the city would be "just like Akron."[6]

At other levels of play—college, town, school, neighborhood, and company—having a team means you're a player. Having a good team means you're a winner. It was Huey Long, governor of Louisiana from 1928 to 1930, who vowed after being elected that Louisiana State University would produce a winning football team: "LSU can't have a losing team because that will mean I am associated with a loser."[7] Long would be pleased today to see that LSU has become a perennial powerhouse in many sports, which routinely earns the school mention and media attention. Political consultant James Carville rarely passes up the chance to talk about the LSU football team. However, perhaps the classic statement of college football prestige was uttered by University of Oklahoma President George

L. Cross (1943–1968), who said he hoped "to build a university our football team can be proud of."[8]

Winning in sports is too often equated to winning in life. While we may protest this reality, it is a fact of life about American society and many other political systems as well. Sports successes and failures matter to so many. It is as if sport outcomes generate collective emotional states of mind and feeling. In professional baseball, the steroid abuse scandal has threatened the value of home-run records and cast doubt on the legitimacy of the game. When umpires discovered former Chicago Cubs' slugger Sammy Sosa's bat was corked in June 2003, the nation groaned. Like the steroid problem, it was evidence of cheating, and it mattered collectively as a reflection on American society.

On the other hand, when the New England Patriots won the Super Bowl following the terrorist attacks in 2001, it was a symbol of a wounded nation battling back. The Patriots' insistence on being introduced as a team with no one person commanding the spotlight (an approach since emulated) projected a moving picture of unity the nation embraced. More than once, team owner Robert Kraft told America that "we are all Patriots." The Dallas Cowboys may have held the honor in the past, but suddenly the Pats were America's team.

The power of sports to shape a nation's image is also apparent in international play. No one who watches World Cup Soccer, the Olympics, Tennis Grand Slam tournaments, or other high-profile multinational events can ignore the influence of sport on a nation's psyche. When Argentina, long a soccer power, was knocked out of the 2002 World Cup games early, it was a gut blow to a country struggling with economic troubles and hungry for financial and emotional solvency. The Olympics is as much about diplomacy and international political, social, and economic prestige as it is about sports. Medal counts matter, all the more against political rivals. It was no accident that in the cold war era, American television focused coverage on medal tallies between the United States and the Soviet Union. In China too sports is viewed as reflecting a moral order crucial to a national image.[9]

As one *USA Today* writer put it the week before the International Olympic Committee voted on a venue, "if investors could buy futures in U.S. Olympic medals, next week's International Olympic

Committee vote on the 2012 Summer Games host would be on every financial ticker."[10] Americans wanted the Olympics in New York to better market and showcase U.S. talent. The French were desperate to host in Paris. When London was announced as the winner on July 6, 2005, a crowd of Parisians who had gathered to celebrate were deflated; as a newspaper headline put it, "Britain Bests Archrival France." A reporter who wrote "it was also a win laced with political significance, with Prime Minister Tony Blair getting the better of French President Jacques Chirac" was stating the obvious.[11] The Olympics, therefore, not only is an arena for constructing gender identities, as Mark Dyerson notes, but also a giant stage that, for the host, links athletic success with international political clout.[12] With the 2008 Olympics to be held in Beijing, China "is preparing for an all-out assault on the medals race, with thousands of athletes training in dozens of state-sponsored training centers."[13]

The influence of sports, particularly in the United States, is difficult to overestimate. We respond when athletes hock products (is there anything Indianapolis Colts quarterback and Super Bowl victor Peyton Manning won't advertise?), praise them when they urge children to study hard in school and steer clear of drugs. The sway of professional athletes over the nation's youth played no small part in prompting Congress to become involved in battling illegal steroid use in professional sports, a point amplified by testimony from parents whose children died from taking steroids, presumably to emulate the greatness of their athletic heroes.

Sports matter because they offer a readily understood image of success and convey social values we can all agree on. Athletics emphasize powerful values of fair play, accepting defeat gracefully, maintaining calm despite the pressure of competition, perseverance, being a team player, self-discipline, and the triumph of hard work. It is no accident that sports metaphors pepper our language and become models for teachers and employers. We are asked to "step up to the plate," and warned not to "drop the ball." We like team players and those who "play strong D." The best stories of athletic success become lessons we clutch like charms. Sports inspire and push us to achieve. After the Red Sox won the 2004 World Series after 86 years of failing to reach that goal, the message to children around Boston was not to give up.

We turn to events like the World Series and the Super Bowl to forge a sense of unity and common purpose. Everybody (almost) watches. We can mourn the splintering of our nation into special-interest groups, red states and blue states, soccer moms and NAS-CAR dads, churchgoers and agnostics, rock or country-music fans, urban or suburban or rural. We can bemoan the failure of citizens to follow politics or world affairs. Yet there is one place many reliably come together. In America, that stage—the biggest stage—is the one on which our athletes play.

Sports Matter to Business Equality

We also choose sports figures to run companies and head organizations, not to mention sell products. Thus sports is a big player in the economic business enterprises that constitute American society.[14] This is obvious, for example, when corporate America pays dearly for athletes to endorse products. It is also why athletes who stray from those values risk losing precious endorsements. NBA star Kobe Bryant, once commander of a squeaky clean image and one of the most marketable players in the league, saw his stock temporarily plummet after being charged with sexually assaulting a woman in a Colorado hotel.[15] Sports marketers estimated Bryant lost $4 million to $6 million in endorsement contracts.[16] That many news outlets covered the Bryant accusations as a business story, not as a legal case, reveals the tight power alignment between sports and business.

Athletics offers more than marketable images, however. Business leaders and politicians see appealing "values" connected to the sports experience. Athletics are considered (as they were in the 1800s by the captains of industry) a proving ground for gaining experience essential to success in other fields. Top athletes are potential CEOs.

Days before Super Bowl XXXVIII, for example, the *Boston Globe* featured New England Patriots coach Bill Belichick on the front of the *business* section. The headline? "Bill Belichick, CEO."[17] Business writer Charles Stein's story enlisted high-profile local and national business executives to analyze Belichick's "management talent," drawing parallels between coaching decisions and tough choices demanded of corporate heads.

Jack Welch, former General Electric chief executive, pointed out Belichick's now historic decision not to meet salary demands of Lawyer Milloy, releasing him days before the first game only to have him picked up by the Patriots' first opponent, the Buffalo Bills. The move, which drew the ire of fans and startled team members, led to a meltdown in which the Pats lost to the Bills 31-0. Still, Welch admired that Belichick was willing to make an unpopular decision which eventually energized the team, allowing them to make it to the Super Bowl. "Whether you are a corporate leader or a football coach, your currency is winning," observed another executive, David D'Alessandro of John Hancock.[18]

There are clear links between skills developed in athletic competition and skills required in the business world. Research suggests psychological skills displayed by successful athletes mesh with business demands, including being able to manage stress, block out distractions, project self-confidence and a strong work ethic, be driven to achieve goals, and work with teammates.[19] Being able to lose one day, retool and come back to face the competition again are game skills prized in corporate America and in public office. In some fields, playing a high school or college sport is considered more relevant in hiring than grades, courses, or rankings.

Actual athletic ability is a tremendous asset in business. Being able to play a competent game of softball for the company team, compete in corporate track relays or marathons, or show some b-ball comfort on the court offers an intangible bonus at work. Of course, one does not have to be of professional caliber; being serviceable (particularly in golf) is enough. A survey of 401 of the nation's top women executives showed 327—81 percent—reported playing organized sports after elementary school, including on competitive school or community teams or in intramural programs.[20]

The value of sports to workplace success is not new. In 1981 the *New York Times* wrote about the phenomenon of corporate softball team competition, including one statistical analyst with the International Telephone and Telegraph Corporation who said playing on the softball team enhanced players' workplace status.[21] In recent years, however, athletics have been viewed more baldly as a strategic tool for career advancement. Whether participation is organized or informal, athletics provide a valued vehicle for networking. One female software CEO described a 5:00 A.M. run with a senior executive while in Tokyo on business. "You get to know each other in a very different way," she said. Another female executive noted that "when you get out of a business suit and into a pair of running shorts, you look at each other on a personal level. It makes friends, and I like to do business with friends."[22]

Similarly, the recognized benefit of being able to play a competent round of golf has spawned an industry of golf schools and programs for business leaders. Obviously, spending four or five hours on a golf course with key people—making emotional connections that mirror the ups and downs of tee-to-green success and failure—forges friendships, trust, and respect.

"Women who are not playing golf are choosing to neglect probably one of the most powerful business and career development tools there is," said Hillary Bruggen, president of a Washington, D.C., company that gives corporate golf workshops. In a 2004 *Golf for Women* magazine survey of 1,000 businesswomen, 73 percent said playing golf has helped them develop key business relationships, 70 percent felt conduct on the golf course was a predictor of how people do business, and 67 percent said golf has increased their confidence in business dealings. Half of those in executive level positions said just being able to talk about golf enhances their success.[23]

Athletic Literacy

Being able to play is great, but in the business world there is value in just *knowing* about sports. Earlier in her career, Ruth Ann Marshall, president of the Americas for MasterCard, became CEO of Buypass, an Atlanta company that processes retailing transactions. One of her first executive decisions was to buy tickets to the Masters Tournament. "I called up the CEOs of petroleum companies and supermarket companies—the people I wanted to do business with—and I said, 'I'd like to invite you to the Masters this spring.' To a person, they said, 'The Masters!' They flew to Atlanta and we drove to Augusta together. We walked the course and watched and talked golf . . . The invitation gained me entry to corner offices I never would have gotten into otherwise. I still see those guys from Shell and Texaco today. And they still remind me about what a great experience it was."[24]

The Masters is but one sports venue for doing business. Probably the ultimate site for business deals and relationship building is the Super Bowl. For example, some 65 percent of those who attended the 2005 Super Bowl were key decision makers in their companies, according to the Jacksonville Super Bowl XXXIX Host Committee.[25] One sports marketing firm counted more than 400 of the nation's *Fortune* 500 companies at Super Bowl XXVIII in Houston, using the venue "to close major deals."[26] The event has become known as "Super Schmooze" with as much action off the field as on with celebrities, business leaders, and politicians making social rounds in days leading up to the big game.

While Ruth Ann Marshall (ranked #41 in *Forbes*'s 100 most powerful women in 2005) regularly plays golf—and plays it very well—her experience, like Super Bowl mania, illustrates the value of being a knowledgeable fan. Too many women bow out of sports talk before they can even get hooked. Yet sports are an ongoing drama with recognizable characters that make it easy to start conversations with people you don't know but want to (or need to) for business reasons.

Sports Matter to Political Equality

Sports are becoming more visible in politics.[27] It takes little probing, for example, on Sen. Jim Bunning's website to learn about his career as a star pitcher for the Detroit Tigers and Philadelphia Phillies and his 1996 induction into the Baseball Hall of Fame. Likewise, it's plain to see how he parlayed athletic cachet into political success. The site boasts photos of Bunning visiting with soldiers in Iraq and schoolchildren—and of him honoring home run king Hank Aaron, speaking in support of awarding Jackie Robinson the Congressional Gold Medal, and hosting members of the Russian Youth All-Star baseball team.

Bunning's biography describes how he first won election by a narrow margin—just 6,766 votes—and his 2004 reelection by earning the most votes ever cast for a U.S. Senate candidate from Kentucky, which, we learn, didn't surprise those who knew him. "Competition is a hallmark of Bunning's life, and he is no stranger to winning," his bio reads, offering a transition into information about his baseball career. We read of Bunning's "competitive spirit" and his "willingness to work hard," qualities that have served him in baseball and in public office. The biography emphasizes the commonalities between athletics and political life: "The same commitment that made Jim Bunning a Hall of Famer also serves him well in public office."[28]

There is no nuance here. Success in sports seems a positively natural precursor to a political career. NFL quarterback Tom Brady is a "leader" on the field, a veritable general marching his team, first down by first down, to victory. The buzz about his having a bright future in elective office is no surprise. Republican Lynn Swann ran for governor in 2006 against incumbent Democrat Edward G. Rendell, based on his popularity as an NFL Hall of Fame player and star wide receiver for the Pittsburgh Steelers. Swann, of course, scored the game-winning touchdown over the Dallas Cowboys in Super Bowl X, the capstone of the 1975 season. Football images dominated Swann's campaign website, which featured his sports-inspired slogan: "Join Lynn's Winning Team Today."[29]

On the campaign trail, our politicians amplify the positive messages of sport, donning caps and jerseys from teams in districts they're wooing. It is the most basic means for forging common ground. During his 2004 campaign, President George W. Bush put on a race jacket and opened the Daytona 500, NASCAR's most prestigious event, while courting Florida voters.[30]

Bush—the first Little Leaguer elected president—in May 2001 began hosting youth at the White House for T-ball games on the South Lawn. The one-inning games administered by Little League of Williamsport, Pennsylvania, are intended to "promote interest in baseball and a spirit of teamwork," according to the White House.[31] And when the WNBA suspended its operations for a month to let players prepare for the 2004 Athens Summer Olympics, one sports columnist described it as "a true act of patriotic sacrifice."[32] It takes little digging to unearth athletic roots in political careers.[33] When President George W. Bush first ran for the Oval Office in 2000, his position as owner and general managing partner of the Texas Rangers filled out his résumé in the executive experience category. His love for baseball—and his collection of signed balls—provided color and burnished an image of the All-American sports fan. After the election, Bush made his distance running—and swift seven minutes per mile pace—a visible part of his presidential persona. He even boasted to *Runner's World Magazine* that his running times improved during the invasion of Iraq.[34]

As citizens, we have come to expect images of presidential athletic outings (whether Bush on his cigarette boat, jogging, or playing golf). The athletic ability of the president is not just about the man, but part of the projection of power, virility, and discipline central to the office. Richard M. Nixon may not have been much of an athlete, but his passion for athletics, particularly football, is legendary, and he often peppered his public comments with observations about sports. Even President Bill Clinton, a self-described "band boy" with little athletic ability, was frequently photographed jogging and playing golf.

While this sports-leadership axis historically has been linked to males, a research project on women in high elective office shows a strong connection between athletic experience and political leadership. The White House Project surveyed 18 female members of Congress and found 14 participated in sports in middle school, high school, or college. The former athletes all credited sports experiences as key contributors to their present roles.[35]

Former Rep. Nancy Johnson, who played baseball, hockey, basketball, and did biking and swimming, insisted in her response that "without the sports programs I was privileged to be part of, I would not be in politics today. Competitive sport teaches a person to demand the very best of themselves, recognize the skills of others and coordinate with teammates, play hard but by the rules, and win or lose gracefully."[36] Former Rep. Karen L. Thurman, a swim team member, said that "athletics play an important role in the leadership development of young women," building, among other skills, "teamwork, discipline, and a competitive edge."[37]

The fact is we want leaders who appear unafraid of adversity, are agile in making decisions, living with the consequences, rebooting, and heading back into the fray. Just as athletic contests offer a drama in which the victor may have been initially underrated, the athlete is a vessel of possibility. The athlete may overcome odds and, based on personal qualities, achieve the unexpected. We embrace athletic achievement as more than it is, as a sign of human superiority. Call it athletic capital. Those who play sports—or coopt the images and language of athletics—may parlay that into social, economic, and political advantage. In a nutshell, however ludicrous it may be, many in American society believe that if a star player can lead a football team in the Super Bowl, why not a nation in the Oval Office?

The Problem: Gender Inequality in Sports

If sports were unconnected to social, business, and political capital in the United States, gender inequality in sports would still be a problem, but would not have the all-encompassing range it currently manifests. The way sports permeates all areas of American life and the way sports in America shapes values outside of the athletic realm, however, mean that gender inequality in sports is as fundamental a problem demanding policy correction as the way educational, employment, and other key arenas have required policy corrections to achieve for women equality with men.

Some sports values, of course, are transferable and highly prized, such as the belief in fair play that permeates work life, from courtroom practice to business ethics. Sports lessons (the best examples, of course) reflect values we embrace in business, in politics, as a nation, and as a culture. We are troubled by dishonorable behavior, in sports or in life.[38] Pete Rose may never gain entrance to the Baseball Hall of Fame because he bet on sports. In his 2004 State of the Union Address, President George W. Bush drew attention to this overlap in values with his demand that team owners, union representatives, coaches, and players "take the lead, to send the right signal, to get tough, and to get rid of steroids now." Sports matter, he said, because high-profile organized athletics set standards for social practice. "To help children make right choices, they need good examples," Bush said. "Athletics play such an important role in our society."[39]

However, there is a problem: sports values are not gender-equitable values. In fact, the opposite is true. Sport is still a male-dominated institution whose standards often conflict with goals of gender equality. The very presumptions that drive organized athletics at virtually every age and skill level presume and enforce a system in which females are second in status to males. There are individual exceptions, some more equitable sports and individual programs, but the *system* of sports—which reflects the fallback mind-set of athletic culture—presumes that males are better athletes than females. From idiosyncratic differences in rules between male and female versions of play that bear no relation to any sex-based physical differences, to the quiet reinforcement of the presumption that male athletic events are more worthy of media coverage and attention, the institution of organized sport constructs and reinforces assumptions that women are inferior to men, thereby maintaining, rather than challenging, stubborn barriers to women seeking equality in society.

There is, of course, nothing inherently male to being a sports fan or a sports participant. And yet, because sport has been a male domain, some women feel they don't belong, a feeling males have done little over the years to change. Thus, traditionally those who support teams, own teams, and are the most visible fans have been men. Still, there have long been female sports fans (baseball teams in the early twentieth century hosted ladies' days to attract women to the ball park and women today work in front offices), even if they have not always been appreciated. In June 1940, a *New York Times* story on the increasing presence of women at sporting events noted that "women not only go to games for much the same reasons as men, but they like the same sports." But, the writer added, "the sports promoters agree that the increase in female attendance is fine for business, but they wish the same gross could be achieved without the ladies."[40]

Twenty years later, in 1960, a syndicated columnist observed "the growing male feeling" that women don't belong at men's sports events and should have "their own baseball teams and football major leagues, their own ice hockey teams, perhaps even their own fishing and hunting preserves—and certainly their own golf courses." While tongue in cheek, the columnist insists "the lady sports fan" is "the most dubious product of the modern equal rights movement."

The columnist quotes unnamed "masculine sports addicts" who claim that "it was kind of cute thirty years ago to take a girl to a football or baseball game. She asked so many dumb questions it made a man feel superior." Now, they argued, "in a single generation the lady sport fan has graduated from a know-nothing to a know-it-all . . . Anybody who sits within shouting distance of two dames at a ball game has numb ears by the third inning." The column is a rant against female fans and backhanded praise of their increased sports knowledge. It conveys the power associated with knowing about sports. The headline reveals male anxiety: "Boyle Suggests: Let Women Vote, But, Fellas, Let's Keep 'Em Out of Sports."[41]

The belief that sports should be a male preserve continues. In 2002, *National Review* financial columnist Stephen Moore wrote about March Madness and the "annoying new features of the tournament that are simply un-American." His top suggestion? "No women." Moore complains that the NCAA allowing female referees for men's games is something "liberals celebrate...as a breakthrough for gender equity," but he sees as "an obscenity. Is there no area of life where men can take a vacation from women?"

Moore also complains about "a bigger and more serious social problem in America: The feminization of basketball generally. Turn on ESPN or even the networks these days and you're as likely to see women playing as men. *USA Today* devotes nearly half its basketball coverage to the gals... Do I have to shout it on a mountaintop? I don't care! No one does. We are being force fed lady hoops." (Moore fails to note that some women's games have earned higher TV ratings than men's NCAA contests.) Women intrude, he says, "during these precious moments of male bonding."[42] And he adds "another travesty: in playground games and rec leagues these days, women now feel free to play with the men." While Moore notes "some of the girls these days are half decent," he says "that's not the point."

Thus too often women who want to "play with the boys" are painted as upstarts. When golfers Annika Sorenstam and Michelle Wie played in all-male PGA events, some objected, casting them as troublemakers. Such threats (even amid overwhelming support) create a climate in which female athletes are made aware of their place, which is to say, second place to men. This discourages all but the bravest from challenging the traditional social order.

Too often male athletic events reinforce the message that male sports are the official form of athletics. In early February, Americans are met with supermarket promotions that rival Thanksgiving, urging shoppers to order football-shaped cakes and snack platters early to be ready for "the game." The fact that no women are participating in the game even as referees is ignored by media and invisible to most spectators.

Male organized sport is celebrated as a reputable, laudable, and glorious institution with a long tradition, while female organized sport is cast as an experimental and perhaps even a temporary enterprise, propped up by good fortune or the benevolence of generous men. This dual view—of legitimate and illegitimate athletic enterprises—reflects social discomfort with serious female athletes. The very pursuit of athletics (as opposed to fitness) has been male. This is changing. In recent years, the public has warmed to fierce female soccer players and applauded lean, muscular female runners, powerful women tennis players, and basketball stars. There is always, however, the note that they are female, and exceptions to the gender norm. Their athleticism is qualified by their sex. No one forgets they are girls and during televised events we often hear about how as children they played in the backyard with older brothers, information that allows us a collective "ah, I see." These girls (and commentators often refer to these women as "girls") are praised for succeeding in spite of their gender. Women, in other words, may compete, but only within a comfort zone that does not threaten male hegemony and is not too successful.

What would happen if the Tennessee Lady Vols basketball team, perennial NCAA championship qualifiers and 2007 winners, insisted on removing the "Lady" from their title and being called the Tennessee Volunteers? (They won't; coach Pat Summitt has built a brand around it, but others have or might consider it.)[43] Should we insist the men's team be the Tennessee Gentleman Vols? Or the Gent Vols for short?

Men Play for Money, Women for Love . . . Really?

For too long, women's employment was assumed to be little more than a sideline to women's roles as wives and mothers. Such a view made it easy to rationalize sex discrimination in employment practices, such as sex discrimination in hiring, promotion, and wages. Since women were not really serious about working, but just supplementing what was presumed to be their husband's income, what difference did it make if they were paid less and kept out of high-level employment positions? More recently, of course, society has accepted the view of women as professionals in their own right who may be earning more than their husbands or living just fine without husbands in the first place. Getting to that perspective rests on laws such as Title VII that make it a federal crime to discriminate on the basis of sex in employment contexts.

So too in sports do we find a parallel situation. We are at the stage where society for the most part views women's participation in sports as beneficial but not as serious as men's participation. This view is reflected in the belief that female athletes play for the love of the game, in part because their inferiority to male athletes limits the degree of professionalism possible for women. By contrast, for male athletes, sports is a serious profession that is the foundation of their economic livelihood and that provides an arena for displays of men's superiority as athletes. The notion of a male college player leaving after one year of schooling (basketball) and entering the NBA draft is considered perfectly reasonable, while a female player cutting short her education to play in the WNBA (despite the public wondering if Candace Parker would) looks silly or at least short-sighted. Similarly, when people buy tickets to see females play, they expect to pay less than to see males play, even if the level of competition is equally compelling, just as female employees used to receive lower wages for doing the same job as men.

Consider, for example, that season tickets advertised online for the University of Tennessee men's basketball team, which has weathered coaching changes and disappointing seasons, ranged from $186 to $298 while tickets for Pat Summitt's women's team—a perennial national NCAA contender—were about half that price, ranging from $95 to $165.[44] At the University of Wisconsin, it may cost $360 to $396 to catch men's Badgers basketball for a season, but attending the women's season is a fraction of that: $45 to $75 for season tickets.[45]

These are but two examples. A 2004 study examining ticket prices for men's and women's Division I NCAA basketball showed fans at 308 colleges and universities analyzed over four seasons paid more than twice as much on average to see male basketball teams play than to see female basketball teams play. The study also showed the gap widened over the four years as ticket prices for men's games rose faster than prices for women's games. Even when researchers accounted for other potential explanations for the discrepancy, they found that "gender of the team is a significant predictor of ticket price." Another component of the study sought input from 82 subjects on the perceived value of tickets. Even when subjects were given fictitious information about teams, ticket price influenced how they valued teams.

"Analyses showed that relative differences in the price of tickets translated into relative differences in the evaluations of teams," researchers said. "When women's tickets cost more than men's, the women's team was rated more positively in relation to the men's team than when the women's tickets cost less than men's. In other words, when participants saw that it cost more to watch the women's games than the men's, they perceived the women's teams as equivalent in value to the men's teams."[46]

The practice of valuing tickets to men's and women's games differently is not limited to basketball. While colleges don't charge for admission to many athletic events, in others they charge a nominal fee. Sometimes it is a few dollars and sometimes it is the same for men's and women's games. At the University of North Carolina, men's and women's soccer games both carry a $5 charge for adults and $3 for students and seniors, even though UNC women's soccer is a national powerhouse and a source of talent for World Cup teams. Others insist, however, on differentiating by sex. At Rutgers, it costs $7 to attend a men's soccer game and only $4 to get into the women's game.[47] Such tiny differences in ticket price can have no real effect on the bottom line or be justified by anything other than that we *expect* women's play to cost less to see. It is a blatant example of the gender logic that prevails and enforces women's inequality.

The perceived higher value of male play—coupled with media attention that embraces this skewed equation—is self-perpetuating. The media coverage of college football brings schools and players huge audiences that increase the regional and national exposure of these athletes and ultimately increase their value on entry into the professional marketplace. This is not necessarily a good thing. The drive to increase broadcasting of college sports may bring more dollars to some campuses, but it raises the question of appropriateness. Are colleges serving as football and basketball minor leagues?

The quasi-professional nature of NCAA Division I sports would seem a distinct issue were it not for the reality that some male athletes (unlike most female athletes) have professional sports opportunities after college. As colleges push harder to compete at higher levels, drawing more media and public attention, this highlights the status differences between male and female athletes. This is most obvious in football. At a June 2005 meeting, the Knight Foundation Commission on Intercollegiate Athletics raised concerns about the Bowl Championship Series, which matches up teams for bowl games that draw huge sponsors and television audiences (and in 2003 netted the conference of each team participating $17 million).[48] As the *Chronicle of Higher Education* reported, "The series makes a sport even for amateur athletes into something resembling a professional-league event, they said."[49] Rather than scaling back, colleges are pushing harder to play at higher levels. In the past 15 years, for example, 13 Division I-AA colleges have moved up to Division I-A and, noted one report, "most of the 13 have made the move for the reasons that Mr. [Sidney A.] McPhee of Middle Tennessee State articulates: Division I-A football buys an institution more room on the sports page and inclusion on ESPN's weekend roundup."[50]

The semiprofessional status of certain men's college sports has fueled competition among schools trying to recruit the best high school athletes. Not surprisingly, revelations of scandal have become almost routine, despite NCAA crackdowns on recruiting practices. No wonder University of Colorado physics professor Carl Weiman, winner of a 2001 Nobel Prize, felt his institution had become "an academic appendage to a football program.[51]

The exalted status afforded accomplished male athletes, however, begins long before college. High schools charge to attend boys' basketball and football games in some cases simply because people are acclimated to the idea that they should pay to see males play those sports. Talented boy athletes are treated like potential future stars. Consider media attention given the Little League World Series. While a few girls play Little League, it remains predominantly male. By the time a team of 12-year-old boys from Saugus, Massachusetts, made it to the final play-off game in the summer of 2003, they had earned regular coverage on local television stations and newspapers. This in turn fed a frenzy of followers who treated these boys as if they were professional athletes. From the *Boston Globe*:

Highlights from their Little League games were even shown on the Jumbotron at Fenway Park. When the team returned home and the bus pulled into the high school parking lot on Aug. 25, the players were greeted by 200 fans. As police held the crowd back, the Little Leaguers signed T-shirts, baseballs, and hats on the back of a pick-up truck that read, 'Saugus Americans, New England Regional Champs.' The team also was honored by the Red Sox, and with a motorcade through Saugus.[52]

And the Saugus kids lost. They weren't even the World Series winners. For the boys from East Boynton Beach, Florida, who actually won the U.S. Championship game, recognition came during Game 3 of the Major League 2003 World Series between the New York Yankees and the Florida Marlins. The boys met President George W. Bush and Florida Governor Jeb Bush, and were recognized at a Miami Dolphins football game. The Florida House of Representatives voted unanimously on a resolution commemorating the team's accomplishments.[53]

The Little League girls' softball league, formed in 1974 when the organization was forced to accept girls into baseball, holds a Little League Softball World Series. It doesn't attract nearly the institutional, media, or public support as Little League baseball. The Girls Big League Softball World Series held in Kalamazoo, Michigan, in 2003 featured a winning team from Waldorf, Maryland, whose victory earned little fanfare, save a posting on a Southern Maryland Online website: "Congrats to the girls of Southern Maryland, Big League Softball USA Champs."[54]

Despite being under the Little League umbrella, sponsors for the girls' World Series and the Little League World Series in 2003 couldn't have been more different. The Softball World Series Committee thanked 11 sponsors, including the City of Kalamazoo, a local credit union, State Farm Insurance, and individuals, among others. Little League Baseball had a dozen big-name sponsors, including Honda, the Russell (athletic) Corporation, Wilson Sporting Goods Company, Masterfoods USA (Snickers and other candy), Bubblicious gum, Capri Sun, and other national brands. Celebrating Little League's stars may seem reasonable, but such hoopla is not without cost or consequences. The idea of fifth grade boys signing autographs and riding a motorcade through town reveals a system out of kilter. It will be virtually impossible for those Little League players to do anything in the future without its being noted that they were members of that team. This may be fine. But it certainly skews any pretense that sports—even Congress-chartered Little League—merely reflect athletic reality. Who can fairly argue that the boys from Saugus or Boynton Beach are superior athletes to the girls from Waldorf, Maryland? Who can say their games are more compelling? Why is their athleticism more highly valued?

Organized sport is not a free market system. Female athletes are not recognized less, paid less, or followed less because they are lesser athletes or offer less compelling play. Rather, male baseball players and male football players are paid hundreds of thousands or millions because we have decided that their games matter more. We have decided male athletes are worth more than female athletes. And we have evolved values and traditions that keep in place practices which enforce athletic, hierarchical gender order, sometimes using public resources to do it.

What Free Market?

The arbitrary, differential monetary rewards provided to male versus female athletes, even at the high school level, refute contentions that the free market accounts for the economic inequalities in the way athletic performances are rewarded. If the initial assumption is that female athletes are inferior to men, which prescribes coerced sex segregation along with easier athletic demands for women compared to men, then it follows that spectators should not be required to pay as much to watch women play sports. Thus the initial assumption that women are inferior to men in sports gets institutionalized not only by the way sports is coercively organized on a sex-segregated principle, including sex segregation in the monetary rewards for playing sports, but also in the way these principles reproduce the initial assumption of women's inferiority in the first place. Usually we assume that things which cost more are of higher quality than things which cost less. Thus if tickets to women's athletic events cost less than tickets for comparable men's events, it must be because women's sports are not of the same high quality as men's.

The problem with the free market logic, however, is that it is a tautology. With no opportunity to "play with the boys," there is no way to see that at least some women are as good or better than male athletes. The lopsided way we pay more to be a spectator at male sporting events on the assumption that such events are "better" than female ones turns out to be verification for the assumption of women's inferiority, which was the rationale for differential monetary rewards in the first place.

Thus the assumption that men are better than women in sports leads to more funding of men's sports, higher ticket prices, and more hype. No surprise that some male sporting events generate more money than female sports at college and professional levels of play. The Women's United Soccer Association (WUSA), for example, folded for lack of funds (it plans to relaunch), and the WNBA struggles financially. As more people flock to women's Division I basketball games, even more watch the men play. And men's professional sports franchises can be huge money makers. What can rival the NFL?

However, what appears to be pure marketing genius by men's professional sports leagues, aided by raw public interest, is more complicated. These major sports have been helped in the past by government intervention as well as a powerful sales tool: cultural tradition. The icon of the strong, successful (and today rich) professional athlete is part of our national identity.[55] We want them to be stars because it amplifies who we are as a nation. We all conspire to make male professional athletes successful because their success is our success. This is not to negate the genius of people like Bert Bell and Pete Rozelle, who understood the power of television and marketing and transformed pro football from a low-profile sport to the center of the athletic entertainment universe. We credit Rozelle in particular for being first to understand how television could excite the public's passion for sports competition.

It was no surprise when the *Sporting News* put George Bodenheimer, president of ESPN, at the top of its 2003 "Power 100" most powerful people in sports. ESPN, which reaches 90 million fans a week, in 2002 became the first network with simultaneous contracts to televise the four major professional sports leagues: the NBA, NHL, NFL, and Major League Baseball.[56] If the idea of a 24-hour sports channel seemed ridiculous a quarter century ago, it now appears visionary with other cable channels now devoted to single sports, from golfing to NASCAR. And this phenomenon is reaching still further as media coverage of college sports explodes. The Big 10 Conference in June 2006 announced plans to create a 24-hour cable network and recent years have seen the arrival of Internet and television outlets dedicated to college sports broadcast and news, including ESPNU, College Sports Television Networks, and Fox College Sports.

This is about more than filming athletic play and putting it on the airwaves. Rozelle understood that athletic contests need to be packaged and narrated. It was not enough to have one game a week. To cultivate fans and followers—investors, if you will—you had to generate news, highlights, and features about players, coaches, and the matchups themselves. The more people found out about Broadway Joe Namath, the more they wanted to know, and it wasn't all about his play. It was about him as an actor on the stage of Sunday afternoon TV football (and anywhere else he might turn up).

The media have the power to create sports celebrities from talented athletes, who by virtue of being widely known can command higher salaries and even more press coverage. It is not, however, a free market of broadcasters giving the public what it wants, but a well-orchestrated popularity campaign that grooms audiences to care about and pay for merchandise and opportunities to see players who have become household names.[57] The televised competition is more than the game. It is the broadcast climax of a well-explicated battle of personalities, hard-luck pasts, come-from-behind personal triumphs, and moving anecdotes designed to make us care, not just about the physical actions of the person wearing a numbered uniform but about the individual facing this moment of intense challenge.

As a result, sports is not a wide-open field but a narrow, well-worn path in which the same schools, the same teams, the same sports, the same players, and the same coaches conspire with the same broadcasters and corporations to shape, package, and sell Americans their image of sport. How can one argue that competition involving top-level female athletes is uniformly less compelling than competitions involving male athletes? Most of America knows too little and has seen too little of the nation's talented women athletes to judge. Certainly the rise of college sports television, cable sports channels specializing in particular sports, and Internet sports coverage and game streaming have brought new attention to sports that had barely been noticed before. But there remains the undisputed power of the prime-time, well-anchored, well-shot (in high definition) broadcast that bestows on certain sports (and even certain athletes) a legitimacy that the increasingly splintered sports media cannot approach. The top broadcasters and writers continue to create our heroes and spur the demand for particular athletes. How do we break down bias that historically has cast male athletes as more worthy of public attention? How do we reorder traditions that are so American we do not consider their gender-power implications?

The president throwing out the first pitch in Major League Baseball or ex-presidents chatting on the anchor desk before the Super Bowl offers a legitimacy that cannot be purchased. The coverage of baseball spring training, the insane detailed analysis given to the NFL combine and draft, only feed the established patterns of stardom, viewership, and power. The corporate connections, the political cachet, and the broadcast rights ensure the decision has already been made about what America will watch, care about, and spend its sporting entertainment dollars on.

Money also matters because it is the reason typically given for why, even at colleges and universities subject to Title IX rules, programs like men's football and basketball deserve more institutional support. That support may mean accommodations ranging from larger operating budgets or capital improvements like new stadiums, to rearranging class schedules to suit broadcast schedules or even quiet efforts to hire professors as tutors to help players improve their grades. Schools routinely justify huge expenditures on men's athletic programs that are considered revenue producers. However, revenue producing is not necessarily profit making, and with the exception of a handful of elite Division I-A college sports programs, most lose money. Still, colleges continue to pour money into high-profile men's sports like football and basketball because, as Sidney A. McPhee, president of Middle Tennessee State University observed, "Athletics really is the front porch of the university. It's not something I'm particularly happy about, but it's the reality."[58]

The irony is that in Middle Tennessee's case, spending millions of dollars to field a Division I-A football team, something done so they can be considered in the same league as a school like Ohio State University, hasn't translated into crowds at games. Attendance between 2001 and 2004 averaged just over 13,000, below a NCAA requirement that Division I-A schools average at least 17,000 fans per game—a rule also altered to help schools like Middle Tennessee essentially save face and stay in Division I-A.[59]

Such maneuvers reveal how willing the NCAA is to alter rules to support the traditional structure and pecking order of athletics on campus. There is little creative thinking about how a college might instead capitalize on a stellar women's team, using it (instead of men's football) as a "front porch" to the school. The grip of football spending is stunning. Only 15 of the 326 Division I schools spend more on all women's sports combined than they do on football.[60]

When players, coaches, and advocates for men's wrestling, gymnastics, and other non-revenue-producing sports complain that Title IX is eliminating their teams, they are missing the boat. They should blame football. It is a budget issue, not a him-versus-her issue. NCAA colleges still spend an average of $31,000 per year on male athletes, 72 percent more than the $18,000 they spend on female athletes.[61] Title IX opened doors but has not yet produced equality. Rather, organized sport remains an institution that perpetuates gender inequality. Sport is not the by-product of a patriarchal society but a central means by which male hegemonic structure is normalized and carried on. It is a vehicle for preserving male power.

Gender Logic

Some scholars describe the taken-for-granted presumption of male athletic superiority as "gender logic." This belief system concludes that females are naturally inferior to males, males are naturally superior athletes, and when females do play sports they are not as exciting to watch because they do not match male performance standards.[62] This belief provides a self-perpetuating reality. For example, men's professional athletic contests are treated in the media as high drama while women's events are presented as less serious or even frivolous. This is beginning to change, particularly in golf and tennis. Still, analyses of televised sports and accompanying commentary are brutally revealing. One study of major golf tournaments showed male events treated in a far more legitimate manner. The leader board was shown three times as often in male events. Commentators in women's events discussed club selection 21 times, compared with 68 times in men's events. During the broadcast, there were 28 descriptions of male strength, compared with eight for women. The men were described in robust terms with such phrases as "two of the most powerful and compelling players in the game," and "quite violent . . . sheer macho. It's huge," and "you just can't hit a seven iron that far." Commentators in women's events were ambivalent when expressing female power with such phrases as "she's a delightful lady who can sure launch it into the air."[63]

Perhaps most telling was commentator reaction to poor shots. When males hit bad shots, announcers mentioned the "poor lie of the ball" and the "impossible pin placements" which study authors noted as attempts to "forgive" male golfers for errors. When females hit poor shots, it was practically expected. The attitude was condescending and suggested the inevitability of poor play because these were women. Researchers found the difficulty of the course mentioned 38 times during men's tournaments, but only three times during women's events.

There was also the matter of sheer coverage: 17.5 hours for men and only 9 hours for women. They also observed that broadcasts of male tournaments were built up to be dramatic television events, when in fact golf can be dull on TV if it's merely filmed. The men's events had more pre- and postplay coverage and employed more slow-motion replays, a device research has shown enhances the drama of the event. Such analysis reveals and highlights what is so ingrained and accepted that it seems reasonable to most Americans: men's events are legitimate contests while women are lucky to be on TV at all. Likewise, women's sports pages in daily newspapers are taken as a sign of progress, a sign media care about women's sports. Yet this merely reveals the underlying social belief that women's sports don't rate coverage in the main pages, or at least not often. Some newspapers are better than others, with *USA Today* notably stronger on women's sports coverage than many.

The problem? No one sees anything amiss. Female athletes accept lower pay, lower status, and less desirable playing conditions.

A 2004 *Forbes* magazine article said, "The income inequality that exists between men and women isn't just taking place in the board-room or on the factory floor—it's also taking place on the playing fields of professional sports."[64] The article notes that "The World's 50 Best Paid Athletes is the only *Forbes* list comprised entirely of men."

With notable historic exceptions like Billie Jean King's tennis strike and members of the 1999 Women's World Cup champion soccer team, women haven't argued about deserving better. Until Wimbledon pay was equalized in 2007, females would play, never balk (the 2005 pay for singles champions at Wimbledon was $806,526 for men and $768,000 for women) and curtsy when they meet the Queen.[65] There are few Billie Jean Kings. Women have not seen this as a matter of equality but focus on the distance trav-eled, the gains made. Triathlete Karen Smyers, two-time women's world champion in 1990 and 1995 and 1995 women's winner of the Ironman Triathlon in Hawaii, which consists of a 2.4 mile ocean swim, 112 mile bike race, and 26.2 mile marathon, doesn't focus on gender inequities.[66] Rather, in junior high school when Title IX was passed, Smyers was grateful to have access to two or three sports by the time she reached high school. She marvels at the sea change.

"Women are now growing up in a culture of 'Hey, I want to be like Mia Hamm,' there are more women's sports pages. I see it getting better," said Smyers, interviewed in her Lincoln, Massa-chusetts, home. "Change happens slowly sometimes."[67] Even as Smyers makes a level-headed observation about progress, she re-flects a common view that women feel they have been given op-portunities and shouldn't be ungrateful or appear too greedy.

When it comes to sports, too many people accept the belief that men are supposed to be better, be paid more, valued more, given better tools, attention and facilities. In November 2003, some 30 years after passage of Title IX, the American Civil Liberties Union announced an agreement in a lawsuit against the city of Grants Pass, Oregon, which required the city to provide a playing field for the Amateur Softball Association's Grants Pass Blaze Softball League.[68]

The lawsuit, *Bellum v. Grants Pass*, was filed by the ACLU in April 2002 on behalf of girls aged 8 to 18 who competed in the amateur softball league. The city had dedicated two high-quality baseball fields to the exclusive use of two boys' leagues, forcing girls to share the remaining fields with all of the city's Little Leagues, the high school softball team, and adult leagues in the community. The settlement corrected the inequality. But in how many other communities across America do such gaps never come to light? In how many towns do people embrace gender logic and fail to question the belief that boys deserve special fields while girls don't because they are assumed to be inferior athletes? Even the mental comparison of male baseball players and female softball players misses the critical point: even as the courts repeatedly uphold legal rights to gender equality, it remains an open secret that such equality is not part of the operational definition of daily community living.

Women are as much to blame as men for accepting this "gender logic." Smyers would like to see equal pay and sponsorship for female athletes but notes it may be out of reach because "sports is a business and it is a private enterprise."[69] It bothers swimmer Emily Watts when she hears of unequal prize money for male and female swimmers, but she ignores dollars in considering her own participation. "I guess maybe because I do this sport because I love it, winning money is nice, but I am not winning it for the money," she said.[70]

It is easy to understand why athletes like Smyers and Watts aren't interested in making an issue out of money: to undertake the grueling competitions they embrace requires dedication not motivated by dollars. And yet money matters. It is a sign of status, prestige, value. Offering the female singles champion at Wimbledon slightly less than the male singles champion was a willfully sexist act that underscored the belief that men's play is worth more than women's play, even when women drew higher television ratings. (The 2002 Wimbledon finals, in which Serena Williams beat her sister Venus Williams, earned a 4.6 Nielsen rating, while the men's singles finals rating ranged from 2.6 to 3.1.)[71]

Annika Sorenstam, one of the most dominant golfers in history, is frequently compared with Tiger Woods. She has become a household name with reliable media coverage. Yet as the top women's golfer she earns about $5 million a year on the course and from sponsors like Callaway Golf and Microsoft. Some 21 male golfers, with far less name recognition, earned more than $5 million in 2003.[72]

The Gender Code: Alive and Well Today

Men are also victims of gendered divisions in sports. Men who participate in "female" sports like ice dancing or volleyball face doubts about their masculinity. One disturbing study of a college men's volleyball team offers an inside view of players' identity crises as they struggled playing a "feminine" or "pussy" sport. The study's author, later the team's assistant coach, described incidents in which players sought to amplify their masculinity by goading teammates who made errors with demeaning gender-typed phrases such as "don't be a pussy, play the ball!" At other times, players used sexually vulgar phrases as a psych-up and bonding exercises. Players even sought out real women to have sex with in one-night rampages that included assaults and appalling encounters in which women were treated as disposable objects. One teammate boasted of urinating on an intoxicated woman.[73] The crude and alarming behavior, a show of exaggerated and inappropriate masculinity that became fodder for discussion and encouragement by teammates, was seen as a means of countering the perception that their sport—and therefore the players themselves—were feminine.

Some rightly see change in the air. Credit the U.S. women's soccer team, for example, for the public unveiling, literally and figuratively, of the new female athlete. It was the image that galvanized a new athletic reality: Brandi Chastain, moments after she fired the winning goal into the net, giving the U.S. women's soccer team a victory over China in a double overtime shootout in the 1999 World Cup, ripped off her shirt and waved it to the frenzied crowd gathered in the Rose Bowl in Pasadena, California. As Chastain dropped to her knees on the field, her arms clenched into a victory pump, photographers captured the picture that would pronounce—for those who hadn't seen it coming—the arrival of the modern female athlete. The photo ran in newspapers and magazines. It was on the cover of *Newsweek* for July 19, 1999, with the screaming headline, "GIRLS RULE!"[74]

The picture of Chastain reveals a well-muscled woman with powerful arms and shoulders—and a girlish blonde ponytail. The juxtaposition of physical power with clear female characteristics (Chastain was photographed in her sports bra) echoed news coverage of the event, which struggled with this new interpretation.

Females, we learned, could now be strong, gutsy, determined, competitive.

However, is this a real change from the twin norms governing women's participation in sports on the basis of natural weakness and heterosexual attractiveness? Not really. As *Newsweek*'s "Girls Rule" headline underscored (variations of which appeared elsewhere), the essential point was that they were still "girls," just larger versions of the ones in ponytails who populate community soccer fields on Saturday mornings. That view rested on the assumption that Chastain, though strong, is not strong enough to "play with the boys." Although it would have shattered Victorian norms for a woman to rip off her shirt in public, given social norms about what make women attractive to men, this was electrifying and acceptable today precisely because it was sexy.

Women athletes have come far since Victorian times—or have they? Despite enormous gains the fundamental norms are still firmly in place: women can play sports as long as their participation reinforces, rather than challenges, the view of women as heterosexually attractive and lesser athletes than men. They may be good or talented, but such recognition must exist within the scope and limits of female play.

Time to Change the Rules

Sports matter precisely because they are more than play. Organized athletics reveal our beliefs and biases and offer a proving ground for the lessons we care about. Sports culture may be steeped in tradition and resistant to reinterpretation. But we must try. We must be able to recast our athletic heroes as girls and women. We must reimagine games and rules and opportunities so that women and men can compete more often on the same field.

The idea of change in sport is as old as the notion of tradition in sport. Regardless of how organic it feels or for how long it has been woven into nationalistic rituals, sport is human-made. Athletic rules change constantly, seeking ways to draw larger audiences, speed up play, or improve player safety. On the eve of Wimbledon in 2003, for example, one newspaper polled tennis fans and concluded "millions are switching off 'boring' tennis" because it had become a

contest of power serves. The newspaper survey of tennis aficiona-
dos, not mere average citizens, revealed half of respondents believed the solution was to adjust the game by reducing the pressure
inside tennis balls to make them slower.[75]

There is, in other words, nothing "pure" or unalterable about
sports. The practice of realigning conferences or jumping divisions
is a constant in organized athletics. Players are traded and teams
carry on. It should not be impossible to set goals at end marks other
than winning a championship or selling more tickets. It should be
possible to make gender equity a goal too.

Sport holds a distinguished place in our society. In his analysis of
American fitness from 1890 to 1940 Donald J. Mrozek observes that
"the genteel preacher, doctor, or teacher came to tolerate the public
display and physical assertiveness of organized sport and athletics
by seeing with them new means for ingraining the principles of
ethical conduct."[76] At the very moment organized sport could have
been rejected as a crude intrusion into American life, it had the
fortune of being seized on by the upper-middle class and cast as a
noble pursuit, an enterprise that developed physical health and
moral character. As a result, Mrozek asserts, organized sport has
become "a key building block of the mass culture."[77]

Sport today, despite its dark side, remains idealized as a vessel of
positive social values. Players, fans, and parents may misbehave at
sporting events, but we continue to emphasize the positive lessons.
We prefer the romanticized image of athletics as a wholesome contest in which the rules are plain, the play fair, and the victors gra-
cious. The clarity of games, whether Saturday morning youth soccer
or the U.S. Open in tennis, is welcomed in a world in which things
are not often as they seem and the final outcome is elusive.

Despite the starry-eyed glamour afforded American sport, despite the good to individual lives, it has been a barrier to gender
equity. The time has come to acknowledge this and rethink the
structure of American sport to support fair play and a just society.
While many point to the progress women have made in terms of
athletic achievement and public visibility, it does not erase the larger
fact: females have been accommodated and tolerated, not treated as
equals and promoted. There have been small adjustments and con-
cessions to "let the girls play," but organized sport has resisted deep
change. The solution is not to "let" females play, but to open our

eyes to inequalities that have become routine business in organized sport that are barriers to women athletes.

We need reform at several levels. It is not work for one segment of society, but for all, from the personal to the governmental, from attitudes of coaches to institutional rules. Here are ten recommendations intended as a starting point.

1. *Accept a new, gender-neutral view of sports.* We must challenge the stereotype that males are naturally superior athletes and consider the individual first. There are more athletic differences among individuals than between athletes which are based only on gender. This means challenging biases that label some sports as female and others as male. Girls can race cars; boys can figure-skate. Parents, teachers, neighbors, community leaders, and others whose impressions shape attitudes from youth must recognize and challenge ingrained stereotypes. Support children in playing whatever sport they choose; encourage girls to play sports that are not traditionally considered female and boys to play in sports that are not traditionally male.

2. *Increase opportunities for coed sports at every level.* We need more events in which males and females play together. At the professional level, we must have more models of sex-integrated sporting events, even if they are initially special promotional events outside of regular circuit play. At recreational, youth, middle and high school levels, we must stop the reflexive sex segregation of sports. There must be more coed teams and more coed opportunities for competition. This means dividing teams by ability with the goal of increasing participation so that more individuals—even those males who are not stellar athletes—may find an appropriate level of competition.

3. *Gender-blind sports rules.* The International Olympic Committee, as well as governing bodies of various men's and women's sports, should eliminate rule differences between male and female versions of a sport which reflect outmoded beliefs about male and female capabilities or that merely serve to differentiate male and female play. Wherever reasonable, the size of play areas, the length of games and races, the points needed to win or other measures in a sport should be the same for males and females.

4. *Require parity in ticket prices, promotion, and salaries at educational institutions.* We must close the gap between pay for

coaches of male teams and coaches of female teams. In addition, there should be no difference in ticket prices between men's and women's college and high school sporting events. College promotions offices should be required to put as much media effort into promoting women's sporting events as they do promoting men's.

5. *Equal television time for women's sports.* Much as the federal government requires broadcasters to devote regularly scheduled time to educational broadcasting for children for the privilege of using the airwaves, broadcasters should be required to devote equal time to programs on women's athletics or to covering women's events. As has happened with children's programming, these demands will likely yield new media stars and capture for broadcasters a new pool of viewers.

6. *Better print and online news coverage for women's sports.* Too many newspapers and mainstream online news and sports sites still cover women's sport events as charity work. The stories of female athletes and competition are just as compelling as stories about male athletes. The more people learn about an athlete, the more they will care and seek coverage. More television coverage of women's sports will drive increased interest in and reporting on female athletes. If sports editors value women's athletics as more than the occasional soft feature, people will look for those stories. They are looking for them now, and they're missing.

7. *Women must "speak" sports.* Athletics are important in our society and women opt out at their peril. Just as it is important to vote and be informed about local, national, and international political events, following sports can promote one's inclusion in business, professional, and everyday public life. Many women are already sports fans, consumers, and participants. They are already benefiting from sports as a key feminist tool.

8. *Feminist power play: bringing athletics into the network.* Men long ago created a power network that includes leaders in business, politics—and sports. Powerful women gather around business and political issues, but we must widen the circle so that there are more frequent and visible networking crossovers among high-profile female athletes, coaches, and team owners, and politicians and business leaders. We must help each other. Ruth Ann Marshall, president of the Americas for MasterCard, for example, decided to have MasterCard sponsor LPGA players like Dottie Pepper and sponsor the

Women's World Cup soccer. Such forward-thinking acts must be replicated by women in power. This is not charity. Raising the profile of female athletes and business and political leaders broadens public recognition for women and normalizes female competence and power.

9. *If you can, buy the team—or at least a ticket.* We need women to support women's athletics. Buy a season ticket to the WNBA franchise. Attend and support female athletic events. Take your children to see women play. If you can afford it, buy a team. More women must be at the owner's table, whether in women's leagues (precious few choices at the moment) or in men's. We must drive change from outside as well as from within. Even an act as simple as having your March Madness office pool include the Women's NCAA basketball tournament—not just the men's—raises awareness of compelling women's play. There is no apologetic stance needed: the women have game and more people need to know about it.

10. *Strengthen Title IX.* Title IX may have seemed appropriate when it was passed in 1972, but it never demanded equality. We now need financial equality, even if that means dramatically scaling back men's college football and basketball programs, some of which hardly resemble programs suitable for educational institutions. If the NFL or the NBA wants a development league, they should build it. Colleges should value men's and women's Olympic sports as part of their educational mission. Title IX also must be more aggressively enforced. And finally, Title IX must *not* permit coercive sex segregation that prevents girls from "playing with the boys."

Sports: The Next Frontier

In the United States, the act of defining sex difference has defined inequality. The long-standing images of women as weak and physically inferior to males has ensured stark sex differentiation and in the past barred females from higher education, kept them from the right to vote, and created barriers in the workplace. In many cases, women embraced these limitations, agreeing it was not their "place" to occupy the same social and economic space as men.

Integrating higher education, permitting women to vote, and outlawing sex bias at work have been crucial steps not just for women, but also for American society. Organized athletics represents the next goal in the quest for equal participation. Familiar arguments of female physical and biological differences drive sex-separate athletic programs, differentiated male and female rules (not based on actual physical differences), and sex-differentiated expectations.

In fact, the barriers female athletes face today are not chiefly physical but social and cultural. One has only to look internationally to see the limiting power of social gender bias. When Lima Azima finished last in the 100-meter race at the World Track and Field Championships in Paris in August 2003, no one blamed her athletic ability. Her victory was in overcoming impressive obstacles to become the first Afghan woman ever to compete in a major worldwide sports event. She wore long baggy pants to other runners' sleek, form-fitting uniforms. She struggled with the starting blocks, had never worn proper running shoes (Adidas donated shoes for the race), and had not been permitted to train outdoors or in front of men. Merely participating was success.[78]

In Bangladesh, the women's soccer team has faced protests from conservative Muslim groups that consider their play immoral. In October 2004, the women's team played despite a demonstration by 500 activists in Dhaka carrying placards reading, among other slogans: "Stop un-Islamic activities, protect sanctity of womanhood." Moulana Abdur Rashid, deputy chief of the Islamic Constitution Movement, warned that "the national sport council will be put under siege . . . if the satanic women's football league is not abandoned immediately."[79]

The pervasive belief that athletics will keep women from being womanly persists. Research at the University of Nigeria found 51 percent of women were concerned that playing a sport would lead them to develop masculine features and therefore they chose not to participate. Many worried that athletics could affect menstruation and reproduction, and that they could be injured, which kept parents from encouraging daughters to play sports.[80]

Females in some minority groups avoid sports because of similar cultural messages. For example, only 43 percent of Hispanic high school sophomore girls play at least one interscholastic sport, compared with 52 percent of non-Hispanic sophomore girls. The issue is not money but cultural habits in which girls are not encouraged to stay after school for sports because they are expected at home to help with family obligations. Raul Hodgers, athletic director at

Desert View High School in Tucson, Arizona (the school is 80 percent Hispanic), noted that "most of these girls are athletically inclined, but it is difficult to acclimate parents to the idea of kids staying after school."[81] And he was referring to girls, not boys.

In some parts of the developing world the demands of daily survival make sports appear trivial, while in other developing nations women are restricted to private spheres of home and child rearing, excluding them from public realms of work and sport.[82] And yet it is clear that athletics can be potent diplomatic and ideological tools.

The Chinese have earned international attention for athletics, winning 32 Gold Medals at the 2004 Athens Olympics, second only to the Americans. The Chinese government urged all Chinese citizens to learn from those athletic victories. "The excellent performance by China's athletes again shows the spirit of the Chinese nation's unremitting efforts to improve itself," the government said in broadcasts on state-run television. "The motherland is proud of you, and the people are proud of you."[83]

Nationalism

The rise of China's athletic profile on the international stage (NBA star Yao Ming has also helped) is seen as clear evidence of a nation on the road to economic dominance. Interestingly, success of Chinese women athletes, in part, has been attributed to a cultural norm in which an athlete's Chinese identity is viewed as more important than her gender identity. "Any polarization of males versus females is therefore overwhelmed by feelings of 'China versus the world,'" noted one researcher. "This is a phenomenon starkly at variance with the historical 'male versus female' dichotomy common in Western sporting nations, but is closer to the situation that existed in much of Eastern Europe and Cuban sport."[84]

It may be socially convenient to differentiate sports by sex. However, it thwarts power sharing and equality between the sexes. When Little League lawyers and physicians in 1974 argued to a New Jersey civil rights hearing officer that "boys like to be with boys and girls like to be with girls" in their failed quest to keep girls off the diamond, they echoed a cultural belief: regardless of whether boys and girls can or should play together, many don't want to.[85]

Although girls are now permitted to play Little League, and modest numbers actually do, most choose softball instead. Talk with parents and you hear similar sentiments: their daughters don't want to play with boys and boys don't want to play with girls. Whether the sport is baseball, basketball, ice hockey, wrestling, or soccer, the presumption is that athletes prefer to compete with players of their own sex. Adults, even in social tennis, gravitate to same-sex play. Organized sport truly is the most sex-segregated secular institution in our society. More than a reflection of actual physical differences between males and females, it reveals cultural norms and our present comfort zone. We have been conditioned—and our children are being conditioned—to believe this is *the right way* to play.

Sharing power depends on sharing turf in the Oval Office, Congress, state houses, local government, boardrooms, CEO suites— and on the playing field. Opening power structures to greater male-female cooperation means including more females in athletic opportunities with males, inviting more women to the business golf outing, seeing more females pick-and-roll in a pick-up, recreational league, or after-work basketball game.

This must start when children are young. Just as the drive for increasing racial and ethnic diversity is considered critical to preparing children for the future, we must teach children from the time they step onto the gymnasium floor on Saturday mornings to play Itty Bitty Basketball that girls and boys can pass to one another, and either can drive to the hoop.

The Family and Community

This requires a new way of thinking and an active effort by parents and youth sports leaders. It is critical we get out of the gender role habits that dominate in sports and the rest of life. It matters for players and for fans. It matters for athletes, coaches, organizers, media members, and sponsors. The challenge, in other words, demands a break from a sex-segregated past that stretches back well more than a century.

The Government

It is recognized now that women can and should have educational opportunities equal with men. This, in turn, serves as a foundation for equal employment opportunities. As a nation we want women to enter nontraditional educational and employment fields, through government and foundation-sponsored programs aimed at encouraging women to enter such fields as math, science, and engineering.

Sports

We must do the same thing in sports. The family, the community, and government must press girls to explore nontraditional sports. We need role models. Girls must see women playing football and being referees in high-profile professional sports, including football, basketball (there's just one), and baseball. Just as the government encourages sex integration—rather than sex segregation—in math, science, and engineering, it must encourage sex integration in athletic programs. Sports is the next battleground in the fight for gender equality. The roots of sex discrimination must be challenged head-on. There are physical biological differences between the sexes. But they are not as great as we have supposed, and the female difference in not necessarily a lacking. Women are not inherently weak and in need of protection.

Not all women will support this drive. In every era, as women sought to gain equal access to education, to voting and workplace rights, other women were their fiercest adversaries. Women didn't want to take on male roles that meant learning, earning, and having a voice in our democracy. We know there is no justice without responsibility. More than ever we need women's voices in the halls of power, at the helms of corporations, and being celebrated for their athletic prowess. Women are starting to gain recognition for physical ability, mental acuity, and the ability to compete. And, yes, *"thank God* we ain't what we was."

However, we are not yet what we ought to be. Females playing sports with males must become standard practice, not the exception. And as surprising, if not difficult, as this idea may be for some, it is an idea that is gaining ground. When sports writer, Dave Anderson, for example, speculated about how Tiger Woods's infant daughter, Sam Alexis, might handle her father's legacy, he noted that "maybe she'll want to try to win the most majors on the women's Tour, *if not the men's Tour.*"[86] *Exactly*. Playing with the boys should be an option, if not the norm, for her and for all girls and women, if we are to become *what we ought to be*.

Table 4.1. Sport Cases, Sex-Segregation Issues, Female Plaintiffs

Case citations and descriptions are primarily (almost without exception) reported verbatim from Karen Tokarz, *Women, Sports, and the Law: A Comprehensive Research Guide to Sex Discrimination in Sports* (Buffalo, NY: William S. Hein, 1986).

Adams by and through Adams v. Baker, 919 F. Supp. 1496 (1975, 1996)

The female student sought to wrestle on her high school's wrestling team that was only open to male student participation. She was prohibited from trying out for the team and then brought her action against defendants. Court ruled that this policy was a violation of Title IX, Title 42, and her right to equal protection.

Beal v. Midlothian Indep. Sch. Dist., 2002 U.S. Dist. LEXIS 8937 (2002)

The students had been denied an equal opportunity to participate in interscholastic athletics and had received unequal treatment and benefit in these programs. The court dismissed plaintiffs' Title IX effective accommodation claims for lack of standing. Yet the court found that the students satisfied the prerequisites of Fed. R. Civ. P. 23(a), numerosity requirement. Lastly, the court found that the students satisfied Fed. R. Civ. P. 23(b)(2), as they only sought injunctive and declaratory relief.

Bednar v. Nebraska School Activities Association, 531 F.2d 922 (8th Cir. 1976)

The court upheld the granting of an injunction that required the school to let girls participate on boys' cross-country team, where defendant's only argument was that she was not good enough to make the team. Evidence supported plaintiff's argument.

Brenden v. Independent School Dist., 742 477 F.2d 1292 (8th Cir. 1973), aff'd 342 F. Supp. 1224 (D. Minn. 1972)

The court held that an athletic association rule barring girls from noncontact cross-country skiing, running, and tennis where no team was provided for girls violated girls' equal protection rights.

Bucha v. Illinois High School Association, 351 F. Supp. 69 (N.D. Ill. 1972)

The court held that there are "rational bases" to justify prohibition of competition between sexes in high school swimming program and to support restrictions applicable only to female contests, under the Fourteenth Amendment and 42 U.S.C. S 1983.

The court took judicial notice that males consistently outperform females on the playing field. The court accepted that physical and psychological differences exist between female and male athletes warranting segregation in order to avoid male domination and to maximize female participation. The court rejected analogy to Title VII employment discrimination cases. From its language, it appears the court's decision would be different under Title IX or a higher level of constitutional scrutiny.

Carnes v. Tennessee Secondary School Athletic Association,
415 F. Supp. 569 (E.D. Tenn. 1976)

The court granted an injunction requiring the association to allow a girl to play on a high school baseball team. For the sake of argument the court accepted the contention that a state may segregate contact sports, but indicated that the classification of baseball as a contact sport was probably unreasonable.

Clinton v. Nagy, 411 F. Supp. 1396 (N.D. Ohio 1974)

The court granted an injunction requiring a city's recreation program to allow an individual twelve-year-old girl to play on a city football team. The defendant association made no showing that the individual plaintiff was unqualified to play football except for her sex. The court observed that all players, male or female, risk serious injury when playing football.

Collins v. Day, 644 N.E. 2d 72 (Ind.) (1994)

Finding that females cannot be prevented from competing with males on noncontact sport teams like track, gymnastics, swimming, and golf.

Cook v. Colgate Univ., 802 F. Supp. 737 (1992)

In 1979, 1983, 1986, and 1988, the women's club ice hockey team applied for varsity status. Their applications were rejected in all four years for the following reasons: (1) women's ice hockey is rarely played on the secondary level; (2) championships are not sponsored by the NCAA at any intercollegiate level; (3) the game is only played at approximately fifteen colleges in the east; and (4) hockey is expensive to fund, and would heavily impact a total intercollegiate program by requiring: increased locker room space, large budget, a full-time coach, and so on. Accepted except for compensatory damages.

Craig v. Boren, 429 U. S. 190 (1976)

In Craig, the Supreme Court considered the constitutionality of an Oklahoma statute which prohibited sale of 3.2 percent beer to men under the age of 21, and women under the age of 18. The Court did not find the sex classification to be substantially related to the state's objective of providing for public safety by limiting the sale of alcohol to males under the age of twenty-one on the basis of statistics showing that 2 percent of men 18 to 21 were arrested for drunk driving, while only 0.18 percent of women the same age were arrested for the same offense.

Darrin v. Gould, 85 Wash. 2d 859, 540 P.2d 882 (1975) (enbanc)

The court held that a school district rule prohibiting qualified girls from playing on the high school football team was unconstitutional under the state equal rights amendment and the Fourteenth Amendment. Although the court did not consider sex to be a "suspect class," it found no rational relationship between a person's sex and the ability to participate in sports.

Dodson v. Arkansas Activities Assoc., 468 F. Supp 394 (1979)

The court held that it is unconstitutional to require high school girls to play half-court basketball. The court held that Arkansas tradition, the only justification offered for significantly different sports for boys and girls, was not constitutionally adequate.

Force v. Pierce City R-VI School Dist., 570 F. Supp. 1020 (W.D. Mo. 1983)

The court found unconstitutional a blanket rule prohibiting all eighth grade females from trying out for the football team. The alleged objective of maintaining safe athletic programs did not bear a sufficiently substantial relationship to the ban on female participation.

Fortin v. Darlington Little League, Inc., 376 F. Supp. 473 (D. R.I. 1974), rev'd and remanded 514 F.2d 344 (1st Cir. 1975)

The district court found sufficient state action to hear claim by ten-year-old girl excluded from recreational league baseball, under 42 U.S.C. S 1983 and Fourteenth Amendment. The district court also took "judicial notice" that baseball is a contact sport and found "material physical differences between boys and girls in 8–12 age bracket" to warrant exclusion of girls for safety reasons. On appeal the First Circuit held that the district court's finding that injury will result from the physical differences between boys and girls was unsupported. The court limited its holding to age group in question, 8–12-year-olds, because athletic ability does not differ greatly in that age range between boys and girls.

(Forton) Michigan Department of Civil Rights ex rel. Forton v. Waterford Township Department of Parks and Recreation, 124 Mich. App. 314, 335 N.W.2d 204, 208 (1983)

The court held that separate basketball leagues for girls and boys are not equal if scheduling differences forced girls, but not boys, to make a choice between playing football or basketball. The court also held that a quota of two members of the opposite sex on each team is not permissible.

Gilpin v. Kansas State High School Activities Association, 377 F. Supp. 1233 (D. Kan. 1973)

The court held that it is unconstitutional to bar a girl runner from a high school cross-country team when there is no girls' team.

Gregoria v. Board of Education of Asbury Park Cause No. A-l277–70 (N.J. Super. Ct. App. Div. 1971), noted in 1 WOMEN'S RIGHTS L. REP. 39 (1972)

The trial court refused to enjoin enforcement of the New Jersey Athletic Association rule prohibiting coed interscholastic sports, including noncontact sports such as tennis. Among the rational bases for the policy, the court cited the psychological impact on males, the need for additional female trainers, and the possibility of insufficient bathroom facilities. The appeals court affirmed the lower court's ruling that the "psychological well-being of girls is a rational reason for exclusion."

Haas v. South Bend Community School Corp., 289 N.E.2d 495, 259 md. 515 (1972)

The court held that an Indiana high school athletic association rule prohibiting participation by girls on boys' teams in noncontact sports, like golf, is unconstitutional under the equal protection clause of the Fourteenth Amendment, when there is no athletic team for girls.

Hollander v. Connecticut Interscholastic Athletic Conference, Inc. Cause No. 12497 (Super. Ct. Conn., New Haven County, 1971), app. dismissed 164 Cons. 654, 295 A.2d 671 (1972) (mem.), noted in 1 WOMEN'S RIGHTS L. REP. No. 2 at 41 (1972)

The court negotiated an agreement with the association to allow girls, including plaintiff female cross-country runner, to compete on boys' teams in noncontact sports. Despite the agreement, the court ruled for defendants on the equal protection claims. The court reasoned that boys would have no thrill of victory by beating girls.

Hoover v. Meiklejohn, 430 F. Supp. 164 (D. Cob. 1977)

The court held that a state athletic association's rule barring girls from a high school soccer team violates equal protection when there is no girls' team. The court based its decision on a denial of equal educational opportunities.

Israel v. West Virginia Secondary Scho. Activities Comm'n., 388 S.E. 2d 480.

A female high school student was prohibited from playing baseball on a boys-only team and was told she should play on the softball team instead. Even after she graduated from high school, rendering her possibility of playing on the boys' high school baseball team moot, the court heard her case on the grounds that the issues could be repeated in another situation and that the case involves important "collateral issues." The court ruled that prohibiting females from playing on baseball teams with boys did violate the equal protection clause of the Fourteenth Amendment and the West Virginia Human Rights Act. The court ruled that the female student had a right to reasonable attorney's fees to be paid to her.

Kelly v. Wisconsin Interscholastic Athletic Association, 367 F. Supp 1388 (1973)

Court held that claim of female students excluded from participation on the male varsity swimming teams because of association rule stated a constitutional claim under the Fourteenth Amendment against individual defendants who, either directly or in their official capacities, allowed enforcement of such rule. However, Court held the plaintiffs failed to state a cause of action on which relief could be granted against the Association because they failed to allege the necessary "state action" against the state superintendent of schools. Note: This case is included because the finding was that sex-segregated sports policies did fall under court review using the equal protection clause, even though in this case, there was no finding of state action.

Kemether v. Pennsylvania Interscholastic Ath. Ass'n., 1999 U.S. Dist. LEXIS 17326 (1999)

Her high school athletic association discriminated against her by refusing her any opportunity to officiate at boys' basketball games and in taking various retaliatory measures against her after she complained to the Equal Employment Opportunity Commission. Court found sex-segregation policy to be violations of Title VII, Title IX, and Pennsylvania Equal Rights Amendment.

Lantz v. Ainbach, 620 F. Supp. 663 (S.D. N.Y. 1985)

The court enjoined enforcement of a New York public high school regulation that prohibited mixed-sex competition in football, as a violation of the Fourteenth Amendment, and permitted a 16-year-old healthy female student to try out for junior varsity football. Although the court acknowledged an important governmental objective in protecting the health and safety of female high school students, it found the regulation was overbroad and lacked reasonable relation to the objective.

Leffel v. Wisconsin Interscholastic Athletic Association, 444 F. Supp. 1117 (E.D. Wis. 1978)

The court held that when both girls' and boys' swimming teams are offered, it is not discriminatory to prevent talented girls from swimming on the boys' team. The court also held that schools should provide separate teams for girls to participate in contact sports.

Mercer v. Duke Univ., 190 F.3d 643 (1999)

She was not permitted to attend summer camp or dress for games, the university's head coach made offensive comments to her, and she was dropped from the team the next season because of her sex. Court found that where appellee university permitted appellant, a female kicker, to try out for a single-sex team in a contact sport such as football, the university was subject to Title IX's prohibition against discrimination on the basis of her sex. Once a sport, any sport, including contact sports, is sex integrated, it must remain so, according to Title IX regulations, according to the Court.

Muscare v. O'Malley Civil No. 76-C-3729 N.D. Illinois (1973)

A 12-year-old girl sought to play football with the boys in a recreational program. In ruling for the plaintiff, the court reasoned that offering a sport for males but not for females is a violation of equal opportunity rights under the Fourteenth Amendment. The court allowed a 12-year-old girl to play tackle football in Chicago Park District football games, even though there was a touch football program available for girls.

Morris v. Michigan State Board of Education, 472 F.2d 1207 (6th Cir. 1973)

The court affirmed a preliminary injunction prohibiting enforcement of a Michigan High School Athletic Association rule that prohibited female students from high school tennis competition with boys. The court specifically reserved the question of separate teams in contact sports. (The Michigan Legislature adopted Act no. 138 of the Public Acts of 1972 allowing females to participate in all noncontact interscholastic athletic activities. Under this statute, girls are permitted to compete for positions on the boys' team, even if the institution has a girls' team. Mich. Comp. Laws Ann. S 340.379(2), 1982 Mich. Pub. Acts 138.)

(NOW) National Organization for Women v. Little League Baseball, 318 A 2.2d 33 (1974)

The New Jersey Superior Court struck down a rule that limited Little League participation to boys 8 to 12 years of age on the grounds that this regulation violated state law against discrimination since the baseball sport in question involved places of public accommodation. The court rejected arguments that there were substantial physiological differences between boys and girls that required prohibiting girls from playing with the boys.

O'Connor v. Board of Education of School District,
No. 23 645 F.2d 578 (7th Cir. 1981), cert. denied 454 U.S. 1084
(1982), on remand 545 F. Supp. 376, 381 (N.D. Ill. 1982)

The district court on remand held that denying an 11-year-old girl the opportunity to try out for sixth grade boys' basketball team was not a violation of equal protection or Title IX, even though only participation on the boys' team would provide the skilled plaintiff with levels of competition to enable her to further develop her skills. The court cited Petrie 75 Ill. App. 3d 980, 394 N.E.2d 855 (1979), which upheld the total exclusion of males from a female-only sports team as constitutional under the Illinois equal rights amendment, as a precedent for upholding the total exclusion of females from a male-only sports team.

Opinion of the Justices to the House of Representatives,
374 Mass. 836, 371 N.E.2d 426 (1977)

The Supreme Judicial Court of Massachusetts rendered an opinion that proposed legislation which would have disallowed "participation of girls with boys on the following contact sports teams: football and wrestling" would be unconstitutional under the state's Equal Rights Amendment. The court specifically reserved the question whether a statute "more limited in its impact" would serve a compelling state interest, for example, whether females could be constitutionally excluded from male teams in a particular sport if they were provided with an equal team.

Packel v. Pennsylvania Interscholastic Athletic Association,
334 A.2d 839 (1975)

The attorney general of Pennsylvania initiated a suit against the Pennsylvania Interscholastic Athletic Association (PIAA) on the grounds that the Association's rules prohibiting girls from competing or practicing against boys "in any athletic context" violated the equal protection clause of the Fourteenth Amendment as well as Pennsylvania's Equal Rights Amendment. The court concluded that it would be futile to conduct a trial because the Association's prohibition "is unconstitutional on its face under the [Pennsylvania] ERA and none of the justifications for it offered by the PIAA, even if proved, could sustain its legality." Since the regulations violated the Pennsylvania ERA so blatantly, the court did not consider whether the regulations also violated the equal protection clause of the Fourteenth Amendment.

Pavey v. University of Alaska, 490 F. Supp. 1011
(D. Alaska 1980) (consent decree)

Female student-athletes brought an action against the University of Alaska, charging the university with discrimination in the operation of its athletic program in violation of Title IX and the Fourteenth Amendment's due process and equal protection clauses. The university filed a third-party suit against the NCAA and the AIAW, which charged that the two associations' inconsistent rules required the university to discriminate in its athletic program in violation of federal laws. In denying the NCAA and AIAW motions for dismissal of the suit, the district court held that the university's suit stated a valid claim, that the university was reasonably trying to avoid a confrontation with the two associations' rules that could cause a disruption in the participation of student athletes in intercollegiate athletics, and that the facial neutrality of the association's rules did not negate the university's claim that the combined effect of those rules forced the institution to discriminate in its athletic program. The parties subsequently settled the claim.

(Penn.) Commonwealth v. Pennsylvania Interscholastic Athletic
Association, 18 Pa. Comznw. 45, 334 A.2d 839 (1975)

The Pennsylvania attorney general obtained an order, under the state's equal rights provision, invalidating a provision in the bylaws of the PIAA which provided that "girls shall not compete or practice against boys in any athletic contest." The bylaws applied to football, cross-country, basketball, wrestling, soccer, baseball, field hockey, lacrosse, gymnastics, swimming, volleyball, golf, tennis, track, softball, archery, and badminton. The court concluded that a female may not be "excluded solely because of her sex without regard to her relevant qualifications." Although the attorney general did not seek to invalidate the bylaw as it applied to football and wrestling, the court voluntarily extended its order to these sports. The court said that exclusion based on sex is improper (at least as to females), whether or not separate teams are offered for females and males in the same sport.

(Power Squadrons) United States Power Squadrons v. State Human Rights Appeal Board, 59 N.Y. 2d 401, 452 N.E. 2d 1199, 465 N.Y.S. 2d 871 (1983)

The court upheld claim of sex discrimination by women denied membership in USPS, a nonprofit foreign corporation whose purposes include promotion of safety and skill in boating, whose activities the court held constituted public accomodation under New York human rights law.

Reed v. Nebraska School Activities Association, 341 F. Supp. 258 (D. Neb. 1972)

The court issued a preliminary injunction to permit female golfers to participate on the male golf team, where the high school has no female team. The court acknowledged that a classification based on sex must have a rational relationship to a state objective, and here no such justification was presented.

Reed v. Reed, 404 U.S. 71 (1971)

The Supreme Court found that an Idaho statute which gave automatic preference to fathers and/or husbands in the administration of a deceased child's estate to be an unconstitutional form of sex discrimination in violation of the equal protection clause of the Fourteenth Amendment.

Ritacco v. Norwin School District, 361 F. Supp. 930 (W.D. Pa. 1973)

The court found that unlike race discrimination, "separate but equal" gender classification in the realm of sports competition is justifiable when there is a "rational basis" for the classification—fostering greater participation in sports based on physiological and psychological differences between females and males. The court assumed the opportunities were equal and denied plaintiff's claim, under 42 U.S.C. S 1983, to play on the boys' high school tennis team, rather than the girls' team.

Ruman v. Eskew, 165 md. App. 534, 333 N.E.2d 138 (1975)

The court denied plaintiff's initial petition for an injunction in aid of appellate jurisdiction, refusing to examine the quality of the separate high school tennis programs. The court also denied plaintiff's interlocutory appeal from denial of the preliminary injunction, holding that girls can be excluded from playing on boys' high school tennis team, when a girls' team exists.

Saint v. Nebraska Sch. Activities Ass'n., 684 F Supp 626 (1988)

Court rejected argument that girls are physically inferior to boys and cannot wrestle with boys, and, even if that were true, this particular individual girl was capable of wrestling with boys.

Simpson v. Boston Area Youth Soccer, Inc. Case No. 83-2681 Super. Ct. Mass (1983)

Plaintiff, a sixth grade female soccer player, sued the soccer association because it excluded plaintiff from the all-male soccer team in her town. Plaintiff had played for three years on coeducational teams; many of her former teammates were on the team; and she maintained that the girls' league would present inferior competition. The case was settled when defendant soccer league agreed to change its constitution and bylaws to allow females to play on male teams, with such teams being entered in the boys' league.

Striebel v. Minnesota State High School League, 321 N.W.2d 400 (Minn. 1982)

The court held that when limited athletic facilities made it necessary to schedule high school boys' and girls' athletic teams in the same sport in two different seasons, and neither season was substantially better than the other, there was no equal protection constitutional violation. The court stated that treatment of the separate teams must be as nearly equal as possible and that separation is allowable only to the extent absolutely necessary to provide equal athletic opportunity for all participants. The court specifically limited its holding to the facts of the case in which the evidence was uncontroverted that access to the pool and tennis courts at most high schools was insufficient to accommodate boys' and girls' teams in the same season. The court reserved the question whether separate seasons would be constitutionally permitted if adequate facilities were available.

Justice Wahl, in dissent, argued that the evidence failed to prove that separate seasons were substantially related to an important governmental interest. According to Wahl, the seasonal structure violated the equal protection clause: the girls' tennis season began before the school year began; coaches for boys' teams averaged 8.1 years experience, while coaches for the girls' teams averaged 4.5 years experience. He further pointed to evidence that sex segregation in athletic programs contributes materially to the failure of females and males to work together in career situations, to occupational sex segregation, and to lower economic status of women. Cf. *Forton v. Waterford Township Dept. of Parks and Recreation, 124 Mich. App. 314, 335 N.W.2d 204 (1983).*

Swann v. Charlotte-Mecklenburg Bd. of Educ., 402 U.S. 1, 2, reh'g denied 403 U.S. 912 (1971)

In this pre-Title IX case, the Supreme Court ruled that gender discrimination cases are analogous to school desegregation and that the goal of the Court, as advanced by the decision in this case, is to eliminate from schools all vestiges of state-imposed segregation because they violate equal protection guarantees, including sex discriminatory policies in athletics programs sponsored in the context of educational institutions.

(VMI) United States v. Virginia, 518 U.S. 515, 546 (1996)

The Supreme Court ruled in this case that the publicly funded Virginia Military Institute (VMI), by excluding females, violated the Fourteenth Amendment's equal protection, despite the fact that its sex-segregation policies did not violate Title IX because of statutory exemption as a military educational institution.

*Yellow Springs Exempted Village School District Board of
Education v. Ohio High School Athletic Association, 647 F.2d
651 (6th Cir. 1981), rev'g on diff. grounds 443 F. Supp. 753
(S.D. Ohio 1978)*

The court held that the use of an irrebuttable presumption that all
females are physically weaker than all males denied plaintiff's
liberty interest, thereby violating substantive due process rights.
The court also determined that under Title IX the athletic association could not bar schools which chose to field mixed teams from
athletic competition. Judge Jones, concurring in part and dissenting
in part, found that the "separate but equal" program for female
athletes at the middle school level violates equal protection and rel-
egates females to inferior girls' teams. He suggested that a stigma
may attach upon the separation of male and female athletes.

Notes

Chapter One

1. Cited in Diane Heckman, "Women and Athletics: A Twenty-Year Retrospective on Title IX," *University of Miami Entertainment and Sports Law Review*, Winter 1992, 34.

2. For early analysis about how sports pervade American society as well as world political systems, historically and today, see Nancy Theberg and Peter Donnelly, eds., *Sport and the Sociological Imagination* (Fort Worth, TX: Texas Christian University Press, 1984); Elaine M. Blinde, "Teaching Sociology of Sport: An Active Learning Approach," *Teaching Sociology*, July 1995, 264–268.

3. Lisa De Moraes, "The Super Bowl's Ratings: Appropriately Decent," *Washington Post*, February 8, 2005, C7; "Career-Low Audience for Bush's State of the Union," February 3, 2005, http://ca.tv.yahoo.com/news/va/20050203/110749470400.html.

4. For this reason, Jeffrey Hill argues that more attention needs to be directed to the way sports contribute to wider political processes. Jeffrey Hill, "Introduction: Sport and Politics," *Journal of Contemporary History*, July 2003, 355–361. See also Lincoln Allison, ed., *The Changing Politics of Sport* (Manchester: Manchester University Press, 1993).

5. Melissa M. Beck, "Notes: Fairness on the Field: Amending Title VII to Foster Greater Female Participation in Professional Sports," *Cardozo Law Journal* 12 (1994): 244.

6. Julia Lamber, "Gender and Intercollegiate Athletics: Data and Myths," *University of Michigan Journal of Law,* Fall 2000–Winter 2001, 154.

7. Barbara Lee, "An Evening of Stars: 5th Annual Celebration of Women in Sports," September 24, 2002, www.barbaraleefoundation.org. As Lee observes, "Did anybody ever urge Billie Jean King to run for office? What about Jackie Joyner-Kersee?" Lee's point is that sports trains people to have such skills as "leadership, hard work, courage, perseverance, and determination." That is, "sports don't train you just to be successful on the field; sports train you to be successful in life" generally and in politics specifically. Thus Lee argues that "just as Title IX has encouraged girls and young women to play sports, women need to encourage other women to run for [political] office."

8. Varda Burstyn, *The Rights of Man: Manhood, Politics, and Culture of Sports* (Toronto: University of Toronto Press, 1999). Also see Jim McKay, Michael A. Messner, and Don Sabo, eds., *Masculinities: Gender Relations in Sport* (Thousand Oaks, CA: Sage, 2000); Jon Swain, "How Young Schoolboys Become Somebody: The Role of the Body in the Construction of Masculinity," *British Journal of Sociology of Education,* July 2003, 299–314.

9. Michael H. Messner, *Power at Play: Sports and the Problem of Masculinity* (Boston: Beacon, 1992); Michael H. Messner, "Masculinities and Athletic Careers," *Gender and Society,* March 1989, 71–88. Also see *Social Approaches to Sport,* ed. Robert M. Pankin (Madison, NJ: Fairleigh Dickinson University Press, 1982); D. Stanley Eitzen, *Fair and Foul: Beyond the Myths and Paradoxes of Sport* (Lanham, MD: Roman & Littlefield, 1999); Eric Dunning, *Sport Matters: Sociological Studies of Sport, Violence, and Civilization* (London: Routledge, 1999); Jan Graydon, "But It's More Than a Game. It's an Institution: Feminist Perspectives on Sport," *Feminist Review,* Spring 1983, 5–16. For explanations of how the social construction of sports is connected to the undervalued labor of mothers and wives, see Shona M. Thompson, *Mother's Taxis: Sport and Women's Labor* (Albany: SUNY Press, 1999); for an assessment of how economic and political influences determine women's interest in and development of bodybuilding at both professional and amateur levels, see Maria R. Lowe, *Women of Steel: Female Bodybuilders and the Struggle for Self Definition* (New York: New York University Press, 1998); for an analysis of how the social construction of masculinity can result in the acceptance of male violence toward women as normal male behavior, see Rosaline Miles, *The Rites of Man: Love, Sex, and Death in the Making of the Male* (London: Grafton, 1991).

10. On this point, see also Mariah Burton Nelson, *The Stronger Women Get, the More Men Love Football: Sexism and the American Culture of Sports* (New York: Harcourt Brace, 1994); Nelson, *Embracing Victory: How*

Women Can Compete Joyously, Compassionately, and Successfully in the Workplace and on the Playing Field (New York: Avon, 1998).

11. For an examination of how the traditional exclusion of women from sports reinforces stereotypical gender role norms, see Earl C. Dudley Jr. and George Rutherglen, "Ironies, Inconsistencies, and Intercollegiate Athletics: Title IX, Title VII, and Statistical Evidence of Discrimination," *Virginia Journal of Sports and the Law*, Fall 1999, 177.

12. Generally, the term "sex" refers to presumed biological differences between men and women while the term "gender" refers to differences resulting from socialization. We often use the terms "sex" and "gender" interchangeably, since in the context of sports, we contend that both sex and gender differences are socially constructed.

13. For an early argument about the need to challenge the way sports policies reproduce the dominant, male-centered organization of sports and society, see Jennifer Hargreaves, *Sporting Females: Critical Issues in the History of Sociology of Women's Sports* (New York: Routledge, 1994).

14. For more on historical ideas of women's bodies as weak, see chapter 6. See also Patricia Vertinsky, *The Eternally Wounded Woman: Woman, Doctors, and Exercise in the Late Nineteenth Century* (Chicago: University of Illinois Press, 1989).

15. For an analysis of the way the social construction of the body becomes the foundation for the social construction of femininity and masculinity, see Trish Gorely, Rachel Holroyd, and David Kirk, "Muscularity, the Habitus, and the Social Construction of Gender: Towards a Gender-Relevant Physical Education," *British Journal of Sociology of Education*, September 2003, 429–448.

16. Maree Boyle and Jim McKay, "You Can Leave Your Troubles at the Gate: A Case Study of the Exploitation of Older Women's Labor and 'Leisure' in Sport," *Gender and Society*, October 1995, 556–575.

17. As Nancy Theberge notes, there are two major critiques of sport. Radical criticisms focus on its authoritarian, excessively competitive, and hence elitist structures, while feminist criticisms focus on the male-dominated and masculine bias common to sports. Her analysis argues that both critiques are inadequate, and she proposes a revised model of sport, much as we do in this book. Nancy Theberge, "A Critique of Critiques: Radical and Feminist Writings on Sport," *Social Forces*, December 1981, 341–353.

18. Rhonda Reaves, " 'There's No Crying in Baseball': Sports and the Legal and Social Construction of Gender," *Journal of Gender, Race, and Justice*, Spring 2001, 283; Galen Sherwin, "Single-Sex Schools and the Anti-Segregation Principle," *New York University Review of Law and Social Change* 30 (2005): 35.

19. Jacques Steinberg, "Imus Struggling to Retain Sway as a Franchise," *New York Times*, Wednesday, April 11, 2007, A1.

20. Selena Roberts, "A First-Class Response to a Second-Class Putdown," *New York Times*, Wednesday, April 11, 2007, C15.

21. Quoted in Roberts, "First-Class Response," C15.

22. For an important analysis of how the Women's National Basketball Association uses marketing devices to depict its players as good, heterosexual white girls as a tactic for deflecting images that WNBA players are either black, lesbian, or both, see Mary G. McDonald, "Queering Whiteness: The Peculiar Case of the Women's National Basketball Association," *Sociological Perspectives*, Winter 2002, 379–396.

23. For an excellent analysis of the advantages of using a principle of intersectionality in research projects, see Ange-Marie Hancock, "When Multiplication Doesn't Equal Quick Addition: Examining Intersectionality As a Research Paradigm," *Perspectives on Politics*, March 2007, 63–79. Also see Rhonda Reaves, " 'There's No Crying in Baseball': Sports and the Legal and Social Construction of Gender," *J. Gender, Race and Justice* 283 (Spring 2001).

24. Barrie Houlihan and Anita White, *The Politics of Sports Development: Development of Sport or Development through Sport?* (London: Routledge, 2002), 3.

25. For an excellent analysis of the range of ways sports matters in contemporary American society, including the partisan political system, see Anne Bolin and Jane Granskog, *Athletic Intruders: Ethnographic Research on Women, Culture, and Exercise* (Albany: State University of New York Press, 2003).

26. Winnie Hu, "Equal Cheers for Boys and Girls Draw Some Boos," *New York Times*, January 14, 2007, A1. Such behavior and policies undermine the potential for cheerleading to constitute a progressive opportunity for integrating women into sports, as discussed by Natalie Adams and Pamela Bettis, "Commanding the Room in Short Skirts: Cheering as the Embodiment of Ideal Girlhood," *Gender and Society*, February 2003, 73–91.

27. Valeri Vecchio, "Class B Finalist Has Female Kicker," *Post-Standard*, November 26, 1993, D3.

28. Nancy Theberge, "It's Part of the Game: Physicality and the Production of Gender in Women's Hockey," *Gender and Society*, February 1997, 69–87; Nancy Theberge, *Higher Goals: Women's Ice Hockey in the Politics of Gender* (New York: State University of New York Press, 2000).

29. Note that the WBNA league in December 2005 voted to make rules changes, beginning in the 2006 season, that bring some women's rules more

in line with men's rules, including changing the shot clock for women from 30 to 24 seconds, to be the same as the men's game, and changing the structure of the game from two 20-minute halves to four 10-minute quarters. The men still play longer, 12-minute quarters. "New WNBA Rules Include Quarters, 24-Second Clock," http://sports.espn.go.com/wnba/news/story?id+2250190.

30. *Official NCAA Rule Book*, 2001, www.olympic-usa.org/sports; see also www.everyrule.com.

31. Mary Jo Festle, *Playing Nice: Politics and Apologies in Women's Sports* (New York: Columbia University Press, 1996), 55.

32. Juliet Macur, "Wimbledon to Pay Equal Prize Money to Men and Women," *New York Times*, February 23, 2007, C10.

33. International Olympic Committee, www.olympic.org.uk/sports/programme/disciplines uk.asp?DiscCode=CM.

34. International Olympic Committee, www.olympic.org.uk/sports/programme/disciplines uk.asp?DiscCode=CM.

35. "Margaret Thompson Murdock," www.usashooting.com/alumni/MargaretMurdock.html.

36. Margaret Murdock, interview, November 13, 2006.

37. International Olympic Committee, www.olympic.org.uk/sports/programme/disciplines uk.asp?DiscCode=CM.

38. Richard F. Johnson, Donna J. Merullo, and Valerie J. Rice, "Relation of Rifle Stock Length and Weight to Military Rifle Marksmanship Performance by Men and Women," *Perceptual and Motor Skills*, October 2001, 479.

39. Sara Greenlee, "Shooting: Tidmore Wins First NCAA Championships in Air Rifle, Army Stops UAF from Winning Seven Straight," press release, March 12, 2005, www.usocpressbox.org/usoc/pressbox.nsf.

40. USA Gymnastics Organization, www.usa-gymnastics.org.

41. "Figure Skating," www.olympic.org/uk/sports/programme/disciplines ik.asp?DiscCode=FS. Emphasis added.

42. "Figure Skating," www.olympic.org/uk/sports/programme/disciplines ik.asp?DiscCode=FS.

43. The difference between the fastest American male runner and the fastest male runner, who was from Kenya, was 6:49.

44. Table tennis is an Olympic sport and the others are recognized as competitive sports by the International Olympic Committee.

45. To be recognized by the IOC, the sport must be sponsored by an organization that belongs to the International Sports Federations, international nongovernmental organizations that administer one or several sports at world level and encompass organizations administering such sports at

the national level. To qualify as a recognized sport, the organizations administering the sport "must apply the Olympic movement Anti-Doping Code and conduct effective out-of-competition tests in accordance with the established [IOC] rules." www.olympic.org/uk/sports/recognized/index_uk.asp.

46. While there are some occasions and categories that provide for mixed-sex teams, the major tournaments and events for all of these sports use formats featuring separate divisions for male and female players. Likewise the World Bridge Federation International Olympic Committee Grand Prix features separate play for women, juniors, and seniors. Although local club bridge competitions do feature men and women as partners or opponents, this high-level play in pursuit of inclusion in the Winter Olympics features separate female play (http://worldbridge.org/competitions/worldchampion ships/teamchampionships.asp). College bowling teams feature separate male and female divisions and even though there are specific mixed-gender categories of play at various levels of bowling, male and female all-time scoring records and typical play exist as separate entities. www.bowlingmembership .com/PDF/bowlers_encyclopedia_Oct0604.PDF.

47. "Juniors" are players up to twenty-five years old; "seniors" are players at least fifty-five years old. "Categories," www.worldbridge.org/categories.

48. Marilyn Yalom, *Birth of the Chess Queen: A History* (New York: HarperCollins, 2004).

49. "Regulations for the 36th Chess Olympiad," www.36chesso-lympiad-daily.com. See also www.fide.com/officialhandbook.

50. Simone de Beauvoir, *The Second Sex* (New York: Knopf, 1957).

51. "Tournament Rules and Format," www.playbca.com/vegas/rules .php.

52. "Ten Toughest Athletes," *USA Today*, www.USAToday.com/sports/graphics/10toughest/flash.htm.

53. "Equestrian," www.olympic.org/uk/sports/programme/index_uk .asp?SportCode=EQ.

54. "USEA Announced 2006 Hall of Fame Inductees," http://useventing .com/aboutus.php?section=convention&id=539.

55. Joanne C. Gerstner, "Ruggiero, Brother Team Up," *Detroit News*, January 27, 2005, www.detnews.com/2005/moresports/0501/27/C01–72111 .htm.

56. "Ruggiero Limited to One Period of Action," http://sports.espn .go.com/espn.

57. Personal correspondence with authors.

58. www.teeballusa.org/rules.asp

59. Melissa A. Landers and Gary Alan Fine, "Learning Life's Lessons in Tee Ball: The Reinforcement of Gender and Status in Kindergarten Sport," *Sociology of Sport Journal* 13 (1996): 87–93.

60. Kathleen Williams, Kathleen Haywood, and Mary A. Painter, "Environmental Versus Biological Influences on Gender Differences in the Overarm Throw for Force: Dominant and Non-dominant Arm Throws," *Women in Sport and Physical Activity Journal* 5 (1998): 29–48.

61. For early challenges to the idea that women's sports participation depends primarily on women's biological or psychological differences from men, see Mary A. Boutilier and Lucinda San Giovanni, *The Sporting Woman* (Champaign, IL: Human Kinetics, 1983); and Betsy C. Postow, ed., *Women, Philosophy, and Sport: A Collection of New Essays* (Metuchen, NJ: Scarecrow, 1983).

62. Cited in Ruth Bader Ginsburg, Biography.corn/id 1 51 50.

63. Cited in Ruth Bader Ginsburg, Biography.corn/id 1 51 50.

64. *Reed v. Reed*, 404 U.S. 71 (1971).

65. In 1976, for example, in *Craig v. Boren*, the high court ruled on an Oklahoma law that allowed women who were 18 to 20 years old to purchase beer containing 3.2 percent alcohol, but did not allow men to make such purchases until they were 21. Oklahoma officials documented that among 18- to 20-year-olds, 11 times as many males as females were arrested for drunk driving; that 10 times more males than females were arrested for public drunkenness; and more male drivers than female drivers preferred beer to other alcoholic beverages (84 percent of males, 77 percent of females). The state of Oklahoma argued that such statistics offered good reason for different policies for males and female, but the Supreme Court ruled that for gender to be used as a "proxy for other more germane bases of classification... [there must be a strong] congruence between gender and the characteristic or trait that gender [is] purported to represent." The Court's message was that despite the state of Oklahoma's evidence, the correlation between gender and drunken behavior was not strong enough to use as a classifying device for the purpose of promoting public safety.

66. For an insightful analysis of how the ideal of equality is defined to be at the "law's heart" in the work of legal scholar Catharine MacKinnon, see Robin L. West, "Law's Nobility," *Yale Journal of Law and Feminism* 17 (2005): 385.

67. Cited in Mark Dyreson, "Nature by Design: Modern American Ideas about Sport, Energy, Evolution, and Republics, 1865–1920," *Journal of Sport History*, Fall 1999, 459.

68. Cited in Dyreson, "Nature by Design," 459.

69. See the chapter entitled "Boys Will Be Boys and Girls Will Not," in Nelson, *The Stronger Women Get*. See also Marilyn Frye, "Sexism," in *The Politics of Reality: Essays in Feminist Theory* (Freedom, CA: Crossing Press Feminist Series, 1983). Also see Geneviève Rail, *Sport and Postmodern Times* (Albany: SUNY Press, 1999).

70. Deborah L. Blake, "A Legal Framework for Single-Sex Education," *Women's Equity Resource Center Digest*, October 1999, http://www.2.edc.org/WomensEquity/pubs/digests/digest-singlesex.html. See also "More Schools Test Single-Sex Classrooms," www.msnbc.msn.com/id/13229488.

71. For an excellent review of the scope and impact of Title IX, see Kimberly Bingman, "Title IX of the 1972 Education Amendments," *Georgetown Journal of Gender in the Law*, Fall 2002, 329; David S. Cohen, "Title IX: Beyond Equal Protection," *Georgetown Journal of Gender in the Law*, Summer 2005, 217.

72. Title IX, implementing regulations. Cited in Williams, 799 F. Supp. (1992), 513, 516.

73. Hank Gola, "Singh Tees Off on Annika, Says Top Female Doesn't Belong," *New York Daily News*, May 13, 2003, 65.

74. "Sorenstam Brings Ratings to USA Network," *USA Today*, May 23, 2003, http://usatoday.com/sports/golf/pga/2003–05–23-colonial-ratings.

75. Festle, *Playing Nice*, 158–159.

76. Larry Schwartz, "Billie Jean Won for All Women," http://espn.go.com/sportscentury/features/00016010.html.

77. "Billie Jean King and Bobby Riggs, U.S. Tennis Players," www.historychannel.com/speeches/archive/speech_372.html.

78. For an excellent review article addressing the way sports policies socially construct not only masculinity but social, economic, and political systems of "hegemonic masculinity" despite the gains of Title IX, see Sohaila Shakib and Michele D. Dunbar, "The Social Construction of Female and Male High School Basketball Participation: Reproducing the Gender Order through a Two-Tiered Sporting Institution," *Sociological Perspectives*, Winter 2002, pp. 353–378. Also, for a superb analysis of the importance for women's equality and actualization of their abilities of images and practices featuring women's physical and mental strengths, see Shirley Castelnuovo and Sharon R. Guthrie, *Feminism and the Female Body: Liberating the Amazon Within* (Boulder: Lynne Rienner, 1988).

79. Schwartz, "Billie Jean Won."

80. Rudy Martzke, "Sorenstam Has Networks Hopping," *USA Today*, May 22, 2005, www.usatoday.com/sports/columnist/martzke/2003–05–22-martzke.

81. Martzke, "Sorenstam."

82. Kevin Paul Dupont, "History Lesson: She Can Hang with the Boys," *Boston Globe*, May 23, 2003, E1.

83. Kevin Paul Dupont, "Regardless of Score, Attempt a Success," *Boston Globe*, May 24, 2003, E1.

84. Jim McCabe, "Sour Note for Swede," *Boston Globe*, May 24, 2003, E7.

85. McCabe, "Sour Note for Swede."

Chapter Two

1. Cited in Deborah Brake, "The Struggle for Sex Equality in Sport and the Theory Behind Title IX," *University of Michigan Journal of Law Reform*, Fall–Winter 2000 (34 U. Mich. J. L. Ref. 13) 01:92

2. Jimmy Golen, "Kraft Blisters Parcells," August 28, 1996, www.s-t.com/daily/08–96/08–28–96/d01sp123.htm.

3. For an analysis of how the construction of masculinity often depends on the denigration of women, see Valerie K. Vojdik, "Gender Outlaws: Challenging Masculinity in Traditionally Male Institutions," *Berkeley Women's Law Journal* 17 (2002): 68.

4. Angelique Chengelis, "Wolverines in the Pink for Iowa," *Detroit News*, October 19, 2005, sports sec.

5. Chengelis, "Wolverines."

6. Researchers have found that boys' fear of being feminine can contribute to their rejection of academic work as an endeavor that is bookish rather than physical. Carolyn Jackson, "Motives for Laddishness at School: Fear of Failure and Fear of the Feminine," *British Educational Research Journal*, August 2003, 583–590.

7. Joe Leigh Simpson, Arne Ljunhqvist, Malcolm Ferguson-Smith, Albert de la Chapelle, Louis J. Elsas, A. A. Ehrhardt, Myron Genel, Elizabeth A. Ferris, and Alison Carlson, "Gender Verification in the Olympics," *Journal of the American Medical Association*, September 27, 2000, 1568–1569.

8. Laura A. Wackwitz, "Sex Testing in International Women's Athletics: A History of Silence," *Women in Sport & Physical Activity Journal*, March 31, 1996, 51.

9. "Mosaic in X & Y," *Time*, September 29, 1967, http://time.com/archive/preview/0,10987,899860,00.html.

10. "Sex Test Disqualifies Athlete," *New York Times*. September 16, 1967, 28.

11. D. B. Dickinson, M. Genel, C. B. Robinowitz, P. L. Turner, and G. L. Woods, "Gender Verification of Female Olympic Athletes," *Medicine and Science in Sports and Exercise*, October 2002, 1539.

12. "Olympics Require Sex Test," *New York Times*, January 30, 1968, 48.

13. Gina Kolata, "Ideas & Trend: Who Is Female? Science Can't Say" *New York Times*. February 16, 1992, http://query.nytimes.com/gst/health/article.

14. Gina Kolata, "Track Federation Urges End to Gene Test for Femaleness," *New York Times*, February 12, 1992, http://query.nytimes.com/gst/health/article.

15. Anne Fausto-Sterling, *Sexing the Body: Gender Politics and the Construction of Sexuality* (New York: Basic, 2000), 1–2.

16. Kolata, "Track Federation Urges End."

17. Boyd Eaton, Blaine A.Woodfin, James L. Askew, Blaise M. Morrisey, Louis J. Elsas, Jay L. Shoop, Elizabeth A. Martin, and John D. Cantwell, "The Polyclinic at the 1996 Atlanta Olympic Village," *Medical Journal of Australia*, December 1997, 599–602.

18. Joe Leigh Simpson, Arne Ljunhqvist, Malcolm L. Ferguson-Smith, Albert de la Chapelle, Louise J. Elsas, A. A. Ehrhardt, Myron Genel, Elizabeth A. Ferris, and Alison Carlson, "Gender Verification in the Olympics," *Journal of the American Medical Association*, September 27, 2000, 1568–1569.

19. J. C. Reeser, "Gender Identity and Sport: Is the Playing Field Level?" *British Journal of Sports Medicine*, May 2005, 695–699. The IOC Committee voted on this in June 1999 at the 109th IOC session in Seoul. "The 109th IOC Session in Seoul," *Olympic Review*, August-September 1999, 6–7.

20. Jere Longman, "Olympics: Drug Sleuths' Surprise Produces a Breakthrough," *New York Times*, December 18, 1994, http://query.nytimes.com/gst/health/article.

21. "Lausanne Declaration on Doping in Sport," www.sportunterricht.de/lksport/Declaration_e.html.

22. Neil Amdur, "Women Facing More Than an Athletic Struggle," *New York Times*, December 21, 1980, S1.

23. Amdur, "Women Facing."

24. For an early analysis of the significance of the construction of gender in sports by means of the marginalization of women coaches, see Nancy Theberge, "The Construction of Gender in Sports: Women, Coaching, and the Naturalization of Difference," *Social Problems*, August 1993, 301–313.

25. Theresa M. Wizemann and Mary-Lou Pardu, eds., *Exploring the Biological Contributions to Human Health: Does Sex Matter?* (Washington, D.C.: National Academy Press, 2001), 21.

26. Anne Fausto-Sterling, *Sexing the Body: Gender Politics and the Construction of Sexuality* (New York: Basic, 2000), 30–31.

27. Robin Herman, "Controversy over Renee Richards Adds Dimension to Sex Role in Sports," *New York Times,* August 31, 1976, 31.

28. Herman, "Controversy over Renee Richards."

29. For an excellent analysis of transsexualism in relation to sports, see Emily Q. Shults, "Sharply Drawn Lines: An Examination of Title IX, Intersex, and Transgender," *Cardozo Journal of Law and Gender,* Fall 2005, 337.

30. J. C. Reeser, "Gender Identity and Sport: Is the Playing Field Level?" *British Journal of Sports Medicine,* May 2005, 695–699; Patricia Del Ray, "Apologetics and Androgyny: The Past and the Future," *Frontiers: A Journal of Women's Studies,* Spring 1978, 8–10.

31. Eva Moore, Amy Wisniewski, and Adrian Dobs, "Endocrine Treatment of Transsexual People: A Review of Treatment Regimens, Outcomes, and Adverse Effects," *Journal of Clinical Endocrinology & Metabolism,* August 2003, 3468, 3469.

32. "Transgender in Sport," www.ausport.gov.au/women/ftrans.asp.

33. Arne Ljungqvist and Myron Genel, "Transsexual Athletes—When is Competition Fair?" *The Lancet,* December 2005, S42-S43.

34. Moore, Wisniewski, and Dobs, "Endocrine Treatment," 3467–3473.

35. Reeser, "Gender Identity," 695–699.

36. Jere Longman, "Pushing the Limits: A Special Report: Someday Soon, Athletic Edge May Be from Altered Genes," *New York Times,* May 11, 2001, www.query.nytimes.com/gst/health.

37. Stefan Lovgren, "Olympic Gold Begins with Good Genes, Experts Say," *National Geographic News,* August 20, 2004, http//:news.nationalgeographic.com/news/2004/08/0820_olympics_athletes.html.

38. Stefan Lovgren, "The Science of Lance Armstrong: Born, and Built, to Win," *National Geographic News,* July 22, 2005, http//:news.nationalgeographic.com/news/2005/07/0722 050722 armstrong.html.

39. Longman, "Pushing the Limits."

40. Robert McG. Thomas Jr., "Flo Hyman, Volleyball Star for 1984 U.S. Olympic Team," *New York Times,* January 25, 1986, 10.

41. Natalie Angier, "New Clues Emerge on a Fatal Hereditary Disease," *New York Times,* July 26, 1990, http://query.nytimes.com/gst/health/article.

42. Judith Lorber, "Believing Is Seeing: Biology as Ideology," *Gender and Society,* December 1993, 568–581.

43. Sandra L. Hanson and Rebecca S. Kraus, "Women, Sports, and Science: Do Female Athletes Have an Advantage?" *Sociology of Education,* vol. 71, no. 2 (Apr., 1998) pp. 93–110.

44. "Body Measurements," National Center for Health Statistics, Centers for Disease Control, www.cdc.gov/nchs/fastats/bodymeas.htm.

45. William P. Ebben and Randall L. Jensen, "Strength Training for Women: Debunking Myths That Block Opportunity," *The Physician and Sports Medicine*, May 1998.

46. Ebben and Jensen, "Strength Training for Women."

47. Ebben and Jensen, "Strength Training for Women."

48. Lynda B. Ransdell and Christine L. Wells, "Sex Differences in Athletic Performance," *Women in Sport & Physical Activity Journal*, March 31, 1999, 56.

49. The association of masculinity with testosterone, studies have shown, lead women to perceive masculine faces as markers of testosterone, which in turn women associate with indications of good health and aesthetic preferences as positive features on one hand, but also with negative features such as male dominance and distasteful personality traits. Researchers concluded that there is a distinction between masculinity defined as facial dominance and presumed testosterone levels reflecting males' perceived status and men's physical attractiveness to women. Nick Neave, Sarah Laing, Bernhard Fink, and John T. Manning, "Second to Fourth Digit Ratio, Testosterone, and Perceived Male Dominance," *Proceedings: Biological Sciences*, October 2003, 2167–2172.

50. R. C. Schafer, "Special Considerations in Female Athletes," http://chiro.org/pplaces/RC_Schafer/mono-10.htm.

51. Ransdell and Wells, "Sex Differences," 67.

52. Ellen B. Brandt, "Coed Sports: Is Equality the Answer?" *The Physician and Sportsmedicine*, September 1999, 121. See also Ransdell and Wells, who cite sources suggesting elite male distance runners have as little as 5 to 10 percent body fat while elite female distance runners have 9 to 15 percent body fat.

53. Ebben and Jensen, "Strength Training for Women."

54. Ransdell and Wells, "Sex Differences," 60.

55. Ransdell and Wells, "Sex Differences," 7.

56. Ebben and Jensen, "Strength Training for Women."

57. Nancy C. Rich, "Female Strength and Neuromuscular Response Time: A Review," *Women in Sport & Physical Activity Journal*, March 31, 1994, 48.

58. Wilmore cited in Nancy C. Rich, "Female Strength and Neuromuscular Response Time: A Review." *Women in Sport & Physical Activity Journal*, March 31, 1994. Vol. 3, No. 1: 49. See also J. R. Morrow Jr., A. S. Jackson, W. W. Hosler, and J. K. Kachurik. 1979. "The importance of strength, speed, and body size for team success in women's intercollegiate volleyball." *Research Quarterly*. 50: 429–437.

59. C. S. Fulco et al., "Slower Fatigue and Faster Recovery of the Adductor Pollicis Muscle in Women Matched for Strength with Men," *Acta Physiologica Scandinavica*, November 1999, 233–239.

60. Ransdell and Wells, "Sex Differences," 65.

61. M. C. Riddell, S. L. Parington, N. Stupka, D. Armstrong, C. Rennie, and M. A. Tarnopolsky, "Substrate Utilization during Exercise Performed with and without Glucose Ingestion in Female and Males Endurance Trained Athletes," *International Journal of Sport Nutrition and Exercise Metabolism*, December 2003, 407–421.

62. Mark A. Tarnopolsky, "Gender Differences in Physiology: Introduction to the Symposium," *Canadian Journal of Applied Physiology*, August 2000.

63. Tarnopolsky, "Gender Differences."

64. B. Kendall and R. Eston, "Exercise-Induced Muscle Damage and the Potential Protective Role of Estrogen," *Sports Medicine*, February 2002, 103–123.

65. Ransdell and Wells, "Sex Differences," 62.

66. Charlotte A. Tate and Robert W. Holtz, "Gender and Fat Metabolism during Exercise: A Review," *Canadian Journal of Applied Physiology*, December 1998, 570–582.

67. Ransdell and Wells, "Sex Differences," 65.

68. For an excellent analysis of the sex-integration of baseball, see Susan E. Jennings, " 'As American as Hot Dogs, Apple Pie, and Chevrolet': The Desegregation of Little League Baseball," The Journal of American Culture, 4:4 (Winter, 1981), 81.

69. Richelle Taylor, "News flash: Women are different from men," The Lantern, 5/30/97, http://media.www.thelantern.com/media/storage/paper333/news/1997/05/30/Column/News-Flash.Women.Are.Different.From.Men =42151.shml, accessed 7–10–07.

70. Richelle Taylor, "News flash: Women are different from men," The Lantern, 5/30/97, http://media.www.thelantern.com/media/storage/paper333/news/1997/05/30/Column/News-Flash.Women.Are.Different.From.Men =42151.shml, accessed 7–10–07.

71. Shirley Castelnuovo and Sharon R. Guthrie, *Feminism and the Female Body: Liberating the Amazon Within* (Boulder, Co: Lynne Rienner, 1988), p. 1.

72. Shirley Castelnuovo and Sharon R. Guthrie, *Feminism and the Female Body: Liberating the Amazon Within* (Boulder, Co: Lynne Rienner, 1988), p. 13.

73. "UW–Badwater Ultramarathon 135 Miles: Pam Reed Wins Race Outright for Second Time," http://ultramarathonworld.com/news_2003/n26jyo3b.htm.

74. Mark Poepsel, "Pam Reed Completes 300 Mile Run," March 29, 2005, www.kold.com/Global/story.asp?S=3136042&nav=14RTY0WP.

75. "Anchorage Daily News Iditarod Hall of Fame," *Anchorage Daily News*, www.adn.com/iditarod/guide/hall/story/764104p-817202c.html.

76. "Libby Riddles: Libbymania Helped Propel Race," *Anchorage Daily News*, February 20, 2001, www.adn.com/iditarod/hall/story/764092 p-817024c.html.

77. Ransdell and Wells, "Sex Differences," 60.

78. D. J. Dutto and J. M. Cappaert, "Sex Differences in Crawl Stroke Swimming," *Medicine and Science in Sports and Exercise* 26, no. 5 (1994): 1098.

79. Richard Severo, "Gertrude Ederle, the First Woman to Swim Across the English Channel, Dies at 98," *New York Times*, December 1, 2003, www .nytimes.com/2003/12/01/sports/othersports/01EDER.html.

80. "Alison Streeter Swims English Channel—Again!" srichinmoyraces .org/channel/news/alison_successful. See also "A Glorious, Brave, and Dotty Obsession," *London Guardian*, August 27, 2001, http://sport.guardian.co.uk.

81. Records from Catalina Island Swim website, www.swimcatalina .org.

82. Information from records posted at U.S. Masters Swimming website, www.usms.org/longdist/records.html.

83. Emily Watts, interview, May 2003.

84. Race results from Manhattan Island Foundation website, www .nycswim.com/events/results.aspx?Event_ID=2.

85. Laura Pappano, "Closing the Gender Gap," *Boston Globe Magazine*, September 28, 2003, 10.

86. USGWA national rankings, http://usgwa.com/rankings.

87. Pappano, "Closing the Gender Gap."

88. Ron Wilmot, "Hutchinson Steals Thunder," *Anchorage Daily News*, February 5, 2006, http://fhsw.com/Michaela%20Hutchison%20wins% 20Alaska%20state%20title.htm.

89. Kristin Dizon, "The Adventures of Spider Woman: Ace Climber Lynn Hill Tells Her Tale of a Life on the Rocks," *Seattle Post-Intelligencer*, May 20, 2002, D1. See also Ed Douglas, "Where There's a Hill," *Observers Sports Magazine*, May 5, 2002, 40.

90. Account from Lynn Hill, "El Capitan's Nose Climbed Free," *American Alpine Journal*, 1994, www.stanford.edu/~clint/yos/nosehill.htm.

91. Ransdell and Wells, "Sex Differences," 58.

92. Nancy C. Rich, "Female Strength and Neuromuscular Response Time: A Review," *Women in Sport and Activity Journal*, March 31, 1994, 54.

93. Rich, "Female Strength," 54.

94. S. E. Always, J.D. MacDougall, D. G. Sale, J. R. Sutton and A. J. McComas., "Functional and Structural Adaptations in Skeletal Muscle of Trained Athletes," *Journal of Applied Physiology* (March) 64, no. 3 (1988): 1114–1120.

95. Prince, Hikida, and Hagerman cited in Rich, "Female Strength," 69.

96. Jon C. Henry and Christopher Kaeding, "Neuromuscular Differences between Male and Female Athletes." *Current Women's Health Reports* 1 (2001): 241–244, www.biomedcentral.com/content/pdf/cr-wr1326.pdf.

97. E. J. Steele Cowling, Jr., "Is Lower Limb Muscle Synchrony during Landing Affected by Gender? Implications for Variations in ACL Injury Rates," *Journal of Electromyography and Kinesiology*, August 2001, 263–268.

98. Dr. Bertram Zarins, interview, August 14, 2003.

99. L. Y. Griffin, J. Agel, M. J. Albohn, et al., "Non-contact Anterior Cruciate Ligament Injuries: Risk Factors and Prevention Strategies," *Journal of the American Academy of Orthopedic Surgery* 8, no. 3 (2000): 141–150; cited in Henry and Kaeding, "Neuromuscular Differences."

100. Dr. Arthur Boland, interview, August 22, 2003.

101. Theresa M. Wizemann and Mary-Lou Pardu, eds., *Exploring the Biological Contributions to Human Health: Does Sex Matter?* (Washington, D.C.: National Academy Press, 2001), 14.

102. Wizemann and Pardu, eds., *Exploring*, 29.

103. Wizemann and Pardu, eds., *Exploring*, 18.

104. Dr. Bertram Zarins, interview, August 14, 2003.

105. John Steinbreder, "No Guts, No Glory: When It Comes to NFL Offensive Lines These Days, Big Is Definitely In," *Sky*, December 1996, 86–90.

106. Erik Brady, "She's the Family Tree: McCarville Sprouts Out of Tight Household to Become All-American at Minnesota," *USA Today*, December 14, 2004, C1.

107. Brady, "She's the Family Tree," C2.

108. Sally B. Donnelly, "Meet The Power Sisters," *Time*, August 30, 2000, www.time.com/time/arts. See also Pagan Kennedy, "The Strongest Woman in the World," *New York Times Magazine*, July 28, 2002, 38–40.

109. Cheryl Ann Haworth biography, www.msbn.tv/USAVision/displaypage.aspx?id=448. See also Cecil Bleiker, "Haworth Fourth at Weightlifting Worlds," *USA Weightlifting*, October 7, 2007, www.usoc.org/11645_49437.htm.

110. Greg Garber, "Holley Mangold Fights Perception to Succeed," November 22, 2006, http://sports.espn.go.com/espn.

111. Brady, "She's the Family Tree," C1.

112. Dr. Carol Otis, interview, August 25, 2003.

113. Dr. Carol Otis, interview; Laura Pappano, "Closing the Gender Gap," *Boston Globe Magazine*. September 28, 2003, cover story.

114. "NBA Notebook: They're Tall; But Too Wide?" *Seattle Times*, http://seattletimes.nwsource.com/html/sonics/200220 1574 nbanotes09.htm.

115. Lynda Ransdell, interview, July 30, 2003. At the time Ransdell was associate professor of exercise and sport science at the University of Utah.

116. Orlando Molina, "Hockey Not Phase for Saxon," *Contra Costa Times*, www.tallahassee.com/mld/cctimes/sports/youth/2817712.htm.

117. "Woman Gets Kick Out of Making History," *Boston Globe*. December 26, 2002, C6.

118. Katie Hnida, college sports profile, www.collegesports.com/schools/nm/sports/m-footbl/mtt/hnida katie00.htm.

119. "Female Scorer Breaks the Ice," *Boston Sunday Globe*, February 2, 2003, C6.

120. Joanne C. Gerstner, "Ruggiero, Brother Team Up," *Detroit News*. January 27, 2005, www.detnews.com/2005/moresports/0501/27/C01–72111.htm.

121. Jason Dunbar, "No Backing Down as Nelson Steps In," *Boston Globe*, August 8, 2003, E10.

122. Becky Dubin Jenkins, "British Woman Weathers Record Sail," *USA Today*, February 8, 2005, C1.

123. Matt Weeks, "One Giant Leap for Women's Basketball," *USA Today*, March 31, 2004, C1.

124. Yi-Wyn Yen, "Do Balls Matter? Get Your Mind Out of the Gutter: One Woman Proves She Can Bowl with the Boys," *Sports Illustrated*, April 4, 2005, 14.

125. "Sorenstam Crosses $20 Million in Career Earnings," www.lpga.com/content_1.aspx?pid=8034&mid=2.

126. Dave Anderson, "At 13, She Already Has Tiger in Her Sights," *New York Times*, June 28, 2003, A1.

127. "Wie Wins Men's US Open Qualifier," BBC Sport, May 16, 2006, http://news.bbc.co.uk/sport2/hi/golf/4986104.stm.

Chapter Three

1. Senator McGovern, *Congressional Record*, 30158, August 5, 1971.

2. Jane Gross, "Miss Lopiano a Leader in Women's Sports," *New York Times*, January 8, 1980, C12.

3. Donna Lopiano, "Growing Up with Gender Discrimination in Sports," in Richard E. Lapchick, ed., *Sport in Society: Equal Opportunity or Business As Usual?* (Thousand Oaks, CA: Sage, 1996), 83–95.

4. Lopiano, "Growing Up," 83.

5. "Ford Formally Admits Girls to Little League," *New York Times*. December 27, 1974, 66.

6. "Schools Get Guidelines to Bar Sex Bias in Sports and Books," *New York Times*, November 13, 1974, 91.

7. National Coalition for Women and Girls in Education, *Title IX at 25*, www.ncwge.org/pubs.htm.

8. "H.E.W. Head Says Title IX Won't 'Bankrupt' Schools," *New York Times*, June 27, 1975, 15–16.

9. Many are still unhappy about possible policy consequences of Title IX. Richard A. Epstein, "Forward: Just Do It! Title IX as a Threat to University Autonomy," *Michigan Law Review*, May 2003.

10. Janet Sayers, *Biological Politics: Feminist and Anti-Feminist Perspectives* (London: Tavistock, 1982), 12.

11. Sayers, *Biological Politics*, 10.

12. Edward H. Clarke, *Sex in Education, Or, A Fair Chance for Girls* (Boston: Osgood, 1873), 32–33.

13. Clarke, *Sex in Education*, 22, 33–39.

14. Patricia Schroeder, quoted in Letty Cottin Pogrebin, *Family Politics* (New York: McGraw-Hill, 1983), chap. 6.

15. Zine Magubane, "Which Bodies Matter? Feminism, Poststructuralism, Race, and the Curious Theoretical Odyssey of the Hottentot Venus," *Gender and Society*, December 2001, 816–34.

16. Brendan O'Flaherty and Jill S. Shapiro, "Apes, Essences, and Races: What Natural Scientists Believed about Human Variation, 1700–1900," Columbia University, Department of Economics, Discussion Paper Series no. 0102–24, March 2002, 36.

17. Stephanie A. Shields, "Functionalism, Darwinism, and the Psychology of Women: A Study in Social Myth," *American Psychologist* 30 (1975): 740.

18. G. J. Romanes, "Mental Differences between Men and Women," *Nineteenth Century* 21 (1887): 655. Quoted in Shields, "Functionalism," 741.

19. Stephen Jay Gould notes flaws in Broca's work, observing that "brain weight decreases with age and Broca's women were, on average, considerably older than his men at death." Also, he noted, brain weight increases with height and the men in Broca's sample, on average, were considerably taller than the women. Using multiple regression analysis to correct for age and height, Gould found differences in brain sizes of the men and women in Broca's study was reduced by 36 percent. See "Measuring Heads: Paul Broca and the Heyday of Craniology," in Stephen Jay Gould, ed., *The Mismeasure of Man* (New York: Norton, 1996), 137–138.

20. Cited in Gould, *Mismeasure*, 136–137.

21. Cited in Viola Klein, *The Feminine Character: History of an Ideology* (London: Routledge, 1946), 48.

22. Gould, *Mismeasure*, 147.

23. Quoted in Gould, *Mismeasure*, 136.

24. Quoted in Gould, *Mismeasure*, 418. For excellent analysis about how the development of civilization in relationship to sports reflects biased assumptions about gender, particularly the superiority of men compared to women, see Jennifer Hargreaves's excellent work, *Sport, Culture and Ideology* (London: Routledge, 1982); *Marxism, Cultural Studies, and Sport* (London: Routledge, 2007); and *Heroines of Sport: The Politics of Difference and Identity* (London: Routledge 2001).

25. For example, women were prohibited from working as bartenders. See chapter 7.

26. Mary Wollstonecraft, *A Vindication of the Rights of Woman* (1792; Mineola, NY: Dover, 1996).

27. Mildred H. McAfee, "Segregation and the Women's Colleges," *American Journal of Sociology*, July 1937, 16–22.

28. McAfee, "Segregation," 16–22.

29. Suzanne Mettler, *Soldiers to Citizens: the G.I. Bill and the Making of the Greatest Generation* (Cambridge: Oxford University Press, 2005), 3.

30. www.gibill.va.gov/education/GI Bill.htm

31. www.pbs.org/newshour/bb/military/july-decoo/gibill_7-4a.html

32. Benjamin Fine, "14 Billion Spent in 7 Years to Educate 8,000,000 G.I.'s," *New York Times*, July 22, 1951, 1.

33. Fine, "14 Billion Spent," 1.

34. Mettler, *Soldiers*, 7.

35. The mammoth expenditures allocated by the federal government for the GI Bill do not fully reveal the program's impact. To appreciate the scope of opportunities supported by the GI Bill, consider that of the men born in 1920, "fully 80 percent were military veterans." And military veterans used the GI Bill in record percentages. Fully 51 percent of World War II veterans, or 7.8 million, used the GI Bill to further their education or training. Mettler, *Soldiers*, 7.

36. Andrea Stone, "Panel's Decision Reheats Women-in-Combat Debate," *USA Today*, May 19, 2005, 7A.

37. Ann Scott Tyson, "Bid to Limit Women in Combat Withdrawn," *Washington Post*, May 26, 2005, A1. The cultural debate over who should bear the risks, as well as the rewards, of dangerous military service is not new. Joseph Califano, former adviser to President Lyndon Johnson, believed in applying standards of equity to military service, asserting that "it's very

important that we have a system that requires every social and economic group in this country and every class to bear their fair share of the dangers of dying in escapades that we think involve our national interest." www.pbs.org/newshour/bb/europe/jan-june99/service_4–8.html.

We have never had such a system and still don't. In 1971, for example, this idea was tested when several men eligible for the Vietnam draft contended a male-only draft was a form of sex discrimination. Why, they asked, should they be required to risk their lives for their country just because of their sex? In *Rostker v. Goldberg,* the Court considered the constitutionality of Congress limiting the draft to males. *Rostker v. Goldberg,* 453 U.S. 57 (1981). The Court declared that it is constitutional to draft only men.

The restriction of women from combat positions, as the Court noted, meant that "women may not be assigned to duty on vessels or in aircraft that are engaged in combat missions" (*Rostker,* p. 76). The Court concluded the reason Congress does not require women to register for the draft is not because of their sex, but because they belong to a group not eligible for combat duty. Thus the Court ruled, "men and women, because of the combat restrictions on women, are simply not similarly situated for purposes of a draft or registration for a draft" (*Rostker,* p. 78). Selection of only men was not unconstitutional sex discrimination.

38. Mettler (p. 30) states that women constituted less than 2 percent of the military in World War II. Using 2 percent as the component of the military that is women indicates, therefore, that there were 16,600,000 people in the military, 16,268,000 of whom were men and 332,000 women. Some estimate the number of women to be 350,000, which would not change the percentages appreciably. www.liblncsu.edu/exhibits/gibill/eOpportunity .html.

39. userpages.aug.com/captbarb/femvets5.html

40. userpages.aug.com/captbarb/femvetsalso.html

41. William Paul Skelton and Nadine Khouzam Skelton, "Women Prisoners of War," *Military Medicine* 160, no. 11 (1995): 558–560.

42. Franklin D. Roosevelt, "Roosevelt on Rights Bill," *New York Times,* June 22, 1944, 32.

43. *VA Health Care for Women: Despite Progress, Improvements Needed,* General Accounting Office report GAO/HRD-92–23, January 1992, 1.

44. *1998 Advisory Committee on Women Veterans Report,* Appendix A. Center for Women Veterans, U.S. Department of Veterans Affairs, http://www1.va.gov/womenvet/page.cfm?pg=43.

45. userpages.aug.com/captbarb/femvetsalso.html

46. *VA Health Care for Women: Despite Progress, Improvements Needed*, General Accounting Office report GAO/HRD-92–23, January 1992, 1.

47. *Actions Needed to Insure That Female Veterans Have Equal Access to VA Benefits*, General Accounting Office report GAO/HRD-82–98, September, 1982, 8. Many women veterans were entitled to GI Bill benefits, but because there was virtually no effort to inform them, an estimated one-third of qualified female veterans, over 100,000 women, "did not even know they were eligible for the G.I. Bill." *Waves National G.I. Bill Survey, 1995–2003*, Operational Archives Branch, Naval Historical Center, Washington, D.C., www.history.navy.mil/ar/whiskey/waves.htm. The failure to inform female veterans of their rights—or to inform them with the same gusto that male veterans were informed—was cited as a lingering problem in the 1982 GAO report. The report noted the Veterans Administration failed to contact all members of a women's veteran's group "or provide accurate information," leaving "some female veterans . . . confused about what benefits they were eligible for." A September 1982 General Accounting Office report, *Actions Needed to Insure That Female Veterans Have Equal Access to VA Benefits*, GAO/HRD-82–98, details inequalities, including a failure to make outreach efforts to female veterans on the same basis as male veterans and the failure to measure "female veterans' awareness of benefits, as it has for male veterans" (p. 3). The report also details instances in which female veterans were denied medical care to which they were entitled and cites disturbingly high rates of gynecological cancer among female veterans. Women were also denied medical care for routine pregnancy and childbirth, even if they were pregnant upon discharge from the military.

Not surprisingly, a 1985 Louis Harris survey of female veterans found 57 percent did not know they were eligible for VA services. *1998 Advisory Committee on Women Veterans Report*, Appendix A. Center for Women Veterans, U.S. Department of Veterans Affairs, http://www1.va.gov/womenvet/page.cfm?pg=43.

48. Quoted in Mettler, *Soldiers*, 144.

49. *1998 Advisory Committee on Women Veterans Report*.

50. Mettler, *Soldiers*, 147. Rather than expand women's educational and professional opportunities, in contrast to men, the end of World War II put pressure on women to be properly situated as wives and mothers at home. Thus women, after experiencing the hardships of war, came home to experience the "hardships of public opinion." userpages.aug.com/captbarb/femvets5.html. The war disrupted American life and inadvertently revealed American women to be physically, intellectually, and emotionally as capable as American men. However, a kind of amnesia about those capabilities

set in as the nation sought return to prewar roles. The result was a hyperdemonstration of gender assignment. If victory was reflected in postwar production of consumer goods and idealized domesticity, women were conscripted to play their part. As fervently as they had been ordered into factories, they were ordered back home.

Men who served could open up newspapers and learn of their GI Bill benefits in columns and articles. Women too learned of their duties, sometimes even on the same page. In the *Independent-Record* in Helena, Montana, a July 1944 story outlining American Legion efforts for the GI Bill is positioned next to an urgent message to American women. The headline outlines the task: "Women Can Control Any Inflation, Auxiliary Is Told: Mrs. Hurlburt Anderson Tells 200 Delegates Women Will Quit Jobs," *Independent-Record,* July 24, 1944, 5. As this story, representative of others at the time, suggests, it was women's duty to return to their homes after the war and give the jobs to returning veterans. Working, women suddenly learned, was un-American. Their contribution was at home, where purchasing decisions "may either hasten or prevent inflation." Women's wartime contributions were eagerly forgotten. The men were back, and women could best serve the nation by shopping well.

51. Mettler, *Soldiers*, 147. As Mettler reports, 38 percent of the female veterans she interviewed who did not use the GI Bill cited familial roles as the reason, while 28 percent said they "preferred to work" (p. 148).

52. Mettler, *Soldiers*, 147.

53. These calculations are derived from information contained in Suzanne Mettler's book, which states that 51 percent of male veterans used the GI Bill but only 40 percent of female veterans (p. 145). As already noted, there were 332,000 women veterans and 16,268,000 male veterans. Although some research sources report slightly different figures for the relative numbers of women and men veterans, those differences do not significantly alter the claim that there is an immense gap between women and men's usage of the GI Bill.

54. Mettler, *Soldiers*, 156–157.

55. The Civil Rights Act of 1964 greatly expanded, among other initiatives, the Civil Rights Division that had been established as part of the Civil Rights Act of 1957, where the latter had been the first civil rights legislation passed by Congress since the aftermath of the Civil War in the days of the first reconstruction (Days 1084, 991). For an excellent analysis of the first and second reconstructions, see Richard M. Valelly, *The Two Reconstructions: The Struggle for Black Enfranchisement* (Chicago: University of Chicago Press, 2004).

56. Title I of The Civil Rights Act of 1964 was included to protect the voting rights of African Americans, and the next year Congress passed additional legislation to protect with even more detail those voting rights. Hugh Davis Graham, *The Civil Rights Era: Origins and Development of National Policy, 1960–1972* (New York: Oxford University Press, 1990); Hugh Davis Graham, "The Origins of Affirmative Action: Civil Rights in the Regulatory State," *Annals of the American Academy of Political and Social Science: Affirmative Action Revisited,* September 1992, 50.

57. *Brown v. Board of Education,* 347 U.S. 483 (1954), p. 495.

58. Title VII of the Civil Rights Act of 1964, www.eeoc.gov/policy/vii.html.

59. www.eeoc.gov/abouteeoc/35th/milestones/1965.html

60. "Is Section 1981 Modified by Title VII of the Civil Rights Act of 1964?" *Duke Law Journal,* December 1970, 1230–1238.

61. www.eeoc.gov/abouteeoc/35th/milestones/1965.html

62. Nicholas Pedriana, "Help Wanted NOW: Legal Opportunities, the Women's Movement, and the Battle over Sex-Segregated Job Advertisements," *Social Problems,* May 2004, 187.

63. www.congresslink.org/print_basics_histmats_civilrights64text.htm (emphasis added).

64. Some make the point that proponents of including "sex" in Title VII played on racist views in the House by pointing out that this title, without the word "sex," would privilege black women above white women. As women's rights advocate Rep. Martha Griffiths of Michigan stated, "I rise in support of the amendment . . . because I feel as a white woman when this bill has passed . . . that white women will be the last at the hiring gate." Griffith drew on historical comparisons between racism and sexism to illustrate that when push comes to shove, combating sexism by congressional legislation too often is sacrificed for the sake of combating racism. She referred to Reconstruction legislation following the Civil War in which Congress passed the Fifteenth Amendment guaranteeing that no state could prohibit the right to vote on the basis of race, but, by omitting the word "sex," allowing states to continue to prohibit the right to vote on the basis of sex. Comparing the past with the present, she argued, "When the colored woman shows up and she is qualified, she is going to have an open entrée into any particular field . . . White men have done this before . . . your great-grandfathers were willing as prisoners of their own prejudice to permit ex-slaves to vote but not their own white wives." Southern representatives such as Rivers of South Carolina were apparently swayed by such arguments, Rivers stating that he would support adding "sex" to Title VII in order to make it "possible for the white Christian woman to receive the same consideration for employment

as the colored woman." All quotes from Serena Mayeri, "A Common Fate of Discrimination: Race-Gender Analogies in Legal and Historical Perspective," *Yale Law Journal*, April 2001, 1045.

65. Nicholas Pedriana, "Help Wanted NOW: Legal Opportunities, the Women's Movement, and the Battle over Sex-Segregated Job Advertisements," *Social Problems* 51 (2004): 187.

66. Pedriana, "Help Wanted," 182.

67. Pedriana, "Help Wanted," 189.

68. gos.sbc.edu/f/fuentes.html

69. *The Feminist Chronicles*, www.feminist.org/research/chronicles/fc1967.html.

70. Pedriana, "Help Wanted," 190, emphasis added.

71. John Herbers, "For Instance, Can She Pitch for the Mets?" *New York Times*, August 20, 1965, 1.

72. Pedriana, "Help Wanted," 191.

73. Herbers, "Can She Pitch?" 1.

74. Pedriana, "Help Wanted," 191.

75. Pedriana, "Help Wanted," 191.

76. *The Feminist Chronicles*, www.feminist.org/research/chronicles/fc1967.html.

77. "Key Events in the Women's Rights Movement," www.infoplease.com/ipa/A0875322.html.

78. EEOC, *Compliance Statement and Plan*, smallbusiness.findlaw.com/business-forms-contracts/form2–5.html.

79. Sharon M. McGowan, "The Bona Fide Body: Title VII's Last Bastion of Intentional Sex Discrimination," *Columbia Journal of Gender and Law* 12 (2003): 77.

80. See *Diaz* v. *Pan-American Airlines*, 442 F.2d 385 (5th Cir. 1971); *Wilson* v. *Southwest Airlines*, 517 F. Supp. 292 (N.D. Tex. 1981).

81. "Developments in the Law: Employment Discrimination and Title VII of the Civil Rights Act of 1964," *Harvard Law Review*, March 1971, 1183.

82. "Developments in the Law: Employment Discrimination and Title VII of the Civil Rights Act of 1964," *Harvard Law Review*, March 1971, 1182.

83. See *Weeks* v. *S. Bell Tel. & Tel. Co.*, 408 F.2d 228 (5th Cir. 1969).

84. McGowan, "Bona Fide Body," 38.

85. McGowan, "Bona Fide Body," 38.

86. "Developments in the Law," 1183.

87. "Developments in the Law," 1183.

88. "Developments in the Law," 1185.

89. "Developments in the Law," 1186.

90. Quoted in McGowan, "Bona Fide Body," 39.

91. Derived from graph in *Hearings before the Special Subcommittee on Education of the Committee on Education and Labor,* House of Representatives, Ninety-First Congress, Part I, June 1970, p. 25.

92. Title IV of the Civil Rights Act reads, "Nothing in this title shall prohibit classification and assignment for reasons other than race, color, religion, or national origin" omitting the word "sex" and thus allowing discrimination on the basis of sex (Sen. Bayh, citing Title IV, *Congressional Record,* 30403, August 6, 1971).

93. *Congressional Record,* 39252, November 4, 1971. In addition, Harvard complained it would need to build "additional dormitories" were women admitted on an equal basis with men (Rep. Griffiths, *Congressional Record,* 39254, November 4, 1971).

94. Rep. Bella Abzug, *Congressional Record,* 39258, November 4, 1971.

95. www.usdoj.gov/cft/cor/coord/titleixstat.htm

96. Sen. Birch Bayh, *Congressional Record,* 5807, February 28, 1972.

97. ailiwick.lib.uiowa.edu/ge/historyRe.html

98. Dan Wakefield, "All Boys Aren't Athletes, and Some Survive," *New York Times,* May 11, 1975, S2.

99. Joseph B. Treaster, "Girls a Hit in Debut on Diamond," *New York Times,* March 25, 1974, 67.

100. Nadine Brozan, "Girls on the Athletic Field: Small Gains, Long Way to the Goal," *New York Times.* January 12, 1976, 46.

101. Regulations read, "A recipient may operate or sponsor separate teams for members of each sex where selection for such teams is based upon competitive skill or the activity involved is a contact sport. However, where a recipient operates or sponsors a team in a particular sport for members of one sex but operates or sponsors no such team for members of the other sex, and athletic opportunities for members of that sex have previously been limited, members of the excluded sex must be allowed to try-out for the team offered unless the sport is a contact sport. For purposes of this part, contact sports include boxing, wrestling, rugby, ice hockey, football, basketball and other sports the purpose or major activity of which involves bodily contact."

102. Title IX Regulations, *Federal Register* 65, no. 169 (August 30, 2000): 52872–57873.

103. Title IX Regulations, *Federal Register* 65, no. 169 (August 30, 2000): 52872–57873. Full sentence reads, "However, where a recipient operates or sponsors a team in a particular sport for members of one sex but operates or sponsors no such team for members of the other sex, and athletic

opportunities for members of that sex have previously been limited, members of the excluded sex must be allowed to try out for the team offered unless the sport involved is a contact sport."

104. Deborah Brake, "The Struggle for Sex Equality in Sport and the Theory behind Title IX," *University of Michigan Journal of Law Reform*, Fall 2000–Winter 2001, 13; Kimberly Bingaman, "Fourth Annual Review of Gender and Sexuality Law: Education Law Chapter: Title IX of the 1972 Education Amendments," *Georgetown Journal of Gender and Law*, Fall 2002.

105. For an analysis of how the major men's sports undermine the ability of Title IX to promote gender equity in sports, see Michael A. Messner, *Taking the Field: Women, Men, and Sports* (Minneapolis: University of Minnesota Press, 2002). For an analysis of how Title IX demands more than equal treatment because of its educational context, see Julia Lamber, "Gender and Intercollegiate Athletics: Data and Myths," *University of Michigan Journal of Law Reform* 34 (2000): 151–229.

106. What is important to keep in mind about proportionalities is that it does not refer to an equal number of teams. It is not that there have to be five teams for men and five teams for women, but rather it has to be that the participation opportunities for men and women in student body as a whole are equitable. So if the student body is proportionate of 55:45 and there are 400 athletic participation opportunities provided then there should be a proportionate amount of 220 slots for male athletes and 180 for female athletes provided. It might be that all 220 men would be participating on two teams and 180 women might be participating on six teams. But the idea is that of the athletic opportunities that are provided by the school there should be proportionate distribution of men and women in those opportunities. Another aspect of proportionality is that scholarship dollars that are provided to male and female athletes also should be proportional to athletic participation. So if a college is spending $400,000 per year on athletic scholarships and half of the athletic participants are women then half of that amount, $200,000, should be funding athletic scholarships for women. The third point is that institutions must provide equal benefits for male and female athletes in terms of athletic equipment, uniforms, supplies, provision of quality coaches, practice and competitive facilities, and scheduling travel between other athletic program areas. It is not that an equal dollar benefit is required but that the institution must spend whatever is required that women are provided with the same quality of uniform and equipment as that provided to male athletes. So, for example, if it costs $1,000 to outfit a male football player, it is not required that the institution pay $1,000 to outfit a female basketball player if in fact it does not cost $1,000 to provide quality equipment to a basketball player (Women's

Sports Foundation 2). For a critique of the proportionality requirement, see Kimberly A. Yuracko, "One for You and One for Me: Is Title IX's Sex-Based Proportionality Requirement for College Varsity Athletic Positions Defensible?" *Northwestern University Law Review*, Winter 2003, 731.

107. www.now.org/titleix.html. Also see Erin E. Buzuvis, "Survey Says . . . A Critical Analysis of the New Title IX Policy and a Proposal for Reform," *Iowa Law Review*, March 2006.

108. Suggs Welch, "New Policy Clarifies Title IX Rules for Colleges; Women's Group Objects," *Chronicle of Higher Education*. April 1, 2005, A47.

109. Jessica E. Jay, "Women's Participation in Sports: Four Feminist Perspectives," *Texas Journal of Women and the Law* 7, no. 1 (1997).For a discussion of how Title IX policies affect male athletes, see Deborah J. Anderson and John J. Cheslock, "Institutional Strategies to Achieve Gender Equity in Intercollegiate Athletics: Does Title IX Harm Male Athletes?" *American Economic Review*, May 2004.

110. In terms of school budgets and student participation, athletics is the most prominent extracurricular activity at the high school level. Alison J. Tracy and Sumru Erkut, "Gender and Race Patterns in the Pathways from Sports Participation to Self-Esteem," *Sociological Perspectives*, Winter 2002, 445–466.

111. Some have discounted Title IX's influence in women's sports participation, arguing that women were entering sports in greater numbers before its implementation. See Jessica Gavora, *Titling the Playing Field: Schools, Sports, Sex, and Title IX* (San Francisco: Encounter, 2002). Others, however, including many female athletes, continue to cite Title IX as a key to developing an interest in sports.

112. Erik Brady and MaryJo Sylwester, "More and More Girls Got Game: Percentage of Females Playing Varsity Sports Rising Slowly," *USA Today*, July 1, 2003, C1.

113. This holds even though studies still show that among adolescents, girls do not participate in sports to the same degree as boys, even when controlling for socioeconomic background, siblings, family background, year in school, type and size of school, region of the country, urbanization, and so on. Tami M. Videon, "Who Plays and Who Benefits: Gender, Interscholastic Athletics, and Academic Outcomes," *Sociological Perspectives*, Winter 2002.

114. For a critique of Title IX, see Erin E. Buzuvis, "Survey Says . . . A Critical Analysis of the New Title IX Policy and a Proposal for Reform," *Iowa Law Review*, March 2006, 821. For a discussion of the relationship between Title VII and Title IX, see Earl C. Dudley Jr. and George Ruther-

glen, "Ironies, Inconsistencies, and Intercollegiate Athletics: Title IX, Title VII, and Statistical Evidence of Discrimination," *Sports and Law*, Fall 1999.

115. *USA Today*, March 15, 2004, 15E–24E.

116. *Annual Report to Congress, Fiscal Year 1997*, U.S. Department of Education, Office for Civil Rights, www.ed.gov./about/offices/list/ocr/AnnRpt97/edlite-index.html.

117. Title IX complaints, www.womenssportsfoundation.org.

118. Suggs, *Annual Report on Gender Equity*.

119. Brad Wolverton, "Crying Foul Over Postseason Opportunities," *Chronicle of Higher Education*, July 28, 2006, A26.

120. *Title IX and Women's Athletic Opportunity: A Nation's Promise Yet to Be Fulfilled*, National Women's Law Center, June 2002, www.nwlc.org/pdf/PromiseJune2002.pdf.

121. *State-of-the-Art Field for Boys; Inadequate Field for Girls*, Office for Civil Rights, www.edgov/print/about/offices/list/ocr/success-t9athletics.html.

122. As Shakib and Dunbar note, in post–Title IX high school basketball, the goal of gender equity is undermined by the continuation of such practices as an emphasis and naturalization of sex group differences and lower expectations for women athletes compared to men, producing a two-tiered basketball institution at the high school level that perpetuates inequality for women instead of correcting it. Sohaila Shakib and Michele D. Dunbar, "The Social Construction of Female and Male High School Basketball Participation: Reproducing the Gender Order through a Two-Tiered Sporting Institution," *Sociological Perspectives*, Winter 2002, 353–378.

Chapter Four

1. *Hollander* v. *Connecticut Interscholastic Athletic Conf.* (1971) 164 Conn. Supp. 57 (1971); appeal dismissed, 164 Conn. 654, 295 A. 2d 671 (1972).

2. Alexis de Tocqueville, *Democracy in America*, ed. Richard Hefner (1835; New York: Mentor, 1984), 126. Cited in William E. Thro, "Judicial Paradigms of Educational Equality," 174 *Ed. Law Rep.* 1 (April 24, 2003) p. 1

3. www.blueshoenashville.com/suffragehistory.html

4. www.blueshoenashville.com/suffragehistory.html

5. www.law.umkc.edu/faculty/projects/ftrials/conlaw/nineteentham.htm; see also www.blueshoenashville.com/suffragehistory.html

6. The critique of formal equality by legal scholars, political scientists, and others is vast. However, for a brilliant critique and unusually insightful analysis, see Robin L. West, "Law's Nobility," *Yale Journal of Law and Feminism* 17, no. 385 (2005).

7. Andrea Campbell, *How Policies Make Citizens: Senior Political Activism and the American Welfare State* (Princeton, NJ: Princeton University Press, 2005), 2.

8. Suzanne Mettler and Eric Welch, "Civic Generation: Policy Feedback Effects of the G.I. Bill on Political Involvement Over the Life Course," *British Journal of Political Science*, July 2004, 497–501

9. Suzanne Mettler, *Soldiers to Citizens: The G.I. Bill and the Making of the Greatest Generation* (Cambridge: Oxford University Press, 2005); Robert C. Lieberman, *Shifting the Color Line: Race and the American Welfare State* (Cambridge: Harvard University Press, 1998); Jacob S. Hacker, *The Divided Welfare State: The Battle over Public and Private Social Benefits in the United States* (New York: Cambridge University Press, 2002).

10. From *Civic Mission of Higher Education: From Outreach to Engagement*, Kettering Foundation, 2001, quoted in *Fulfilling the Promise*, Social Science Colloquium Series, 2003–2004, Bucknell University, www.departments.bucknell.edu/vp_academic_affairs/programs/Sscs/this.html.

11. Social policies can also be established by executive orders issued by the president, such as President Truman's Executive Order 9981 in 1948 to integrate the military racially. President Eisenhower used an EO to racially desegregate schools; presidents John F. Kennedy and Lyndon Johnson used EOs to prohibit race discrimination in hiring, contracting, and housing; Ronald Reagan used an executive order to ban the use of federal funds for providing information about abortion services; President Bill Clinton overturned Regan's abortion gag EO with an EO of his own; and President George W. Bush reinstated the abortion gag order with yet another EO, issued within 24 hours of taking office after the disputed 2000 presidential election. See www.trumanlibrary.org/9981.htm, www.thisnation.com/question/040.html; see also www.sfgate.com/cgi-bin/article.cgi?file=chronicle/archive/2001/01/22/MN96633.DTL.

12. For a review of the way feminist legal theorists can contribute particularly salient perspectives to an analysis of women's oppression in sport, see "Cheering on Women and Girls in Sports: Using Title IX to Fight Gender Role of Oppression," *Harvard Law Review*, May 1997, 1627–1644.

13. *Plessy v. Ferguson*, 163 U.S.A. 537 (1896).

14. The relevance of these intangible factors had been established by the Court in *Sweatt v. I*, 339 U.S. 629 (1950); Julie M. Amstein, "United States v. Virginia: The Case of Coeducation at Virginia Military Institute," *American University Journal of Gender and the Law*, Fall 1994, (3 Am. U. J. Gender & L. 69).

15. *Brown v. Board of Education,* U.S. Supreme Court (1954). Citation from http://usinfo.state.gov/usa/infousa/facts/democracy/36.htm.

16. *Koremetsu v. United States,* 323 U.S. 214 (1944).

17. *Reed v. Reed,* 404 U.S. 71 (1971).

18. The Supreme Court uses three levels of scrutiny to assess the constitutionality of equal protection claims: strict scrutiny, intermediate scrutiny, and the rational basis test. In the case of race, the Court invokes strict scrutiny, which means there must be a compelling state interest to justify the use of racial classifications, a level of scrutiny that nothing short of a national emergency usually warrants. The Court invokes intermediate scrutiny when considering sex-discrimination issues, which requires a state to have a legitimate goal for its sex-discriminatory policies and that the use of sex-discriminatory policies is the most narrowly tailored means for achieving the state's legitimate goal. It is not impossible for a state to produce such a justification, but it is very difficult. For a discussion of the disconnections between the level of review the Court invokes for Equal Protection versus Title IX claims, see Julie Kocaba, "The Proper Standard of Review: Does Title IX Require 'Equality' or 'Parity' of Treatment When Resolving Gender-Based Discrimination in Prison Institutions?" *N.E. Journal on Crim. and Civ. Con.,* Summer 1999. For a discussion of the way the proportionality rule established to implement Title IX (as discussed in chapter 3) may be a "heuristic shortcut for equal treatment borrowed from the context of racially segregated education," see Kimberly A. Yuracko, "One for You and One for Me: Is Title IX's Sex-Based Proportionality Requirement for College Varsity Athletic Positions Defensible?" *Nw. U. L. Rev.,* Winter 2003.

19. *Reed,* p. 76.

20. *Craig v. Boren,* 429 U.S. 190 (1976).

21. *Craig,* p 198.

22. *Craig,* p 199.

23. *Craig,* p. 202.

24. *Geduldig v. Aiello,* 417 U.X. 484 (1974).

25. *Geduldig v. Aiello,* 417 U.X. 484 (1974), Id. at 496–497, n. 20.

26. *Geduldig v. Aiello,* 417 U.X. 484 (1974), Id. at 496–497, n. 20.

27. *General Electric Company v. Martha Gilbert,* 429 U.S. 125 (1976).

28. *Gilbert,* p. 134.

29. *Hogan,* 458 U.S. 718 (1982).

30. Dana Robinson, "A League of Their Own: Do Women Want Sex-Segregated Sports?" *Journal of Contemporary Legal Issues,* Spring 1998; (9 *J. Contemp. Legal Issues* 321), 334–335.

31. *Hogan,* p. 743.

32. *Hogan,* p. 743.

33. 518 U.S. 515 (1996)

34. Amstein, "United States v. Virginia,".

35. Lee Schottenfeld, "The Fate of Separate but Equal in the Athletic Arena," *University of Miami Business Law Review,* Spring–Summer 2002, 666.

36. Amstein, "United States v. Virginia,"

37. Julius Menacker, "Equal Educational Opportunity for Women: How Should It Be Defined?" www.abanet.org/publiced/lawday/schools/lessons/docs/hseeow.doc; article adapted from one originally appearing in *Update on the Courts* 4, no. 3 (1996).

38. American Association of University Women, ww.aauw.org/issue_advocacy/actionpages/positionpapers/singlesex.cfm. For a discussion of why educational segregation based on sexual orientation might be constitutional, see "Why Segregated Schools for Gay Students May Pass a 'Separate but Equal' Analysis but Fail Other Issues and Concerns," *Wm. and Mary J. of Women and Law,* Fall 2005.

39. *United States v. Virginia et al.,* 518 U.S. 515 (1996), neuro.law.cornell.edu/supct/search/display.html?terms=virginia%20and%20militar. For an excellent analysis of the implications of the VMI case for single-sex education, see Linda L. Peter, "Note: What Remains of Public Choice and Parental Rights: Does the VMI Decision Preclude Exclusive Schools or Classes Based on Gender?" *California Western Law Review* 33 (1997): 249; Rosemary C. Salomone, "Feminist Voices in the Debate over Single-Sex Schooling: Finding Common Ground," *Michigan Journal of Gender and Law* 11 (2004): 63; Jolie Land, "Not Dead Yet: The Future of Single-Sex Education after United States v. Virginia," *Stetson Law Review,* Summer 1997, 297; Carolyn B. Ramsey, "Subtracting Sexism from the Classroom: Law and Policy in the Debate over All-female Math and Science Classes in Public Schools," *Texas Journal of Women and the Law,* Fall 1998, 1; Laura Fortney, "Public Single-Sex Elementary Schools: Separate but Equal in Gender Fifty Years Following Brown v. Board of Education," *Toledo Law Review,* Summer 2004, 857.

40. Other sex discrimination concerns related to the implementation of Title IX are sex-specific issues, such as sexual harassment, pregnancy, abortion, rape, sexual violence (14 percent); employment issues in general (not related to sports) (9 percent); disciplinary issues, such as drug testing and academic standing (4 percent). The remainder are miscellaneous, such as a case involving earring policies: does a school policy that allows males to wear stud earrings but not dangling earrings, but allows girls to wear dangling earrings violate the no sex discrimination principle of Title IX?

41. As legal scholar Jamal Greene notes, "The disparity between what the Constitution permits of public schools and what Title IX permits . . . is . . . unquestionably stark." Jamal Greene, "Hands Off Policy: Equal Protection and the Contact Sports Exemption of Title IX," *Michigan Journal of Gender and Law* 11, no. 133 (2005).

42. Patricia Werner Lamar, "The Expansion of Constitutional and Statutory Remedies for Sex Segregated Education: The 14th Amendment and Title IX of the Education Amendments of 1972," *Emory Law Journal*, Fall 1983, 1113. Granted, Lamar made her prediction in 1983. Thus we may conclude that a constitutional basis exists for prohibiting sex-segregated educational policies even though development of such constitutional foundations seems unlikely, given the composition of the Supreme Court in 2007.

43. Lee Schottenfeld, "The Fate of Separate but Equal in the Athletic Arena," *University of Miami Business Law Review*, Spring–Summer 2002, 650.

44. Dana Robinson, "A League of Their Own: Do Women Want Sex-Segregated Sports?" *Journal of Contemporary Legal Issues*, Spring 1998, 321.

45. As some law scholars argue, however, securing equality for women in sports policies also requires passage of a federal-level Equal Rights Amendment (ERA). Richard H. Yetter III, "Equal Rights Level Playing Field: What Title IX Money Cannot Buy," *Sports Lawyers Journal*, Spring 2003, 135.

46. *Brenden* no. 20, p. 1299.

47. The following states have an ERA: Alaska, Arizona, California, Colorado, Connecticut, Hawaii, Illinois, Louisiana (no unreasonable sex discrimination), Maryland, Massachusetts, Montana, New Hampshire, New Mexico, Pennsylvania, Texas, Utah, Virginia, Washington, Wyoming.

States with statutes prohibiting sex discrimination in educational sports programs: Alaska, California, Colorado, Connecticut, D.C., Florida, Hawaii, Idaho, Illinois, Iowa, Louisiana, Maine, Massachusetts, Michigan, Minnesota, Montana, Nebraska, New York, North Carolina, Oregon, Rhode Island, South Dakota, Washington, Wisconsin. States with statutes prohibiting sex and race discrimination in public accommodations: Alaska, Arizona, California, Colorado, Connecticut, Delaware, D.C., Idaho, Illinois, Indiana, Iowa, Kansas, Kentucky, Louisiana, Maine, Maryland, Massachusetts, Michigan, Minnesota, Missouri, Montana, Nebraska, Nevada, New Hampshire, New Jersey, New Mexico, New York, North Dakota, Ohio, Oklahoma, Oregon, Pennsylvania, Rhode Island, South Dakota, Tennessee, Utah, Vermont, Washington, West Virginia, Wisconsin, Wyoming.

48. *Swann,* 402 U.S. 1, 2, reh'g denied 403 U.S. 912 (1971).

49. These cases are *Clinton v. Nagy,* 411 F. Supp 1396 (1974); *Darrin v. Gould,* 85 Wn. 2d 859; *Muscare v. O'Malley* Civil No. 76-C-3729 N.D. Illinois; *Force v. Pierce City* are R-VI School Dist., 570 F. Supp. 1020; *Lantz v. Amback,* 620 F. Supp. 663; *Mercer v. Duke Univ.,* 190 F. 3d 643.

50. *Force v. Pierce City R-VI School District,* 570 F.Supp. 1020, 1023.

51. *Force,* p. 1024.

52. *Force,* p. 1024.

53. *Force,* p. 1028.

54. *Force,* p. 1028.

55. *Force,* p. 1030.

56. "State's First Female Gridder Practices," *Syracuse Herald-Journal,* October 22, 1985, D5.

57. *Lantz v. Ainbach,* 620 F. Supp. 663 (S.D. N.Y. 1985), p. 665.

58. *Lantz,* p. 665.

59. *Lantz,* p. 665.

60. *Lantz,* p. 666. The ten cases are *Lawful v. Wisconsin Interscholastic Athletic Assn.,* 444 F. Supp. 1117 (1978); *Clinton v. Nagy,* 411 F. Supp. 1396 (1974); *Hoover v. Meiklejohn,* 430 F. Supp. 164 (1977); *Force v. Pierce City,* 570 F. Supp. 1020 (1983); *Reed v. Nebraska School Activities Assn.,* 341 F. Supp. 258 (1972); *Morris v. Michigan State Board of Education,* 472 F.2d 1207 (1973); *Haas v. South Bend Community School Corp.,* 289 N.E.2d 495 (1972); *Commonwealth v. Penn Interscholastic Athletic Assn.,* 334 A.2d 839 (1975); *Darrin v. Gould,* 540 P.2d 882 (1975); *Attorney General v. Mass. Interscholastic Athletic Assn., Inc.,* 393 N.E.2d 284 (1979).

61. "Judge Rules Girl, 16, Can Join Football Team," *Syracuse Herald-Journal,* October 29, 1985, A10.

62. "State's First Female Gridder Practices," *Syracuse Herald-Journal,* October 22, 1985, D5.

63. For an excellent analysis of the Mercer case, see Abigail Crouse, "Equal Athletic Opportunity: An Analysis of Mercer v. Duke University and a Proposal to Amend the Contact Sport Exception to Title IX," *Minnesota Law Review,* June 2000, 1655.

64. Kate Stone Lombardi, "Somewhere over the Goal Post a Girl's Dream Lies," *New York Times,* September 26, 1993, WC1.

65. Valeri Vecchio, "Class B Finalist Has Female Kicker," *Post-Standard,* November 26, 1993, D3.

66. Lombardi, "Somewhere," WC1.

67. *Mercer v. Duke University,* 190 F.3d 643 (1999), p. 645.

68. *Mercer,* p. 645.

69. *Mercer,* p. 645.

70. *Mercer*, p. 647.

71. *Mercer*, p. 648.

72. "Knight Inks Deal with Cleveland-based IMG," *Chronicle-Telegram* (Elyria, OH), October 13, 2000, B8.

73. For an insightful analysis of the implication of the Mercer case for challenging sex-segregation policies in sports in general, see B. Glenn George, "Fifty/Fifty: Ending Sex Segregation in School Sports," *Ohio State Law Journal* 63 (2002–2003): 1107.

74. These cases are *Saint v. Nebraska Sch. Activities Ass'n.*, 684 F. Supp. 626 (1988); *Barnett v. Texas Wrestling Ass'n.*, 16 F. Supp. 2d 690 (1998); *Adams by and through Adams v. Baker*, 919 F. Supp. 1496 (1975, 1996).

75. *Adams*, no. 2, p. 1499. Her high school offered sports for boys (football, soccer, basketball, wrestling, tennis, baseball) and sports for girls (volleyball, soccer, tennis, basketball, softball, and cheerleading.) The school's track, cross-country, and golf teams were coed.

76. 1 *Adams* 919 Supplement F 1496, 1500 *Adams*.

77. *Adams* 919 F. Supp. 1496, 1500.

78. 8 *Adams* 1503.

79. 8 *Adams* 1503.

80. 9 *Adams* 1504.

81. 12 *Adams* 1504.

82. 13 *Adams* 1505.

83. 14 *Adams* 1504–1505.

84. Gary Abbott, e-mail communication, May 19, 2005. According to Abbott, only Texas and Hawaii have official state high school championships for girls and have all-girl divisions in their states. Some states, such as California and Florida, have all-girl teams but, said Abbott, "a majority of girls who wrestle still train and compete with boys."

85. David Oliver Relin, "Girl Gladiators: Some Girls Have to Fight Just to Wrestle for the School Team," *Syracuse Post Standard*, March 12, 1996, sports sec.

86. Relin, "Girl Gladiators."

87. www.britannica.com/original?email=1&content_id=1506

88. In 1978, the Major League Baseball commissioner tried to enforce a policy that prohibited female sports reporters from clubhouse locker rooms in city-owned stadiums. When a courageous female reporter who wished to interview the New York Yankees challenged this policy in court, she won on the grounds that she had "a fundamental right to pursue her profession" and that prohibiting her from access to baseball players was an "unreasonable interference" of a fundamental right that violated the Equal Protection Clause of the Fourteenth Amendment, *Ludtke v. Kuhn*, 461 F. Supp.

86 (S.D. N.Y. 1978), cited in Karen Tokarz, *Women, Sports and the Law: A Comprehensive Research Guide to Sex Discrimination in Sports* (Buffalo, NY: Hein, 1986).

89. "Contact sports under the Title IX regulation include boxing, wrestling, rugby, ice hockey, football, basketball and other sports in which the purpose or major activity involves bodily contact," Office for Civil Rights, *Requirements under Title IX of the Education Amendments of 1972*, U.S. Department of Education, www.ed.gov/about/offices/list/ocr/docs/interath.html

90. Title IX, implementing regulations, cited in *Williams v. The School District of Bethlehem, PA*, 799 F. Supp. (1992) 513, 516.

91. Gerald Eskinazi, "Title IX Rules Issued for Equality in Sports," *New York Times*, June 4, 1975, 29.

92. Nancy Hicks, "House Panel Rejects Some Rules on Sex Discrimination in Schools," *New York Times*, July 9, 1975, 61; Hicks, "House Reverses Itself to Allow Integration of Sexes in Schools," *New York Times*, July 19, 1975, 21.

93. Hicks, "Title IX Exemptions Unlikely for Revenue-Producing Sports," *New York Times*, October 2, 1975, 64.

94. National Organization for Women, press release, "Good News and Bad News for Title IX," March 31, 2005, www.now.org/issues/title_ix/033105titleix.html.

95. "Judge Says ABC Okay on Decision," *Daily Courier* (Connellsville, PA), July 6, 1973, 9.

96. "Pookie Loses, Can't Play Ball," *Newport Daily News*, May 15, 1974, 18. The decision was overturned on appeal (*Plaintiffs v. Darlington Little League*, 514 F.2d 344; decided March 31, 1975).

97. *Fortin v. Darlington Little League, Inc.*, 514 F.2d 344 (1st Cir. 1975).

98. *Carnes v. Tennessee Secondary School Athletic Association*, 1976.

99. "Boys on Team Hail Girl's Return," *New York Times*, March 29, 1978, B6.

100. "Girl Challenges Sex Segregation," *Daily Intelligencer* (Doylestown, PA), March 29, 1978.

101. "Boys on Team Hail Girl's Return."

102. For an excellent overview of the answer to this question, see Adam S. Darowki, "For Kenny, Who Wanted to Play Women's Field Hockey," *Duke Journal of Gender Law and Policy*, Spring 2005, 153.

103. *Williams* 799 F.Supp. (1992), 513.

104. "Court Denies Boy's Bid to Play Girls' Field Hockey," *Syracuse Herald-Journal*, September 24, 1993, C11.

105. *Williams* 998 F.2d 168 (1993).

106. *Williams* 1993, 173. See also, Adam S. Darowski, "For Kenny, Who Wanted to Play Women's Field Hockey," *Duke J. Gender Law and Policy*, Spring 2005.

107. *Williams* 1993, 176.

108. *Williams* 1993, 178.

109. Rick Burton, "He Played and Played but He Can't Join the Girls' Team," *Syracuse Post-Standard*, May 8, 1980, B5.

110. *Mularadelis v. Haldane Central School Board*, 74 A.D.2d 248, 427 N.Y.S.2d 458 (1980), 256.

111. See appendix for more detail on these and other cases.

112. *Petrie v. Illinois High School Association*, 75 Ill. App. 3d 980, 394 N.E.2d 855, (1979), 984.

113. Jamal Greene, "Hands Off Policy: Equal Protection and the Contact Sports Exemption of Title IX," *Michigan Journal of Gender and Law* 11 (2005): 135.

114. For excellent discussions about whether or not single-sex education provides developmental benefits to women, see Keri McWilliams, "Education Law Chapter: Single-Sex Education," *Georgetown Journal of Gender and the Law* 7 (2006): 919; Sharon K. Mollman, "The Gender Gap: Separating the Sexes in Public Education," *Indiana Law Journal*, Winter 1992, 149. For the constitutional future of single-sex education, see Lisa A. Gerson, "Single-sex Education," *Georgetown Journal of Gender and the Law* 6 (2005): 547; Jenny L. Matthews, "Admission Denied: An Examination of a Single-Sex Public School Initiative in North Carolina," *North Carolina Law Review*, September 2004, 2032. For a discussion of segregation in the context of homosexuality, see Louis P. Nappen, "Why Segregated Schools for Gay Students May Pass a 'Separate but Equal' Analysis but Fail Other Issues and Concerns," *William and Mary Journal of Women and the Law*, Fall 2005, 101. For a discussion of school segregation in the construction of race and gender, see Verna L. Williams, "Reform or Retrenchment? Single-Sex Education and the Construction of Race and Gender," *Wisconsin Law Review*, 2004, 15.

115. Samuel L. Odom and Mary A. McEvoy, "Mainstreaming at the Preschool Level: Potential Barriers and Tasks for the Field," *Topics in Early Childhood Special Education*, 1990, 49.

116. Anne M. Hocutt, "Effectiveness of Special Education: Is Placement a Critical Factor?" *The Future of Children* 6, no. 1 (1996): 79. The least restrictive environment (LRE) clause of IDEA states, "Each state must establish a procedure to assure that, to the maximum extent appropriate, children with disabilities . . . are educated with children who are not disabled, and that special education, separate schooling, or other removal of children

with disabilities from the regular educational environment occurs only when the nature or severity of the disability is such that education in regular classes with the use of supplementary aids and services cannot be achieved satisfactorily" (20 U.S.C. § 1412 [5] [B]); Steven G. Little and K. Angeleque Akin Little, *Legal and Ethical Issues of Inclusion*, in Steven I. Pfeiffer and Linda A. Reddy, eds., *Inclusion Practices with Special Needs Students: Theory, Research, and Application* (Binghamton, NY: Haworth, 1999), 127.

117. Thomas Lombardi and Diane Woodrum, "Inclusion: A Worthy Challenge for Parents, Teachers, Psychologists, and Administrators," in Pfeiffer and Reddy, eds., *Inclusion*, 174. Some distinguish between mainstreaming and integration. Mainstreaming refers to the placement of disabled children in the regular classroom for abled children; integration refers to the placement of an abled child in a classroom designed specially for disabled children so that the abled child can serve as a peer model for the disabled children. See Odom and Speltz 1983; M. J. Guralnick and J. M. Groom, "Peer Interactions in Mainstreamed and Specialized Classrooms: A Comparative Analysis," *Exceptional Children* 54 (1988): 415–425.

118. Federal definitions of special education disability categories are as follows:

Specific learning disability: a disorder in one or more of the basic psychological processes involved in understanding or using language, spoken or written, which may manifest itself in an imperfect ability to listen, think, speak, write, spell, or to do mathematical calculations. This category includes perceptual handicaps, brain injury, minimal brain dysfunction, dyslexia, and developmental aphasia, but does not include learning problems resulting from visual, hearing, or motor handicaps, or from mental retardation.

Seriously emotionally disturbed: exhibiting behavior disorders over a long period of time which adversely affect educational performance. These include an inability to learn that cannot be explained by intellectual, sensory, or health factors; an inability to build or maintain satisfactory interpersonal relationships with peers and teachers; inappropriate types of behaviors or feelings under normal circumstances; a general pervasive mood of unhappiness or depression; and/or a tendency to develop physical symptoms or fears associated with personal or school problems.

Speech impaired: exhibiting communication disorders, such as stuttering, impaired articulation, and/or language or voice impairments, that adversely affect educational performance.

Mentally retarded: characterized by significantly subaverage general intellectual functioning with concurrent deficits in adaptive behavior which were manifested in the developmental period and adversely affect educational performance. This category includes students who are partly sighted and those who are completely blind.

Visually impaired: having a visual impairment that, even with correction, adversely affects educational performance. This category includes students who are partly sighted and those who are completely blind.

Hard of hearing: having a hearing impairment, permanent or fluctuating, that adversely affects educational performance but is not included in the deaf category.

Deaf: having a hearing impairment so severe that it interferes with the processing of linguistic information through hearing, with or without amplification, and therefore adversely affects educational performance.

Orthopedically impaired: having a severe orthopedic impairment that adversely affects educational performance, including impairments caused by congenital anomaly, disease, or other causes.

Other health impairments: having limited strength, vitality, or alertness, as a result of chronic or acute health problems, that adversely affects educational performance, including impairments caused by congenital anomaly, disease, or other causes.

Multiply handicapped: exhibiting concomitant impairments, the combination of which causes such severe educational problems that students possessing them cannot be accommodated in special education programs solely for one of the impairments. This category does not include students who are deaf/blind.

Deaf/blind: exhibiting concomitant hearing and visual impairments, the combination of which causes such severe communication and other developmental and educational problems that students possessing them cannot be accommodated in special education programs solely for deaf or blind students." Public Law 94-142. 89 Stat 773 (an act to amend the Education for All Handicapped Children Act of 1975). November 29, 1975. Mary M. Wagner, "Outcomes for Youths with Serious Emotional Disturbance in Secondary School and Early Adulthood," *Future of Children*. 5, no. 2: 93.

119. Mark R. Shinn, Gerald A. Tindal, and Deborah A. Spira, "Special Education Referrals as an Index of Teacher Tolerance: Are Teachers Imperfect Tests?" *Exceptional Children* 54, no. 1 (1987): 32–40.

120. Richard A. Villa and Jacqueline S. Thousand, "The Rationales for Creating Inclusive Schools," in Richard A. Villa and Jacqueline S. Thousand, eds., *Creating an Inclusive School* (Alexandria, VA: Association for

Supervision and Curriculum Development, 1995), 35. See also the Council of Great City Schools, 1986, as cited in Alan Gartner and Dorothy Kerzner Lipsky, "Beyond Special Education: Toward a Quality System for All Students," in Thomas Hehir and Thomas Latus, eds., *Special Education at the Century's End,* Harvard Education Review Reprint Series no. 23 (Cambridge, 1992), 129.

121. White and Calhoun 1987; as quoted in Gartner and Lipsky, "Beyond Special Education," 123–151.

122. Davis and Shepard 1983 and Ysseldyke et al 1979; as cited in Gartner and Kerzner Lipsky "Beyond Special Education," 123–151, in Hehir and Latus, eds., *Special Education.* Researchers examining a Colorado program for special needs children reached the same conclusion, finding a lack of statistical or valid clinical criteria for defining or identifying perceptual or communicative disorders. Sheppard and Smith 1981; cited in Gartner and Lipsky, "Beyond Special Education." Another factor that accounts for the inability of test scores to validate classifications of children as abled or disabled is the way teachers use special educational classifications to remove some children from their classroom as a way to make the teaching of the remaining children easier. In this case, the criterion is not so much what child needs special attention outside the regular classroom the most as it is which child does the teacher want to remove the most, as determined by the teacher's own biases. Maggie Coleman, Jo Webber and Bob Algozzine, "Inclusion and Students with Emotional/Behavioral Disorders," in Pfeiffer and Reddy, eds., *Inclusion Practices,* 25–47.

123. *Brown v. Board of Education,* 347 U.S. 483 (1954), p. 493.

124. *Brown,* 1954, p. 493.

125. Jacqueline Thousand and Richard A. Villa, "Inclusion: Welcoming, Valuing, and Supporting the Diverse Learning Needs of All Students in Shared General Education Environments," in Pfeiffer and Reddy, eds., *Inclusion Practices,* 73–108.

126. Jonathan Kozol, *Savage Inequalities: Children in America's Schools* (New York: HarperCollins, 1991); Tomas S. Serwatka, Sharian Deering, and Patrick Grant, "Disproportionate Representation of African Americans and Emotionally Handicapped Classes," *Journal of Black Studies,* March 1995, 492–506; Spyros Konstantopoulos, Manisha Modi, and Larry V. Hedges, "Who Are America's Gifted?" *American Journal of Education,* May 2001, 334–382.

127. Beth A. Ferri and David J. Connor, "Tools of Exclusion: Race, Disability, and (Re)segregated Education" (2005), www.digitaldivide.net/comm/docs/view.php?Doc=ID=312, last accessed 7-26-07.

128. For an analysis of how the special treatment of women in sports constitutes a form of affirmative action, see Jim McKay, *Managing Gender: Affirmative Action and Organizational Power in Australian, Canadian, and New Zealand Sport* (Albany: State University of New York Press, 1997).

129. Little and Little, "Legal and Ethical Issues of Inclusion," in Pfeiffer and Reddy, eds., *Inclusion Practices*, 125–143. This legislation states: "A school system shall educate, or shall provide for the education of, each qualified handicapped person in its jurisdiction with persons who are not handicapped to the maximum extent appropriate to the needs of the handicapped person. A school system shall place a handicapped person in the regular educational environment unless it is demonstrated that the education of the person in the regular environment with the use of supplementary aids and services cannot be achieved satisfactorily. Whenever a school system places a person in a setting other than the regular education environment, it shall take into account the proximity of the alternative setting to the person's home" (34 C.F.R. § 104.34 [a]).

130. ADA, 42 U.S.C. § 12132, www.usdoj.gov/crt/ada/publicat.htm.

131. ADA, Title 28 (28 C.R.F § 35.130 [b] [1]), www.ed.gov/policy/rights/reg/ocr/28cfr35.pdf.

132. Little and Little, "Legal and Ethical Issues of Inclusion."

133. In 1983, for example, in *Roncker v. Walter* 700 F.2d (6th Cir.), the court established that integrated education is the norm and segregation is the exception, and, even then, segregation is acceptable only in the most limited circumstances. Similarly, in 198, the U.S. Court of Appeals considered the case of *Timothy W v. Rochester School District*, 875 F.3d 954, in which Timothy was a student who, school administrators decided, was too disabled to be educable. The court ruled otherwise, however, declaring it the responsibility of school districts "to educate *all* children and specified that the term *all* included in IDEA meant all children with disabilities without exception."

134. Thousand and Villa, "Inclusion," 73–108.

135. Thousand and Villa, "Inclusion." The few instances where courts have allowed more restrictive environments for disabled students tend to be when the disabilities involve emotional and behavioral disorders, see Little and Little 1999.

136. Margaret C. Wang and Edward T. Baker, "Mainstreaming Programs: Design Features and Effects," *Journal of Special Education* 19, no. 4 (1985–1986): 503. "*Performance effects* included measures of achievement in academic subject areas such as mathematics, reading, language arts, and social studies, and measures of the quality of play for preschoolers. *Attitudinal*

effects included measures of students' self-concept and/or their attitudes toward learning and schooling, attitudes of mainstreamed disabled students toward their nondisabled classmates, attitudes of nondisabled students toward mainstreamed disabled students, and attitudes of teachers and parents toward mainstreaming. *Process effects* included measures of classroom processes, such as the type of interactions between teachers and students and among students" (p. 508).

Other studies show that mainstreaming works when the adults involved have positive, constructive attitudes toward disabled students, the necessary resources to work with disabled students are available, and the curriculum is suitable. Nancy K. Klein and Linda Gilkerson, "Personnel Preparation for Early Childhood Intervention Programs," in Jack P. Schonkoff and Samuel J. Meisels, eds., *Handbook of Early Childhood Intervention* (New York, 2000), 460.

137. Odom and McEvoy, "Mainstreaming," 48–61.

138. M. E. Snell, "Schools are for Kids: The Importance of Integration for Students with Severe Disabilities and Their Peers," in J. W. Lloyd, A. C. Repp, and N. N. Singh, eds., *The Regular Education Initiative: Alternative Perspectives on Concepts, Issues, and Models* (Sycamore, IL: Sycamore, 1990), 137–138; Linda A. Reddy, "Inclusion of Disabled Children and School Reform: A Historical Perspective," in Pfeiffer and Reddy, *Inclusion Practices*, 12.

139. Jennifer York, Terri Vandercook, Cathy MacDonald, Cheri Heise-Neff, and Ellen Caughey, "Feedback about Integrating Middle-School Students with Severe Disabilities in General Education Classes," *Exceptional Children* 58, no. 3 (1992): 254.

Chapter Five

1. As Frey and Eitzen note, sport reflects the inequalities characterizing gender and race relations in society. James Frey and D. Stanley Eitzen compare the prominence and appeal of sports as a pivotal institution in society to that of religion. James H. Frey and D. Stanley Eitzen, "Sport and Society," *Annual Review of Sociology* 17 (1991): 503–522.

2. For an excellent analysis of the intersection of race and sport in Britain, see Dan Carrington and Ian McDonald, eds., *"Race," Sport, and British Society* (New York: Routledge, 2001).

3. Douglas Hartmann, *Race, Culture, and the Revolt of the Black Athlete: The 1968 Olympic Protests and Their Aftermath* (Chicago: University of Chicago Press 2003), 454.

4. Hartmann, *Race, Culture,* 454.

5. Quoted in Ed Siegel, "Is It an Error to Equate Art with Athletics? Taking a Hit for a Sports Comparison," *Boston Globe*, October 8, 2005.

6. Hartmann, *Race, Culture*, 454–455.

7. Hartmann, *Race, Culture*, 455.

8. Hartmann, *Race, Culture*, 457. Washington and Karen make the argument that despite the economic and cultural centrality of sport, it is a relatively neglected and undertheorized area of sociological research. Robert E. Washington and David Karen, "Sport in Society," *Annual Review of Sociology* 27 (2001): 187–212. John Wilson persuasively argues that sport requires academic analysis to understand the strong relationships between the state and sport policies that are responsible for the social construction of race, class, and gender identities. John Wilson, *Playing by the Rules: Sports, Society, and the State* (Detroit: Wayne State University Press, 1994).

9. Hartmann, *Race, Culture*, 457.

10. Hartmann, *Race, Culture*, 457.

11. Hartmann, *Race, Culture*, 458.

12. Hartmann, *Race, Culture*, 467–468; Robert L. Simon, *Fair Play: Sports, Values, and Society* (Boulder: Westview, 1991).

13. As Lüschen notes, sport is an institution based on the acquisition of skills and the implementation of strategies. Günther Lüschen, "Sociology of Sport: Development, Present State, and Prospects," *Annual Review of Sociology* 6 (1980): 315–347.

14. For too long, of course, most sports did not include individuals identified by subordinate racial classifications. The literature is vast, but in the case of cricket, see Jack Williams, *Cricket and Race* (Oxford: Berg, 2001).

15. See Shari L. Dworkin and Michael A. Messner, "Introduction: Gender Relations and Sport," *Sociological Perspectives*, Winter 2002, 347–352.

16. For one of the first works to analyze the anthropology of sport, including the prehistory and early history of sports in chiefdoms, primitive states, and archaic civilizations, see Kendall Blanchard and Alyce Cheska, *The Anthropology of Sport: An Introduction* (South Hadley, MA: Bergin & Garvey, 1984). For an analysis of the relationship between sport and immigration, beginning with the seventeenth century, see George Eisen and David K. Wiggins, eds., *Ethnicity and Sport in North American History and Culture* (Westport, CT: Greenwood, 1994). For an analysis of the derivation of African sport, see William J. Baker and James A. Mangan, eds., *Sport in Africa: Essays in Social History* (New York: Africana, 1987). For an ethnographic approach to the intersection of sport and gender, see Alan M. Klein, *Little Big Man: Bodybuilding Subculture in Gender Construction* (Albany: SUNY, 1993).

For the application of feminist theory to sports, see M. Ann Hall, *Feminism and Sporting Bodies: Essays on Theory and Practice* (Champaign, IL: Human Kinetics, 1996). For pioneer works that were among the first to demonstrate how social institutions used to exclude or limit women's participation in sports were deemed to be based on "natural" sex group differences, see Susan K. Cahn, *Coming on Strong: Gender and Sexuality in Twentieth-Century Women's Sport* (New York: Free Press, 1994); and Gai Ingham Berlage, *Women in Baseball: The Forgotten History* (Westport, CT: Praeger, 1994).

For discussions about issues in the study of the history of sports, see Lincoln Allison, *Amateurism in Sport* (London: Frank Cass, 2001); Douglas Booth, *Australian Beach Cultures: The History of Sun, Sand, and Surf* (London: Frank Cass, 2001); Tony Collins and Wray Vamplew, *Mud, Sweat, and Beers: A Cultural History of Sport and Alcohol* (Oxford: Berg, 2002); Rudy Koshar, ed., *Histories of Leisure* (Oxford: Berg, 2002); Michael Oriard, *King Football: Sport and Spectacle in the Golden Age of Radio and Newsreels, Movies and Magazines, the Weekly and the Daily Press* (Chapel Hill: University of North Carolina Press 2001).

17. Elliot J. Gorn and Warren Goldstein, eds., *A Brief History of American Sports* (Urbana: University of Illinois Press, 1993), 47. For a narrative history of British sports, see Neil Tranter, *Sport, Economy, and Society in Britain, 1750–1914* (Cambridge: Cambridge University Press, 1998); and Derek Birley, *Playing the Game: Sport and British Society, 1910–45* (Manchester: Manchester University Press, 1995).

18. Clifford Putney, *Muscular Christianity: Manhood and Sports and Protestant America* (Cambridge: Harvard University Press, 2001).

19. Steven W. Pope, "Negotiating the 'Folk Highway' of the Nation: Sport, Public Culture, and American Identity, 1870–1940," *Journal of Social History*, Winter 1993, 327–340; David Black and John Nauright, *Rugby and the South African Nation* (New York: St. Martin's, 1998). For an interesting historiography of sport history, see Stephen A. Riess, "The New Sport History," *Reviews in American History*, September 1990, 311–325.

20. Mark Dyreson, "Nature by Design: Modern American Ideas about Sport, Energy, Evolution, and Republics, 1865–1920." *Journal of Sport History*, Fall 1999, 460.

21. For an analysis of the relationship between the working class and sports in interwar Britain, see Stephen G. Jones, *Sport, Politics, and the Working Class: Organized Labor and Sport in Inter-War Britain* (Manchester: Manchester University Press, 1988).

22. *The American Boy's Book of Sports and Games: A Repository of In-and-Out-Door Amusements for Boys and Youth* (New York: Dick & Fitzgerald, 1864), 3–4.

23. See Steven A. Riess, *City Games: The Evolution of American Urban Society in the Rise of Sports* (Champaign: University of Illinois Press, 1989); J. A. Mangan and Roberta J. Park, eds., *From" Fair Sex" to Feminism: Sport and the Socialization of Women in the Industrial and Post-Industrial Eras* (London: Frank Cass, 1987).

24. James Naismith, "Basket Ball," *American Physical Education Review*, May 1914, 339–340; as cited in Allen Guttman, *A Whole New Ball Game: An Interpretation of American Sports* (Chapel Hill: University of North Carolina Press, 1988), 70–71.

25. Dyreson, "Nature by Design," 448.

26. Elliot J. Gorn and Warren Goldstein, *A Brief History of American Sport* (Urbana: University of Illinois Press, 1993), 82.

27. Gorn and Goldstein, *Brief History*, 140.

28. Michael Oriard, *Reading Football: How the Popular Press Created an American Spectacle* (Chapel Hill: University of North Carolina Press, 1993). For a parallel analysis about hockey in Canada, see Richard Gruneau and David Whitson, *Hockey Night in Canada: Sport Identities and Cultural Politics* (Toronto: Garamond, 1993).

29. Sal Ruibal, "Tiny Hawaii Looms as Giant in Football," *USA Today*, November 10, 2004, 1.

30. Dahn Shaulis, "Pedestriennes: Newsworthy but Controversial Women in Sporting Entertainment," *Journal of Sport History*, Spring 1999, 31.

31. Gorn and Goldstein, *Brief History*, 188.

32. Gorn and Goldstein, *Brief History*, 136.

33. Mark Dyreson, "American Ideas about Race and Olympic Races from the 1890's to the 1950's: Shattering Myths or Reinforcing Scientific Racism?" *Journal of Sport History*, Summer 2001, 174.

34. Michael MacCambridge, *America's Game: The Epic Story of How Pro Football Captured a Nation* (New York: Random House, 2004), 165–166.

35. Patricia Vertinsky, *The Eternally Wounded Woman: Women, Doctors, and Exercise in the Late Nineteenth Century* (Chicago: University of Illinois Press, 1989), 43.

36. Vertinsky, *Eternally Wounded Woman*, 43.

37. Vertinsky, *Eternally Wounded Woman*, 44.

38. Vertinsky, *Eternally Wounded Woman*, 43.

39. Vertinsky, *Eternally Wounded Woman*, 43.

40. Colette Dowling, *The Frailty Myth: Women Approaching Physical Equality* (New York: Random House, 2000) 16–17.

41. Dowling, *Frailty Myth*, 14.

42. Julia Ward Howe, *Sex in Education* (Boston: Roberts, 1874); as cited in Vertinsky, *Eternally Wounded Woman*, 52.

43. Howe, *Sex*, as cited in Vertinsky, *Eternally Wounded Woman*, 51.

44. Nancy Cole Dosch, "The Sacrifice of Maidens or Healthy Sportswomen? The Medical Debate over Women's Basketball," in Joan S. Hult and Marianna Trekell, eds., *A Century of Women's Basketball: From Frailty to Final Four* (Reston, VA: American Alliance for Health, Physical Education, Recreation and Dance, 1991), 130.

45. *As One Girl to Another* (International Cellucotton Products, 1940), 6–7.

46. Mary Jo Festle, *Playing Nice: Politics and Apologies in Women's Sports* (New York: Columbia University Press, 1996), 55. For an analysis of sports' contribution to the emancipation of women in England, see Kathleen E. McCrone, *Sport and the Physical Emancipation of English Women, 1870–1914* (New York: Routledge, 1998).

47. Jon Sterngass, "Cheating, Gender Roles, and the Nineteenth-Century Croquet Craze," *Journal of Sport History*, Fall 1998, 407.

48. Joan Paul, "Clara Gregory Baer: Catalyst for Women's Basketball," in *A Century of Women's Basketball*, 39.

49. Festle, *Playing Nice*, 50.

50. Pete DeWolf, "Jumping through Hoops: The Cranky Pete Edition," www.hoopsworld.com.

51. Eleanor Flexner and Ellen Fitzpatrick, *Century of Struggle: The Woman's Rights Movement in the United States* (Cambridge: Belknap Press, Harvard University Press, 1996), 78.

52. Flexner and Fitzpatrick, *Century of Struggle*, 79.

53. Festle, *Playing Nice*, 17; Mabel Locke, obituary; Sharon L. Van Oteghen, "Mabel Locke, 1907–2003," *Journal of Physical Education, Recreation & Dance*, September 1, 2003, http://statichighbeam.com/j/joperdthejournalofphysicaleducationrecreationampda.

54. Scraton analyzes how female physical educators in the United Kingdom also hampered the development of women's sports programs by reinforcing patriarchal, if not homophobic, principles, Sheila Scraton, *Shaping up to Womanhood: Gender and Girls' Physical Education* (Buckingham, U.K.: Open University Press, 1992).

55. Festle, *Playing Nice*, 15.

56. Rules, Dorothy Bruno Hills Indoor Tennis League, http://dbhitl.org/rules.html.

57. Betty Spears, "Senda Berenson Abbott: New Woman, New Sport," in Joan S. Hult and Marianna Trekell, eds., *A Century of Women's Bas-*

ketball: From Frailty to Final Four (Reston, VA: American Alliance for Health, Physical Education, Recreation and Dance, 1991), 25.

58. Spears, "Senda Berenson Abbott," 27.

59. Joan S. Hult, "The Governance of Athletics for Girls and Women: Leadership by Women Physical Educators, 1899–1949," in *A Century of Women's Basketball*, 53.

60. Mabel Craft, "College Girls Play Basket-Ball," *Leslie's Illustrated Weekly*, May 7, 1896, 313. Sally Fox Collection, 2005-m73, Folio and Box 12. Schlesinger Library, Radcliffe Institute for Advanced Study, Harvard University.

61. Robin Bell Markels, "Bloomer Basketball and Its Suspender Suppression: Women's Intercollegiate Competition and Ohio State, 1904–1907," *Journal of Sport History*, Spring 2000, 37.

62. Markels, "Bloomer Basketball," *Journal of Sport History*, Spring 2000, 36.

63. Cahn, *Coming on Strong*, 92–93.

64. Helen Frost and Hazel Cubberley, *Field Hockey and Soccer for Women* (New York: Scribner's, 1923). xiv.

65. Frost and Cubberley, *Field Hockey*, xv.

66. Frost and Cubberley, *Field Hockey*, xvi.

67. David Welky, "Viking Girls, Mermaids, and Little Brown Men: U.S. Journalism and the 1932 Olympics," *Journal of Sport History*, Spring 1997, 29.

68. Joan S. Hult, "The Story of Women's Athletics: Manipulating a Dream, 1890–1985," in M. Costa and S. Guthrie, eds., *Women and Sport: Interdisciplinary Studies in Human Kinetics* (Champaign, IL: Human Kinetics, 1994), 84.

69. Welky, "Viking Girls," 29.

70. Festle, *Playing Nice*, 19.

71. Cited in Cahn, *Coming on Strong*, 114.

72. Welky, "Viking Girls," 29.

73. Cahn, *Coming on Strong*, 114.

74. Festle, *Playing Nice*, 11.

75. Festle, *Playing Nice*, 11.

76. Festle, *Playing Nice*, 12.

77. "Cleve Abbott," USA Track & Field Hall of Fame, www.usatf.org/HallOfFame/TF/showBio.asp?HOFIDs=2.

78. Jennifer H. Lansbury, "The Tuskegee Flash and the Slender Harlem Stroker: Black Women Athletes on the Margin," *Journal of Sport History*, Summer 2001, 233–252.

79. Patricia Vertinsky and Gwendolyn Captain, "More Myth Than History: American Culture and Representations of the Black Female's Athletic Ability," *Journal of Sport History*, Fall 1998, 532–561.

80. Sam Lacy, "Has Althea Gibson Conquered Herself?" *Baltimore Afro-American*, June 29, 1957, magazine sec. Cited in Vertinsky and Captain, "More Myth Than History," 540.

81. Vertinsky and Captain, "More Myth Than History," 541.

82. Editorial, *NCAA News*, July 15, 1975, 2; cited in Festle, *Playing Nice*, 180.

83. Festle, *Playing Nice*, 189.

84. Festle, *Playing Nice*, 180.

85. Festle, *Playing Nice*, 175.

86. For a discussion of how ice hockey can contribute to breaking down sex barriers in sports, see Cynthia Fabrizio Pelak, "Women's Collective Identity Formation in Sports: A Case Study from Women's Ice Hockey," *Gender and Society*, February 2002, 93–114.

87. "Dangerous 'Turns' by Women May Be Stopped in England," *New York Times*, July 1, 1906, X6.

88. Mary Lou LeCompte, "Home on the Range: Women in Professional Rodeo: 1929–1947," *Journal of Sport History*, Winter 1990, 324–325.

89. Harvey Araton, "For a Girls Team, the Learning Curve Is Full of Extreme Angles," *New York Times*, February 2, 2007, C14.

90. "Girls in Athletics Joining the Boys," *New York Times*, April 30, 1972, 87.

91. "Girls in Athletics," 87.

92. " Starting at Right Tackle: Ms. Jones," *New York Times*, September 28, 1972, 64.

93. "Starting at Right Tackle," 64.

94. "Starting at Right Tackle," 64.

95. Pennsylvania Education Committee, *Report: June 25, 1973*, National Organization for Women papers, National Task Force on Sports file (31.10), Schlesinger Library, Radcliffe Institute for Advanced Study.

96. Marcia Federbush, handwritten note to NOW, November 1, 1973, National Organization for Women papers, National Task Force on Sports file (31.10), Schlesinger Library, Radcliffe Institute for Advanced Study.

97. Article 19 of *PA Athlete*, May 1973. Reprinted in Pennsylvania Education Committee, *Report: June 25, 1973*, National Organization for Women papers, National Task Force on Sports file (31.10), Schlesinger Library, Radcliffe Institute for Advanced Study.

98. Lillian Faderman, *Odd Girls and Twilight Lovers: A History of Lesbian Life in Twentieth-Century America*. Cited in Markels, "Bloomer Basketball," 43.

99. "Athletic Girls Do Not Suit Elliot: Tendency of Young Women in College to Imitate Their Brothers Condemned," *Evening Dispatch*, February 16, 1904, sec. 2, 1. In Markels, "Bloomer Basketball," 43.

100. Spears, "Senda Berenson Abbott," 30.

101. For an analysis of the way heterosexual principles contribute to sexism, see Lisa Disch and Mary Jo Kane, "When a Looker Is Really a Bitch: Lisa Olson, Sport, and the Heterosexual Matrix," *Signs*, Winter 1996, 278–308.

102. Cahn, *Coming on Strong*, 165.

103. Susan K. Cahn, "From the Muscle Moll to the Butch Ballplayer: Mannishness, Lesbianism, and the Homophobia in U.S. Women's Sport," *Feminist Studies*, December 31, 2001, 347.

104. For an analysis of the way contemporary gay athletes deal with discrimination, see Eric Anderson, "Openly Gay Athletes: Contesting Hegemonic Masculinity in a Homophobic Environment," *Gender and Society*, December 2002, 860–877.

105. Shari Lee Dworkin and Faye Linda Wachs, "The Morality/Manhood Paradox: Masculinity, Sport, and the Media," in Jim McKay, Michael A. Messner, and Don Sabo, eds., *Masculinities, Gender Relations, and Sport* (Thousand Oaks, CA: Sage, 2000), 55.

106. Dworkin and Wachs, "Morality/Manhood Paradox," 57.

107. Cahn, *Coming on Strong*, 350.

Chapter Six

1. Dave Kindred, "Joe Louis' Biggest Knockout," *Sporting News*, February 10, 1999, www.sportingnews.com/archives/sports2000/moments/140271.html.

2. Written on a building wall, Manhattan, New York, visible from West Side Drive, around 45th Street, January 2007.

3. Douglass Hartmann, "What Can We Learn From Sport If We Take Sport Seriously as a Racial Force? Lessons from C.L.R. James's *Beyond a Boundary*," *Ethnic and Racial Studies*, May 2003, 462. For an elaboration of the paradox, namely, how sport can reinforce gender and racial hierarchies as well as challenge them, see Margaret Gatz, Michael A. Messner, and Sandra J. Ball-Rokeach, *Paradoxes of Youth and Sport* (Albany: State University of New York Press, 2002).

4. In *Forty Million Dollar Slaves: The Rise, Fall, and Redemption of the Black Athlete* (New York: Crown, 2006), William C. Rhoden argues persuasively that the political capital of black athletes has been squandered.

5. "Fight Excitement Causes 12 Deaths," *New York Times*, June 21, 1936, S1.

6. "Harlem Disorders Mark Louis Defeat," *New York Times*, June 20, 1936, 34.

7. "Goebbels Hails Victor," *New York Times*, June 20, 1936, 10.

8. "Germany Acclaims Schmeling as National Hero for His Victory over Louis," *New York Times*, June 21, 1936, S11.

9. "Schmeling Guest of Hitler at Lunch," *New York Times*, June 28, 1936, S4.

10. "All Reich 'Likes' Schmeling," *New York Times*, June 19, 1938, 62.

11. Joe Louis (as told to Meyer Berger and Barney Nagler), "Life Story of Joe Louis: Sees Roosevelt," *New York Times*, November 10, 1948, 41.

12. Dave Kindred, "Joe Louis' Biggest Knockout," *Sporting News*, February 10, 1999, www.sportingnews.com/archives/sports2000/moments/140271.html.

13. James P. Dawson, "Louis Defeats Schmeling by a Knock Out in First," *New York Times*, June 23, 1938, 1.

14. "Street Dance in Chicago; Negroes in Gay Celebration of Louis' Triumph," *New York Times*, June 23, 1938, 14.

15. Kindred, "Joe Louis' Biggest Knockout."

16. "Race Barriers Down," *New York Times*, March 20, 1946, 20.

17. Joe Donatelli, "Motley Never Got His Due," *Intelligencer Record* (Doylestown, PA), July 13, 1999, B1, B4.

18. "Rams Sign Washington, Negro Star," *Oakland Tribune*, March 22, 1946, 12.

19. Michael MacCambridge, *America's Game: The Epic Story of How Pro Football Captured a Nation* (New York: Random House, 2004) 17–18.

20. Roscoe McGowen, "Florida City Bars Montreal Negroes," *New York Times*, March 22, 1946, 31.

21. For a provocative account showing that the "inspirational reel" provided by such African American sports heroes as Jackie Robinson, Arthur Ashe, and Muhammad Ali is but half the story, the other half being a tale of black athletes adrift like a lost tribe in a white culture, see Rhoden, *Forty Million Dollar Slaves*.

22. MacCambridge, *America's Game*, 165–166.

23. Ruth M. Sparhawk, Mary E. Leslie, Phyllis Y. Turbow, and Zina R. Rose, *American Women in Sport, 1887–1987: A 100-Year Chronology*

(Metuchen, N.J.: Scarecrow, 1989), 14. See also Ellen Klages, "The Girls of Summer," www.exploratorium.edu/baseball/mitchell.html.

24. "Extra! Extra! Girl Fans Babe and Lou," *Zanesville (OH) Signal*, April 3, 1931, 14.

25. "Her Curves Confused the Mighty Babe," *Helena Independent*, April 5, 1931, first sports page.

26. Klages, "Girls of Summer."

27. "Whatever Happened to . . . Margaret Gisolo," *Sheboygan Press*, March 24, 1961, 14.

28. Emma Jane Osler, "ISTC Instructor Was in Midst of Baseball Furor," *Indiana (PA) Evening Gazette*, July 10, 1948, 7.

29. "She's Eligible," *Frederick (MD) Post*, July 10, 1928, first sports page.

30. "Whatever Happened to . . . Margaret Gisolo." See also Gai Ingham Berlage, "Yes, Virginia, Little Girls Were Allowed to Play Baseball before 1974: The Story of Margaret Gisolo" (presentation at Iona College), http://aafla.org/sportslibrary/NASSH_Proceedings/NP1993j.pdf.

31. "Blonde German Girl Threatens to Win Men's Fencing Title," *Lima (OH) News*, February 25, 1935, 8.

32. "Sport Slants," *Dothan (ALA) Eagle*, April 4, 1935, 8.

33. "Champion Fencer Excited over Home Trip," *Reno Evening Gazette*, January 23, 1936, 9.

34. Jean Lyon, "Foils and Foibles," *Independent Woman*, January 1938, 12.

35. "Girl May Race Men Olympians," *New York Times*, March 9, 1924, XX2.

36. "Woman Breaks Man's Record for First Time in Swim History," *New York Times*, October 9, 1922, 19.

37. "Greeks, Girls, and 1944," *The Nation*, February 27, 1924, 222.

38. For a review of the history of discrimination against women in sports in the context of the development of Title IX and a doctrine of formal equality, see Jessica E. Jay, "Women's Participation in Sports: Four Feminist Perspectives," *Texas Journal of Women and the Law*, Fall 1997, 1.

39. "Girl May Race Men Olympians."

40. Mark Dyreson, "Scripting the American Olympic Story-Telling Formula: The 1924 Paris Olympic Games and the American Media," *Olympic Perspectives*, October 1996, 62.

41. "Greeks, Girls, and 1944," 222.

42. "Girl May Race Men Olympians."

43. "Youthful Maid Passes Away at Chicago Today: 23-year-old Mermaid; Ill for 92 Days, Dies after Contracting Cold," *Davenport Democrat and Leader*, January 31, 1927, 7.

44. Copeland C. Burg, "Sybil Bauer's Death Caused by Exertions," *Danville(VA) Bee*, February 18, 1927, 7.

45. "Sybil Bauer Ordered to Take Long Rest," *Oakland Tribune*, March 2, 1926, B1.

46. "Participated in by Eleven Women, All over 75 Years of Age," *Newark (OH) Advocate*, April 13, 1905, 1.

47. "The Walking-Match," *New York Times*, November 18, 1876, 2.

48. Dahn Shaulis, "Pedestriennes: Newsworthy but Controversial Women in Sporting Entertainment," *Journal of Sport History*, Spring 1999, 33.

49. "Misc. news items," *Chester (PA) Daily Times*, December 14, 1878, 1.

50. Dahn Shaulis, "Women of Endurance, Pedestriennes, Marathoners, Ultramarathoners, and Others: Two Centuries of Women's Endurance (1816–1996)," *Women in Sport and Physical Activity Journal* 5 (1998): 1–27

51. "Female Pedestrians," *New York Times*, March 27, 1879, 5.

52. "The Woman's Walking Match: Only Seven Now on the Track—One of Those Who Retired Seriously Injured, and Another Insane," *New York Times*, April 1, 1879, 2.

53. Shaulis, "Pedestriennes," 33.

54. Shaulis, "Women of Endurance," 1–27.

55. Eleanor Flexner and Ellen Fitzpatrick, *Century of Struggle: The Woman's Rights Movement in The United States* (Cambridge: Belknap Press, Harvard University Press, 1996), 288.

56. Helen Kendrick Johnson, *Woman and the Republic* (1913; 2000) The text has been reformatted, redesigned, and hyperlinked to add to its usefulness as a research document. This version: Copyright 2000 Jone Johnson Lewis. All Rights Reserved. http://womenshistory.about.com/library/etext/bl_watr_ch11.htm.

57. Phyllis Schlafly, "Careers, Choices, Costs, and Biases," *Phyllis Schlafly Report*, July 2002, www.eagleforum.org/psr/2002/july02/psrjuly02.shtml.

58. Schlafly, "Careers, Choices."

59. Schlafly, "Careers, Choices."

60. For a discussion of how disturbing it is when feminists settle for sex-segregated sports policies and the difficulties of using either the Equal Protection Clause of the Fourteenth Amendment or Title IX for correcting sex discrimination in sports, see Dana Robinson, "A League of Their Own: Do Women Want Sex-Segregated Sports?" *Journal of Contemporary Legal Issues*, Spring 1998.

61. Mary Jo Festle, *Playing Nice: Politics and Apologies in Women's Sports* (New York: Columbia University Press, 1996), 85.

62. Festle, *Playing Nice*, 85.

63. Festle, *Playing Nice*, 85.

64. Ying Wushanley, "The Olympics, Cold War, and the Reconstruction of U.S. Women's Athletics," *Bridging Three Centuries: Fifth International Symposium for Olympic Research*, 2000, 119.

65. "Why Can't We Beat This Girl?" *Sports Illustrated*, September 30, 1963. In Festle, *Playing Nice*, 92.

66. Festle, *Playing Nice*, 99.

67. Researchers found this bias present in nonsport media arenas as well. A study of nonsport popular men in women's magazines revealed that the most common images portrayed by advertisers and media publishers emphasized power and performance sports for men in contrast to pleasure anticipation activities for women, thereby reinforcing rather than challenging existing gender relations. Timothy J. Curry, Paul A. Arriagada, and Benjamin Cornwell, "Images of Sport in Popular Non-Sport Magazines: Power and Performance Versus Pleasure Anticipation," *Sociological Perspectives*, Winter 2002, 397–413. Also see Anna Archer, "From Legally Blonde to Miss Congeniality: The Femininity Conundrum," *Cardozo Journal of Law and Gender*, Fall 2006.

68. "American Legion Baseball," www.baseball.legion.org/history.htm.

69. Lance Van Auken and Robin Van Auken, *Play Ball! The Story of Little League Baseball* (University Park: Penn State Press, 2001), 203–204.

70. Little League Baseball Historical Timeline, www.littleleague.org/history.

71. Van Auken and Van Auken, *Play Ball*, 79.

72. Keith H. Klepfel, "Put Me In Coach, I'm Ready to Play! The Story of Girls and Little League Baseball," May 5, 2005, www.archiva.net/hist300ay/papers/klepfel.doc.

73. Van Auken and Van Auken, *Play Ball*, 154–156.

74. Van Auken and Van Auken, *Play Ball*,145.

75. "She Was in a League of Her Own in '63," *New York Times*, March 31, 1974, 65.

76. Matthew Goodman, "Little League Justice: Three Cheers for Maria Pepe, Baseball's Susan B. Anthony," *Utne Reader*, September–October 1990, 118.

77. "Court Decision is Awaited in Little League Test Case," *New York Times*, June 30, 1973, 24.

78. "Michigan Girl's Suit Filed against Little League Ban," *New York Times*, June 21, 1973, 88.

79. "Girl Loses Little League Plea," *New York Times*, October 31, 1974, 36.

80. "Hoboken Was Home to First Girl to Play Little League," *Hoboken Reporter*, November 6, 2005, www.hudsonreporter.com/site/news.cfm?newsid=15531945&BRD=1291&PAG=461&dept_id=551343&rfi=6.

81. "Little League to Honor Maria Pepe," November 7, 2003, www.cnn.com/2003/US/Northeast/11/07/little.league.Ap/index.html.

82. "Hoboken Was Home."

83. Robert Reinhold, "Sharon's Brief Baseball Career: Town Wasn't on Her Side," *New York Times*, July 7, 1971, 26.

84. Murray Chass, "Mets, Yanks Back Girls in Little League," *New York Times*, April 2, 1974, 49.

85. Joan Cook, "Jersey Bids Little League Let Girls Play on Teams," *New York Times*, November 8, 1973, 51.

86. Summary of proceedings for hearing, State of New Jersey, Department of Law and Public Safety, Division on Civil Rights, November 8, 1973, 2. National Organization for Women papers, National Task Force on Sports file (31.10), Schlesinger Library, Radcliffe Institute for Advanced Study.

87. Cook, "Jersey Bids Little League," 51.

88. Summary of proceedings for hearing, State of New Jersey, Department of Law and Public Safety, Division on Civil Rights.

89. Summary of proceedings for hearing, State of New Jersey, Department of Law and Public Safety, Division on Civil Rights.

90. Richard Phalon, "50 Girls Join 175 Boys at Tryout for Little League," *New York Times*, March 28, 1974, 83.

91. Joseph B. Treaster, "Judge Chides Little League Lawyer as Out of Tune on Girls," *New York Times*, March 26, 1974, 45.

92. Joseph B. Treaster, "Girls a Hit in Debut on Diamond," *New York Times*, March 25, 1974, 67.

93. Treaster, "Girls a Hit."

94. "Ford Formally Admits Girls to Little League," *New York Times*, December 27, 1974, 66.

95. For an analysis of how separate is not equal in the context of women's educational experiences, see Shannon N. Ball, "Separate but Equal Is Unequal: The Argument against an All-Women's Law School," *Notre Dame Journal of Law, Ethics, and Public Policy* 15 (2001): 171.

96. Pennsylvania Education Committee, *Report: June 25, 1973*, National Organization for Women papers, national task force on sports file (31.10), Schlesinger Library, Radcliffe Institute for Advanced Study.

97. "Plan to Eliminate Sex Discrimination in High School Interscholastic Athletics," National Organization for Women, Twin Cities chapter, October 1973, National Organization for Women papers, National

Task Force on Sports file (31.10), Schlesinger Library, Radcliffe Institute for Advanced Study.

98. Mary Lee George-Geisser, *Athletics: Equality for Females,* undated (context of letter dates it January 1974), National Organization for Women papers, National Task Force on Sports file (31.10), Schlesinger Library, Radcliffe Institute for Advanced Study.

99. Marcia Federbush, note to National Organization for Women, November 1, 1973, National Organization for Women papers, National Task Force on Sports file (31.10), Schlesinger Library, Radcliffe Institute for Advanced Study.

100. Federbush, note to National Organization for Women, November 1, 1973.

101. Eleanor Smeal, letter to "Penn. N.O.W. Chapter pres., convener, sports or education chair-one," November 14, 1973, National Organization for Women papers, National Task Force on Sports file (31.10), Schlesinger Library, Radcliffe Institute for Advanced Study.

102. "Plan to Eliminate Sex Discrimination in High School Interscholastic Athletics."

103. Joseph B. Treaster, "Little League Baseball Proving Just a First Step for Girl Athletes," *New York Times,* June 23, 1974, 40.

104. Treaster, "Little League Baseball," 40.

105. Treaster, "Little League Baseball."

106. Jan Cunningham, letter to "Women in Sports Task Force People," February 21, 1975, National Organization for Women papers, National Task Force on Sports file (31.10), Schlesinger Library, Radcliffe Institute for Advanced Study.

107. Welch Suggs, *A Place on the Team: The Triumph and Tragedy of Title IX* (Princeton: Princeton University Press, 2005).

108. Reinhold, "Sharon's Brief Baseball Career."

109. Leonard Buder, "Scribner Would Let Girls Play against Boys in Some Sports," *New York Times,* February 4, 1971, 44.

110. Nadine Brozan, "Girls on the Athletic Field: Small Gains, Long Way to the Goal," *New York Times,* January 12, 1976, 46.

111. Marilyn Bender, "Gym's Not Bore It Used to Be—It's Coed," *New York Times,* November 7, 1969, 54.

112. Photos by Don Hogan Charles and Bill Aller, *New York Times,* November 7, 1969, 54.

113. William E. Farrell, "State Backs Coed Noncontact Sports," *New York Times,* March 1, 1969, 29.

114. Buder, "Scribner Would Let Girls Play."

115. Alfonso A. Narvaez, "Regents Allow Girls to Compete with Boys in Noncontact Sports," *New York Times*, March 27, 1971, 12.

116. Buder, "Scribner Would Let Girls Play."

117. "Results of the NISO Poll No. 4: Some Thumbs Up, Some Thumbs Down," *Senior Scholastic*, May 10, 1971, 2.

118. Treaster, "Little League Baseball."

119. "High Schools Suspended for Girls on Boys' Teams," *New York Times*, June 5, 1977, S3.

120. "A Judge Rules for Coed Sports," *New York Times*, January 11, 1978, A15.

121. Treaster, "Little League Baseball."

122. Treaster, "Little League Baseball."

123. For an insightful analysis from global perspectives of how power relations are embodied in sport and how women circumvent a wide array of barriers, see Jennifer Hargreaves, *Heroines of Sport: The Politics of Difference and Identity* (New York: Routledge, 2000).

Chapter Seven

1. Quoted by feminist attorney and author Sonia Fuentes, "The Legal Revolution in the Employment Rights of Women in the United States Since the Mid-Sixties" (presentation to the School of Industrial and Labor Relations, Cornell University, April 12, 2000), http://gos.sbc.edu/f/fuentes.html.

2. Tyler Kepner, "From Big Apple to Bay Area, It's Battle for Bragging Rights: Distraction-Free Clemens Handles Mets with Ease," *New York Times*, June 29, 2003, sec. 8, pp. 1, 4.

3. As early as 1747, John Broughton, a great boxing champion who also considered himself a "professor of athletics," beseeched Britons to eradicate foreign effeminacy by taking up boxing, which he described as " 'that truly British art.' " Christopher Johnson and Henry Fielding, "British Championism: Early Pugilism and the Works of Fielding," *Review of English Studies*, August 1996, 351.

4. Clyde Brown and David M. Paul, "The Political Scorecard of Professional Sports Facility Referendums in the United States, 1984–2000," *Journal of Sport and Social Issues* 26, no. 3 (2002): 248.

5. Rick Eckstein and Kevin Delaney, "New Sports Stadiums, Community Self-Esteem, and Community Collective Conscience," *Journal of Sports and Social Issues* 26, no. 3 (2002): 235–247.

6. Eckstein and Delaney, "New Sports Stadiums."

7. As quoted in John R. Thelin, *Games Colleges Play: Scandal and Reform in Intercollegiate Athletics* (Baltimore: Johns Hopkins University Press, 1994), 73.

8. Joe McGuff, "Are Athletics Too Big?" *NCAA News* 17, no. 9 (1980): 2. See also David W. Levy, "The Wit of George Lynn Cross," *Sooner Magazine* 15, no. 2 (1995): 22–26.

9. Susan Brownell, *Training the Body for China: Sports in the Moral Order of the People's Republic* (Chicago: University of Chicago Press, 1995); Shiva Balaghi, "Football and Film in the Islamic Republic of Iran," *Middle East Report,* Winter 2003, 54–56.

10. Vicki Michaelis, "U.S. Games Boost Bottom Line," *USA Today,* June 30, 2005, 9C.

11. "Notes: Britain Bests Archrival France," *USA Today,* July 7, 2005, www.usatoday.com/sports/olympics/summer/2005-07-07-notes-britain-vs-france_x.htm.

12. Mark Dyerson, "Icons of Liberty or Objects of Desire? American Women Olympians and the Politics of Consumption," *Journal of Contemporary History,* July 2003, 435–460.

13. Michaelis, "U.S. Games."

14. The literature is vast. For a useful review, see Mike Cronin, "Playing Games? The Serious Business of Sports History," *Journal of Contemporary History,* July 2003, 299–314.

15. Chris Sheridan, "NBA Uses Bryant Case to Warn Rookies," *Toronto Star,* August 3, 2003, www.thestar.com.

16. Patrick O'Driscoll, "Kobe Bryant, Accuser Settle Her Civil Lawsuit," *USA Today,* March 2, 2005, www.usatoday.com/sports/basketball/nba.

17. Charles Stein, "Bill Belichick, CEO," *Boston Globe,* January 28, 2004, D1.

18. Stein, "Bill Belichick."

19. For example, Daniel Gould and Kristen Diffenbach, "Psychological Characteristics and Their Development in Olympic Champions," *Journal of Applied Sport Psychology* 14, no. 3 (2002): 172–204; Caroline M. Petherick and Daniel A. Weigand, "The Relationship of Dispositional Goal Orientations and Perceived Motivational Climates on Indices of Motivation in Male and Female Swimmers," *International Journal of Sport Psychology* 33 (2002): 218–237; Nicholas L. Holt and John M. Hogg, "Perceptions of Stress and Coping during Preparations for the 1999 Women's Soccer World Cup Finals," *Sport Psychologist* 16 (2002): 251–271; Donfanf Chie-der, Steve Chen, Chou Hung, and Chi Li-kang, "Male and Female Basketball Players' Goal Orientations, Perceived Motivational Climate, Perceived Ability, and the Source of Sport Confidence," *Sport Journal* 6, no. 3 (2003), www

.thesportjournal.org/2003/journal/Vol6-No3/confidence.htm; Corey D. Bray and Diane E. Whaley, "Team Cohesion, Effort, and Objective Individual Performance of High School Basketball Players," *Sport Psychologist* 15 (2001): 260–275.

20. "From the Locker Room to the Boardroom: A Survey on Sports in the Lives of Women Business Executives," press release, February 4, 2002.

21. Judy Klemesrud, "Who's on First? Liz from Inventory," *New York Times*, August 5, 1981, C1.

22. Del Jones, "Many Successful Women Also Athletic," *USAToday*, March 26, 2002, 1.

23. *Golf for Women*, January–February 2004, www.golfdigest.com/gfw/gfw.

24. Susan Reed, "At the Top of Her Game," *Golf for Women*, January–February 2004, www.golfdigest.com/gfw/gfw.

25. Regan Stewart, "Sport Cities: How Sports Can Make a City a Better Place for Your Business," www.facilitycity.com/busfac/bf_05_02_cover.asp.

26. "Business: The Super Bowl. Sales, Not Just TV Ads," Profnetwire.com.

27. For an international and historical analysis of the relationship between sports and politics, see Allen Guttmann, "Sport, Politics, and the Engaged Historian," *Journal of Contemporary History*, July 2003, 363–375.

28. U.S. Senator Jim Bunning, http://bunning.senate.gov/index.cfm?FuseAction=Biography.Home.

29. Lynn Swann, www.lynnswann.com.

30. "President Bush Makes Stop at Daytona," February 16, 2004, http://nascar.com.

31. "White House South Lawn Tee Ball," http://cripexi.info/tball/index.html.

32. Les Carpenter, "WNBA Makes a Patriotic Choice," *Seattle Times*, August 2, 2004, http://seatletimes.nwsource.com/html/sports.

33. For example, Senator Bill Bradley traded on Olympic and NBA fame to win a Senate seat and to run for president in 2000. Former congressman Tom McMillan (D-Maryland) was a University of Maryland All-American basketball player and NBA star. Buffalo Bills quarterback Jack Kemp served in the House (R-New York) and ran for president in 1988. University of Nebraska Football Coach Tom Osborne serves in the House (R-Nebraska). Seattle Seahawks wide receiver Steve Largent served a term in Congress (R-Oklahoma) and ran unsuccessfully for governor of Oklahoma in 2002. Kansas Republican and former Olympic track star Jim Ryun won election to Congress in 1996. Former University of Oklahoma star quarterback J.C. Watts "served four terms in the U.S. Congress and is now head of an

international communications company bearing his name—and his sports-laden message: "From leading his Oklahoma Sooners football team to two consecutive Orange Bowl titles, to his distinguished 4-term career as a leading U.S. Congressman, J.C. Watts has proven he can deliver big wins in a diverse range of arenas. Now, through J.C. Watts Companies and strong alliances with key international companies, he and his team are uniquely positioned to help your organization win big." www.jcwatts.com/home.html.

34. "Runner's World Interviews President Bush," www.ultramarathonworld.com/news_2002/n22au02a.htm.

35. The White House Project/Women's Leadership Forum, unpublished project data, provided courtesy of the White House Project, as of 2002.

36. The White House Project, survey form from Nancy L. Johnson. Johnson was first elected in 1982.

37. The White House Project, survey form from Karen L. Thurman. Thurman served from 1993 to 2003.

38. For a historical analysis of scandal and reform in sports, see John R. Thelin, *Games Colleges Play: Scandal and Reform in Intercollegiate Athletics* (Baltimore, MD: Johns Hopkins University Press, 1994).

39. George W. Bush, excerpts from the State of the Union Address, *Boston Globe*, January 21, 2004, A17.

40. Elizabeth Duval, "Woman's Place Is Also in the Grandstand," *New York Times*, June 30, 1940, 87.

41. Hal Boyle, "Boyle Suggests: Let Women Vote, But, Fellas, Let's Keep 'Em Out of Sports," *Lima News*, August 31, 1960, 9.

42. Stephen Moore, "March Madness: Seven Ways to Make It Even Better," *National Review*, March 19, 2002, www.nationalreview.com.

43. Christine Brennan, "What's Ladylike in Floor Burn? Gender Distinctions Confine Women to 2nd Class Status," *USA Today*, April 4, 2007, 2C.

44. Ticket prices obtained online, http://utsports.collegesports.com/tickets/tenn-tickets.html.

45. Ticket prices obtained online, www.uwbadgers.com/tickets/headlines/index.aspx.

46. Michelle R. Hebl, Traci A. Guiliano, Eden B. King, Jennifer L. Knight, Jenessa R. Shapiro, Jeanine R. Skorinko, and Anjali Wig, "Paying the Way: The Ticket to Gender Equality in Sports," *Sex Roles: A Journal of Research* 51, no. 3–4 (2004): 227–235.

47. Ticket prices obtained online, www.scarletknights.com/tickets. There is also a gap between ticket prices for men's and women's basketball at the school. Season tickets to the men's team ranged from $120 to $442, and to the women's team from $78 to $221 during the 2006–2007 season,

the year in which the Rutgers women played in the NCAA Championship game.

48. Steve Weisberg, "What USA's Top Prep Players Are Thinking," *USA Today*, December 31, 2003, 3C.

49. Eric Wills, "Knight Commission Criticizes Growth of College Spending on Sports," *Chronicle of Higher Education*, June 10, 2005, A29.

50. Welch Suggs, "The Cost of Empty Seats," *Chronicle of Higher Education*, March 4, 2005, A39.

51. Whitson and MacIntosh argue that the professionalization of policy making in Canada in the context of Olympic sports marginalizes nonelite interests. David Whitson and Donald MacIntosh, "Rational Planning vs. Regional Interests: The Professionalization of Canadian Amateur Sport," *Canadian Public Policy*, December 1989, 436–449.

52. "Newsmakers of 2003: Saugus American Little League," *Boston Globe*, January 1, 2004, N6.

53. "Little League U.S. Champions Honored during Yankee-Marlins World Series: Event Was the Latest in a Long Series of Tributes," press release, www.littleleague.org/media/archive/boyntonhonored.htm.

54. "Maryland District 7 Is the 2003 Big League Softball World Series Champion," http://forums.somd.com/archive/topic/14396-l.html.

55. For an interesting analysis of how women figure into America's national identity, see Mark Dyreson, "Icons of Liberty or Objects of Desire? American Women Olympians and the Politics of Consumption," *Journal of Contemporary History*, July 2003, 435–460.

56. Stuart Miller, "TSN's Power 100," www.sportingnews.com/features/powerful2003/l.html.

57. This is true not only in the United States but around the world; see Matthew B. Karush, "National Identity in the Sports Pages: Football and the Mass Media in 1920s Buenos Aires," *The Americas*, July 2003, 11–32. Lawrence A. Wenner shows how sports provides the foundation of an entertainment economy in his edited volume, *MediaSport* (London: Routledge, 1988)

58. Suggs, "Cost of Empty Seats."

59. Suggs, "Cost of Empty Seats."

60. Peter Keating, "Boys Don't Cry," *ESPN The Magazine*, June 24, 2002, http://espn.go.com/magazine/vol5no13titleixessay.html.

61. Peter Keating, "Boys Don't Cry," *ESPN The Magazine*, June 24, 2002, http://espn.go.com/magazine/vol5no13titleixessay.html.

62. Karen H. Weiller and Catriona T. Higgs, "Television Coverage of Professional Golf: A Focus on Gender," *Women in Sport and Physical Activity Journal* 8, no. 1 (1999): 83.

63. Weiller and Higgs, "Television Coverage."

64. Kurt Badenhausen, "Uneven Playing Field," June 28, 2004, www.forbes.com/2004/06/28/cz_kb_0628gender.

65. Women's Sports Foundation, *Women's Sports & Fitness Facts & Statistics*, April 1, 2005, 26.

66. Smyers was Women's World Triathlon Champion in 1990 and 1995. www.guinnessworldrecords.com/content_pages/record.asp?recordid=44262&Reg=1. Smyers won the 1995 Ironman Triathlon, finishing in 9:16:46.

67. Karen Smyers, interview, August 3, 2000.

68. "A League—and a Field—of Their Own: ACLU Wins Equality for Girls' Softball League," ACLU press release, November 20, 2003.

69. Karen Smyers, interview, August 3, 2000.

70. Emily Watts, interview, May 2003.

71. "Williams Sisters Bring Viewers to Wimbledon," July 9, 2002, www.medialifemagazine.com/news2002/jul02/jul08/2_tues/news7tuesday.html.

72. Badenhausen, "Uneven Playing Field."

73. Stephen J. Harvey, "The Construction of Masculinity among Male Collegiate Volleyball Players," *Journal of Men's Studies* 5, no. 2 (1996): 131.

74. Mark Starr and Martha Brant, "Girls Rule!" cover; Starr and Brant, "It Went Down to the Wire...and Thrilled Us All," *Newsweek*, July 19, 1999, cover; 46–54.

75. Anthony King, "Wimbledon Fans Falling Out of Love with the Power Game," *Daily Telegraph*, June 23, 2003, 7.

76. Donald Mrozek, "Sport in American Life: From National Health to Personal Fulfillment, 1890–1940," in Kathryn Grover, ed., *Fitness in American Culture: Images of Health, Sport, and the Body, 1830–1940* (Rochester, NY: Margaret Woodbury Strong Museum, 1989), 19.

77. Mrozek, "Sport in American Life," 24.

78. "Runners Make History," *Syracuse Post-Standard*, August 21, 2004, 6; "Track and Field," *Syracuse Post-Standard*, August 24, 2003, D2.

79. "Bangladesh Group Protests against Women's Soccer," *Gleaner* (Kingston, Jamaica), October 18, 2004, 12.

80. S. U. Anyanwu, "Issues and Patterns of Women's Participation in Sport in Nigeria," *International Review for Sport Sociology* 15 (1980): 878–895. Cited in R. Chappell, "Sport in Developing Countries: Opportunities for Girls and Women," *Women in Sport and Physical Activity Journal* 8, no. 2 (1999): 1.

81. MaryJo Sylwester, "Hispanic Girls in Sports Held Back by Tradition," *USA Today*, March 29, 2005, 1.

82. Chappell, "Sport in Developing Countries."

83. "Chinese Athletes Cash in on Medalist Status: China's Communist Rulers Cast Olympians as Model Workers," www.msnbc.msn.com/id/5867721.

84. James Riordan, "Chinese Women and Sport Success, Sexuality, Suspicion," *Women in Sports and Physical Activity Journal* 9, no. 1 (2000): 87.

85. Dr. Thomas Johnson, psychiatrist from San Diego testifying in support of Little League. Summary of proceedings for hearing, State of New Jersey, Department of Law and Public Safety, Division on Civil Rights, November 8, 1973, 3, National Organization for Women papers, National Task Force on Sports file (31.10), Schlesinger Library, Radcliffe Institute for Advanced Study.

86. Dave Anderson, "Now Woods May Be Compared to Nicklaus as a Father," *New York Times*, Thursday, June 21, 2007, e16, emphasis added.

Index

Note: Italicized numbers represent tables